THE COLLECTED PLAYS

DERMOT HEALY

THE COLLECTED PLAYS

Edited, with an Introduction,

by Keith Hopper & Neil Murphy

DALKEY ARCHIVE PRESS

First edition, 2016

Library of Congress Cataloging-in-Publication Data

Names: Healy, Dermot, 1947-2014, author. | Hopper, Keith, editor, writer of introduction. | Murphy, Neil, editor, writer of introduction.
Title: The collected plays / Dermot Healy ; edited with an introduction, by Keith Hopper & Neil Murphy.
Other titles: Plays
Description: First edition. | Victoria, TX : Dalkey Archive Press, 2016.
Identifiers: LCCN 2016010775 | ISBN 9781564789303 (softcover : acid-free paper)
Classification: LCC PR6058 .E19 2016 | DDC 822/.914--dc23
LC record available at https://lccn.loc.gov/2016010775

Partially funded by a grant by the Illinois Arts Council, a state agency.
The Collected Plays received financial assistance from the Arts Council of Ireland.

www.dalkeyarchive.com

Victoria, TX / McLean, IL / Dublin / London

Dalkey Archive Press publications are, in part, made possible through the support of the University of Houston-Victoria and its programs in creative writing, publishing, and translation.

Printed on permanent/durable acid-free paper

For Helen

CONTENTS

Editors' Introduction: Waiting for Dermot

> Once, the [local parish priest in Cavan] devoted an entire sermon to Beckett's *Waiting for Godot*; he'd gone to see a performance in London. We all wait for the messenger, he said. We wait, despite the fact that no one comes.
>
> —Dermot Healy, *The Bend for Home*, 1996

In his acclaimed memoir *The Bend for Home*, Dermot Healy recalls eking out a living in London in the late 1960s while dreaming of becoming a writer. In one comic and theatrical vignette, Healy returns home to Cavan for a wedding, where he ends up sitting beside the editor of the local newspaper, the *Anglo-Celt*:

> How is the writing going on? he asked.
> Oh fine, I said.
> He filled me out another glass of wine.
> I'm glad to hear it, he said.
> Thank you.
> So will we be seeing a book out soon?
> Not yet. (*Pause.*) But I have a play finished.
> And is it going on?
> Yes.
> Where? In the Abbey?
> Oh no. I searched round frantically. On TV.
> TV, he said.
> ITV actually.
> Well that's wonderful.

I got a thousand pound.
You're made up. He raised his glass. What's it called?
Night-crossing, I said.
To *Night-crossing*, he said.
We touched glasses.
It starts with two lads leaving Ireland on the Holyhead boat.
Sounds good. (59)

A week later, back in London, one of Healy's friends presents him with a copy of the *Anglo-Celt*: "And there I was on the front page with a cigarette in my mouth over a small headline that read: CAVAN AUTHOR FINDS FAME." Digging himself an increasingly deeper hole, Healy invents an ITV producer and even sets a broadcast date for his imaginary play: "The more of the story I invented, the more real it became" (60). In desperation, he eventually conjures up funding problems and production difficulties, and the TV programme quietly disappears. Nonetheless, long after the fuss had died down, the invented drama gave way to something much more real and enduring: "I had set myself a duty. Everything I write now is an attempt to make up for that terrible lie. Had I not lied I might never have tried my hand at fiction. The truth is the lie you once told returning to haunt you" (60).

Dermot Healy (1947-2014) was born in Finea, Co. Westmeath, and grew up in Cavan near the border with Northern Ireland. Outside of Ireland, Healy is probably best known as a novelist, but he was also an accomplished poet, short story writer, screenwriter, actor, director, and playwright. A generous and gregarious man, Healy was a natural literary enabler: he founded and edited the regional journals *The Drumlin* and *Force 10*, and taught creative writing classes for prisoners as well as for local community groups – a collaborative spirit which is very much evident throughout his theatrical work.

Throughout a prolific career, Healy remained fascinated by borderland spaces and liminal states of mind, and he frequently transgressed the formal boundaries between poetry, fiction and drama, while foregrounding the gap between representation and reality. In all of Healy's writings there is a productive tension between the depiction of complex lives and events, and the desire to find new ways of expressing the rich subjectivity of those lives – a tension which animates his plays as much as his fiction.

Healy's interest in drama was deep and longstanding, and remained central to his ongoing development as a writer. In 1979, he co-founded The Hacklers Theatre Group in Cavan, and their ambitious debut production – Beckett's *Waiting for Godot*, which Healy produced and directed – won the award for Best Play at the All-Ireland Drama Festival in 1980. As a result, the play ran for five nights at the Peacock Theatre in Dublin (the Abbey Theatre's more adventurous junior affiliate) – a quite remarkable achievement for a fledgling amateur company.

In the early 1980s Healy returned to London and became director of The International Theatre Company, a fringe company which included members of the National Theatre and the left-wing agitprop group, 7:84; he also founded Erbury Square, a company of all-Irish actors based in London. Healy moved to Sligo in the mid-1980s, where he eventually settled down, and began writing plays for various amateur and professional theatre groups. From 1983, he was associated with the Peacock Theatre in Dublin, providing in-rehearsal critique and programme notes for a series of groundbreaking plays written by Tom Mac Intyre and directed by Patrick Mason: *The Great Hunger* (1983), *Rise Up Lovely Sweeney* (1985), and *Dance for your Daddy* (1987). Healy also wrote the programme notes for a number of important productions at the Peacock and the Abbey, including Neil Donnelly's *The Silver Dollar Boys* (1986), Thomas Kilroy's *The Death and Resurrection of Mr Roche* (1989), and Michael Harding's *Amazing Grace* (1998).

Throughout Healy's theatrical career, Samuel Beckett remained an important aesthetic touchstone (Healy later directed *Krapp's Last Tape*, *Rockaby*, and *Footfalls* at the Sligo Trades Club and the Hawk's Well Theatre in Sligo). As he noted in an interview in 1980, about his experience of directing

Waiting for Godot for the Hacklers: "I learnt a lot from Beckett and the way he raises the most clichéd language to imaginative status. [. . .] All the movement is in the lines and you've just got to feel it out, move, and stand still between the pauses" (quoted in Sennett, n. pag.). However, in Healy's own plays, this formal appreciation of Beckett's spatial abstractions and dramaturgical astringencies is supplemented by a more Brechtian sense of social and political engagement. Indeed, one of the most striking features of the thirteen plays contained in this present volume is their unabashed spirit of community collaboration and their strong social conscience. As the scholar and theatre critic Michelle Paull has noted, "In all these plays there is a sense of Healy acting as a guiding voice: an enabler of disenfranchised communities and the conduit speaker for unheard voices whose life experiences are rarely presented on stage" (Paull, 365).

Healy's first play, *Here, and There, and Going to America*, which he also directed, was performed at the Sligo Youth Centre in 1985 by a local community group, the Dole Q Company. Like Beckett's *Godot*, this is essentially a play where nothing happens twice: in Act I, two young brothers, Michael (a punk) and Sean (a skinhead), scam some money from the Dole Office in Sligo to enable them to move to London; in Act II, they end up in a similar Dole Office in London, dreaming of going to America but rarely leaving the confines of their squat. Throughout the piece, *Waiting for Godot* is deliberately echoed in some of the lines; in one scene, when the brothers first arrive in London, they end up waiting in a train station for their friend to arrive:

> MICHAEL: There's no point asking anyway. We'll just wait till Paddy comes.
> SEAN: Fucking Paddy never comes.

Although the language is a little brash at times, this is very much in keeping with the punk spirit of the central characters, and also Healy's generous collaboration with the original cast (all of whom were unemployed amateurs). At the very least, Healy finally fulfilled his promise to the editor of the *Anglo-Celt* almost two decades earlier: like his imaginary play *Night-crossing* – which purported to start "with two lads leaving Ireland on the Holyhead boat" (cf. *The Bend for Home*) – Healy's first play captures something of the Irish emigrant experience, and of life in London at the height of the Thatcher era.

His second play, *The Long Swim*, was commissioned by, and performed at, the Hawk's Well Theatre in 1987. It was first produced by the Acorn Theatre Company, Sligo, and directed by Healy himself. The play focuses on the character of Matti, a drama lecturer and writer who is suffering from Alzheimer's disease. Over the course of three acts – entitled "Consecutive Time," "Fragmented Time," and "Continual Time" – we watch as Matti's once formidable mind and sense of self gradually begins to disintegrate, and we witness the terrible effect the illness has on her and her family over a six-year period. At times, Matti resembles an archetypal Beckett protagonist, impotently raging against the dying of the light and chattering on regardless; at other times, she self-consciously reflects on the nature of her condition, as in the scene where she writes – and rehearses out loud – a final lecture on drama for her students:

> MATTI: And this is drama. You, the audience, are the ones with faith. Should the players fail you, it makes no difference. You will look elsewhere until you find your faith restored. In *Antigone* the chorus goes: "Of happiness the crown and chiefest part is wisdom, and to hold the gods in awe." The chorus is our key, our memory, the source of all. In the drama we are trapped in someone else's memory, which in time becomes our own, for the period of performance, and beyond.

One of the most interesting things about *The Long Swim* is the way in which Healy has already begun to incorporate a more daring yet organic sense of dramaturgy into the proceedings. In his stage directions at the beginning of the text, he proposes a strong objective correlative between the drama and its design:

> *Set*: *Four flats on one side, four flats on the other, each can pivot round a central screw so entrance and exit can occur both sides of a single flat. The interior of each flat can contain appropriate designs but all flats are white on the far side, out of view.* [. . .] *No entrance is ever made again through a door gone white. They are closed forever. The back wall should be completely white so that in the final scene we have a complete white-box area.*

At the end of the play – in a scene reminiscent of Brian Friel's early drama *The Loves of Cass McGuire* (1967) – the unbridgeable gap between Matti and her devoted husband Taig is movingly depicted through a simple configuration of lights, small physical gestures, and low-key sound effects:

> MATTI *goes into a foetal position. A spotlight hovers over her bed. The rain begins as at the beginning of the play. As the rain begins, the spotlight over the bed starts to increase. As it does, another spotlight starts increasing stage right.* TAIG *is standing in the second spotlight.* MATTI *turns in the bed, lifts up her head, and looks to where* TAIG *is. But already his spotlight has begun to dissolve. She returns to a foetal shape.*
> [*Darkness.*]
> [*The rain continues a little while.*]
> END

The struggle between darkness and light is very much the theme of Healy's 1989 version of *Blood Wedding*, which he adapted from the original 1933 play by Federico García Lorca. (In conversation with the present editors in March 2014, Healy said that he adapted the text from an (unspecified) English translation, and then sat down with a Spanish academic and checked his version against Lorca's original Spanish.) It was first performed in June 1989 at the Hawk's Well Theatre by the Seven Woods Theatre Company, Sligo, and directed and designed by Frank Conway. A dark and brooding tragedy about sex and violence, choice and deception, *Blood Wedding* shows that Healy's debt to European modernism goes well beyond Beckett and Brecht. Moreover, it situates Healy within a particular Irish tradition of creative adaptation, one which speaks to the violence of the Northern Irish Troubles without ever mentioning that conflict directly. As the *Irish Times* drama critic Fintan O'Toole wrote in his original programme notes for the Seven Woods production:

> The eighties has been the great decade of translation in the Irish theatre, a period in which Irish language has been melting into the European classics, making for a synthesis that is both Irish and foreign. Brian Friel, Thomas Kilroy, Derek Mahon and Frank McGuinness, among others, have enriched the Irish theatre with the meeting of minds and cultures between themselves and writers as diverse as Chekov, Lorca, Ibsen and Molière. Dermot Healy's version of *Blood Wedding* joins these ranks and it is appropriate that Lorca, the great unifier, should be the subject of this act of union. (n. pag.)

Lorca is still regularly revived by amateur and professional theatre groups in Ireland, and any Irish company wishing to tackle *Blood Wedding* in the future would be well advised to consider Healy's stark but poetical version.

His fourth play, *On Broken Wings*, was first performed in Ennis, Co. Clare, in January 1992 by Theatre Omnibus, and directed by the playwright himself. Theatre Omnibus were founded in Ennis in 1981 and, as the Irish Theatre Institute note in their online *Playography Ireland*, they "developed a unique style of visual theatre which featured a large degree of community involvement. Besides touring new Irish writing throughout the country, the company also produced puppet theatre, community pageants and puppet and mask making workshops" (n. pag.). In this respect, it is easy to see how Healy and Theatre Omnibus would be a perfect fit, and their subsequent collaboration allowed Healy the opportunity to explore more expressionistic and surrealistic forms of theatre. In his "Playwright's Note" for the original programme – which we have reproduced in full as a preface to the extant script – Healy wrote:

> [*On Broken Wings*] takes its title from a popular song of the 1930s, a period in which some of the scenes are set. It opens in contemporary Ireland with an old masked figure – Timothy Lavell – seated by the hearth of a cottage on the Mullet peninsula. The fireplace opens and in strides his mother, father, and himself as a young boy. We follow in Act I scenes from Timothy's childhood, including his trip by boat to Scotland, and his sojourn there potato-picking. [. . .] In Act II we follow Timothy Lavell's life in America. [. . .] His experiences, his failed love affair, his hallucinations, and his fears are explored. Eventually he returns to Ireland. [. . .] He is back as he was at the beginning of the play. It's a simple story told in a visual style with masks used to portray the many characters and the ageing process. Humour and pathos and fatalism are the main ingredients of Timothy Lavell's life. He is a stubborn survivor of another age.

As in many of Healy's works – and this is as true of his novels as it is of his dramas – the play ends where it began, in this case with the elderly man staring into the ashes of the hearth and conversing with his dead parents. Typically though, Healy resists easy sentiment or fake melancholy: like the best of his fiction, *On Broken Wings* is ultimately a hymn to the troubled ecstasy of ordinary lives, and a celebration of the whole gift of existence. Or as Timothy's mother quietly puts it, "Isn't life delectable?"

On the Ramparts was first performed by the Drogheda Youth Theatre at the Droichead Arts Centre in 1994, and was directed by the playwright himself. As an article in the *Drogheda Independent* later recalled, Healy spent two months as writer-in-residence at the Droichead Arts Centre, "and wrote the play from his experiences of the people and places of Drogheda." The article also quoted the director of the Arts Centre, Paul O'Hanrahan: "It is an abstract play, a bit like *Waiting for Godot*. It features Drogheda people talking about life in Drogheda and young people's experiences" (n. pag.). Although the ramparts of the title are left unspecified, the play would seem to be set in and around the historic Millmount Fort in Drogheda, overlooking the river Boyne. In a rather Beckettian prologue, three nameless figures stand watch over the monument, bearing mute – and, between themselves, not-so-mute – witness to the travails of history:

> *As the first light wanes, small lights gradually come up over* FIGURE I *(female),* FIGURE II *(male) and* FIGURE III *(female). They are situated stage left, in a half-circle, with* FIGURE I separated *somewhat from the other two. The three figures wear flat masks with minimal features and large mouth openings. They are seated in three stone-coloured partitions. They cannot see each other. They all wear black. At an appropriate moment, after a beat of stick on wood,* FIGURE I *moves her foot,* FIGURE II *moves his arm, and* FIGURE III *moves her head. Silence.* FIGURE I *and* FIGURE II *raise their arms onto their laps.*
> FIGURE 1: Is he there?
> [FIGURE 3 *knocks on partition separating her from* FIGURE 2. *She knocks again.* FIGURE 2 *does not move.*]

Despite its embedded historical allusions, *On the Ramparts* is as much about the experience of young people growing up in contemporary Ireland as it about the ghostly burden of Irish history. Throughout the play, the teenagers bicker and gossip, and these everyday squabbles take place against the backdrop of the monument itself. As in Healy's debut novel *Fighting with*

Shadows, the landscape seems to retain a trace memory of past conflicts and traumas, which impinge on the characters in ways they are barely conscious of.

Last Night's Fun (1996) saw Healy reunited with Theatre Omnibus. In their online synopsis in *Playography Ireland*, the Irish Theatre Institute summed it up as follows:

> Declan works nights. His wife Gloria keeps a washing line of pots in the kitchen and could be back in Herefordshire if she wanted. He is convinced she is having an affair with the apothecary. His mother Maggie lives in a granny flat, listening to the deaths on the local radio (she is uncertain whether her missing husband is dead). When they sleep the women have scandalous dreams; Declan never sleeps, but turns into a musical instrument. Gloria, to stop his outbursts, turns to acoustics.

This summary, though lucid and fair, barely does justice to the manic energy of this musical farce. Throughout the play, the characters communicate by banging gongs, blowing whistles, and tapping out their joys and frustrations on a washing line strung with pots and pans. More than any other Healy play, *Last Night's Fun* depends to a great degree on audience participation, both spontaneous and orchestrated. As he outlined in his detailed stage directions at the opening of the text:

> *All movements are choreographed by sound. Audience participation may or may not take place. Workshops prior to performance would allow a group of five or six performers to sit among the audience. These performers may be conducted from the stage to play various instruments at particular moments, giving single notes, melodies and discordant tunes. In the absence of audience participation, allowance has been made for the actors themselves to create the same musical text on stage.* [. . .]

> *So the text contains possibilities for audience participation or its alternative.*

Healy's passion for music, and his growing awareness of the boundless possibilities of dramatic form, resurfaced in *The Music Box*, which was first performed at the Peacock Theatre in Dublin on 24 January 1998. *The Music Box* – a.k.a. *Boxes* – formed part of a trilogy of short plays entitled *Swans, Boots, and Boxes*, written by Eugene McCabe, Éilís Ní Dhuibhne, and Dermot Healy respectively. The extant script included in this volume is described by the author as "A Prose Treatment of a Play," and indeed this hybrid text could easily have been included in the edited volume of Healy's *Collected Short Stories*. The drama is structured as a kind of Yeatsian fairytale, where a young man, Jack Straw, encounters a series of archetypal figures – a peddler, a washerwoman, and a king – all of whom struggle to take possession of three mysterious music boxes. At the end of the play, the king throws open all of the boxes, and in one simple movement we get the distilled essence of Healy's musical and lyrical conception of theatre: "The sea and the storm and the music pour forth. All gather in pace together. One by one they stop, the music last of all, in darkness."

Mr Staines, Healy's eighth play, was first performed in September 1999 at the Samuel Beckett Theatre, Dublin. It was produced by the award-winning Pan Pan Theatre Company, Dublin, and directed by Gavin Quinn. Best described as a piece of knockabout metatheatre, *Mr Staines* is the most obviously Beckettian of all of Healy's dramas, with a pinch of Pirandello's *Six Characters in Search of an Author* thrown in for good measure. As Pan Pan noted in their online "Archive Scrapbook":

> *Mr Staines* [. . .] is a play within a play. It is set on a stage, where the characters are actors rehearsing their roles. The play is interrupted many times by shouts wafting from the wings, when the characters forget their lines. Throughout, Mr Staines ponders his

> existence and his role in life, not to mention his role in the play. [. . .] One of the most novel and interesting conventions of the play is that the women and the men are never on stage at the same time. Yet they manage to comically communicate with each other from the wings. [. . .] The play ends with Mr Staines continuing his search for the answers. But what were the questions again?

This carnivalesque sense of play – and the enforced separation of men and women – is also evident in one of Healy's most ambitious and engaging dramas, *Men to the Right, Women to the Left* (2001). The play was written in collaboration with the Clones Drama Group from Co. Monaghan, and first performed in the Abbey Theatre Bar, Dublin, as part of Bealtaine, the Season of Creativity in Older Age, in May 2001. It was later broadcast on RTÉ Radio 1 in 2002, and was revived at the Peacock Theatre, Dublin, as part of the 2003 Bealtaine Festival. The script was published in 2005 by the Outreach and Education Department of the Abbey Theatre – the only Healy play published until now – under the general title of *Stories of the Drumlins.* At the end of that volume, the editor, Sharon Murphy, includes a fascinating mini-essay entitled "Reflections on the Process." Murphy notes how the Clones Drama Group initially met once a week at a day care centre in Monaghan, and developed the project over a three-year period. The primary aim was "to introduce the older people to process-based drama and to link their stories and concerns with those played out in the Abbey Theatre productions they attended on a regular basis" (144). As the project developed, Dermot Healy "was selected by the group and subsequently commissioned by the Abbey to develop a script in collaboration with that group" (147). As Murphy describes it:

> They worked together over a period of just three months. Dermot encouraged the participants to write about an incident or incidents in their lives that they remembered, asking them to focus on specific details

> of character, situation and setting and in particular to focus on writing dialogue. Using tape recorders and journals the participants began to write. Though initially they all said they found it challenging, with encouragement and practice the words began to flow. Many participants wrote their stories in letter form to Dermot, many writing several letters. The letters provided the raw material from which Dermot wrote *Men to the Right, Women to the Left.* (147)

Healy clearly relished the collaborative process, and *Men to the Right, Women to the Left* remains one of his most compelling and subtle plays. This is partly due to the graceful manner in which Healy gathered and wove together his material, but it is also a direct consequence of what is not said: those underlying silences, gaps and omissions in the collective narrative that speak volumes about recent Irish history and culture. As one of the elderly participants, Mollie Kearns, later reflected: "The drama was a wonderful experience, an awakening of memories both pleasant and sad. Drama seemed to reach into our souls and capture the community spirit I thought lost in today's world" (154).

This sense of community spirit in the face of an unkind history is also at the heart of Healy's longest and most epic drama, *Metagama* (2004). It was first performed by Theatre Hebrides, Stornoway, on the Isle of Lewis, Scotland, on 18 August 2004 at Studio Alba, Stornoway, and was directed by Muriel Ann Macleod. The play is named after a transatlantic steamship, the Metagama, which transported poor Scottish crofters to Canada during the great wave of emigration from the Western Isles in the 1920s. In a 2004 article in *Northings: Arts and Culture in the Highlands and Islands of Scotland*, one of the co-founders of Theatre Hebrides, Peter Urpeth, reflected on how the play was commissioned and made:

> The name Metagama is totemic in the history of the Outer Hebrides [. . .]. If the play was to work, the writer would have to be able to struggle with some of

> the most enduring and painful episodes in Hebridean history and would have to be able to wring something new from the familiar in order to engage with his or her audience. (n. pag.)

The commission went out to international tender, and applications and treatments arrived from the USA, Canada, Israel, and elsewhere. Healy's "unsentimental" treatment was the unanimous choice of the company's reading panel, and over the course of several months he visited Lewis and "researched his work in both the conventional manner of seeking documents, photos and interviews, and reading of swaths of history and oral accounts; but also his research was unconventional, involving an engagement with the landscapes and seascapes of the islands" (Urpeth, n. pag.). The final draft of the text included in this volume suggests that Healy was an inspired choice. Healy's vivid sense of place is absolutely central to his understanding of the world, and throughout his writings he retained an almost anthropological fascination with local habitats, dialects, customs, and codes of behaviour. In the case of *Metagama*, Healy's empathy for the islanders and their tragic history manifests itself most powerfully in the earthy yet lyrical language, which combines English with phrases of Scottish Gaelic. Like many of Healy's works, *Metagama* is structured in two parts, each of which mirrors the other – in this case, we follow a group of islanders struggling to maintain their lives and dignity, first in the Hebrides and then in Canada. Once again, the play ends where it began, with the transplanted islanders still chanting their work songs on the other side of the Atlantic:

> ALL: Se feamainn tha 'nam chasan. (My feet are made of kelp.) Togail an fheamainn, tionndadh an fheamainn. (Lifting the kelp, turning the kelp.)
>
> [*The work gains momentum, as they sing. Then suddenly they all stop. They take leave of each other, shaking hands. Then one by one they leave the stage.* [. . .] *Enter* MacTAVISH. *He walks around the space.*

> *Looks out at the audience with his lamp. Returns to the door. Hits the switch. Darkness. The sound of the sea starts in the dark, and a far distant sound of bells. Then everything stops.*]

Where *Metagama* was epic and spacious, *Serious* (2005) was – out of site-specific necessity – much more intimate and claustrophobic. *Serious* emerged from Healy's stint as writer-in-residence at Castlerea Prison, Co. Roscommon, and was performed inside the prison in December 2005 by the inmates themselves. Healy worked closely with the prisoners for several months, and the final script captures their experiences and expectations in a manner that is both compassionate and tough-minded. At times the play is very funny, and their endless banter acts a temporary respite to their grim surroundings:

> JER: It's been downhill since James Bond became an Irishman – that's what my Da used ta say. I didn't know he was Irish, did you?
> DANNY: Who, your father?
> JER: Fuck sake.

For the most part, though, the play is deeply serious, and it deftly explores the concept of seriousness both as a euphemism for depression and as a metaphor for mental entrapment:

> DAVE: Do you know what bitterness is?
> MATTIE: Yeh, I can hear it in your voice.
> DAVE: Wanker.
> DANNY: Bitterness is real s-e-r-i-o-u-s.
> OLLIE: Fuck sake.
> DANNY: What happen is you – [*Points at OLLIE.*] – start talking to the wall.
> OLLIE: Hey – watch it.
> DAVE: Okay, Ollie, you tell us what bitterness is.
> OLLIE: Alright, let me think. [*Pause.*] Bitterness is the disease that stops you breaking life's chain.

The idea of bitterness as a form of social disease also informs Healy's 2006 play, *A Night at the Disco*. As part of a "Writers in Schools Project" sponsored by Amnesty International, Ireland, the play was written and directed by Healy in collaboration with the teachers and students of St Mary's Secondary School in Ballina, Co. Mayo. In his "Playwright's Note" for the original programme – which again is reproduced in full as a preface to the extant script – Healy recalled the process of collaboration:

> Like everyone else involved in the project, I did not know what to expect when I arrived. It was up to them to direct me towards what might be occupying their minds. We did a couple of hours work, role-playing, improvising movement and language, and before long a pattern began to emerge: this jarring jaunt the girls reluctantly took by bus each weekend to a disco in Crossmolina, because at the time there was no disco or no cinema available for their age group in Ballina town. [. . .] It may be local, and appear trivial, but to them at the time it was all important. [. . .] They wrote it, and I listened in.

Healy's final play, *Where Are You?* (2010), was also conceived with young people in mind. It was first performed by Sligo Drama Circle Young People's Theatre at The Factory Performance Space, Sligo, on 27 April 2010, and directed by Peter Milne. In an RTÉ documentary about Healy's work, *The Writing in the Sky* (dir. Garry Keane, 2011), there is a short clip of the cast of *Where Are You?* in rehearsal, flapping their arms and hissing like geese. This image of the wild geese becomes the central conceit of the play, and is inspired by Healy's acclaimed volume of poetry, *A Fool's Errand* (2010) – a linked sequence of sonnets which centres on the annual migration of the barnacle geese near Healy's home in Ballyconnell, Co. Sligo. In *Where Are You?*, the natural cycle of the flock's departure and return is juxtaposed against the social rituals of a group of teenagers who are alienated from themselves and the world around them. Throughout the piece, the characters act like avatars trapped within a sinister computer game, and they gradually lose their grip on reality. This thematic fascination with shifting identities and virtual realities is cleverly echoed through the frame-breaking dialogue, which recalls Healy's abiding fondness for the metatheatre of Pirandello and Beckett:

> SHELLEY: Did you ever get the feeling that. . .
> GEORGINA: That we are being watched?
> SHELLEY: And that we. . .
> GEORGINA: Really don't know what we are at?
> SHELLEY: Exactly. You could not have put it better.
> GEORGINA: I'm made up.
> SHELLEY: You are. You were invented.

Yet again, the play ends as it began, with the characters trapped on stage and prevented from leaving by unseen forces. This time, however, Healy implicates the audience in his mischievous *danse macabre*:

> ROBERTO: Please turn off your mobiles. [*He looks straight out to the back of the audience, and heads off in a circle around the stage.* ROBERTO *prepares to head off stage left but a hand comes up, flat palm upward, signalling that he cannot exit.*] Excuse me. . . Is this starting all over again? [*He faces the hand. He bows his head with resignation.*] Come on now. You're joking. [*He is very serious, nearly angry. The hand grows firmer.*] I want to get off, you hear me? [*Pleading softly.*] Why can I not continue on the way I was going? [*He stands listening. The hand slowly drops, and as it does so the lights go down slowly, in time to the hand, as if the hand was conducting the light. When the hand at last goes back in behind the curtain, the lights go out. Silence.*]

Although the settings and idioms of Healy's plays are often local by design, their energy and vision invariably transcend those boundaries. Moreover, the experimental impulse is always balanced and kept in check by a clear ethical commitment, with a fruitful dialectic between dialogue and dramaturgy. As Michelle Paull remarks:

> Healy's drama is evocative, lyrical and disturbing. Working with specialist groups on local subjects does not limit his theatrical reach but instead widens the dramatic resonance. By allowing the local to speak for the national, his work points to the underlying connections between personal stories and international events. While his narrative fiction celebrates the evocative nature of language, his drama explores the visceral impact of that which cannot be captured on paper, using sound, visual imagery, and music to offer the audience the feeling of an experience rather than simply present a rational or intellectual explanation of things. Healy's theatre is above all a theatre of the physical and, as such, his work deserves to remain at the centre of contemporary stage practice and design. (381)

The thirteen plays collected here show the origins and evolution of Dermot Healy's subtle and complex style, and serve as a written record of a substantial theatrical *oeuvre*. But these plays were obviously written to be performed, and so our ultimate wish in compiling this volume is to see some of these works being revived in the near future. In this respect, the publication of *The Collected Plays* should be of interest not just to scholars and devotees of Irish theatre, but to all practitioners of contemporary drama.

—Keith Hopper & Neil Murphy,
Oxford and Singapore, 2016

Works Cited

Anon. "Award for Writer of Drogheda Play." *Drogheda Independent* (27 June 2002): <www.independent.ie/regionals/droghedaindependent/news/award-for-writer-of-drogheda-play-27115775.html> [accessed 15 February 2016].

Anon. Entry for "Theatre Omnibus." *Playography Ireland: A comprehensive database of new Irish plays produced professionally since 1904*. Irish Theatre Institute: <www.irishplayography.com/company.aspx?companyid=209> [accessed 15 February 2016].

Anon. Entry for "*Last Night's Fun*." *Playography Ireland: A comprehensive database of new Irish plays produced professionally since 1904*. Irish Theatre Institute: <www.irishplayography.com/play.aspx?playid=713> [accessed 15 February 2016].

Anon. Entry for "Mr Staines". *Current Archive Scrapbook for Press*. Pan Pan Theatre Company website: <http://panpantheatre.com/shows/mr-staines/> [accessed 15 February 2016].

Healy, Dermot. *A Fool's Errand*. Oldcastle, Co. Meath: Gallery Press, 2010.

———. *The Bend for Home: A Memoir*. London: The Harvill Press, 1996.

———. *The Collected Short Stories*. Edited, with an Introduction, by Keith Hopper & Neil Murphy. Illinois/London/Dublin: Dalkey Archive Press, 2015.

———. *Fighting with Shadows*. Edited, with an Introduction, by Neil Murphy & Keith Hopper. 1984; Illinois/London/Dublin: Dalkey Archive Press, 2015.

———. "Playwright's Note." Programme for the Theatre

Omnibus production of *On Broken Wings*, Ennis, Co. Clare (January 1992). Programme courtesy of the Healy Estate.

Keane, Garry. Dir. *The Writing in the Sky* [documentary on Dermot Healy]. Ireland: RTÉ, 2011. 54 mins. DVD.

O'Toole, Fintan. Programme Notes for the Seven Woods Theatre Company production of Dermot Healy's adaptation of *Blood Wedding*, The Hawk's Well Theatre, Sligo (June 1989). Programme courtesy of the Healy Estate.

Paull, Michelle C. "Dermot Healy: Local, National and International Drama." *Writing the Sky: Observations and Essays on Dermot Healy*. Edited, with an Introduction, by Neil Murphy & Keith Hopper, with a foreword by Neil Jordan. Texas/London/Dublin: Dalkey Archive Press, 2016. 365–81.

Sennett, Graham. "The Hacklers Rise." *Evening Press* (7 June 1980). The Hacklers Collection, Cavan Library: <www.cavanlibrary.ie/file/Local-Studies/Library-Scanned-Docs/The-Hacklers-Collection.pdf> [accessed 15 February 2016].

Urpeth, Peter. "Dermot Healy delivers on *Metagama*." *Northings: Arts and Culture in the Highlands and Islands of Scotland* (14 July 2004): <http://northings.com/2004/07/14/metagama/> [accessed 15 February 2016].

A Note on the Texts

In March 2014, Dermot Healy provided the editors with the most up-to-date typescripts of all thirteen of his plays. He also supplied us with some miscellaneous production notes and background information, which proved invaluable in the editing of this collection. The original typescripts were collated by the playwright himself with the assistance of Helen Gillard Healy and Eileen O'Toole, and were presented to us in various formats (both hard copy and digital). Given that the plays span a period of twenty-five years (1985–2010), and include an ad hoc mixture of final revised drafts and rehearsal scripts, the formatting and presentation of these base texts varied considerably from play to play. Thus, for the purposes of this volume, we have standardised and reformatted the texts in the conventional manner for published plays, and in accordance with the Dalkey Archive Press house style. The original typescripts contained a considerable number of typographical errors, mostly relating to punctuation and spelling, and these have been silently sub-edited throughout. The cast lists, in particular, were often a little erratic: given the collaborative nature of Healy's theatrical process, the scripts sometimes evolved to include characters not initially listed, and in several plays the main actors played multiple but unlisted roles. Consequently, all characters are now listed in order of their appearance on stage. In all cases, though, we have stayed true to the dialogue and stage directions as written down by the playwright in the original typescripts provided. One particular Healyism is worth mentioning: occasionally a character will ask a rhetorical question, which Healy often presents without a question mark, thus making the sentence more quietly declarative, e.g. "Is that so." As far as possible, we have followed this convention.

One play, *Metagama*, proved particularly problematic. The extant script is the final rehearsal version dated 26 July 2004, on which new lines were scribbled in and existing lines and scenes were scribbled out. We have retained as much of the original script and marginalia as possible, and disentangled the rather muddled cast list (each of the seven core actors plays multiple parts, not all of which were clearly delineated). Throughout the rehearsal script the characters speak a mixture of English and Scottish Gaelic, but the improvised use of Gaelic was intermittent and rather ad hoc. Moreover, Healy's rough, phonetic rendering of Scottish Gaelic was sometimes incomprehensible, all of which effectively precluded any future productions. Consequently, we have tightened up the Gaelic text considerably, and appended the following editorial note: "For the most part, their speech in the text is presented in English. Depending on the linguistic ability of the actors, they can introduce some Gaelic phrases at appropriate points. Any line of Gaelic spoken should be immediately followed by its translation into English. In some key scenes, Gaelic is spoken for dramatic and thematic effect, and these lines have been tidied up and retained."

Each play in this volume is prefaced by a short note outlining the date and the basic details of its first production; where possible, we have indicated the status of the extant text as being either a revised draft version or a final rehearsal script.

Acknowledgements

This volume of *The Collected Plays* was conceived and initiated with Dermot Healy's blessing and assistance in July 2013. Dermot had kindly agreed to comment on the final draft typescript and galley proofs; sadly, following his untimely death in June 2014, this was not to be. We do hope that this collection would have met with Dermot's approval, and that its publication will, in some small way, serve as a tribute to his memory. We are very grateful to his family and friends for their encouragement and support in bringing this volume to fruition; any errors in the text are entirely our own.

Immense gratitude and admiration are also offered to Dermot's wife, Helen Gillard Healy, who was deeply involved in this venture from the outset, during early discussions in Singapore and Sligo, and thereafter by phone, email and in person – none of this would have been possible without her help and commitment.

Seán Golden's friendship with Dermot spanned more than four decades, as did his familiarity with the intensely nuanced topography of the work – we have been extremely fortunate to find in Professor Golden a most helpful and gracious guide through the labyrinths of print and myth. Brian Leyden has also been an invaluable presence for which we are, and continue to be, extremely thankful. Eileen O'Toole helped Dermot to gather together and collate all of the original typescripts, and provided much-needed logistical support. We are also grateful to Frank Conway, Marianne Fahey, Siobhan Dooney, John Gaffney, and Noreen Egan for helping Dermot to fill in some of the gaps in the production notes and bibliography. Without the assistance of those who were familiar with Dermot's work and life down through the years, our work would have been, at the very least, far more challenging.

We owe a special debt of thanks to Paddy Murray, one of the original members of the Hacklers Theatre Group, Cavan, for generously providing us with newspaper clippings and photographs of the group's award-winning production of *Waiting for Godot*. Paddy, with the help of Mags Amond and Nollaig Amond Murray, kindly supplied us with the photograph which adorns the cover of this volume. Thanks also to David Chaplin and James Connolly for their help in cleaning up and digitizing the image.

The cover photograph was taken by Beth Rigdell (14 June 1980), and now forms part of The Hacklers Collection, Cavan Library: <www.cavanlibrary.ie/file/Local-Studies/Library-Scanned-Docs/The-Hacklers-Collection.pdf>. We have tried to track down Ms Rigdell, without success, so we hope that this acknowledgment will act as a thank-you for her fine group portrait of the Hacklers (Dermot Healy is on the far right of the picture gazing off into the distance). We are grateful to the Hacklers Theatre Group for allowing us permission to reproduce this image.

Thanks too are offered to John O'Brien for his visionary Dalkey Archive Press, with sincere gratitude for his continued support of this venture, and for his ongoing contribution to literature that matters. We are also indebted to Jeff Higgins and the production team at Dalkey Archive for their diligence and patience in producing this and the three other books in the multi-volume sequence devoted to Dermot Healy.

We are very grateful to Dr Michelle Chiang, who offered much-needed support and dedication in preparing the text for publication.

Emma Wilcox, the English subject librarian at the School of Humanities and Social Sciences library, NTU, has, as always, been extremely supportive. Thanks also to Prof Lance Pettitt, Dr Michelle Paull, Prof Shaun Richards, Donal McCay, and everyone in the Centre for Irish Studies at St Mary's University, Twickenham, for their encouragement and advice. Thanks also to Dr Catherine McGuinn, Dr Rhona Trench, and Dr Una Mannion at the Institute of Technology, Sligo, for inviting us to discuss Dermot Healy's plays with their Performing Arts students.

Katie Moriarty-Hopper commented on some of the early typescript versions of the Healy plays, and her theatrical expertise – as well as her keen editorial eye – proved invaluable. We are grateful, once again, to Dr Jack Fennell for his linguistic expertise, and for helping us with some of the Scottish Gaelic phrases in *Metagama*.

One of the plays in this collection, *Men to the Right, Women to the Left*, was originally published as *Stories of the Drumlins: A Collaborative Theatre Project Developed by the Abbey Theatre, Positive Age and the Health Service Executive*, ed. Sharon Murphy (Dublin: Outreach/Education Department of The Abbey Theatre, 2005), 155pp. We are grateful to Phil Kingston and the Abbey Theatre's Outreach and Education Department for allowing us permission to reprint this play.

This work was completed with the assistance of a Singapore MOE, ACRF Tier 1 grant, awarded to the editors in 2014, for which thanks and acknowledgement are registered.

Deepest gratitude, as always, is offered to Niamh Moriarty and Su Salim Murphy, for their constant support and encouragement.

THE COLLECTED PLAYS

Here, and There, and Going to America

First performed at the Sligo Youth Centre in 1985 by the Dole Q Company, Sligo. Directed by Dermot Healy.

CAST

MICHAEL O'DONNELL	a punk
SEAN O'DONNELL	a skinhead
MAGGIE	
IRISH DOLE OFFICER	Mr McManus
VARIOUS YOUNG PEOPLE	
A PORTER	
ENGLISH DOLE OFFICER	
OLD WOMAN	
OLD FELLOW	
A YORKSHIREMAN	
A COCKNEY	a man
A POLE	a man
A SCOT	a man
A LIVERPUDLIAN	a man
A NORTHERN IRISHMAN	
PRIEST	
NEIL	a hippy busker
FIDO	a female busker
PADDY McMORROW	and his punk band
WOMAN DOLE OFFICER	
MAN IN THE QUEUE	
SECOND MAN IN THE QUEUE	
TINA	from Donegal
GRAINNE	from Donegal

Mode: Each scene is announced by a character in top hat and tails who will turn over the pages on a noticeboard where in legible scrawl are the names of the scenes.
Style: Street language; crowd scenes.

SCENE 1
The Sligo Train

We are on an embankment beside the railway. Even before the lights come up we hear the sound of a train in the distance. On stage are a party of young people (maybe about seven of them) variously scattered about, drinking cider and handing around cigarettes; SEAN *and* MICHAEL *are stage right. The train comes, climaxes, and passes. This sound should fill the place, then recede, and the lights dim accordingly.*

SCENE 2
The Home

Table is mid-stage, MICHAEL *stage left,* SEAN *stage right, both seated. It is night-time. Various tics – drumming with the hands on the table, feeling their hair, etc., and* MICHAEL *provides some hysterical outbursts of nonsense. We open on one of these.*

MICHAEL: Go long. Go long. Do tell me. Oh certainly, certainly. [*Adopts English accent.*] My good man. [*Back to Irish accent.*] Bejazus now. I'll break your face. And of course we all have our problems, and you'll be alright – just keep taking the tablets and vomit in the street, do you hear, not in the house, not on your person, but find a nice spot of your own and show your skills, demonstrate to me your skills, if you please, and not a moment too late, he came up behind me, the bastard . . .

SEAN: [*He has not been listening.*] Do you know, I think you're right sham.

MICHAEL: Of course I'm right.

SEAN: And what could we do there?

MICHAEL: Where would we get off?

SEAN: If it's New York, do we go to Boston?

[*Pause.*]

MICHAEL: What would the work be like?

SEAN: You could get a job in a casino, something like that, maybe.

MICHAEL: Maybe.

SEAN: We'd be skint anyway.

MICHAEL: You can be sure of that.

SEAN: And how do we go in?

MICHEAL: We could go by Mexico.

SEAN: The Mexican prison is not very clean. They'd beat the head of you there.

MICHAEL: And if we went in the legal way how would that work out?

SEAN: That's a problem.

[*Pause. They consider this. A bottle comes out of a bag, is quickly shared, and then put back in again.*]

MICHAEL: I think I know.

SEAN: How?

MICHAEL: We go in by England. [*Pause.*] We go in by England, pick up the few bob there, and just head off. [*Pause.*] What we have to do is get to England first.

SEAN: Well there's nothing for us here.

MICHAEL: And that means a letter.

SEAN: How come, Sham?

MICHAEL: A letter to the Dole from some class of an uncle inviting us over.

SEAN: You could ask Paddy McMorrow, he's in some kip in London.

MICHAEL: Paddy can't write.

SEAN: He can fairly play the bass.

MICHAEL: But Maggie could type us up a version and Paddy send us a stamp, and they'd be happy enough with that down at the dole.

SEAN: We could ask around.

MICHAEL: The very first thing in the morning, Sean.

SEAN: Right Sham.

[*Pause.*]

MICHAEL: I want out of this hole.

SEAN: You'd get depressed.

MICHAEL: And then we'll be on the waves. It'll be cheery-bye.

SEAN: And no loss.

MICHAEL: You have to look after the little things. The very first thing in the morning, Sean. Right?

SEAN: Are we bringing anyone else with us?

MICHAEL: No, only ourselves. [*Pause.*] They can come over later. We'll be alright. You'll see.

[*Lights down.*]

SCENE 3

The Gay Byrne Hour

The kitchen by morning. SEAN *standing by the table, emptying pockets, but coming up with little. If possible, Gay Byrne speaking in the background on the radio.* SEAN *is looking to see what money he has left and you can tell he is distressed.*

SEAN: Ah shit. [*He sits with a mug of tea.*] It was all talk anyway. [*Takes out the teabag. Picks up a guitar maybe, puts it down.*] Ah no. [SEAN *can whinge.*]

MICHAEL: [*Off.*] Hey, give us a hand.

[*Enter* MICHAEL *and* MAGGIE *with typewriter. They set it up on the table.*]

SEAN: You're serious.

MAGGIE: Hallo there, Sean.

SEAN: You know what's going on, Maggie?

MAGGIE: Aye.

SEAN: And what will the mother say?

MICHAEL: I saw her before she went to work. She said she'd be glad to see the end of us. [SEAN *sits. He puts on loud music.*

MAGGIE *sits behind the typewriter, slips a sheet of paper in, takes out a fag, and waits.*]

MICHAEL: [*Shouts.*] Will you shut that thing, I can't hear myself think.

[SEAN *cuts off radio.*]

[*Silence.*]

MAGGIE: C'mon lads.

[*Silence.*]

MICHAEL: Fuck you Sean, say something.

SEAN: Number 1, The Siding, Beecher Street, Kensington.

MAGGIE: Well that will do for a start.

SEAN: Dear Mr McManus.

MAGGIE: Dear Mr McManus.

MICHAEL: Dear who? Dear Christ. Who is writing to Mr McManus?

SEAN: The Uncle is.

MICHAEL: No, he's not you idiot.

SEAN: Well who is he writing to?

MICHAEL: He's writing to us, for fuck sake.

MAGGIE: Ah so it'll be Dear Sean.

SEAN: Yes that'll do.

MAGGIE: And Michael.

SEAN: Aye. [*Pause.*] Well he might enquire how we are, like.

MICHAEL: Exactly. He'd ask whether you were the same bollix you always were.

MAGGIE: That's nice.

SEAN: I thought youse might be interested to know.

MICHAEL: What are you on about?

SEAN: That's how he'd start. The Uncle is a plain man, he gets right to it.

MAGGIE: I thought you might be interested to know . . .

MICHAEL: That we have two vacancies.

SEAN: No.

MICHAEL: No what?

SEAN: You don't have vacancies on a building site.

MICHAEL: And what do you have?

SEAN: Situations.

MICHAEL: Situations?
SEAN: Yeh.
MAGGIE: That we have two situations. That sounds mad.
SEAN: Vacant.
MAGGIE: Vacant.
SEAN: At present, like. If you are interested. What else would he say? He'd say like "How is the Mammy?" Is he from Sligo? Would he ask about the town and that crack? He'd say something like "How are things about the town? Is it still the same hole?"

[MAGGIE *lights up another cigarette.*]

MAGGIE: C'mon lads.
MICHAEL: I'll keep the jobs open till I hear from. You.
MAGGIE: Yours sincerely.
SEAN: Uncle Stephen.
MICHAEL: Uncle George.
SEAN: No, he's got to be a Stephen. A George 'id be too grand.
MAGGIE: So now. [*She flicks page up.*] 1, The Sidings, Beecher's Street, Kensington. Dear Sean and Michael, I thought you might be interested to know that since you last wrote to me asking for work nothing came up till the last few days. I have now two situations vacant and will hold the jobs open till I hear from you. How is your mother? Tell her Elizabeth sends her regards, and is looking forward to seeing her this summer in Sligo which she says is the most beautiful place in the world. I'll sign off here, yours, Uncle Jim.
SEAN: You're some woman, Maggie.

[*Lights off.*]

SCENE 4

The Sligo Dole Office

Desk, phone, ledgers, such posters as would be proper. DOLE OFFICER *keeps taking off and putting on magnificent bottle-glasses. He has a tic of cleanliness. The two lads are in their Sunday best, they'd sit up straight, hair a bit flattened down, but always on the verge of rebelling. It's the weight of Sligo and familiarity on them. We open on* DOLE OFFICER *standing stage right, his desk is stage left, he is in actual fact pinning a poster to the back wall as part of the scene change. Knocking sound.*

DOLE OFFICER: Come in. [*They enter.*] Sit down over there, I'll be with you in a while. [*He finishes pinning up the poster, stands back, espies. Checks desk for file.* MICHAEL *sits.* SEAN *stands.*] Hold on there a second. The O'Donnells, isn't it? [*He exits.*]

MICHAEL: [*Quietly.*] I'll do the talking.

[DOLE OFFICER *returns with the files. Sits. Looks at them.*]

DOLE OFFICER: And what can I do for you?

MICHAEL: I got this letter in the post the other day from England. [*He hands it over, sits.*]

DOLE OFFICER: And the envelope, please. [MICHAEL *hands it over, sits.* DOLE OFFICER *commences to read, disturbs files, reads there, returns to letters, back to files.*] How much are you getting on the dole?

MICHAEL: We get thirty-four pounds each. The father is dead.

SEAN: We've jobs promised over there.

MICHAEL: We're unemployed two years.

SEAN: This is our chance to make a go of things.

DOLE OFFICER: [*Glasses on/off.*] Hold on for a minute will you. Let me finish. [*Two boys awkward. He lays down the glasses.*] Have you been in this line of work before?

MICHAEL: We've had no work before.

DOLE OFFICER: Have you been in England, how do you think you'd settle there?

SEAN: Sure don't we look like them.

DOLE OFFICER: I suppose you do.

MICHAEL: The Uncle is alright.

DOLE OFFICER: And you've spoken to your mother.

MICHAEL: We told the mother this morning.

DOLE OFFICER: [*Hesitancy.*] And what do you think you'll find over there that you won't find here?

MICHAEL: That's obvious.

DOLE OFFICER: And if you were only thinking of having a holiday at our expense, I have to tell you that you'd be cut off for a while should you return.

MICHAEL: We are not thinking of coming back, Mr McManus.

DOLE OFFICER: Wait outside, please. [*He taps with a pencil. The boys leave to corridor outside.* DOLE OFFICER *checks stamp on envelope, and lifts the phone.*]

SEAN: I don't like this one bit.

MICHAEL: Take it easy.

SEAN: I'd give anything for a fag.

MICHAEL: Just keep your mouth shut.

[SEAN *gives a karate kick towards his brother's head. Then they both enter into a series of funny walks and stances.*]

DOLE OFFICER: [*On phone.*] I've got the two young O'Donnells here. From St Joseph's. Yes. Up the hill. Seemingly they have an Uncle Stephen in the painting and decoration trade in Peckham. Oh it seems genuine enough. Yes, I have a phone number. Should I bother? What do you think yourself? The stamp is from England, all right.

[*In the corridor, they break into exercise.*]

SEAN: Fuck, he's taking his time.

MICHAEL: What if he calls the number?

SEAN: I'm going.

MICHAEL: [*Grabbing him.*] I'll break your neck, you rat.

[*Meanwhile,* DOLE OFFICER *has replaced the phone and rung another number.*]

SEAN: He's taking a long time.

MICHAEL: What's he at in there?

SEAN: Who knows? [SEAN *stands on his head.*]

DOLE OFFICER: Hallo, CIE? Hallo, could I book two seats to London? This is McManus here, Social Welfare. Hallo, yes. For Monday, fine. Yes, indeed, coach and boat. In the names of, just a sec, yes, Michael and Sean O'Donnell. Yes, that's them. Oh there's plenty of them about. [*Chuckles good-manneredly.*] And you can charge it to the Health, the Department of Health. Thank you. What's that? Oh yes, one way. [*Replaces phone. Gets up immediately, enters corridor to find* SEAN *on his head, and* MICHAEL *doing push-ups. Blackout.*]

SCENE 5

The Going-Away Party

A whole hive of young people, all types, arranged around the stage, sitting, standing, wafting. We are in Sligo graveyard. Each person as they enter carries in a gravestone. One lad puts a bowl of flowers by one. A drape is thrown over the dole office desk to make a mausoleum and on it is placed a skull. SEAN *sits there, dangling his legs. There are about seven or eight people on stage. Four lads huddled and one woman stage right. Two girls centre stage at back.* SEAN *has a bottle of cider sitting on the mausoleum beside him. This scene will depend on improvised words. There are some lines of importance though.*

MICHAEL: [*Explaining to the lads.*] Patrick McMorrow will be meeting us at Victoria.

GIRL: Are you going to go into music, Sean?

SEAN: You never know. But everyone says my songs are too morbid.

LAD: Fuck, so they are.

SEAN: Well I don't mean them to be.

MICHAEL: [*He breaks into English-accented gibberish which no-one passes any heed to.*] Hallo mate. Where'd you get the earrings then? Fucking great party. Got any old dope? Bloody awrful party. No, that's not right. It's a great bloody party. [*He thumps ground with can.*]

LAD: It's a good job you don't drink Michael.

MICHAEL: I met this bloke right? He was running with blood. Right? Right down over his shirt, see? I said, what's this mate? He said bugger off, bastard. My name is George the First.

GIRL: I can see youse now.

SEAN: So can I.

[*Enter at distance the sound of train. It passes very quietly, returns with more strength. Group prepares to leave. Various words from songs.*]

VOICE: See you Michael.

VOICE: See you Sean.

SEAN: Good luck, Sham.

[*They turn the grave stones around, and on them is written Manchester, Birmingham, Edinburgh, etc., with train timetables (they are all angled stage left). All this is done in the half-light. A bucket of papers is emptied over the two lads who sit stage centre at the back. This also in half-light. The train reaches its peak, recedes, lights come up but not full.*]

SCENE 6

Victoria Station

The desk that became the mausoleum is now a rack for cases and a PORTER *is hauling it away from stage left to stage right. There is complete silence. It is packed with an assortment of bags. The two lads watch him haul.* SEAN *is sitting with his bag between his legs,* MICHAEL *standing with his bag beside him. They are pretty ruffled and out of focus. People come to inspect the timetables (i.e. on the gravestones), and walk off again. Loudspeakers give the times. Lights go down some, then revive.* SEAN *is lying out asleep with his head on his bag;* MICHAEL *is sitting on his bag, with a stranger standing beside him.*

FIRST LOUDSPEAKER: The six-thirty for Brighton will be leaving from Platform 9.

SECOND LOUDSPEAKER: The ten-thirty to Southampton is leaving in three minutes from Platform 2.

THIRD LOUDSPEAKER: Will Mr Jenkins please come to the information desk?

[*Lights go down, revive,* SEAN *is sitting alone chewing a hamburger, and* MICHAEL *backs in from stage right.*]

SEAN: Well?

MICHAEL: There's no reply.

SEAN: Are you sure you know how to work the phones over here?

MICHAEL: Don't be a fucking pain.

SEAN: Well, where is the bastard?

FOURTH LOUDSPEAKER: If Patrick McMorrow is in the station will he please come to the information desk. [*Repeat.*] If Patrick McMorrow is in the station will he please come to the information desk.

[SEAN *surprised, laughs, they sit on their bags waiting.* PORTER *approaches.*]

SEAN: Is it far to Peckham, mister?

[*The* PORTER *is taken aback. Nervous of skinhead.*]

PORTER: Yes, man, yeh. It's a long way. [*He moves off a bit.*]

SEAN: Thank you anyway.

PORTER: [*Stops, turns.*] And you can't get a train from here, man. You gotta go to Euston, change there, and take the underground to The City, and you can get an overground to Peckham, changing over at Forrester, there. OK?

SEAN: Yeh fine, thanks.

PORTER: No problem.

[*He goes off,* SEAN *sits by* MICHAEL.]

MICHAEL: There's no point asking anyway. We'll just wait till Paddy comes.

SEAN: Fucking Paddy never comes.

[PORTER *reappears dragging desk emptied of cases behind him. This time places it stage right. He begins taking away in the half-light the destination signs, while whistling. The boys watch him intently. He places a chair in front of the desk, surveys the scene, the train sound goes away, with one quick flourish he whips blankets away, and lights immediately go off.*]

SCENE 7

The Westminster Dole Office

SEAN *seated,* MICHAEL *standing. There is much tension in the air. They face the desk at stage right. At rear of stage a lone* OLD

WOMAN *sits with many plastic bags completely immobile on a forum. At times they might look at her but the pace of the exchange is very fast, the scene much different than that in Sligo.* DOLE OFFICER *wears a poppy in his buttonhole. The boys look wild. Open scene with them staring at each other, adversaries.*

DOLE OFFICER: And where are you staying at the moment? [*He stands behind his desk.*]

SEAN: Victoria Station.

MICHAEL: We haven't got a place yet.

DOLE OFFICER: You can't get off a train from Ireland and expect her Majesty's Government to take care of you.

SEAN: We had a fellow was supposed to meet us. [*He gestures.*]

MICHAEL: We have jobs coming.

DOLE OFFICER: And why did you not go directly to your source of employment?

MICHAEL: [*A small moment's hesitancy.*] We will not be getting the go-ahead for two weeks.

DOLE OFFICER: And where did you expect to stay in the meanwhile?

SEAN: Oh hey Sham, that's what we are here for.

DOLE OFFICER: You should have thought of that before you came over.

MICHAEL: Aren't we entitled to it?

DOLE OFFICER: I'll decide what you are entitled to.

SEAN: And what was all this talk about the EEC? Hey? [*He gestures.*]

MICHAEL: You mean we are going to get nothing?

DOLE OFFICER: Come back in the morning and we'll see.

MICHAEL: Lookat here.

SEAN: Where can we go to?

MICHAEL: We're going no place. We're staying here.

DOLE OFFICER: There's nothing I can do for you till tomorrow.

MICHAEL: Look we've been here waiting all day.

SEAN: We've no place else to go.

DOLE OFFICER: You should have thought of that – at the risk

of repeating myself – before you came.

MICHAEL: We're not moving Sham, till we get our rations.

SEAN: You tell him, Michael.

DOLE OFFICER: You are not the only ones who have problems. It's impossible. I can't attend to your problem till tomorrow.

OLD WOMAN: [*Suddenly, without looking at them.*] And then it'll be the day after tomorrow.

[*All conversation stops.* DOLE OFFICER *sits, waiting for them to go away.*]

MICHAEL: I demand to see your boss. [*No reply.*] I demand to see the manager.

DOLE OFFICER: You're in no position to demand anything. And anyway, he'll only repeat what I've told you.

SEAN: [*Tapping table.*] Send him down here and we'll talk to him.

DOLE OFFICER: [*He looks at the two of them. Rises.*] I'm sorry, I'll have to ask you to leave.

SEAN: Well fuck you.

[*He gets up, tears a sleeping bag out of his bag and spreads it on the floor. For the first time the* OLD WOMAN *takes note of this fellow. She nods, resumes her reverie.* SEAN *disappears into his sleeping bag.*]

MICHAEL: And that goes for me.

DOLE OFFICER: Okay, have it your own way. You leave me no alternative except to call in the police. [*He exits from behind desk.*]

SEAN: I don't want – [*Head appearing.*] – to spend the night in a cop-shop.

MICHAEL: I'm not backing down. They want to give us the run-around.

[SEAN *sits up, wondering.*]

MICHAEL: I know my rights.

[SEAN *climbs out of sleeping-bag.* DOLE OFFICER *reappears, takes in scene, then sits.*]

DOLE OFFICER: Okay now, if you are in a more obliging frame of mind can we start from the beginning again. [*He lifts his pen, looks up.*]

SEAN: [*Sitting.*] My name is Sean O'Donnell and this is my brother Michael . . . [*At this stage an* OLD FELLOW *with a fag in his mouth enters with a tray of delph. He deposits it on* DOLE OFFICER's *desk. Then from stage left he pulls another table with places set onto the stage. Passing no remarks* SEAN *tells his tale.*] We came over from Sligo the other morning looking for work, no, we were going to work. We have jobs out in Peckham to go to. We were looking for a place to stay. [*Meanwhile, simultaneous with this, various other men emerge, the lights start to go down, and the* OLD FELLOW *reappears ringing bell.* DOLE OFFICER *takes jacket off the back of his chair, puts on hat, and we move simultaneously into the hostel scene with* SEAN *speaking and guiding us through.*]

SCENE 8
The Hostel Scene

This is a dowdy place. Eight men eventually seated around two tables. The OLD WOMAN *brings in the steaming pots of tea, the* OLD FELLOW *shuffles about, sweeping.* SEAN *continues talking, breaking for the one intervention of the bell ringing.*

OLD FELLOW: [*Whispers.*] Breakfast, dol-de-do. [*Shouts.*] Breakfast up.

[SEAN *remains where he is seated, as does* the YORKSHIREMAN. *Two men take other their places at the table,* MICHAEL *goes to sit in a chair but* . . .]

COCKNEY: Oi, you can't sit there, that's my chair.

SEAN: [*Continuing to speak.*] Then we spent two nights at Victoria Station.

COCKNEY: Well you'd want to watch your bum there, mate.

SEAN: And then we got emergency accommodation.

[*At first table on left* is the YORKSHIREMAN, *at the back is the* COCKNEY, *right is* SEAN, *and at the front is a* NORTHERN IRISHMAN. *Next table left is a*

LIVERPUDLIAN, *back* MICHAEL, *right a* SCOT, *and front (with back to audience) is a* POLE. OLD WOMAN *brings out the steaming bowls of porridge. The* SCOT *is in the rats.* MICHAEL *goes for the sugar, so does the* SCOT, MICHAEL *leaves it to him. There is silence until the* POLE *starts a lament, only partly in his own language.*]

POLE: La za motay, en due fornicay, malakay, duo. Nanze Magi. Oh. Neno parakowsky. Neduo en dorso, nanze magi. [MICHAEL *looks up thinking it's directed at him; everyone else passes no remarks.*] Ish konfo kawzi. [*Sighs as if in romantic take*]. Ill kuno day, nanze magi. [MICHAEL *aghast, not knowing what to answer.*]

SCOT: That's it Leki, you tell him.

POLE: Maza koffe tu, brigand az tonfay, jettison and Ardlougher, mallme, ikist. Ill me penseroso, tu. Nanze magi. [*Sadly.*] Nanze magi.

LIVERPUDLIAN: Will you shut your hole. Every morning it's the same thing.

POLE: [*Continues in lower mumble.*] Us tay pay sans dearth, us tay pay. Navum Scouse. [*Shrieks.*] Nanze magi.

[SEAN *laughs.*]

COCKNEY: And what the hell are you laughing at?

NORTHERN IRISHMAN: [*Roots in his bags – the same bags the* OLD WOMAN *had in the previous scene.*] It's five hundred miles from London to Glasgow, give or take a few.

SEAN: Is it.

NORTHERN IRISHMAN: Give or take, and London to Liverpool – three hundred and fifty.

LIVERPUDLIAN: The other fellow is off now.

[POLE *continues in a low chanting key.*]

NORTHERN IRISHMAN: Birmingham to Manchester – one hundred and sixty. Dover to Bristol – two hundred.

[COCKNEY *interrogates the racing page.*]

YORKSHIREMAN: Would you be interested in a radio? [*He takes a small radio out of his pocket and places it before* SEAN.]

SEAN: Does it work?

YORKSHIREMAN: Course it does, course it does.

[SEAN *turns the dial and it comes on at a blast.* OLD FELLOW *on forum at back nearly drops cup.*]

LIVERPUDLIAN: Ah, Jock, you know what I mean.

[*Radio remains on.*]

SCOT: Shut it off Paddy.

SEAN: [SEAN *knocks it off.*] I don't have the bread.

[YORKSHIREMAN *replaces the radio in his pocket.*]

YORKSHIREMAN: We can speak of these things again. Is yourself and your mate long on the road?

SEAN: He's my brother.

YORKSHIREMAN: No lack of respect intended.

COCKNEY: Take a decko at this. [*He just continues reading.*]

YORKSHIREMAN: What part of Ireland? I've got plenty of friends over there, yes plenty . . .

[*Scowl and bitter laugh from* COCKNEY.] What part of Ireland are you from?

SEAN: St Joseph's, St Joseph's in Sligo.

NORTHERN IRISHMAN: I don't know Sligo but I know Donegal.

YORKSHIREMAN: And what did you come over here for?

SEAN: To go to America.

[*The* SCOT *has a spluttering fit.*]

SCOT: Say that again. [*Silence.*] I say Paddy, where did you say you were going?

SEAN: America.

COCKNEY: Well you're a bit out of your way, a little bit off course.

SEAN: Well that's where we're going.

MICHAEL: Shut your face, Sean, you half-wit.

LIVERPUDLIAN: And how about passports, visas? [*He turns round to* SEAN *who is directly behind him.*]

SEAN: [*Bad-temperedly.*] Ask me brother.

MICHAEL: No, we haven't got them yet. That's in the long term.

COCKNEY: We've got two right ones here.

SCOT: Youse are all fucking mad anyway.

[OLD FELLOW *and* OLD WOMAN *begin collecting the*

cups, etc., and the POLE*'s voice emerges from the throng as if saying grace after meals. He strikes his heart three times and, strangely enough, everyone remains silent until he ends.*]

POLE: Iosagan san kawxa, king dul mayer, is on Kurosawa dunta, is on ego briste. Nosay. Nosay. Nosay Lana Turner may bless, ish moribund, la un say tray kish dun, duntay. [*He enters a silent reverie.* LIVERPUDLIAN *rises to his feet, turns his chair round next to* SEAN.]

LIVERPUDLIAN: Would you like a game of cards?

NORTHERN IRISHMAN: [*To* MICHAEL.] Come over and sit down Sligo. Aye.

SEAN: A game of cards would go down nice after the breakfast. [*This statement raises eyebrows.*]

NORTHERN IRISHMAN: And what's your names, lads?

SEAN: My name is Sean.

NORTHERN IRISHMAN: How are you Seanie?

SEAN: [*Taking note of* MICHAEL *reluctantly pulling his chair over.*] And my brother's name is Michael.

NORTHERN IRISHMAN: Aye, Mihawl. Over here you have to think in distances, see. See me, I'm from the Ormeau Road myself, I'm over here twenty-five years. It was a wee small matter I don't want to go into. Dear old Belfast.

SCOT: A fucking shithole.

NORTHERN IRISHMAN: Aye. [*He gives a big mad laugh.*] [SEAN *gives* MICHAEL *a funny look.* MICHAEL *has sat on* SEAN*'s left.* YORKSHIREMAN *remains where he is.* LIVERPUDLIAN *is on* SEAN*'s right.* COCKNEY *and* NORTHERN IRISHMAN *remain where they are.* SCOT *stands watching.*]

NORTHERN IRISHMAN: The drink is cat over here.

MICHAEL: Is this a friendly game?

SCOT: [*Sniggers.*] Are you serious?

YORKSHIREMAN: Quit the crap, Jock.

LIVERPUDLIAN: Who's dealing?

COCKNEY: Me.

SEAN: What's the fucking story? What are we playing?

SCOT: Bridge.

NORTHERN IRISHMAN: [*Another mad laugh.*]
LIVERPUDLIAN: Will you catch a grip of yourself?
COCKNEY: There'll be murder at this table yet.
SCOT: Are you not feeling well?
SEAN: No, I'm pure paranoid.
[COCKNEY *cuts cards himself, shuffles, considers* MICHAEL.]
COCKNEY: Mate, I think you should change seats with the Ripper.
MICHAEL: No problem.
[*The* YORKSHIREMAN *and* MICHAEL *exchange seats.*]
LIVERPUDLIAN: Five pence all up.
COCKNEY: Jacks to open.
[*Meanwhile the* COCKNEY *is dealing.*]
LIVERPUDLIAN: Pass.
SEAN: These cards are ridiculous.
YORKSHIREMAN: No.
NORTHERN IRISHMAN: You must be joking.
MICHAEL: Well I'm opening.
COCKNEY: You what?
MICHAEL: I'm opening. [*Throws down.*] For two bob.
[*Everyone at the table consider this.*]
SCOT: Watch it lads, here comes the reverend. [*Immediately all the cards are dumped,* COCKNEY *hauls money in.* MICHAEL *in consternation, his cards pulled out of his hand, it's all over in an instant.*] Good morning Father.
[*Enter jolly chap from stage right in jeans and t-shirt with some American university slogan on it.*]
CHORUS: [*Everyone from table except* MICHAEL *and* SEAN.] Good morning Father.
PRIEST: Good morning, Good morning. [*He claps hands.*] I believe ye must be the new lads from Ireland. Well I'm Father Ryan, a Cavan man myself.
SEAN: Right Father.
PRIEST: Now I'd like to have a few words with these lads in private. Come along, Leki.
[*The others get up, depart in their respective ways (with the chairs), but the* POLE *stalls, turns at door, and sourly addresses*

the PRIEST.]

POLE: Ko sa lingere faldo.

PRIEST: Yes I'm sure Leki. [POLE *gives him the finger, departs.*] And yours. [PRIEST *repeats gesture.*] And now a few basic rules lads. [*He takes the* COCKNEY*'s chair by the back.*] No drinking in the hostel, no bringing in women – it doesn't matter who they are, whether they're your cousin or aunt – no women. If you're out late you'll have to bring the key, you can have the key once a week and that for a one-pound fee – how much money have you got with you?

MICHAEL: Only a few shillings.

PRIEST: Be that as it may. If you want to work and sign on you can do so, but if you get caught you'll be in trouble.

SEAN: Right Father.

PRIEST: We've had all the types, we know them all, there's nothing you can get up to would shock me. You understand?

SEAN: Yes Father.

PRIEST: Let me see, yes, if you're doing nothing tonight there's a dance at the Irish Centre in Camden Town. The bus will leave the door at 7.30. It's a jolly old get-together. Anything else? [*Silence.*] That's everything now and anything you want, you know where I am.

SEAN: Sound Father.

PRIEST: As you're from soccer country I suppose youse are soccer fans?

MICHAEL: Who wants to see twelve idiots running round after a ball?

PRIEST: Twelve? Eleven surely.

MICHAEL: Well now you know how much we know about soccer.

PRIEST: [*Dropping patronizing tone.*] Have you made arrangements about the dole?

MICHAEL: Yes, we have.

PRIEST: [*He prepares to go.*] And if you're having a drink, don't come back drunk, and if you're offered drugs don't take them. [*He goes out the door, then returns.*] Do you take drugs?

SEAN: Oh no Father.

PRIEST: I'll see you at 7.30 then. [*He departs.*]

SEAN: [*To* MICHAEL.] Hey Sham, this is worse than lock-in.

[MICHAEL *and* SEAN *pull both tables back against the back wall. They sling two sheets over them. Hurl their sleeping bags onto them (this action can commence before the* PRIEST *leaves).*]

MICHAEL: The first chance I get I'm getting out of here.

[*They tidy their beds. Insert a little desk between the beds. Put their bags in.* MICHAEL *commences blow-drying his hair.* SEAN *begins his karate kicks. Light suddenly out.*]

SCENE 9

The Drunk Scene

This takes place in the two beds as prepared before. Performed in dim light with city shadows. As the others roar abuse at them, MICHAEL *will continue to imitate their accents and break into their gibberish. It is essentially his scene. The brothers' playing-acting should lend itself to the nightmarish and stress their wasteful rebellion (right up until the* PRIEST*'s high-mindedly cold interruption), but it might also display their indifference and yet their concern for the others. Open with* SEAN *drunkenly singing the Sid Vicious version of "My Way." He is advancing towards the audience.*

SEAN: [*Singing.*] There were times . . .
I'm sure enough . . .
When I bit off . . .
More than I could chew . . .

COCKNEY: [*Off.*] Shut your bleeding arsehole.

MICHAEL: Oi, take a decko at this. [*Sitting up drinking in bed.*]

SEAN: [*Still singing.*] I did it my way.

[*Boot lands on stage.*]

SEAN: [*Still singing.*] I did it my way.

[*He propels himself back for cider. Gropes, nearly falls, kept upright by* MICHAEL.]

COCKNEY: Hey lads, that's enough now.

MICHAEL: Oi you can't sit there, that's my chair.
SCOT: You're looking for it, Paddy.
MICHAEL: Here comes the reverend.
SCOT: [*Off.*] I won't take much more of this.
MICHAEL: This one is about solidarity, Jock.
SEAN: [*Replenished, singing again.*] There were times I'm sure enough . . . Hold on where am I?
POLE: Kaza muclchi! Klapper own!
MICHAEL: Nanze magi.
NORTHERN IRISHMAN: [*Gives the huge mad laugh.*]

[SEAN *is in bits with the laughter. Another missile lands.* SEAN *lifts it, hurls it back.*]

POLE: [*Screams.*] Sona funka buy ach.
SCOT: I'm going to paste you round the walls if you don't fucking stop Paddy.
SEAN: I did it my way . . .

[*Suddenly lights come fully on.* SEAN *is standing in Y-fronts centre stage with bottle.* MICHAEL *has jumped out of bed, we see him do it, and* PRIEST *enters.*]

PRIEST: What's going on here? [*He takes bottle from* SEAN.] I thought I told you – no drink.
SEAN: [*Swaying.*] Oh Father I forgot.
PRIEST: Get your stuff packed and get out.
SCOT: You tell them Father.
SEAN: We were thinking of going anyway.
PRIEST: Well go now, and if you don't have your stuff packed this minute, you can leave it here and collect it tomorrow.
COCKNEY: Right on, Father.
MICHAEL: I'll have the bottle. [*He takes it, shoves it in his bag.*]
PRIEST: Are you not ashamed of yourself?
MICHAEL: Fuck you and your hostel. C'mon Sean.

[SEAN *dithering, pulling clothes on.*]

PRIEST: Get out, do you hear me? [*Laughs from off-stage.*] You break my trust, that's what you get.

[MICHAEL *takes* SEAN *and bags.*]

SEAN: Goodbye Tom.

[*Catcalls and whistles from off-stage.*]

MICHAEL: Fuck off bastards.

[*Carrying each other, they depart stage right.*]

PRIEST: And if your giros come during the week, you can come here to collect them. After that I don't want to see you ever again. You hear me? [*Meanwhile, shouting at them as they depart, he is hauling the beds off-stage, one to the left, one to the right, while sounds off-stage from other sleepers build up into one great, multi-voiced jeer. He surveys the empty stage.*] You came in rough lads and you'll have to get out rough. [*He stands, surveys the space, flicks light off.*]

SCENE 10

The Underground Scene

If possible, there should be layers of posters on the back wall, advertisements, etc. SEAN *and* MICHAEL *are in their sleeping bags, stage right, lying parallel to back wall.*

SEAN: Aw, aw. [*Silence. He looks up and around, digs back into sleeping bag. He is next to the wall.* MICHAEL *turns on his side so we can see his face. First one woman passes, going one way, then a man with a briefcase going the other way. Far off is the swishing sound of the underground.*] Aw, Michael. [MICHAEL*'s eyes are open but he says nothing.*] You know what I think Michael?

MICHAEL: [*Someone passing.*] What do you think Sean?

SEAN: I think you have to watch what you're saying over here. You have to see what the crack is. [MICHAEL *does not reply.*] I wish I was back in Sligo. [MICHAEL *closes his eyes.* SEAN *sits up.*] You hear me Michael?

MICHAEL: I hear you, you rat.

[*The people passing seem like hallucinations, in the wrong clothes, with masks, with limps, flurrying, whatever, and this is terrifying* SEAN. *Every so often his head comes up to see.*]

SEAN: Ah Jaysus, Michael. [*Enter a hippy busker,* NEIL, *and his girlfriend,* FIDO, *with their instruments. They lay down their collection hat, start tuning, and burst into a quick, short instrumental.* SEAN *lifts head, looks, shakes* MICHAEL.] Hey Michael.

[MICHAEL *does not budge. The buskers finish the short piece.*]

SEAN: [*Sitting up.*] Hey, do you know The Pogues?

NEIL: How does it go?

[MICHAEL*'s eyes open,* SEAN *climbs out.*]

SEAN: Hold on. [*He joins them.* MICHAEL *looks around.*]
[*Sings.*] I met my love by the gas-works' wall . . .
[*All join in.*]
Dreamed a dream by the auld canal . . .
I kissed my girl by the factory wall . . .
Dirty old town, dirty old town . . .
[*Song peters out.*]
I forget the rest.

NEIL: Hey that was good. [*He pulls a joint out of pocket and drops on his hunkers,* MICHAEL *sits up,* SEAN *on his bag,* FIDO *standing.*] Here, have a draw.

SEAN: [*Being ironic.*] This is real cool. Do you mind? [*Indicating* MICHAEL.]

[SEAN *passes joint to* MICHAEL*, then* MICHAEL *to* SEAN, SEAN *to* MICHAEL, MICHAEL *to* FIDO *who squats in front facing them, making a circle, then she hands it to* NEIL, *then* NEIL*, after taking gargantuan drags, gives it to SEAN.*]

NEIL: I'm Neil.

FIDO: I'm Fido.

SEAN: Hallo, I'm fed up with telling people our names, from now on we've got to find new names.

MICHAEL: That's right. It's all these geometrical vibes. [*Joint passes to him, now miniscule.*] I feel the need for speed.

SEAN: What's that?

MICHAEL: I'm not talking to you.

SEAN: Who are you talking to?

MICHAEL: I'm talking to Fido.

SEAN: Oh.

FIDO: Have you no place?

SEAN: No.

FIDO: Well we could help you, couldn't we?
NEIL: Sure.
[SEAN *suddenly jerks his head.* FIDO *rolling a joint.*]
MICHAEL: What's the matter with you?
SEAN: I'm hungry.
FIDO: Well you can come back with us.
SEAN: Have you any grub back at your place, Neil?
MICHAEL: Jesus Sean, you're an embarrassment.
NEIL: There's lentils and beans in the fridge.
SEAN: I'll ate anything.
MICHAEL: Oh Christ.
FIDO: Relax, have another blast.
SEAN: Give us a whiff of that. Hi Sham, did you ever hear of Stiff Little Fingers, a great band from Belfast, I know what they mean. [*He starts laughing.*] There's a place called The Blue Lagoon where we come from, can you imagine that – The Blue Lagoon.
NEIL: Far out, man.
MICHAEL: And The Silver Swan.
SEAN: I'm milled.
FIDO: What?
SEAN: I feel weird.
NEIL: That's what it is, man.
SEAN: And you can have that for nothing for the rest of your life? I don't know. [*Pause.*]
MICHAEL: Where do you live?
FIDO: In a squat in Brixton.
MICHAEL: How did you manage that?
NEIL: You just change the locks and move in.
SEAN: Could we get a squat?
[*Meanwhile, people are passing by.*]
NEIL: No problem. Just break in the door. [*He opens a bag.*] You see man, there's a hatchet. You just break your way in. There's a place next door to us.
SEAN: That sounds the right thing to do, alright.
NEIL: You just fix the electricity, and that's it.

SEAN: Is there water?

FIDO: What are you talking about?

MICHAEL: Stop it, Sean. You're just confusing people. Just sit down. Stop moving around. [SEAN *makes karate stance.*] Do you want to fight?

SEAN: Ah Jazus, Michael.

NEIL: I wonder what you would be like on the acid.

SEAN: Can I tell you something? I never met two nicer people than ye. No, I mean it.

FIDO: Sure Sean.

SEAN: No I think youse are great. Aren't they Michael?

MICHAEL: Yes, Sean. [*To* FIDO *and* NEIL.] He's just tired.

SEAN: No, I'm not, I'm pure paranoid.

NEIL: Well when we finish up here, you can move into your new quarters.

SEAN: Good on you, Neil.

MICHAEL: And I'll go out to find Paddy McMorrow.

SEAN: And to think only last week we were drunk in Sligo.

FIDO: And now you're stoned in London.

SEAN: It's strange, when you think of it, like.

[*Lights slowly go down on the triangle. People passing by place a table, some chairs and a number of blankets stage left. The underground sound rises to climax.*]

SCENE 11

The Pure Paranoid Scene

Their new squat. SEAN *seated in huge tattered armchair, placed stage right against the back of the space. Beside him a table with an old oil cloth on it. Some egg-boxes and other comparable, incongruous matter on the table. Sufficient light to see* SEAN, *from a candle on table. Sudden crashing sound.*

SEAN: What the fuck was that. Is that the council? Well I'm not going for a look. Fuck, where's Michael? [*Smaller distant crash.*] It could be the guards. I feel pure paranoid. Saying they've caught Michael. Ah no, Michael is too fly. Old horse. But if they have him, he'll rat. They'll know I'm in here. [*The *candle on the table goes out.*] Fuck. [*Strikes match, stares with the mad eyes.*] Just think, Sean. I wonder do we ever get home. You'll be alright. The other fellow will be along any minute. With some grub, and some drink. [*Pause.*] Jazus, that stuff has me head done in. If I had the medical card I'd be down to the doctor to see if I'm okay. But sure I only had it the once. Me hands look funny, I don't feel right. Me face is numb, what's happening to me? [*Pause.*] Where the fuck is he? What time is it? You need a clock in these places, you could listen to the time. He must be gone three hours. God, if you get me out of this I'm never going to . . . wank again. [*Pause. Whistles a tune to himself. Then starts humming. Stands up, paces, hands in pockets, goes through his pockets.*] Jesus, we are the right idiots. [*Lifts up an old newspaper.*] Jesus. [*Crumples it, throws it away. Sits back in big armchair. Suddenly lights come on. He lets out a ferocious scream.* MICHAEL *and* PADDY McMORROW *enter. He flings himself at* MICHAEL, *and* PADDY *– a tall punk – backs off.*] Ye're back, ye're back.

MICHAEL: C'mon Sean, stop it.

SEAN: I was scared here to death. [*Puts arms around* MICHAEL.]

MICHAEL: Say Hallo to Paddy.

SEAN: Hallo Paddy.

PADDY: Hallo Sean.

SEAN: Ah Jazus, Michael. [*He releases* MICHAEL.] Jazus Paddy, it's good to see you.

PADDY: How are you Sean, is it getting to you?

MICHAEL: Paddy did the lights for us.

SEAN: I thought youse were the council.

[PADDY *sits down.* MICHAEL *opens parcel. Takes out tape recorder.*]

MICHAEL: See what we got.

SEAN: Did you thieve it?

MICHAEL: You know yourself. [*He hands him a bottle.*]

SEAN: What's this tack?

PADDY: That there's Tequila Sunshine.

SEAN: Oh boy.

MICHAEL: The only trouble is we have only the one tape.

SEAN: And I thought you had deserted me.
PADDY: That's the big city.
SEAN: It's good to see youse, anyway.
MICHAEL: Is there a socket anywhere?
PADDY: That's the way Sean. [SEAN *hands bottle on to* PADDY. MICHAEL *crawls under table. Lights give slight dip.*] Your power is a bit dicey.
MICHAEL: Now have a listen to this.
PADDY: This music would relax you.

[*They wait a minute. On comes a Hari Krishna chant. It continues on through the setting up of the next scene – The Dole Queue Scene – which heightens the incongruity.*]

SCENE 12
The Dole Queue Scene

Stage right, the dole queue comes up from the auditorium and onto the playing space. People sign on at a wire-grid cubicle, then cross stage left to receive their money at a second cubicle. They then go down and around the auditorium to the end of the queue and back on to the stage again, ad infinitum.

Description of queue: All various types, shuffling, impatient, reading the horses, rolling up, coughing, silent, distracted, arrogant, etc. NEIL *plugged into radio. Different people take it in turns.*

1.
WOMAN DOLE OFFICER: [*First cubicle.*] Name?
SCOT: Jimmy, Jimmy Flynn.
WOMAN DOLE OFFICER: Have you worked since you last signed on?
SCOT: Not a chance.
WOMAN DOLE OFFICER: Sign here.

[*He approaches second cubicle where all is conducted in silence. Some count their money, others stuff it in their pockets or hold it in their hand as they exit.*]

2.

WOMAN DOLE OFFICER: Name?
NEIL: Sidney Arthurs.
WOMAN DOLE OFFICER: Have you worked since you last signed, Sidney?
NEIL: Sign here is it? [*He hears nothing, jigs to music.*]

3.
WOMAN DOLE OFFICER: Name?
PORTER: Linnus Joseph and before you ask me, have I been working, I want to say – who would employ me?

4.
WOMAN DOLE OFFICER: Name?
MICHAEL: Michael O'Donnell.
WOMAN DOLE OFFICER: Have you worked?
MICHAEL: Worked the head, that's all. [*Big stupid laugh.*]

5.
WOMAN DOLE OFFICER: Name? [*He does not answer.*] Oh it's you Mr McVictor. Yes, thank you. Now go on, you'll get your money, over there.

6.
WOMAN DOLE OFFICER: Name?
COCKNEY: What's this? It's always the same. Am I for your computer?
WOMAN DOLE OFFICER: Name please.
COCKNEY: What am I, just a number?
WOMAN DOLE OFFICER: If you want any money you'll have to give me your name.
COCKNEY: You know well enough who I am. I've been coming in here for years.
WOMAN DOLE OFFICER: You and a thousand others.
COCKNEY: Alright then. You want to know how I am.
WOMAN DOLE OFFICER: Yes please.
COCKNEY: Well I'm bloody awful. [*Pause.*] I'll tell you my

name if you'll tell me yours.

MAN IN THE QUEUE: Mate, will you move on, just tell her who you are okay?

COCKNEY: Smythe, with a T.

WOMAN DOLE OFFICER: Thank you Mr Smythe. Have you worked since . . . [*He cuts her off.*]

COCKNEY: No. [*As he signs he glares backward.*] Filth, fucking bastards. This bleeding country is diabolical. Bleeding Ken Livingstone, bleeding lesbians, bleeding Paddies. Ken Livingstone, the prick.

WOMAN DOLE OFFICER: That'll be all, Mr Smythe.

7.

WOMAN DOLE OFFICER: Name?

MAN IN THE QUEUE: Darren Watts. It takes all kinds, doesn't it?

WOMAN DOLE OFFICER: Will you sign there, Mr Watts?

MAN IN THE QUEUE: There's no opportunities Miss, is there? It's bleeding assholes like him should be out of work, not people like me. He'd drive you mental, wouldn't he?

WOMAN DOLE OFFICER: Thank you, Mr Watts.

MAN IN THE QUEUE: All right then, I get the point. It's alright for you, isn't it? The jungle. Isn't that right Mate? [*He turns to* SEAN.]

SEAN: Aye, aye, that's right, Jack.

MAN IN THE QUEUE: Not another one.

8.

WOMAN DOLE OFFICER: Name?

SEAN: Sean O'Donnell.

WOMAN DOLE OFFICER: Have you worked since you last signed on?

SEAN: No, no I haven't.

WOMAN DOLE OFFICER: Have you got your social insurance number?

SEAN: Not yet missus, it's been sent on. I have applied for it, it's

somewhere at home. It should be in the post, like.
WOMAN DOLE OFFICER: Sign here, no there, just there. Thank you Mr O'Donnell.
SEAN: Yes thank you.
WOMAN DOLE OFFICER: And as soon as you get it bring it in to me.
SEAN: Yes, missus.
WOMAN DOLE OFFICER: Next please, next please.

9.
WOMAN DOLE OFFICER: Name?
ANOTHER MAN IN THE QUEUE: Henry James.
WOMAN DOLE OFFICER: Henry James, Henry James. I'm sorry Mr James, your giro has not come through.
MAN: What do you mean?
WOMAN DOLE OFFICER: I'm afraid I can't help you. You'll just have to come back next week.
MAN: But it was supposed to be here today.
WOMAN DOLE OFFICER: I'm sorry.
MAN: The woman is going bananas.
WOMAN DOLE OFFICER: I can't help you, you can see for yourself.
MAN: [*Distressed.*] What time next week?
WOMAN DOLE OFFICER: The same time, Mr James.
[*He walks away, shattered but accepting it.*]

10. [Same as 1.]
WOMAN DOLE OFFICER: Next, name?
SCOT: Jimmy, Jimmy Flynn.
WOMAN DOLE OFFICER: Have you worked since you last signed on?
SCOT: Not a chance. [*Etc.*]
[*Lights begin slowly going down as the circle begins to complete itself and the audience have time to see that the whole sequence is about to be repeated. As this happens, pop music of a vulgar type begins to play. The scene ends with murmur of voices from*

the queue, complaining, being drowned out.]

SCENE 13
The Pub Scene

*The dole queue take out some chairs and sit facing the audience in tiers. Bring the entire cast on, sitting there waiting. Silence after settling of chairs, then from back of the hall comes the sound of a guitar (*PADDY *and his punk band.) The audience will swing round to see behind them to see as the dole queue on stage claps along.*

PADDY: [*On bass.*] And now we'll have "Back to the Future" by Sean O'Donnell. Give a big hand for Sean O'Donnell. C'mon up here Sean.
[*The dole queue goes ecstatic.* SEAN *rises, marches through audience. His moment. Joins band and sings "No Future" by the Sex Pistols. When the audience turns back to stage at the end we have returned to the squat.*]

SCENE 14
The Girls' Scene

London squat. Stage in Darkness. Whispers and movement, people walking into chairs, etc.

SEAN: [*Off-stage.*] Hold on girls, the lights will be on in a flash.
TINA: In a flash. [*Nervous laugh.*]
MICHAEL: [*Off-stage striking match.*] Shut up you dope, I'll do it.
TINA: Jesus, only for I'm jarred I wouldn't be here.
GRAINNE: Definitely.
TINA: Where are you?
GRAINNE: Stop that will you?
TINA: Oh is that you?

[*The lights suddenly come on.*]
GRAINNE: Oh my god.
SEAN: [*Entering.*] What do you think of the place?
GRAINNE: It's a shit-hole.
SEAN: Home is where the heart is.
GRAINNE: Where's the heart?
MICHAEL: Sit down over here.
TINA: Have you a cup I could drink out of?
MICHAEL: Get up off your hole, Sean.
GRAINNE: And I suppose I'll want one too.
MICHAEL: Okay.
[*The boys leave. When* SEAN *gets up* TINA *takes his chair to be beside* GRAINNE *at the table.*]
TINA: [*Whisper.*] What have we let ourselves in for?
GRAINNE: [*Loudly.*] You brought me here.
TINA: I didn't. It was them that brought us here.
GRAINNE: You started talking to them first.
TINA: Let's not argue about it.
GRAINNE: It was you brought it up.
[*Pause.*]
TINA: The skinhead is nice.
GRAINNE: The other fellow is nicer.
TINA: You'd disagree with me always. [*Pause.* SEAN *and* MICHAEL *return with cups in saucers, and two old mugs richly decorated.*] Did your cleaning lady not come today?
GRAINNE: Who wants some? [*She unearths a vodka bottle from bag.*]
TINA: It's bloody cold.
SEAN: Do you want a blanket?
TINA: Yeh give us one. [*He gives her a blue blanket. She wraps herself up in, one hand holding it about her, the other holding her cup.*] That's better.
GRAINNE: You look like a tramp.
TINA: Why don't you go over to him? [*Indicating* MICHAEL.]
GRAINNE: Pass no heed on her. [*Nervously to* MICHAEL.] She's only trying to shift him. [*Indicating* SEAN.]

TINA: [*Laughing.*] I'll shift him alright. [*Skittish glance at* SEAN.]

MICHAEL: Youse are very forward.

[*Pause.*]

GRAINNE: What brought you over here?

SEAN: Oh we're going to America.

GRAINNE: Go way you liar you.

MICHAEL: [*Embarrassed.*] We're just getting the money together.

GRAINNE: You go to America? Huh.

[*Pause.*]

TINA: What are you working at now?

MICHAEL: Oh we're not working at the moment.

[TINA *eyes* SEAN. *There are giggles.*]

TINA: And he just told me an hour ago that he was a class of a chef.

MICHAEL: Never mind him, he's a spoofer.

SEAN: It's the drink.

MICHAEL: You're as bad as your mother.

GRAINNE: Talk about gobshites.

TINA: A place like this must take up all your wages paying rent.

[*The two girls crease into ironic laughter.*]

MICHAEL: Give us another drink before I crack up.

GRAINNE: [*Not forthcoming.*] Is that all you can think of?

MICHAEL: Yes most of the time.

SEAN: When we have the money.

TINA: Give them a drink. They're breaking my heart. Here, pass me the bottle.

[TINA *gets up with the bottle and holding the blanket to her.*]

GRAINNE: You never know Tina what you might get from that thing.

TINA: [*Pouring.*] Is that enough?

SEAN: I never get enough.

TINA: Enough of what?

SEAN: This, that and the other.

TINA: In all departments.

GRAINNE: Control yourself.

TINA: I can't. It's the drink . . . [*She explains pouring for* MICHAEL.]

SEAN: Curse it anyway.

TINA: Would youse mind awfully if I take off my shoes?

GRAINNE: Everyone hold their noses.

TINA: Don't be cheeky, you bitch.

MICHAEL: Take it easy girls.

[*Pause.*]

TINA: It's a good job I don't have to work in the morning.

GRAINNE: Why? Are you thinking of staying the night?

TINA: Aye, yeah surely.

SEAN: Great.

GRAINNE: You're very sure of yourself.

TINA: Ah, he wouldn't like to see a young girl walking home on her own. [SEAN *starts coughing.*] Hard nights, Sean.

SEAN: Yeah I suppose.

MICHAEL: I can't get a word in here edgeways.

GRAINNE: Well what do you want to say?

[*Silence.*]

TINA: We could talk about home.

[*Silence.*]

GRAINNE: I don't want to talk about home – it brings back bad memories.

TINA: Jesus I miss it.

GRAINNE: Well I don't, but I hate this place. Give us a fag.

TINA: How about ye, do ye miss it?

SEAN: Well, I didn't want to come here in the first place.

MICHAEL: Don't start on that.

TINA: Well I can't stand being out of work. It pisses me off. I can't imagine going round without money. I like my sociable drink. Isn't that right Grainne, we like our crack at the weekend. I don't like staying in. As a matter of fact I hate being alone. I get depressed, I don't know what to do with myself. Did you ever get like that?

SEAN: Constantly, this week especially.

TINA: I suppose you think I'm raving.

MICHAEL: We all get depressed now and then.

SEAN: The minute I entered the pub I felt bad.

TINA: Well I wouldn't give up my job for the world. I can't imagine getting up at two o'clock in the day and doing nothing. I know people in the situation – it depresses me just thinking about them. You have to keep yourself occupied.

SEAN: You do.

TINA: I know what I'm talking about. [*Silence.*] I like getting up in the morning. I like coming out at the end of the week with a couple of quid in my pocket. I keep all my pay slips. They tell me who I am. [*She drinks.*] It beats Donegal. [*Climbs down out of her reverie.*] I'm not going to be a victim. [*Laughs at herself.*] Help yourselves, lads. That's courtesy of Mr Halpin. I think I'm drunk, but I'm happy. Tomorrow morning I'll probably have regrets.

MICHAEL: We all have regrets.

GRAINNE: Tina goes on a bit.

TINA: Wait till she starts. [*She gets up, faces audience, pulls back (imaginary) curtain.*] Do you know what we should do?

SEAN: What's that, Tina?

TINA: We should go for a walk – London is gorgeous by night.

MICHAEL: Would you not be afraid of the muggers?

GRAINNE: Not our Tina. She's the romantic type.

TINA: [*Smiling.*] Amn't I.

[*Lights come slowly down as* TINA *pulls the blanket tighter about her.*]

END

The Long Swim

First performed in October 1987 by the Acorn Theatre Company, Sligo. Directed by Dermot Healy. Commissioned by, and performed at, the Hawk's Well Theatre, Sligo. The extant script is a revised version dated "January 1989."

CAST

MATTI	a lecturer and writer, wife of TAIG
TAIG	a mechanic, husband of MATTI
ROSE	sister of MATTI, a housewife
MICHAEL	a civil servant, husband of ROSE
SHEILA	sister of MATTI, a bank clerk
JOEJOE	a labourer
MR P	a neighbour from MATTI's childhood
MRS P	wife of MR P and a patient in hospital
MR RODGERS	waterworks man
DR JOHN FARRELL	
NURSE	
MALE NURSE	

Note: MATTI *never leaves the playing area.*

Set: Four flats on one side, four flats on the other; each one can pivot round a central screw so that entrance and exit can occur both sides of a single flat. The interior of each flat can contain appropriate designs but all flats are white on the other side, out of view. Every turn to white is noted in the text, and flats are numbered 1 to 4 on each side (working out from upstage to downstage). No entrance is ever made again through a door gone white. They are closed forever. The back wall should be completely white so that in the final scene we have a complete white-box area.

Author's note: Since the text does not contain any direct reference to Alzheimer's disease, perhaps the walls of the theatre could display some facts relating to the illness (e.g. "One-tenth of everyone in the theatre will die of Alzheimer's" (cf. Jonathan Miller), etc.).

ACT I

Consecutive Time

A newly-acquired house by the sea, housewarming just over, general untidiness. Front room. 1980's, but a sense of the restricted present. Moments of darkness between scenes, spliced.

ACT II

Fragmented Time

Same room, some attempt has been made at decoration. Working space for MATTI. *Bed has gained a frame. Perhaps two years later. Darkness between scenes, but* MATTI *always lit.*

ACT III

Continual Time

Six years later. Same room, but spareness predominates. No light changes throughout, but complete scene change done in full light to hospital ward. The only light change is at the end of the play. MATTI*'s own bed becomes the hospital bed. Nothing new is introduced in this change except sheets and bedspread.*

Note: The flats are like doors of perception. The perspective is MATTI*'s. Some things go, others return – but there is often no link.*

Sound: If possible there should be an inaudible hum throughout the play, increased where noted, and turned off where noted, in the text. The sound of rain begins and ends the play.

Furniture: Chairs green. Table green. Last colour remaining is green chair by hospital bed; it then is removed.

Note: Bed belonging to couple can immediately turn into hospital bed by having the iron bedstead already in place at beginning of ACT II, *but disguised.*

On the disease: Alzheimer's disease is a physical disease, so patients by right should not be consigned to asylums but inevitably are due to lack of funding. The sufferer undergoes extremes of memory loss but always tries to compensate, despite their lack of self-awareness in the long run. They are great actors. Normality is the role they play when in the public eye. Eventually they succumb via pneumonia, etc., and die. Often they go silent.

ACT I

Consecutive Time

SCENE 1

Scene: Bedroom-cum-sitting room. Mattress on floor, stage right, parallel with backdrop. Table with small hand mirror propped against a pile of books, downstage left. Tray of drinks sits to side of table. Two tea chests, one bursting with clothes, the other with bric-a-brac – one front stage right, the other centre upstage. Three chairs sit on top on each other, at the rear. Three more chairs: one in front of table, the second downstage of table, and the third, upstage beside tea chest at centre stage left. Various collages may hang from flats. Women's and men's clothes are scattered throughout the room. An air of fly-by-night. All furniture is green. Room is very colourful and bright. Bedspread of patchwork.

Inaudible hum switched on.

As houselights drop, simultaneously the sound of falling rain, on pebbles, on galvanise, everywhere. It reaches stereo heights in the darkness. Sound recedes as lights come up.

Lights come up slowly. Early morning. Mattress is on floor, upstage right. Two figures might be seen lying there. As rain recedes MATTI *comes up onto her elbow to study* TAIG*'s face. She adopts a playful accent.*

MATTI: Thou hast pleased me . . . [*She searches for his name as she touches his face.*] Sir Jed.

TAIG: Oh. [*He too enters the scenario with a reciprocal accent.*] My dearest . . . Nancy.

MATTI: Thou hast pleased me well.

TAIG: You give me the lightness of the head, my unmentionable.

MATTI: Ah but let love prevail, Sir Jed. [*She comes onto her knees.*] Your happiness cannot exceed mine.

TAIG: [*Vaguely introducing reality but still succumbing to the fantasy.*] And yet dare I say it, Nancy, the two are of a different kind.

[*This breaks her concentration. She rises, and with backward looks, walks across to the table to prepare her face.*]

MATTI: [*Backward look.*] You make my juices fall.

TAIG: I beg you, not the juices.

MATTI: [*Backward look.*] Oh yes, the juices.

TAIG: [*Sitting up.*] Of what fruit, pray?

MATTI: Why the juices of the pomegranate . . . and the juniper. [*She sits.*]

TAIG: Oh Nancy.

MATTI: The white flower of the wild strawberry.

TAIG: It is too much.

MATTI: [*Into the mirror.*] And your moist and gentle insistence, my sweet.

TAIG: I fear for my senses.

MATTI: And I for mine. [*Looking back in fun.*]

[*She walks across to the bottom of the bed, and perched provocatively, arms crossed, considers him.*]

MATTI: And does your Nancy not please you?

TAIG: My Nancies are so many, which one shall I compliment, for I fear the others might suspect me of deceit.

MATTI: Just speak to one, Sir Jed, and I shall tell the others not to dismay.

TAIG: Then let me say Nancy, it was beyond reportage.

MATTI: [*Provoking.*] And pray, Sir Jed [*Said with irony.*], of those strangers that did occupy my pleasure when I lay with you, none stood in your way?

TAIG: Their presence but increased my joy.

MATTI: Then I am glad. [*Next she pretends to delicate inquisitiveness, one finger tipping her lower lip, face wholly innocent.*] Our nakedness is good?

TAIG: [*Exaggerating the cliché.*] And yet, my Nancy, are we ever truly naked?

MATTI: Your maleness is my folly.

TAIG: And mine when it doth perturb you.

MATTI: But now, I pray, only wantonly.

TAIG: In your words I find myself.

MATTI: Then hopefully my words will be adequate to your means.

TAIG: They could not be more so.

MATTI: But surely you find yourself, in yourself, also.

TAIG: No, only in you, my Nancy. [*He reaches for clothes.*]

MATTI: And do I reside in you?

TAIG: I cannot presume.

[*She stops playacting. Stands midway between bed and table.*]

MATTI: Then let me say I wish I could travel round in you and no longer be myself. [*She throws everything to the wind.*] Not even a self, but only a part of you.

TAIG: [*He looks at her uncertainly.*] You frighten me, Nancy.

MATTI: And then . . . [*Lifting skirt.*] . . . I would never have responsibility for this world.

TAIG: It is a terrible thing you say.

MATTI: It is what I believe nevertheless. [*She selects blouse, returns to dressing table, and begins buttoning it.*]

MATTI: [*Reassuringly.*] Ah Sir Jed.

TAIG: My Nancy.

[*She sighs. Stares at mirror as if seeing herself for the first time, looks back at him, then looks at him through the mirror as he gets out of bed.*]

MATTI: I cannot do it.

TAIG: Do what, my sweetness?

MATTI: Though I am honoured . . .

TAIG: As I am, I'm sure.

MATTI: . . . I cannot run with you away.

TAIG: You cannot?

MATTI: I fain would but . . .

TAIG: You feel ill today.

MATTI: Yes, I fear the vapours.

TAIG: How cruel the world that they should light on you. Tomorrow perhaps?

MATTI: Once I have you today I am satisfied.

[*Having more or less finished dressing he walks over behind her and kisses the top of her head with his hands on her shoulders. She puts her two hands on top of his. There is something a little panicky in her smile but it passes.*]

TAIG: [*In normal voice.*] Are you happy?

MATTI: I've never been so happy. [*In normal voice.*] But I don't know where to start.

[*He sits at the edge of the mattress watching her button her

blouse.]
[*Hold image.*]
[*Darkness.*]

SCENE 2

A few minutes removed from previous scene. TAIG *with newspaper lying in bed.* MATTI *fully dressed in sharp new light.* ROSE *enters through flat 2 upstage left.*

ROSE: [*Off-stage.*] Can I come in?
MATTI: Yes, of course.
ROSE: I'm not intruding? [*Enters with man's raincoat over her shoulders.*]
MATTI: No.
ROSE: Good morning Taig.
TAIG: Rose.
ROSE: And what force wind was that?
TAIG: Force eight about.
MATTI: Did you sleep well?
ROSE: I spent the night in a fridge.
MATTI: What?
ROSE: [*Meandering around.*] I found myself in a fridge. In fact, I stepped in and pulled the door after me. I intended to defrost the bloody machine, but then I found myself inside. It was terribly cold, but despite that everything was going off.
TAIG: Then?
ROSE: Then I woke up. [*She sits.*] Michael had taken all the clothes to his side.
MATTI: And how is the civil servant this morning?
ROSE: He's in there playing with himself.
MATTI: Never!
ROSE: And his snoring is getting worse.
MATTI: [*To* TAIG.] You snore too you know.
ROSE: In a just world they would be sleeping together.
[*Pause.*]
MATTI: Now I remember.

ROSE: What?

MATTI: What I was dreaming. Not just part of it, but the whole thing. It's strange that it should be so crystal clear – there are two labouring men, one with a straw hat, and one with a scarf. The one with the scarf is Mr Rodgers, he works with me. The other is Joejoe.

TAIG: Joejoe, the waterman.

MATTI: Then there is a middle-aged couple. Do you know who they are? Mr and Mrs P.

ROSE: God above.

MATTI: He's talking of eels of all things. Then there's you and me. [*She looks at* TAIG.]. Sometimes in a pub, sometimes a railway station, and we are all talking away and everything makes perfect sense. It's like it all happened at different times but now it's coming together. I must have been dreaming it over and over – it's so familiar, but this is the first time I remembered it. The place changes but the people don't – it makes me lonesome to think of them.

TAIG: I don't dream at all.

ROSE: And it shows, Taig, it shows.

MATTI: Enough. Let's not talk of it anymore. It frightens me. [*She starts tidying.*]

ROSE: [*Unconcerned.*] And what have you planned for us today?

MATTI: We can't swim.

TAIG: That's out.

MATTI: And we can't walk.

ROSE: And we can't stay here.

MATTI: Why not?

ROSE: Because I'm on holiday.

[*Pause.*]

TAIG: We could go drinking again.

ROSE: I don't know whether I could face another day like yesterday.

MATTI: How does that song go?

TAIG: What song?

ROSE: You're not going to break into song?

MATTI: Next door does when she's depressed.

ROSE: [*Coming to her feet.*] I'd go mad living out here all the time. It's too romantic and uncivilized.

TAIG: We'll get used to it.

ROSE: I suppose I had better get Michael up. I'm not getting anywhere here. [*She exits through flat 2 upstage left.*]

[MATTI *immediately stops what she has been doing. She looks long at* TAIG.]

MATTI: I want to ask you something.

TAIG: Is it going to be in a foreign language?

MATTI: No, it's a simple question. That will be my undoing.

TAIG: Fire ahead.

MATTI: Don't laugh.

TAIG: I won't.

MATTI: And keep your voice down.

TAIG: Alright Matti. [*Forced whisper.*]

MATTI: [*She looks at him wondering whether she will or not.*] First, when Rose said she couldn't face another day like yesterday I had a terrible blank.

TAIG: Go on.

MATTI: I felt for a second as if I'd just been thrown out of bed.

TAIG: It's the Bacardi.

MATTI: Well then I have a problem.

TAIG: No, you haven't.

MATTI: It is a struggle for me Taig.

TAIG: It happens.

MATTI: It happens to me more than I care to mention.

TAIG: It'll come back, it always does.

MATTI: All that comes back is the dream, as if I'd stepped into another place and I'm trapped there.

TAIG: Matti.

MATTI: Yes. [*She is ill-at-ease, but struggles through.*] Oh never mind. It was leading nowhere. I know that. [*Sits.*] I thought we were going to have one of those really quiet days, I forgot we had company. [*Pause.*] There's something else I want to ask you.

TAIG: Yes.

MATTI: Don't think me helpless.

TAIG: No.
MATTI: And you must never bring it up in an argument.
TAIG: I won't.
MATTI: You promise.
TAIG: I promise.
[*Pause.*]
MATTI: You will never leave me, no matter what happens.
TAIG: No.
MATTI: Say "I will never leave you."
TAIG: I will never leave you.
MATTI: "No matter what happens."
TAIG: No matter what happens.
MATTI: You mean it.
TAIG: Yes.
[*Pause.*]
MATTI: And it's strange – don't get me wrong – but even that does not satisfy me.
TAIG: There's things I'd rather not hear.
MATTI: If I ever lost you . . .
TAIG: You'd get over it.
MATTI: [*Vehemently.*] No. Never. [*She puts one hand out and touches his shoulder.*]
[*Hold image.*]
[*Darkness.*]

SCENE 3

Same set as before. Continuation of previous. MATTI *on her feet.* TAIG *returns to lie on the bed.*

MATTI: How did we end up speaking like that? It's my fault, all that moping and self-pity. Forget I ever said a word, will you? Let's start this day all over again . . . [*She turns.*] Right from this very minute.
TAIG: If I can I will.
MATTI: Right from this very second.
MICHAEL: [*Off-stage.*] Hallo. [*Loud-hailer type roar.*] Hallo.

MATTI: Yes Michael.
TAIG: A good time to start.
MICHAEL: [*Head round corner of flat 2 upstage.*] Ah the lovebirds. Are you respectable?
ROSE: [*Coming in behind him.*] Would it make any difference?
TAIG: And how are you feeling?
MICHAEL: It was some housewarming.
MATTI: And your inner self?
MICHAEL: Chastened. Like the story of the nurse and her bicycle.
ROSE: It sounds lewd.
MICHAEL: It's not. It's a true story.
MATTI: That's what they all say.
TAIG: Nurse who?
MICHAEL: Nurse Liz. [*He takes one of the chairs of the three piled up, turns back, sits.*] Nurse Liz was working in St James Hospital. She was a trainee nurse. Each day she locked her bike to the railings and went into work. Some days she locked her bike by the back wheel and some days by the front. This day she locked it by the back wheel and started to pull the bicycle away. Only to find it wouldn't budge. It was locked by the front wheel. This was a conundrum. This was beyond Nurse Liz. So she looked at the bike wondering whether it was hers. It was hers alright. She looked at the lock in her hand. She tried to retrace her steps of that morning. She stood around wondering what to do. And then she went in to find the porter. When she came out with him her bike was gone.
[*Silence for a moment.*]
TAIG: Say that again.
MICHAEL: She had locked her back wheel with her own lock, she unlocked it only to find there was a lock on the front wheel.
ROSE: That doesn't make sense.
MICHAEL: Then she came out with the porter from the hospital to find her bicycle locked to the railings gone.
TAIG: And who put the lock on the front wheel?

MICHAEL: The bloody bicycle thief, that's who.
ROSE: She should have locked it again before she went for the porter.
MATTI: It would have been the practical thing to do, but it wouldn't strike you would it?
ROSE: Well she should have realised.
MICHAEL: I don't think this is going to be my day. [*Pause. He pulls back flat 3, stage left, and looks out.*] No, definitely not.
MATTI: What's wrong?
MICHAEL: Hallucinations.
ROSE: And next will come refuge in drink.
MICHAEL: Yes, I'd like a glass of gin somehow. Taig, there is an unseemly man across the street looking straight over here at the house, and I'd swear he's got binoculars.
TAIG: [*Not moving.*] We know him. That's Pat the Post. His excuse is Brent geese. We've been told about him.
MATTI: A voyeur, Michael, not an hallucination.
MICHAEL: I'm glad to hear it. [*Replaces flat.*] But talking of voyeurs – were ye rehearsing – I was on my way to the John and I couldn't believe my ears – were ye rehearsing some fairly lascivious piece of Shakespeare – or what – this morning? [*Laughter.*] I questioned your dear sister Rose – "I'm preoccupied," she said. I said: nevertheless, they're out there in the bedroom speaking of the damndest things in the most incredible language.
MATTI: Not Shakespeare, Michael, but Jonson.
MICHAEL: Lo and behold! I am astonished at your range Taig.
MATTI: He's quite adept.
MICHAEL: And I didn't know you brought your work home to the bedroom.
MATTI: Ah but his work is more pleasurable than most.
TAIG: A trifle decadent, maybe.
MICHAEL: I see. Isn't Jonson the right blaggard?
ROSE: Michael is very curious. You are always investigating.
MICHAEL: My brain will not let me rest. [*He opens flat 2, stage left.*]
ROSE: And that's only the half of it.

MICHAEL: There goes that boyo again. [*Closes flat 2.*] Lord knows there is nothing worse than to be attacked by an allergy you can't place.

MATTI: Like hormonal discomfort.

MICHAEL: The same. The very same. Sex is the crux. Only for that we would all get on. It's a pity when we earned these big overweight brains which they claim we have – through better eating, self-regard, high-protein or whatever – it's a pity they didn't close up the other apertures.

MATTI: Where would you start?

TAIG: There'd be very little fun.

ROSE: Like all drunks Michael is a puritan at heart.

[MICHAEL *leans down confidentially to* MATTI *in mock manner.*]

MICHAEL: Is he looking after you?

MATTI: He's a good friend.

MICHAEL: Well don't be alone no matter what.

MATTI: No, Michael.

MICHAEL: Good. [*Off again.*] Rose has a theory.

ROSE: Have I?

MICHAEL: Maybe a better word for it, to avoid argument, would be intuition.

TAIG: Yes?

ROSE: [*To* TAIG.] This will concern some invasion of my privacy.

MICHAEL: That we are all mirrors of each other. There is a primal shape toward which we aspire. And we choose to love those in whom we can the better see ourselves.

ROSE: [*To* MATTI.] See what a mistake I made.

MICHAEL: [*To* ROSE.] But didn't I put it well.

ROSE: You surprised me.

MATTI: I would go further than that.

ROSE: [*Sits.*] You were always competitive.

MATTI: That if you were given to someone, we live in them and they in us.

TAIG: I'm sure it would be no joy for you to travel round in my troubled soul.

MATTI: [*Turning her back on him.*] I'm sorry to disappoint you Taig – I meant the body not the soul.

[*Pause.*]

MICHAEL: She has you there, Taig. She is well able for you.

ROSE: And why ever not?

[*Pause.*]

MATTI: [*Turning.*] Taig, let's go nowhere today.

TAIG: I don't think we were going anyplace.

ROSE: Why ever not Matti?

MATTI: Because . . . [*Faltering.*] I don't mind going out if you bring me with you.

MICHAEL: Afraid you might miss something?

MATTI: That's it, Michael.

ROSE: Well I don't get you.

MATTI: If I was to walk out that door alone right now, when I'd come back I fear I might not know you. You might not know me. Everything must have changed.

MICHAEL: There's very little chance of that, unfortunately.

[*Pause.*]

ROSE: But why should we leave you behind.

MATTI: I don't know. Hangovers make me panic, maybe. It's all this newness.

[*Pause.*]

TAIG: [*Getting up.*] Would anyone like a hot whiskey? [*Repeats.*] Would anyone like a hot whiskey?

MICHAEL: Yes, give us a hot whiskey. And Taig?

TAIG: [*Lifting tray of drinks.*] Yes.

MICHAEL: Could I have a cold one while I'm waiting?

[*Laughter.*]

[*Hold image.*]

[*Darkness.*]

SCENE 4

Same room as before, but much later that night, or the next night, or the night after. MATTI *seated by table reading and writing by aid of bedside lamp. Notebook and pen. "Two Jewish Reels" by De*

Danann is playing on a tape recorder. Mood is homely and relaxed. MATTI *has drink at hand. All of a sudden the light goes off, the tape spins down . . .*

MATTI: Taig, the lights have gone. Taig, Taig, where are you? [*Sounds of people and doors. Laughing.*] Jesus Christ, what's going on. [*More movement in background. Whispers.*] Come on, what's happening? [*Silence.*] Taig, I know you're there. [*A birthday cake appears with all the candles lit.*] I don't believe this.

[*Lights come on, and with that the tape recorder starts chugging into power again.* MICHAEL, ROSE, *and* SHEILA *enter.*]

MICHAEL: Look what the cat brought in.

MATTI: [*Looking at* SHEILA *who's holding the cake.*] You're joking.

SHEILA: What day is it?

ROSE: You don't know?

MATTI: I don't know.

SHEILA: It's March 25th.

MATTI: That's not my birthday!

MICHAEL: Yes, but let's pretend.

[MATTI *breaks into small jig.* MICHAEL *heads to drink tray carrying bottles.* ROSE *pulls table forward.*]

SHEILA: [*Placing cake on table.*] Blow them out.

[MATTI *bends double in very tomboy fashion and blows.* ROSE *blows with her.* MICHAEL *is pouring drinks.* TAIG *enters, spreads chairs.* ROSE *stops, looks at* MATTI. ROSE *kisses* SHEILA. MICHAEL *hands glasses round.* MATTI *kisses* TAIG. *Then she kisses* MICHAEL. *Then at last* ROSE. *The mood is one of improvised affection.* TAIG *turns and puts tape to low.*]

TAIG: Let me propose a toast.

[*They come to their feet. Glasses in hand.* TAIG *keeps* MATTI *sitting by keeping a hand on her shoulder.*] To Matti.

OTHERS: To Matti.

[MATTI *downs her own glass quickly, as do the others.*

MICHAEL *replenishes glasses.*]

MATTI: Thank you everyone. I was worlds away.

SHEILA: Whereabouts actually?

MATTI: For a while with William Faulkner, and then Eudora Welty.

SHEILA: [*As they sit.*] And how is the writing coming on?

MATTI: I can't seem to bring myself round to it.

ROSE: She's working at the university where she does not need to be. Do you?

MATTI: It keeps me sane.

ROSE: She doesn't need the money.

TAIG: I do.

MATTI: I need the people.

MICHAEL: I can understand that.

ROSE: You could take redundancy.

MATTI: My writing is not working out. It gives me a headache. I spend half my time jealous of those that can. And the other half trying to pretend to be modest.

ROSE: [*Wild laugh.*] That must come as a chore.

MATTI: Have you been drinking Rose?

ROSE: Just a tincture. [*Further wild laugh.*]

MATTI: Where did you find Sheila?

SHEILA: They found me sitting in front of the box watching "The Avengers."

[*Pause.*]

MICHAEL: Well, I can no longer bring myself to read the *Irish Times.*

TAIG: What else is there?

MICHAEL: There's the radio.

ROSE: It's because the women have come to their own in the *Irish Times.*

MATTI: Where they always repeat themselves.

ROSE: Coming from you that sounds patronising. Some things need repeating.

[*Pause.*]

TAIG: Let's not go up that road, not tonight.

MATTI: And look at the class background of those ladies that write for the *Irish Times*.

ROSE: Never mind. Let the women get in first, and then we'll worry about their class background.

MICHAEL: The cart before the horse.

ROSE: No, the women before the men.

MICHAEL: Either way the country's fucked.

SHEILA: And I'm secretly envious of Lady Di.

MATTI: Oh Sheila.

[*Laughter, general hilarity.*]

[*Hold image.*]

[*Darkness.*]

SCENE 5

As previous scene. Continuation, but slight mood change, a little more introspection, as if the characters have moved into private obsessions that they know each other to have.

MICHAEL: The country is given to bald yuppies.

ROSE: I have nothing against yuppies.

SHEILA: Most are priests.

ROSE: Well I wouldn't be found dead in a church.

SHEILA: If you want to get into the graveyard, I believe you have to sit a while on the altar.

ROSE: I intend to get burnt. And not as a witch.

MICHAEL: I didn't say a thing.

MATTI: I imagine that a person's despair is greater within a church than outside it.

ROSE: Do you say so.

MATTI: Well if you've dared to join others in your belief, to find it become disbelief, and you still belong to the believers – that must be something awful.

SHEILA: Then you just leave.

MATTI: They don't leave, they know that this despair is just a part of it, a part of their faith.

ROSE: This is too much. Have we a born-again in our presence?

MATTI: When I saw mother die, she was still going to chapel of a Sunday. She prayed every day. Prayer for her was to wish another well. Who was I to deny her that?

SHEILA: And yet she was afraid, Matti.

MATTI: That's the despair I'm talking of.

[*Pause.*]

MICHAEL: Well, we can let children decide for themselves.

ROSE: Who are you to speak of children?

MICHAEL: I was just making a statement about them in general.

ROSE: Especially when you have none of your own.

SHEILA: Some count that a blessing.

ROSE: [*To* SHEILA] Did I ever tell you why we didn't have children?

SHEILA: I have the most peculiar sensation.

ROSE: Because he was impotent. Aren't you Michael? Lock, stock and barrel.

MICHAEL: Never mind, Rose, you'll be alright in the morning.

[*Pause.*]

[*General air of embarrassment, but the argument is an old tiff, and is seen as such.*]

MATTI: We did not have children.

ROSE: Yes, but you had a grandiose reason – your career, wasn't it.

MATTI: Not exactly.

ROSE: Well?

MATTI: There were a number of reasons.

ROSE: Miss Prim. But I know the reason why. Don't I Matti?

TAIG: This is Matti's birthday, Rose.

ROSE: Is something troubling you? [*To* TAIG. *To* MATTI.] C'mon Matti, out with it. [*To the others.*] She's afraid of madness. You always were.

MATTI: If you say so.

ROSE: I know you were. But I wasn't. Do you understand? I wasn't. [*Loudly.*] Ever.

[*Pause.*]

SHEILA: [*Indifferently.*] They were always like this – Matti got the schooling Rose didn't.

MICHAEL: And Rose got the civil servant.

TAIG: And Matti the mechanic.

SHEILA: And I go no-one.

ROSE: You're lucky. [*Pause.*] [*To* TAIG.] Me and Matti go back a long way – do you understand?

TAIG: [*Coldly.*] I can't dispute that.

ROSE: So in any argument I will take her side. [*She points slightly drunkenly at* MATTI.] Have you got that? [*To* TAIG.] I'll be there after you're gone.

TAIG: I've no intention of going anywhere.

ROSE: I may have a cretin for a husband. [*Said with drunken fondness.*] But I have Matti.

MICHAEL: You'll be alright in the morning, Rose.

ROSE: Matti, do you come . . . [*A drunken intimacy.*] . . . with him?

SHEILA: God help us, Rose.

ROSE: [*Low conspiratorial voice.*] Do you hear me, Matti?

MATTI: I hear you.

ROSE: Tell us then. [*A grin.*] Do you come when Taig lies on top of you?

SHEILA: Could someone please explain the missionary position?

MATTI: No matter what I say, Rose, you will not be satisfied.

ROSE: I just want to hear the truth.

[*Pause.*]

TAIG: Does Rose come, Michael?

MICHAEL: Now and then.

[*Pause.* ROSE *visibly disorientated. Goes to speak, but doesn't.* MATTI *calm.*]

MATTI: And as for us, now and then. Are you happy with that? Now and then, Rose. Happy?

[ROSE *gets up, glass in hand, moves to rear wall. She turns, looks straight at* MATTI.]

ROSE: If you are Matti.

MATTI: Yes, I am.

ROSE: Happy birthday, then Matti, Happy birthday.

[*Quite resolutely* ROSE *marches over and turns tape up high.*]
[*Hold image.*]
[*Darkness.*]

SCENE 6

MATTI *sits where she has been, lifts her papers and waits. She begins her lecture when the last person has left the stage, and in the growing spot she watches everything intently – as if everything has to be memorised. Then the abrupt end of the music signals the beginning of her lecture at rostrum.*

MATTI: The offense to the human psyche for Antigone is contained in the line "Oh sister, you know how heavy the hand of God is upon us." How woman must suffer for the father. And be ruled by conscience.

And even if we were to forget this, that the voice can never be filled without the help of God, then it would not matter, someone else would remember, someone else would elicit the help of the Higher Power, someone else will intercede on our behalf.

But the time comes when we too must lift the body of our brother. Even if we too risk death by stoning. That is how we are tempted into the drama: we take a chance, put ourselves in the hands of others, and this is how the otherness begins.

On one side sit the gods who know all, on the other are situated those consumed by faith and are by faith related to the gods, and below are those on the lowest platform of all who are blinded by their own sense of freedom. We watch them knowing that all their acts are in vain. The drama will end. Their despair, when they find it, was all an illusion, and will be unbearable. So either they must declare their faith and join those others delicately balanced in between, or else they perish.

And this is where humour begins: for those with faith find those with none to be mere idiots. Their laughter fills the open air. Step back, the freedom lovers say to each other, hold on to each other, let us test our solidarity. But who are they against the gods? The lowest of the low – mere mortals. Then we see where tragedy comes from, and hence that strong aphrodisiac: fatalism.

Can we not hear it – as we listen to their idiotic chants of freedom – the whimpering of the he-goat, the song of the buck cut off from the source of pleasure, doomed to wander the island without saying anything to please the senses, with nothing to fill his stomach?

Indeed it is tragic to be cut off from the gods. But there is a chance of escape to a higher plane. And this can happen. Except it depends where one is standing. For if you are among the freedom lovers you will despise those gone beyond humour and tragedy. For if you are within the tragedy or the comedy, you do not know your surroundings. You, in fact, think the world is emanating from you. But those who see the tragedy cry, those who see the comedy laugh, and the ones with faith who have gone beyond all tragedy and comedy are assured a place with the gods.

And this is drama. You, the audience, are the ones with faith. Should the players fail you, it makes no difference. You will look elsewhere until you find your faith restored. In *Antigone* the chorus goes: "Of happiness the crown and chiefest part is wisdom, and to hold the gods in awe." The chorus is our key, our memory, the source of all. In the drama we are trapped in someone else's memory, which in time becomes our own, for the period of performance, and beyond.

[*She stands back, folds her papers, looks around. Gives a small*

smile.]
[*Hold image.*]
[*Darkness.*]
[*End of* ACT I.]

ACT II
Fragmentary Time
SCENE 7

Same space as ACT I, *but it looks more lived-in and unreal. A new Irish-patterned shawl is thrown over the bed. Coats and jumpers hang from hangers placed strategically along the back, and on some of the flats. A typewriter sits on the table before the mirror. A huge map of the world hangs on the centre of the back wall. The tea chests are gone. Two of the flats on both sides of the stage stand open. These have reproductions of "Connemara Folk" by Jack Yeats, "Seas off Achill" by Paul Henry, "A Photograph of Tinker Children" by Belfast photographer Donovan Wylie, and a reproduction of a portrait of John Clare, the poet. All are blown up to larger-than-usual size. A gas heater purrs – it is winter. A pile of books sit by the bed waiting to be put away.*

MATTI: It's awful. It's a cliché – all of this is a cliché.
TAIG: Then change it.
MATTI: When he stood there I had the awful sensation of wanting to throw my skirt into the air. I had to really stop myself.
TAIG: You did fine considering what was on my mind.
MATTI: And do you know what stopped me?
TAIG: Your future.
MATTI: No, it was the fact that I would not know how to explain it to you. It's fine when it's a joke but if it had really happened, it would have been obscene.
TAIG: Anyway, he has a sense of humour, he laughed a little.
MATTI: His laugh is serious. The less said about that the better.
TAIG: It's not an experiment anymore?
MATTI: It's business – he's my publisher.

TAIG: And you trust his judgement?

MATTI: I don't know, I don't know. The book to me just seems full of resentments. That's not what I want. And when he was talking to me I realised that this was going to be the same old thing. Another part of me was saying, "No, this time it'll be exciting, the magic will happen," but the thought of it – the memory of it – made me feel sick Taig, I actually felt sick. [*She stamps the ground.*] Sick.

TAIG: You didn't show that.

MATTI: And then for a moment I heard this strange voice coming out of my mouth, unbidden – I was speaking with that Sir Jed and Nancy voice. I could have died. [*She smiles over at him, and tips off her shoes with her toes at the heels.*] Things were easier when I was going round in my pinafore and blouse and starched shirt.

TAIG: As a matter of fact, you sounded quite confident and mature.

MATTI: I wonder have I aged without knowing it. [*She sits.*] I still dream of exams. I dream of Mr and Mrs P. One part of me is going back, back – I can even remember being in my cot and my mother leaning over to change me. [*She gets up and takes his hand.*] You'll always stay with me?

TAIG: Yes, I will.

MATTI: Sometimes I have been very wrong.

TAIG: We're all wrong at times.

MATTI: You are very kind to me.

TAIG: It's because I love you.

MATTI: There must have been something beautiful between us from the very beginning.

TAIG: I thought I was sensitive. As a matter of fact I was like stone.

MATTI: And I felt lost. [*She lets go his hand, sits, and looks back at him.*]

MATTI: On the train, not only did I forget where my seat was, I could not tell whether we were going backwards or forwards. Then each empty seat I saw seemed to be facing the wrong way. And though I was carrying an awful lot . . . [*Pause.*] . . .

I did not sit down but toured the train looking for what I'd lost, and then there you were, just as I'd left you.

TAIG: I'm happy for you. [*He crosses behind her.*] You found me.

MATTI: [*She stands.*] But I have the feeling that you can go on without me.

TAIG: [*Crossing again.*] That's not true Matti.

MATTI: [*Following him.*] Something tells me that I can't go on.

TAIG: [*Stops and faces her.*] You're just being morbid. [*Then passes her again.*]

MATTI: [*Turning.*] Is that it? Well it's no fun. There's no art in being sick, being in the middle of this morbid situation.

TAIG: [*Turning to face her.*] It will pass.

MATTI: I hope so, as long as I have you.

TAIG: Well you have me.

MATTI: Are you sure?

TAIG: I am.

MATTI: I love you dearly, Taig.

TAIG: Do you know what's wrong with Ireland?

MATTI: What's that?

TAIG: Too much white bread. [*She laughs. She goes back and sits. He advances back to his chair.*] That's it, too much white bread. [*She turns her head merrily to look at him as he sits.*] That's why the dog takes fits. [*He points a finger in mock delivery of lesson.*] Isn't it wonderful how the mind can think, and it not right? Isn't it wonderful how the shell of the scallop can grow?

[*Pause.*]

[*Hold image.*]

[*Darkness.*]

SCENE 8

MATTI *before the typewriter.* TAIG *is evident by his absence: newspaper open on his chair, a pair of men's shoes sitting in front of the chair, his jacket over the back of the chair.*

MATTI: [*Types three words.*] Sometimes as creatures we are so hopeless and plain. [*She types eight words.*] This is our present predicament I think. [*She types ten words.*] And yet I am so fond of you. [*She types two words.*] What more, I wonder, will there be to endure? [*She types slowly – significantly, three letters and then a fourth.*] Taig!

TAIG: [*Off-stage.*] Yes. Hold on a minute.

MATTI: [*To herself, normally.*] We must stop fighting – it's all my fault. I frighten myself by thinking that we are destroying each other. [*She stiffens, tries to shake it off. He looks in through flat 2, stage right.*] When are we going to make money?

TAIG: Ah-ha. [*His head disappears.*]

MATTI: Taig.

TAIG: [*Head appearing again.*] Yes.

MATTI: Are you sorry we never had children?

TAIG: No. [*He disappears again. She types.*]

MATTI: A delicate association came between them, a desire to see it out. They felt they were against great odds, even in their own natures. [*She ponders the page.*] Oh my God. [*Gets up, opens flat 2, stage right, and looks out.*] I see Mrs Philips cleaning her windows again, and she with her gloves on. [*Shrieks in gaiety. Back to typewriter. Stands looking at it. Goes back to flat 2.*] He told me – this Belfast man – how this woman he met in Portrush, when he was there on his holidays, became his lover. She had on a long black glove which she always wore. She was never without it. Eventually she took it off and there was a wee baby's hand. [*Copying Belfast accent.*] "And there was a wee baby's hand. And I gave that wee baby's hand a kiss." [*She sits.*] The same man was a musician once. Now he drives a digger. Said playing the levers in the digger was like playing a musical instrument. [*Types five words.*] "La nostalgie de la boue." [*Types five words.*] La nostalgie de la boue. [*Types four words, then one.*] La nostalgie de la boue. [*Enter* TAIG *in mechanic's blue smock, much soiled, places newspaper on chair, sits.*] Yesterday the sight of a schoolboy going by in his school uniform and struggling with plastic bags of groceries gave me such a feeling of nostalgia that my heart went out to him. [*Breathless.*]

TAIG: Tell me again what you used to wear to school.

MATTI: Well my pinafore was blue, and then we had a blouse, that was white, and the jumper was royal blue and had two little yellow stripes on the collar.

TAIG: [*Fondly.*] Two little yellow stripes.

MATTI: One day we stole three pairs of bloomers belonging to the nuns from their washing line. We ran down the road with them and threw them into Devaney's hardware shop.

TAIG: And you look so innocent. [*He laughs.*]

MATTI: The boy was well fit to carry the bags – that was what made it so sad. Is this the woman I am, I thought, and tried to turn my mind to other things.

TAIG: You should stand up to Rose.

MATTI: I have an admission to make. I am lost among women. I can never argue with them. I can fight with a man, but never a woman. That's a terrible thing.

TAIG: [*Relaxing into the fragmentary vein.*] The buck-goat is a dreadful creature. He will drink his own urine. Drink it with his head between his legs.

MATTI: How you come up with these things I'll never know.

TAIG: And all of no account.

[*Pause.*]

MATTI: Tell me about the first time you touched a girl.

TAIG: Put such thoughts out of your head.

MATTI: Was she pretty?

TAIG: You'll only make yourself dizzy.

MATTI: Just one small anecdote.

TAIG: No.

MATTI: You'll never know what I'll give you.

TAIG: No.

MATTI: And then I'll tell you of all the boys I loved when I was seven or eight.

TAIG: No.

MATTI: Or when I was thirteen.

TAIG: Never.

MATTI: Well then, will you put on a dress for me?
TAIG: I will not.
MATTI: One with a huge bust in it, and then down the street with you. [*She grins.*] Can we go to Bundoran? Blackpool?
[*Laughter from both of them.*]
[*Hold image.*]
[*Darkness.*]

SCENE 9

Same area. Typewriter has been moved out of sight. Pages piled on floor. She is going through the papers trying to find something. She is obviously impatient and upset. She crosses the room looking for what she has lost and gets nowhere. Sits, tries to collect herself and TAIG *enters.*

MATTI: Are you still here?
TAIG: I am.
MATTI: I thought you were somewhere outside.
TAIG: No, I was next door.
MATTI: Do you not go to work anymore?
TAIG: Oh I'm always hanging around you.
MATTI: And for what I can't tell.
TAIG: Ah but you can.
MATTI: I've lost page sixteen.
TAIG: Hold on. [*He exits. Come back with page through flat 2, stage left.*] Is this it? [*He hands it to her.*]
MATTI: Yes, where did you find it?
TAIG: It had blown off the sill into the bath.
MATTI: I'm sorry you found it. Now I've no excuse.
TAIG: Next time I won't bother.
MATTI: Humour me Taig.
TAIG: It's becoming a strain.
MATTI: In a little while I'll be finished, and everything will be back to normal.
TAIG: Normal? I don't mind if life isn't normal. I've lost the

criterion. I just want some security – I can't take some of the things you've been telling me.

[*Pause.*]

MATTI: Will you be loyal to me?

TAIG: Why do you ask?

MATTI: Because I had a dream. I was with someone. And I was searching in my memory to see if I had enjoyed being in bed with him. He said: "We are immature these days, we remember what doesn't happen."

[TAIG *looks distraught.]*

TAIG: [*He sits.*] You see. [*Opens hands pleading.*]

MATTI: There's always someone else.

TAIG: What we are is other people.

MATTI: So it goes.

[*Pause.*]

TAIG: [*Calmly.*] When it comes down to it you've got to admit that you made love to someone else.

MATTI: He forced himself on me.

TAIG: That is always your excuse.

MATTI: He did not enter me.

TAIG: So you say.

MATTI: I don't want to talk about this. [*She slaps page sixteen on the table.*] You put words in my mouth.

TAIG: [*Sneering.*] You told him he was the sort of person you could fall in love with.

MATTI: Did I tell you that?

TAIG: So you've forgotten already.

[*She registers his self-satisfaction and wonders is he lying.*]

MATTI: If I'd known it would lead to this I would never have told you.

TAIG: But you did.

MATTI: This is impossible.

[*Pause.*]

TAIG: Did you tell him that night or in the morning?

MATTI: Please stop Taig, stop.

TAIG: That's what I want to know. Did you tell him that you

could love him just before you fell asleep or just after you woke?

MATTI: It was a sordid lapse.

TAIG: So were they all.

MATTI: I was enacting fantasy without regard to its real meaning.

TAIG: What does that mean?

MATTI: I wanted a friend.

TAIG: He stopped moving. He said he "didn't want a relationship."

MATTI: There's no time left to go into all of that.

TAIG: How many other lies have you told?

MATTI: It's not lies.

TAIG: The story changes every time.

MATTI: [*Screams.*] What right have you!

TAIG: You let all your previous lovers down, and now, I'm next in line.

MATTI: I have been very wrong, I'm sorry.

TAIG: He unbuttoned your dress. You had nothing on underneath except a pair of tights.

MATTI: I was pretending to myself that I could sleep with him in a companionable way. I say pretending because I should have had more sense. I said no, but I didn't stop him.

TAIG: It is infuriating to find how much your mind is given over to him.

[*Pause.*]

MATTI: Taig, please, we've been both ravaged by jealousy. [*He faces her, plainly overwrought, nearly violent.*] I know I've done wrong, I've done something that we won't get over for a long time. I'm sorry.

TAIG: You'll always keep one part of yourself free to be disloyal. It's the only thing can save you facing yourself.

MATTI: No, this time I mean it.

TAIG: You can't. It's not in you. My Nancy.

MATTI: [*Breaking down.*] You shouldn't. You shouldn't! You'll destroy everything.

[*She wants to go on, but doesn't.*]

[*Hold image.*]
[*Darkness.*]

SCENE 10

Same place as before, but only just. Lights are low, each person as they sit are in a place suitable to their wardrobe. They enter through various flats, slowly, peer around, find their place: JOEJOE *flat 1, stage right;* MR P *flat 2, stage left*; MRS P *flat 3, stage right*; MR RODGERS *flat 4, stage right.* TAIG *and* MATTI *will have already taken up their position, stage right downstage, on chairs.* MR P *and* MRS P *sit centre stage.* JOEJOE *and* MR RODGERS *sit upstage stage left. The elderly visitors are heralded by a disturbance of wind, and then by a beam of light from a torch held by* MR RODGERS.

MR RODGERS: Be the holy. [*The visitors take their places, quite naturally and are at home talking quietly to each other.*] Ah Joejoe.
JOEJOE: Mr Rodgers, how's it going?
MR RODGERS: And who's that beyond?
JOEJOE: That could be Mr and Mrs P.
MRS P: Do you tell me. Indeed you're right – I'm Mrs P.
MR RODGERS: How do you do?
MRS P: And this is MR P.
MR P: That's right, tell the countryside.
MRS P: Hush pet!
JOEJOE: Fierce weather.
MR RODGERS: Hard on the hip.
JOEJOE: You should get a replacement.
MR RODGERS: All you need is one slip – fuh!
MR P: The wonders of medical science, how are you.
MRS P: Hush! [*All of the above are jumbled together during entrance, finding their places and sitting, and having finished they take stock and make themselves comfortable. The next dialogue is raised considerably, as if they had entered a new plane of consciousness – the inner office. Shuffle of feet and coughs die*

out. Lights come up more.] Oh yes.

MR P: So I say right and we came down.

[*Pause.*]

[TAIG *will look over his shoulder now and then.* MATTI *sits looking forward, only to look now and then at* TAIG, *or incline her head to listen. A lot of the listening can be recorded through her expressions.* MR RODGERS *wears a straw hat, and a blue boiler suit with a rose in top pocket and an array of pens.* JOEJOE *has a light tweed jacket, a cap that he places on his knee, outsize jeans and white running shoes – quite incongruous on a man of his age. He rests his hands on his knees, taking stock constantly.* MR P *and* MRS P *both wear brown gabardines and different scarves wrapped round their necks and heads. She wears black laced boots and thick woollen socks over torn nylons. He wears green wellingtons.*]

MRS P: Do you dream?

MATTI: A little.

MRS P: I'd be flying. They say you are not rested.

TAIG: A dream only takes a few minutes.

MRS P: Oh but the journeys I take, it's the damndest thing.

JOEJOE: A bad drinker is the luckiest man ever.

MRS P: In one dream a soldier hit me with a bullet right between the eyes, well I drew out and hit him.

MR RODGERS: It's a struggle in every way.

JOEJOE: If the dog bites you, you'd sleep. Drink will take away your dreams.

TAIG: Milk is the cause of the trouble as regards sleep. Cut out the cow's milk and let the childer sleep at night.

MRS P: What does he mean?

MATTI: It's the goat.

MRS P: Oh yes, it's getting like that – the goat will clear the lungs.

MR P: And worse I believe the boy in the morgue lasts longer these days before going off. I have it from a man in Belfast. He should know.

MRS P: Oh pet.

MR P: It's because of the amount of preservative we eat over the years.

MATTI: That's wild.

MR P: By the time we're done we'll keep for yonks.

MR RODGERS: I spent the summer pulling beets in Fife.

JOEJOE: And one and seven for a hundred yards.

MR RODGERS: I worked the hammer.

JOEJOE: A dread.

MR RODGERS: And the butterfly.

JOEJOE: Worse.

MR RODGERS: Outside Inverness.

TAIG: It's hard to tell where goats will go.

MR P: Yes, it's hard to prognosticate about their surrounds.

MR RODGERS: The Polacks banked off the face at the top. They should not have done that. They should have left a vacancy.

JOEJOE: A dreadful thing.

MR RODGERS: Then the gas built up.

JOEJOE: Oh.

MR RODGERS: Aye.

MRS P: Ah.

MR P: [*Into* MATTI*'s ear.*] She is very fond of me.

JOEJOE: Oh a fast race of tepid people.

MR RODGERS: Aye.

TAIG: Aye.

MRS P: Aye.

MR P: O aye.

MATTI: Ah.

JOEJOE: And long winters shuttering above in Oban.

[*Pause.*]

MR P: [*Recovering from a dream.*] What were we at?

[*Pause.*]

MRS P: [*Getting on with it.*] A banshee follows our family. And I don't mean this fellow here. [*She claps* MR P*'s knee.*] It was a wee woman that size. [*Demonstrates with hand a certain distance from the ground as* MR RODGERS *and* JOEJOE *watch amazed.*] Sitting on a rock combing her hair and crying away. Ah, but once I take my tablets . . . [*Resigned.*] If I did without them I couldn't sleep.

MATTI: You could not.

MRS P: [*Rising note.*] Oh.

JOEJOE: Hahaha.

MR RODGERS: Huh-huh.

TAIG: Hmm.

MR P: Aye [*Last note.*]

MRS P: They relax you. [*Glad to find everyone in agreement.*] They let you lie down. I was given others once. They were the shape of hens' eggs. I thought I was on the waves. [*Tightens hands on lap.*]

TAIG: Aye.

MRS P: That was cheery-bye to them.

MR RODGERS: Indeed.

MRS P: I can tell you.

[*Pause.*]

MR P: [*Laughing triumphantly as if suddenly remembering a joke.*] I'll bet none of you can explain the horse's hair. [*Pause. Note of bewilderment in the others except the smiling and complacent* MRS P, *but* MR P *is quite proud of himself.*] If you take the hair out of a horse – but now it must come out of the tail; indeed, you could use the hair from the tail of a cow, but a horse's hair was how I heard it first – and put it in a bucket of water, and leave it, do you know what will happen?

TAIG: No.

MR P: No? [*Looking round the others.*] Now go one step further. Leave it there for the full duration of three months. And soon you'll see two bruises appear at each end of the hair and a sore come out in the middle. [*He looks about him, and waits.*]

MR RODGERS: [*Hesitantly.*] And then what?

MR P: [*Triumphant – speaking to the ignorant.*] The hair will give out in the middle. Now what have you?

JOEJOE: Hell and tarnation, I honestly do not know.

MR P: You'll have two eels thrashing about in the bucket . . . [*Wild superior laugh.*] . . . that's what you'll have.

JOEJOE: [*Bewildered but cunning.*] Oh right enough.

[MR P *gives him a long disapproving stare. The group relaxes.*]

MATTI: And I was foolish enough to think that you would be able to look after me.
TAIG: You made a bad mistake there.
MATTI: And how is the poor penis.
TAIG: The idle penis resting.
MATTI: Far too idle if you ask me.
MRS P: Look at those pair, at their love talk.
JOEJOE: Isn't it dandy.
MRS P: Do you do any reading?
MATTI: I do.
MRS P: My best friends are on the shelves.
MR P: [*Indignantly remembering.*] Two eels you'll have.
MRS P: Ah the eel. They're great for the skin. And they go – [*She wriggles her hand for the others.*] – like that on the pan.
MATTI: The poor little souls.
MRS P: But the prawn is smashing.
MATTI: It is.
MRS P: [*Gaining momentum.*] And the crab.
MR P: And fish and chips.
MRS P: That too.
MR P: We haven't had any in ages.
TAIG: They're tasty.
MR P: They'd give you an appetite.
JOEJOE: Oh aye.

[*They look out at the world.*]
[*Hold image.*]
[*Darkness.*]

SCENE 11

While the others leave MATTI *remains seated. Distressed, she makes her way with a folder to rostrum. Walk is weary. She is fighting to make sense and clarity but is weighed down by doubt. She looks around the auditorium, half-in and half-out of the previous scene, and she will look back before beginning.*

MATTI: A son of the High King received a blow to the head

in Armagh while fighting in a local skirmish on behalf of his father. The blow that struck poor Cenn Fáelad – head full of wonder – left part of his brain exposed; the part with which you forget things. He was taken to Tomregan Abbey – in fact, one of the first universities. And here Cenn Fáelad was operated on. The surgeon belonged to the old school, which in turn was made up of three schools: law, medicine and barditry. And barditry was the highest of these for it consigned the rules of the other two to memory. Thus medicine and law were put to rhyme. And the surgeon, in line with the appropriate verse, cut off the offending part, and this part – this area of the brain – was the part with which you forget things.

Now Cenn Fáelad had to remember everything. And this was a woeful burden on him, for there was so much that passed between the mind and the tongue, and the eye and the brain. Fortunately, with the advent of Christianity, Latin had arrived, so Cenn Fáelad the warrior turned scholar. He spoke of this new science – writing – as the mirror that might capture the reflection of time, and also ease the great stress on his memory. So he was driven at night to write out his knowledge on white stone, and that's how writing came to Ireland. The mystery moved out of the minds of the bards onto the stone, and later, the parchment of the scholars. Memory had found a new ally: a blow of a sword had given rise to the mark of a pen. So the metaphor is described in the annals.
[*Tiredly,* MATTI *closes the manuscript. Her delivery has been marked by hesitations, culminating in a long pause.*]

Are there any questions? [*Pause.*] You must forgive me if I do not point out the inconsistencies. They hardly matter. Not now. [*She breathes deeply.*]

Oh God. [*Looks at manuscript again.*]
I should add that it was through the power of writing that

Catholicism came to Ireland. He who could write had control over history, and each chieftain was set on having a scribe of his own. And since each scribe was of Roman hue – and had a direct link to trade with England – chieftains immediately accepted the new faith, and thereby had a saint with pen and paper visit them, and set down their battles, marriages and genealogy. Here was fame everlasting. Against this, what could imagination do?
[*She waits, folds manuscript again, untidily, and puts it under her arm. She waits.*]
[*Hold image.*]
[*Darkness.*]

SCENE 12

MATTI *returns from the rostrum to the room where her sisters are waiting. She flings the manuscript folder across the room in manner of flinging a bowl, hand to ankle, cuing it up and throwing it. She is in bad and fragmented humour. She goes directly to the bed and takes the shawl from it. Throws it around her. Sits the edge of the bed, open-kneed and spiteful. The sisters look at each other.* MATTI *switches her mood, palms the shawl ends each side of her.*

MATTI: There is nothing happening. [*Pretend calm.*]
SHEILA: Your work is suffering.
MATTI: Which work?
SHEILA: Your job at the university.
MATTI: Oh that. [*Nervous laugh.*] I don't want to hear anything about that. That was all made up by someone. It makes no difference to me.
ROSE: Look, I don't like interfering in your life but if you've found someone else, you should tell us.
MATTI: Oh.
ROSE: And he . . . [*To* SHEILA.] . . . obviously doesn't like it one bit. Does he?
MATTI: [*Nods.*] Taig is a . . . rare man.
ROSE: He's dragging you down.

MATTI: It's not Taig.

SHEILA: Then what is it?

MATTI: Nothing, nothing at all.

ROSE: It is Taig. [*To* SHEILA.] She will not accept that, you see, what I told you. [*To* MATTI.] He got drunk and drove over to our house to abuse me, Matti. If he speaks to you like he spoke to me you should leave him.

MATTI: He only did that because he thinks you hurt me.

ROSE: See, he's brainwashing her.

SHEILA: Something will have to be done.

ROSE: I intend to speak to him.

MATTI: [*Smiling.*] Oh do.

[*Pause.*]

ROSE: Do you have to sit there with that smirk on your face? [*Shriek.*]

MATTI: I'm sorry.

ROSE: Look, I'm upset, we're all upset, but let's leave Taig out of it. I'm sorry I spoke about him, just please explain.

[*Pause.*]

ROSE: [*Loudly.*] Matti!

MATTI: [*Shocked.*] What?

ROSE: [*Slowly.*] Tell us what is wrong.

MATTI: [*Looks at her a moment.*] There is nothing wrong. At the moment I'm missing something. You know, something small, really.

ROSE: I ran into Feeney from the University. He said that he felt something was wrong.

MATTI: How are things at the bank Sheila?

ROSE: Matti! [MATTI *cowers.*] You have not been yourself. And he felt something must have been wrong at home. He said that you were constantly tired.

MATTI: It must be that stupid diet.

SHEILA: Your students can't follow what you're saying.

MATTI: [*Irritated and defensive.*] That is untrue.

[*Pause.*]

SHEILA: At least you allow that much.

[*Pause.*]

MATTI: It begins just like this: you are sitting there – just where you are – [*She points to* SHEILA.] – and I'm within a fraction of understanding that, but then it fades away . . . I look at a thing and it means nothing.

SHEILA: Have you been to the doctor? [MATTI *nods.*] Has he got you on drugs?

MATTI: No, there's no mention of drugs.

ROSE: Why are you sitting like that? Matti, you are obviously distracted.

SHEILA: We're only trying to help.

MATTI: [*Patiently, begging.*] Just wait a little.

SHEILA: Of course we will.

[*Pause.*]

MATTI: [*Brightening.*] There's apple juice somewhere – if I could lay my hand on it.

ROSE: [*To* SHEILA. *Pause.*] I give up. Matti, please, Matti.

MATTI: Yes?

SHEILA: Are you pregnant?

ROSE: Why are you laughing?

MATTI: At my age? I suppose, of course, I could be. [*She looks at her body.*] It happens to us girls.

ROSE: You're infuriating. [*To* SHEILA.] She makes light of everything.

SHEILA: You never contact us, Matti. You've been in town and never called. Have we done something wrong to you?

MATTI: Oh no.

ROSE: Matti, Matti, Matti, Matti, Matti, please tell us, Taig will be home soon.

MATTI: [*Getting up.*] Taig will explain. [*She starts straightening bed and replacing shawl over it.*]

ROSE: You seem so dependent on him.

MATTI: Oh not really.

ROSE: It's not healthy. [*Pause.*] You've got to lead your own life.

MATTI: [*Beating pillows.*] I do. As you can see.

SHEILA: I can't understand it, if you're not in trouble with Taig, what is it that's wrong?

MATTI: [*Stops what she's at to look around and consider the *question; then thinks otherwise and continues straightening the bed.*] I'm sure you think the house looks dreadful.

SHEILA: A holiday – maybe that's what you need.

MATTI: [*Swinging round – childishly happy.*] A holiday – I would love a holiday.

SHEILA: Then do it.

MATTI: And where will we go? [*Looking from one to another.*]

SHEILA: Go anywhere.

ROSE: Who is the "we"?

MATTI: [*Has to consider question.*] Why you and me and Sheila.

ROSE: And no Taig.

MATTI: I'm sure Taig would like to go too.

ROSE: [*To* SHEILA.] I thought as much. [*To* MATTI.] We are back there again.

MATTI: [*She delivers this standing with her back to flat 1, stage right.*] But don't you understand. Imagine looking into a face and instead of . . . the person there you see their absence. In the sea of faces you know no one . . . you call them by the wrong name and they correct you and you don't remember that new name either . . . there's not a trace of a living soul . . . It's like someone has stolen their identity. And one day you know they will come and steal yours . . . You see?

SHEILA: Have you really been with a doctor?

[MATTI *strides over and sits on the bed again.*]

MATTI: I don't want to see a doctor. There's nothing wrong with me.

ROSE: But look at you. You are just not yourself any more.

MATTI: [*Quickly.*] Yes, I am. [*Considers question.*] Maybe I never was.

ROSE: What does that mean?

MATTI: It doesn't matter anymore. [*Pause.*] Sheila, do you remember the time we tied Rose to the gate and you shouted "Crucify, Crucify!"

SHEILA: She never lets me forget.

MATTI: If only we, if only I, had some drink – we could have a drink.

SHEILA: It's not drink, is it? Christ, it's not the booze.

MATTI: Not that I know of.
SHEILA: You haven't taken to the drink.
MATTI: Oh no, not yet. Taig likes a drink of course.
ROSE: [*Wearily.*] So it's him that's drinking.
MATTI: Yes, and so do I.
ROSE: This is driving me demented. Let's leave it altogether. Matti will tell us all in her own time.
SHEILA: She couldn't be drinking.
ROSE: [*Unsure somewhat.*] Well he is.
MATTI: [*Secretly triumphant.*] And so am I.
SHEILA: [*Giddily seeking anything.*] Do you think it might be depression?
ROSE: [*Vehemently.*] Are you depressed?
MATTI: [*Equally vehement.*] There's absolutely nothing wrong with me.
SHEILA: It's just that we are worried about you.
MATTI: You have nothing to worry about.
ROSE: Let's forget about it.
MATTI: Please.
ROSE: Look Madam, we are your sisters. Not just someone in off the streets . . . We care about you. I can't play any more games . . . I can't speak for Sheila. It's up to you – no one else – you hear me Matti? There's only so far a body can go. [*She sits, worn out and unsure.* SHEILA *bows her head, caught between the two.*]
[*Hold image.*]
[*Darkness.*]

SCENE 13

MATTI *is on stage right while* TAIG *stands with his back to her on stage left. He is leaning down by the side of the table. He reaches in and takes out one bottle of washing-up liquid. Slaps it on table. Then another, slaps it on table, then another and another, fourteen in all, the tempo and the banging building up. Midway through, he looks back at her.*
TAIG: Matti what's this?

MATTI: Oh it's just a mistake.

TAIG: [*Carries on.*] You could wash all the dishes in the street with these. [*Bang, bang, bang. Stops. Hands placed before him on the table.*] Matti! [*Pause.*] What's going on? How did you get through all your wages so quickly? [MATTI *silent. He swings around.*] Matti.

MATTI: Yes.

TAIG: What is happening to us?

MATTI: Stop blaming me.

TAIG: You'll have to see someone.

MATTI: Who do you want me to see? The bloody priest?

TAIG: [*Standing hands on back of chair.*] I spoke to John. I asked him to come round.

MATTI: I don't need to see anyone.

TAIG: Well I told him to come round this evening

MATTI: [*She leaves her position and advances.*] You told him what?

TAIG: In fact I'm expecting him right now.

MATTI: [*Reaching backstage left.*] Well I'll not be here when he comes.

TAIG: Matti – be reasonable. You have headaches. You can't sleep.

MATTI: They'll pass. [*Turns to him.*] Why did you not consult me before you spoke to . . . whoever it is.

TAIG: [*Crossing to stage right.*] Because I knew you would not want to see him.

MATTI: I don't. [*Turns her back.*] And I won't.

TAIG: [*Appeals.*] If you don't see a doctor how will you know what's wrong?

[*Pause.*]

MATTI: [*She turns.*] You think you are a great provider, don't you?

TAIG: No.

MATTI: And you think you are a great lover.

TAIG: No, I don't.

MATTI: Well let me tell you, you're not.

TAIG: I never pretended to be. You make sex sound bad.

MATTI: It was only bad with you.

TAIG: Well fuck you. [*He turns away.*]

[*Pause.*]

MATTI: [*She approaches him, touches his shoulder.*] Taig, no doctors, I'm terrified.

TAIG: [*Struggling.*] I can tell him – I can phone him, and ask him to leave it for again.

MATTI: Please do.

TAIG: I will. [*Turns.*] But you'll promise me you'll go and see him.

MATTI: I will.

TAIG: You promise.

MATTI: I do. [*Pause. She strides off to stage left again and watches him, intently. Her voice comes out quite high.*] Well go and phone . . . Richard.

TAIG: [*Turns.*] Richard – who is Richard?

MATTI: Whoever he is then.

TAIG: [*Advances.*] It's John Farrell.

MATTI: [*Advances.*] Okay. John Farrell. [*They pass each other.*]

TAIG: You went to school with him.

MATTI: Oh him, yes.

TAIG: [*Turning.*] And who is Richard?

MATTI: He must be another one I suppose.

TAIG: [*Both facing each other.*] There is no doctor we know called Richard.

MATTI: He must be someone in the past I suppose.

TAIG: Richard who then?

MATTI: Stop interrogating me. [*Advancing.*]

TAIG: I don't mean to. [*He advances.*] You said Richard, I said John. [*They pass each other.*] And now we have a Richard who may or may not exist.

MATTI: Richard Morgan. [*Her back to him.*]

TAIG: [*Back to her.*] Morgan is it.

MATTI: Yes, he was a friend of my father. [*She goes towards the seat.*]

TAIG: If he was a friend of your father then he's dead.

MATTI: You are cold. [*She sits.*] He was a very polite man.

TAIG: [*Turns.*] I dare say.

MATTI: My father swore by him.

TAIG: [*Slow.*] Your father trusted everyone.

MATTI: Yes, I suppose he did. [*Pause, then jumping up with one wagging finger into his face.*] But if he finds you here he'll put you out.

TAIG: [*Shoving his face at her.*] He won't. [*Backward upward swing of hand.*] I'll go up the chimney first.

[*Combatants part. He stage left, she with her back to him, stage right. Again she turns and watches him intently.*]

MATTI: There is something – I feel it – that you have to do for me.

TAIG: There is. [*He advances.*]

MATTI: [*Watching him.*] What is it then – I seem to have forgotten.

TAIG: [*Passing her on stage right.*] I have to phone John to tell him not to come round.

MATTI: That's it, well, why don't you do it?

TAIG: Because I don't have to.

MATTI: [*Rounding on him.*] Why?

TAIG: [*Face to face.*] Because I only made it up.

MATTI: Why?

TAIG: To get you to promise to go and see him.

MATTI: [*Voltage drops.*] That was cruel. [*Looking at him, face to face.*]

TAIG: Perhaps.

MATTI: And did I promise you?

TAIG: You did.

[*Pause.*]

MATTI: [*Advancing briskly away.*] Well then, I don't have to go.

TAIG: [*Following her.*] You promised.

MATTI: [*Scream.*] But you lied to me. [*She turns and passes him.*]

TAIG: I had to. [*He is left facing the bottles on the table.*] What am I to do with all this washing-up liquid?

MATTI: [*Secure.*] Bring it back. [*Backward sweep of hand, quite snobbish.*]

TAIG: Just like that? I'd feel a fool.

MATTI: [*Still with her back to him.*] Just say I bought too many.

TAIG: [*Turning.*] But every single expedition you made to the shops you must have bought a bottle.

MATTI: [*Nearly leering.*] I must have a fondness for their shape.

TAIG: That, knowing you, should be brought into consideration. [*Pause. Mood change.*] Will you promise me you'll see him?

MATTI: See who?

TAIG: Dr John Farrell.

MATTI: No, and that's final.

TAIG: He could at least give you something to sleep. You know last night I found you in the kitchen. [*He advances.*] The night before I found you sitting on the stairs – you hardly seemed sensible.

MATTI: [*Turns.*] Perhaps I do need to sleep.

TAIG: Then you'll go?

[*She passes him and sits on chair stage left.*]

MATTI: Yes, all we talk of is sleep, because I need my sleep, my beauty sleep. I think sometimes I'm afraid to go to sleep for fear I might never wake up. I want to survive no matter what happens.

[*Hold image.*]

[*Darkness.*]

SCENE 14

Darkness. A capped light, like a street light, begins a very slow descent. Spotlight begins to move from extreme right to extreme left and back again at same momentum. In the background the inaudible hum is slowly switched up. The beam of spotlight will have reached the extreme left at the same time the hum reaches an overpowering shrill sound. Both of these climaxes coincide with the lowest trajectory of street light at upstage centre. Then the hum recedes, the beam slowly swings back from stage left to stage right, and the capped light begins to descend till we reach complete darkness again.

The sounds occur consequentially during the sequence.

1. The hum.
2. A blast of rock music, return to the hum.
3. Pips as in a car indicator; return to the hum.
4. A dog gnawing a bone; return to the hum which is now at its peak.
5. An early morning car radio; short return to hum.
6. Church bells giving way to footsteps; long section of receding hum.
7. A car, which in turn lowers itself to the hum of a fridge.
8. The hum for a few seconds, and then it clicks off.

The whole sequence has a consequential harmony, mixing cliché and isolation and the unexplained.

On the first movement of spotlight we pick up TAIG *sitting stage right.* MATTI *is standing directly beneath the street light which nearly touches her head, she is wearing a coat and carrying a long shopping bag. On the return journey of the beam she is exactly the same but* TAIG *has vacated the chair.*

Darkness.

SCENE 15

MATTI *enters with her shopping bag. She empties the contents on the floor and studies them with her foot. She sits midway through speech.*

MATTI: I would like to have the sense to enjoy fantasy but somehow I can't. It's because of the deprived young men. I must sit. I won't walk – it's too close to falling. And no Taig. Well, it's not so bad in the morning. The girl was over and she was saying that there was nothing better than the bottom ones. And the cows and calves were off and she making out that I was the cause but I made out I didn't hear her. When they go out – you see – they don't bother taking the boxes.

They just take everything with them. [*The mood passes; wearily, she starts collecting her pieces.* TAIG *enters quietly through flat 4, stage right. He stands watching her – she suddenly becomes aware of him.*]

MATTI: Oh Taig, I thought I might never see you again.

TAIG: [*Brushing her away.*] Where were you?

MATTI: I'm so glad to see you.

TAIG: [*Roaring.*] I said where were you?

MATTI: [*Stepping a little way away.*] Oh out, just out walking.

TAIG: You can't . . . A person can't spend the night on the streets. You want to find a bed. And that means finding someone that has one.

MATTI: Oh Taig, what does it matter?

TAIG: Jesus Christ curse you Matti.

MATTI: Taig.

TAIG: Taig, Taig – I can't stand my fucking name on your lips.

[*He slaps her.*]

[*She feels the mark he has left on her face. She returns to her chair and sits in it. He stands left of centre stage, then sits on the edge of the bed.*]

MATTI: Anyway Taig, it's you, you came back.

TAIG: It was you that was away.

MATTI: Oh yes. But I missed you something terrible.

TAIG: Where did you stay?

MATTI: Oh, in a hotel somewhere. I think I crashed the car. Did they tell you? [*He shakes his head.*] Well they will.

TAIG: Are you hurt?

MATTI: Oh no. I'm so glad to see you. [*She stands.*] If you would only come into my arms everything would be alright. Please Taig. [*He gets up reluctantly.*] When you are around me I can do anything. [*He reaches her. She puts her hands on his shoulders.*] It'll never happen again – this is all I have . . . What I see in front of me. We must be tender and intimate . . . Please Taig, take the risk and let's trust each other . . . Do you understand, Taig? Taig, Taig, Taig, Taig.

[*He puts a hand over her mouth aggressively, and one hand behind her neck forcing her mouth into his other hand. Then*

when she stops talking and struggling he lets go. He steps backward, turns and goes out flat 4, stage right, which swings slowly round to white. She watches the white flat, approaches it, and stands still.]
[*Hold image.*]
[*Darkness.*]
[*End of* ACT II.]

ACT III
Continual Time
SCENE 16

Same set as before except table is smaller, chairs are elongated. The prints of the pictures are gone. There is a general spareness. The bed is now a single bed. All the flats are open, except for one white flat – flat 4, stage right – which is closed. The head and foot of the bed stand separately against centre back wall. The feeling is of a deserted place. The gas fire which burned throughout second act is gone. It's summer. Somewhere. Pale blue light.

MATTI *is leaning against a raised pillow, her arms down straight by her sides, and her hands palming the shawl. The shawl has become her companion – wherever she goes, it goes. She has aged somewhat.*

All signs of the writing paraphernalia from the previous two acts are gone. Gone also is the map of the world. A car battery and leads stand on some newspaper on the table. Beside the battery sits the innards of a radio. All light is concentrated on her shawl.

MATTI: Nothing to do but doodle. [*She is quite cheerful.*] On the ceiling. As if they were clouds. A flask of tea, some face, a tree in summer, and . . . Florence, the top of the place where the Jews pray. Every last thing. Then someone comes. [*She listens for the voice.*] "Get up, get up," but I say I am not to be perjured . . . Well they can search in me as much as they want but they won't find who they are looking for . . . Because the whole thing is too beautiful for words. And it all happened before and needs thinning out . . . I can see that. It must be exotic because it's forever changing. Nothing is ever still in their world – and that's as it should be . . . [*Pause.*]

[MATTI *suddenly flings the shawl across the room. Underneath she is fully clothed. She looks for the shawl. This entices her out of bed.*]

[*She has a new walk. Two steps forward, one step back. She touches things, makes little sounds, she is a searcher condemned to search eternally – one thing leads to another until it ends. Then she sits, moves on, tries all the chairs, sits on bed, and at last reaches the armchair. She is partially satisfied that this is her place. She wears a shiny apron with a large pocket, in which she keeps her notebook. The blouse we saw at the beginning of ACT I is now buttoned up wrong, she wears ankle socks, one up, one down.*]

[*Reaching the armchair she remembers the shawl. Its visual sense draws her. She lifts it, cracks it out like a sheet three times, beats it into place – all out of place – into the armchair. Sits down most inelegantly with a thud. Habit is propelling her to repeat gestures with which she is steadily getting unfamiliar.*]

[*She looks sharply back towards the chair and table. "What's wrong here?" her expression says. Then – she lets it all pass.*]

[*Habit makes her look at her hands. She clenches them, and looks wonderingly at the fingertips. Counts the tips of right hand with her thumb, then with her lips, as if after eating a sweet bun. Finished with that she notices her watch. This sets off a new habit. Searches, finds the notebook in her pocket. The pen is attached by string. She writes into the notebook in a logical, precise hand. She reads over what she has written.*]

MATTI: It is 5.15. [*Puts notebook away, but has trouble putting pen away. Sits, waits in isolation, a subtle touch of panic about her, then just quietly waiting. She looks at the table again where the battery sits. She puts her head in her hands for a while, fretting.*]

MATTI: Oh yes. [*Beats her knees bad-temperedly, and begins little rocking motion.*]

MATTI: That too. [*She waits, ceases to rock.*]

MATTI: [*Whisper.*] Oh God.

[*Ruffles her hair. As if preparing to go out. Then gets up, goes back over to bed and lies down. Flatly looks at ceiling. Her head darts up, she looks at the chair. Two steps forward, one step back. She goes over and retrieves the shawl, avoiding everything else in the room. She lies down. Pulls the shawl over her. Sits up. Finds the notebook and the pen on the string. Starts to write but can write nothing. Then sees her watch, and writes as before.*]

MATTI: [*Reads.*] It is 5.20. [*Writes. Reads.*] Since the last time.

[*She replaces the notebook and pen with some effort. Lies beneath shawl. Glances around. Sits up and with an effort looks positively normal, but a little frightened to be alone. She stares in front of her as if trying to find a source out there – or inside herself. Then becomes totally indifferent, all adrenalin gone.*]

[*Suddenly, as before, she flings notebooks and pen across the floor, and turns to the wall.*]

[*Enter* SHEILA *with a white cake-box through flat 1, stage left. She enters very quietly, sits on the bed, and drops a hand onto* MATTI*'s shoulder.*]

SHEILA: Hallo Matti. [MATTI *swings slowly round.*] I came to see you – I'm glad to find you in.

MATTI: The bed will be the death of me – but is there anywhere else?

[SHEILA *looks around. She spots the diary.*]

SHEILA: Is that your diary?

MATTI: It is for the present, but not at hand. [MATTI *follows*

SHEILA's *eye. Then* SHEILA *gets up and retrieves diary. She hands it to* MATTI *who looks down at the notebook as if it were something strange.*] Perhaps it's yours now.

SHEILA: No, it's got your name on it.

MATTI: That may not be me. [*She opens the book, and it becomes familiar.*] If it is, then I have succeeded.

SHEILA: [*As* MATTI *turns the pages.*] You look well.

MATTI: All these words. To keep a distance. [*She shows* SHEILA *the page.*] If I start a sentence I'm afraid it will never end. Before I start it's not there. Then it begins, like this now. [*Closes book.*] Leading now here. [*Smiles.*] Except on the sunny side.

SHEILA: [*After looking around.*] Can I get you something?

MATTI: Perhaps something sweet.

SHEILA: I brought eclairs. [*She opens the box and sits it in front of* MATTI's *nose.*]

MATTI: They smell of my youth. [*She inhales deeply. Spies her watch. Lifts notebook retires into utter privacy. Writes after dropping everything. Reads.*] It is 5.30. [*Hands notebook to* SHEILA, *turns a page, turns another, then another, and returns to where she was.*] I have finished two pages. [*Takes back notebook. Lies back.*] We have made mistakes. [*Sits up.*] I used to think of people who were not there – except in their bodies. Well, I'm not going to indulge myself any longer by thinking that men are to blame. [*She swings her legs out of bed.*] I'm fed up with women talking only of women.

SHEILA: Matti, you're funny.

MATTI: [*She takes* SHEILA's *hands.*] If you are in love you will be as excited as he is. Oh wonders. And won't hold back. The women keep watch – call it – over their bodies. I never. [*Sharp note.*] Their mind – they can't let it out of the body.

SHEILA: Yes, you're right.

MATTI: [*Gets up, walks.*] We are vulnerable then aren't we?

SHEILA: Yes.

MATTI: [*Seated in armchair.*] Well, I will return here no matter what happens. [*Looks back at the shawl and returns for it.*] The vessel is full. Everyone wants to go and see the healing. [*Sits.*]

SHEILA: [*For conversation's sake.*] Taig should be home soon.

MATTI: [*Transformed.*] Taig, oh Taig.

SHEILA: I'll make tea.

MATTI: Oh do. [SHEILA *brings over her notebook,* MATTI *clutches it to her breast when* SHEILA *goes through flat 2, stage left.*] If I could absent myself for long enough it might get done. Who you are is what the world wants. It ends though just before. But if they keep on I won't know – especially in the black-and-white, which is the return journey in the company of the same splendid woman who was there from the start – [*Expansive gesture.*] – except maybe she is tired of her itinerary these last five nights. [*Composed.*] In the night air – [*She listens.*] – the smell crosses the sea from his island to hers, but there is no parallel line. That was common. Only less we cross at thirty-four degrees celcius. That may not be possible. [*Considers.*] Unless you double it. [*Affirms this with strenuous nod. Becomes uncomfortable soon after. There is a stark sense of isolation as if she realizes that this is her last moment alone in her own house. She looks at her watch. Looks at it again.*] Oh jeepers. [*Lifts notebooks.*]

[SHEILA *enters with tea. Laboriously* MATTI *writes.*]

SHEILA: I bought some Bewley's tea for you.

MATTI: [*Reads.*] It is 5.40. [*She struggles to write again, but cannot.*] I can't even write a human sentence, not one. [*She puts her notebook back in her pocket.*] My life is like a story you could put down and forget to return to. [*Pulls shawl about her, looks towards the table, glances upward, hits her knee, then flexes her arm along the side of the chair, looks to the right and left.* SHEILA *hands her the cup. She smells the tea for a long time – this sends her off on a new path.*] What was that programme that was on at 5.30?

SHEILA: On R.T.E.?

MATTI: Well I had myself all settled on the couch to see it. Would it have been *Piggy Longtail*? I had everything done and Mammy came in. She said: "Go up and get us . . .?" It was something, would you believe, to do with paint and wallpapers. White spirits, my God. She wanted me to go to Dooley's for White Spirits and they were at the other end of town. So I ran to the shop. There was a party there buying wallpaper, of all things, and the lady was calling out measurements to the man behind the counter as she shepherded her husband and two children to and fro. The shopkeeper took no notice of me. I tried to get him by the eye. But he was always somewhere else. This lady knew exactly what she wanted. And I stood there for twenty minutes. Only then he asked me what he could do for me. "White Spirits," I said, very crossly. When I got home the Angelus was playing.

SHEILA: Did you not tell Mammy?

MATTI: No, I always do what I'm told. And I had my favourite cushion on the couch got up for behind my head. [MATTI *drinks the tea slowly at first, with some effort, and then liking the taste she holds it to her lips and swallows it all.* SHEILA *pours another.* MATTI *drains it immediately. And holds her cup out for more.*] It's all gone.

SHEILA: I'll make some more.

MATTI: Do. [*Just then* TAIG *enters through flat 1, stage left. She hears him, turns, and on seeing him she immediately rushes towards him. She has not seen him in years. With real joy she throws her arms around him, and they stay like that, holding on to each other.*] Taig, Taig, where were you? – I looked everywhere.

TAIG: I was working on Johnson's car.

MATTI: Well you're here now – and that's all that counts.

TAIG: And then I couldn't find out what was wrong.

MATTI: I can't believe you're here. Don't go away again.

TAIG: I won't.

MATTI: They're talking of things I don't understand. These people.

TAIG: Never mind, I'll look after you.

[SHEILA *puts down tray in embarrassment. She stands for a moment not knowing what to do.*]

TAIG: Sheila.

SHEILA: I was just about to make more tea.

MATTI: Oh Taig.

SHEILA: I'll go and come back later – I have to meet friends somewhere.

TAIG: There's no need.

SHEILA: It's alright – I'll see you soon. [*She approaches them where* MATTI *stands her arms around* TAIG *with her back to* SHEILA *centre stage.*] Goodbye Matti. [*She passes them.*]

MATTI: Goodbye.

[SHEILA *opens flat 1, stage left, and passes through.* MATTI *looks after her. The flat turns to white. Slowly* MATTI *lets go off* TAIG, *walks over – just a step or two – and looks at the white flat in a perplexed wondering manner.*]

TAIG: She said she'd be back later Matti. [*He takes her by the shoulder, turns her round, leads her back to armchair and sits her down. He is hesitant and watchful. He opens flat 1, stage right, and looks out to sea.*] I have something important to tell you.

MATTI: Oh well. [*Brightly.*]

TAIG: They asked me to come to the University.

MATTI: They asked you?

TAIG: They phoned the garage.

MATTI: You talked to them.

TAIG: I drove to Galway.

MATTI: Now for you.

TAIG: And saw the Health Board.

MATTI: That was good.

TAIG: They cannot extend your sick leave. [*She does not reply.*] Now it's nothing as harsh as a dismissal – nothing like that. [*She nods.*] They will pay your full wages to the end of term – then something will be worked out afterwards. [*He goes the whole way.*] But your contract is not being renewed. [*She nods.*] I suppose they did the best they could. [*She picks at her blouse – fatalistic.*] When you get better you can find work elsewhere. [*He goes on his hunkers.*]

MATTI: And you will look after me?

TAIG: Of course I will.

MATTI: I'm so happy to see you.

TAIG: You will get better.

MATTI: I won't cry, don't worry. [*As she speaks he disentangles himself, and moves away – it's something perhaps he's heard a number of times.*] I can't bear anyone that cries, because I am so used to it myself. I hate people that fall sick, because I was always sick as a child. [*He sits in front of the battery, lifts spanner, starts unscrewing cap.*] How does that song go?

TAIG: What song?

MATTI: I'm trying to remember.

TAIG: Hum me a little.

MATTI: I can't.

TAIG: Yes, you can.

[MATTI *hums a little, illuminates; a little time passes.*]

MATTI: Everything will come back, won't it?

TAIG: In time.

MATTI: And then we can return together.

TAIG: Yes.

MATTI: And nothing will have altered.

TAIG: Nothing.

MATTI: That's good to know. I could wear my school uniform again. I love a crisp shirt and good stout churchgoing shoes, like my mother wore.

TAIG: You'll have them.

MATTI: And frost in the yard.

TAIG: And all your friends.

MATTI: That will be nice.

TAIG: How would you like to meet someone you knew?

MATTI: Now?

TAIG: Yes – if you want to.

MATTI: Now will be fine.

TAIG: I can get us something to eat later on.

MATTI: Yes, I'm hungry.

TAIG: Here . . . [*He stands wiping his hands with a cloth.*] . . . let me fix you up.

[*This is a love duet – he straightens her dress after taking off the apron. He unbuttons and re-buttons her blouse, he takes down her socks, kisses her knees, pulls up her socks, strokes her legs, she strokes his head and watches him voyeuristically. Meanwhile they chat.*]

MATTI: It meant so much to me.

TAIG: I understand.

MATTI: I told you they would do this to me but you did not believe me.

TAIG: I was wrong.

MATTI: Should I talk to them?

TAIG: I don't think so.

MATTI: Now I'll have nothing to do.

[*He stands up.*]

TAIG: There – you're fine now.

MATTI: Lips. [*She stands.*]

[*He finds lipstick. He runs it across her lips while she pouts. He wipes away the excess with a tissue, then stands back from her. Turns her armchair towards centre stage, and sits her into it. Goes immediately over to flat 2, stage left, and opens it. Enter a very big man,* DR JOHN FARRELL.]

MATTI: Who is that person? [*Shocked.*]

TAIG: It's Dr John Farrell. Matti, he is going to try and help you.

DOCTOR: Hallo Matti.

[*The shaking of hands is a self-conscious breakable affair.*]

MATTI: Hallo.

DOCTOR: [*Sitting opposite her.*] Do you remember me?

MATTI: How could I forget?

DOCTOR: She was the brightest of us all at Uni.

TAIG: I'll make tea.

DOCTOR: Thank you. [*Exit* TAIG *through flat 2, stage right.*] Now I'm just to ask you a few questions Matti. Nothing formal. Just ordinary things, and I hope, friendly things. You are a couple of years younger than me, aren't you? [*He takes out notebook – she watches this with great interest.*]

MATTI: [*A little slow-paced.*] That's true.

DOCTOR: So what age does that make you?

MATTI: Well I'm not getting any younger.

DOCTOR: The days at university seem a long way away – where are you actually from?

MATTI: Oh I'm a country girl, like yourself.

DOCTOR: Indeed. [*He gestures towards door.*] And where did you meet your husband?

MATTI: The same place he met me.

DOCTOR: And you are a lecturer these days. [*No reply. Up until this point* MATTI *has been enjoying the exchange. She now appears indifferent. He tries a new path.*] Can you describe what you feel – what you think might be wrong with you – if there is anything.

MATTI: [*Looking him squarely in the eye.*] Everybody else has something I have not.

DOCTOR: Could you tell me what that something is?

MATTI: Oh you know yourself.

DOCTOR: Call me John.

MATTI: John.

DOCTOR: Why do you think I have it?

MATTI: Cause I can see it in you. It's dancing in your eye.

DOCTOR: [*He laughs.*] So you'll trust me?

MATTI: Oh yes . . .

DOCTOR: John.

MATTI: John.

[*Pause. New tack.*]

DOCTOR: I'm sure you recall your childhood.

MATTI: We grow out of that.

DOCTOR: But you've written about your childhood.

MATTI: Perhaps I have.

DOCTOR: It's no mean achievement what you did with your life.

MATTI: How do you know so much about me?

DOCTOR: I've read your work. [*She does not reply but shows her earlier indifference. From the pocket of his coat he takes out a book.*] Do you know this book? [*He shoves the book across the table to her.*] You wrote that book.

MATTI: [*Looks at it an instant then looks away.*] Me – never. [*Looks back at it.*] And I don't want to talk about it.

DOCTOR: Why don't you want to talk about it?

MATTI: It means nothing but trouble.

DOCTOR: But Matti – you wrote it.

MATTI: [*She laughs.*] I'm sure it wrote itself. [*Sharpens her face.*] I want to speak to . . . someone else.

DOCTOR: Your husband? And so you shall.

[*Pause. She grows indifferent again. He takes back her novel. Looks at it, pockets it – she watches this, he closes his notebook, arranges the pen on it.*] And have you been writing lately?

MATTI: Oh yes. I have been writing hard, but I found it very difficult.

DOCTOR: What time of the day do you start?

MATTI: Very early.

DOCTOR: And you work till late?

MATTI: Till all hours.

DOCTOR: Does your husband like what you write?

MATTI: I suppose he does. [*Brightens up, then frowns.*] But I don't think he finished the last book.

DOCTOR: What was the title of the last book?

MATTI: You'll have to ask my husband that.

[*Inadvertently she sees her watch, looks at it, looks around the room, lifts her shawl, then takes the notebook out of her pocket, looks into it, sits, finds a page, writes.*]

DOCTOR: You keep a record? [*She nods.*] Towards your next book? [*She nods.*] Could I have a look – please? [*She shakes her head.*]

MATTI: It's private – that part of me is private, you understand?

DOCTOR: I understand, Matti. [*Pause. He pockets his notebook. Looks back towards* TAIG*'s exit.*] Your husband should be back in a moment.

MATTI: He's not here – he's probably off with someone else – the bastard. [*Whisper.*] Whisper! The worst thing about him is – he's anyone's.

DOCTOR: No – Matti – he's next door.

MATTI: [*She laughs.*] The shit. Do you have a cigarette?

DOCTOR: Why yes. [*He hands one across to her. She holds it most ungainly in her mouth. He lights it, she does not pull; he lights it again, she does pull. She is amazed at the whole procedure.*]

MATTI: Thank you most awfully. [*She laughs. Enter* TAIG *with tray.*] Taig, Taig, oh Taig.

TAIG: Matti. [*He puts the tray down.* DOCTOR *retrieves the cigarette where she dropped it.*] Matti – you gave up smoking years ago.

MATTI: Oh Taig, [*Holding him.*] I just felt the need for one. You mustn't stay away, you mustn't.

TAIG: I was just making tea.

MATTI: [*Burying her head into his shoulder.*] Oh Taig.

TAIG: [*Over her shoulder.*] I'll be with you in a minute Doctor.

DOCTOR: Oh never mind me. [*He gets to his feet.*] I'll have a word with you again about Matti.

TAIG: Can you not tell me anything now?

DOCTOR: [*Considering situation.*] Well, because of the strain of looking after Matti by yourself, you might consider having her hospitalized for a time.

TAIG: I'd rather give up my job first.

MATTI: [*Letting him go but facing him.*] Taig.

DOCTOR: Unfortunately, it may come to that. [*Pause.*] You see, Matti will have to be nursed. Doctors are no use to her. I am no use. Nursing is essential, you understand. As are sedatives for sleep. We can't have you wandering around the house, can we Matti?

MATTI: No.

TAIG: [*Passing* MATTI.] And will she always be like this?

DOCTOR: If it is what I think it is – it's a physical disease – we will just have to wait and see. I can't say anything more at the moment.

[MATTI *sits down in* TAIG's *chair slightly turned away.*]

MATTI: What made me like that?

DOCTOR: We don't know.

MATTI: And what's the cure?

DOCTOR: There is no cure – at present. Taig, I will speak to you soon – it's early days yet. [*He walks over to* MATTI.] Goodbye Matti, we will try everything.

MATTI: [*Turns.*] Goodbye.

[*She watches the doctor walk out flat 2, stage left. The flat swing round to white. She turns her head immediately as if not wanting to see.* TAIG *sits down by the table. They sit, each in their own world, for a while.*]

TAIG: Matti.

MATTI: Oh my love. [*She gets up – throws her arms around him.*] They can do something for me.

TAIG: They will try everything.

MATTI: [*Breaking free.*] It's awful. [*Suddenly irritable.*] I can't bear this. [*Stamps foot.*] I am without, or nearly without, my voice. I hear nothing but a fucking new voice. [*She stamps foot.*] And I don't want it. Fuck it! [*Stamps foot.*] Oh Jesus, Taig. Why can't they do something for me?

[*He watches her for a moment.*]

TAIG: [*Lifting battery off table.*] The rain came anyway.

MATTI: It came just in time.

TAIG: [*Opening flat 3, stage right.*] Did you hear the cuckoo?

MATTI: I did, and I heard the corncrake.

TAIG: [*Leaving battery out.*] And how could you hear the corncrake, it's too early for him yet.

MATTI: [*Standing by her armchair.*] Well I heard the corncrake.

TAIG: [*Lifting radio off the table.*] You have good ears.

MATTI: Sure the cuckoo is the corncrake.

TAIG: [*Leaving radio out.*] Is that so?

MATTI: When he's grown old.

TAIG: [*Stopping midway.*] He's the cuckoo with a beard.

MATTI: Yes, and there's plenty of them about. [*Pause. She sits; he sits.*] Fuck, fuck, shit, fuck. You will be sorry.

TAIG: Of course I will be sorry.

[*She starts coughing and trying to swallow. The spasm ceases. She smiles over at him in recognition.* TAIG *gets up to sort out the bed.*]

MATTI: Is it night or day?

TAIG: It's night.

MATTI: That's good. We can sleep together. We never sleep together.

TAIG: We do.

MATTI: That's good.

TAIG: You on the inside.

MATTI: Is that where.

TAIG: And me on the outside.

MATTI: Now for you. [*He walks over and stands beside her. She stands. He takes the shawl and spreads it over the bed.*] I'm frightened.

TAIG: Would you like some apple juice?

MATTI: No. I'd love one.

TAIG: Here . . .

[*She drinks furiously. He sits on the bed.* MATTI, *holding the glass, goes over and sits beside him.*]

MATTI: I don't know who I am. [*He puts his arm round her.*] Or what I am. [*Determined.*] But I'm not lost. [*She looks at him as if to blame him.*] Why can't they do something for me?

TAIG: They are trying.

MATTI: It's intolerable. [*She stands, wraps her arms around herself.*] I can't stand this. [*She kicks the floor with her heel.*] What's happening to me? [*He begins undoing her blouse. She watches his face.*] Yes, it's true.

TAIG: What is?

MATTI: You are going to turn into a bird.

TAIG: A bird with a beak?

MATTI: The beak is just beginning.

TAIG: [*Opening her dress – goes on to his knees.*] I suppose it will be a blue beak.

MATTI: That's right.

TAIG: With a twist to it?

MATTI: [*Stepping out of dress.*] And it will be this long. [*She taps his nose and draws finger out a little distance.*]

TAIG: I love you Matti.

[*She climbs into bed. Watches him – again very interested – as he undresses.*]

MATTI: You'd look lovely. In a dress.

TAIG: And what colour will it be?

MATTI: It will be navy blue. And your top will be royal blue.

TAIG: And what else?

MATTI: I don't know. But please don't stop flirting. Don't be spoken for – no matter what. [*He climbs into bed. A spotlight isolates them from their surroundings. He puts his arm around her.*] They breathe in my hand.

TAIG: Do they?

MATTI: Oh yes, in and out. In and out. [*He closes his eyes. She perches on her elbow and traces his face with her fingertips slow and accurately.*] Didn't you know? [*He does not answer. She finishes with his face and lies down. Her eyes are wide open and one hand is holding the corner of the shawl. Suddenly she looks at him, jumps out of bed, and the lights come up.*] The bed is wet.

TAIG: [*Tiredly.*] Yes.

MATTI: [*Drawing the shawl away.*] I wet the bed, didn't I?

TAIG: Yes, but it doesn't matter. [*He swings his legs out of bed and puts his head into his hands. She watches him.*]

MATTI: Why don't you ever kiss me?

TAIG: But I do.

MATTI: [*Feeling really slighted.*] Why don't you ever kiss me or make love to me?

TAIG: I do, I do, I do. [*He hauls his trousers on and goes to his chair.*] Matti, stop it, please.

[*She watches him, then sits into her armchair with her shawl.*]

MATTI: [*Quite practical – as if talking to a stranger.*] You were the sort of boy I might have picked up in my dancing days.

TAIG: [*Concentrating on not breaking.*] That's an honour.

MATTI: There again, I might have missed you.

TAIG: I would have been hiding in a corner someplace.

MATTI: I'm sure I would have found you.

TAIG: I'm sure you would.

[*He gets up, gathers her clothes. He stands in front of her as before. She stands as before.* ROSE *enters, as* TAIG *is opening* MATTI*'s blouse to put on her.*]

ROSE: Oh, I'm terribly sorry.

TAIG: Rose.

ROSE: Let me do that. [*He hands her the clothes.*] Hallo Matti.

MATTI: Hallo.

ROSE: [*Goes to put blouse over* MATTI *who is wearing only knickers.*] Do you know who I am?

MATTI: Oh I know who you are alright.

ROSE: Could you lift your arms?

MATTI: [*Suddenly backs away.*] I must have the same clothes on as I had yesterday.

ROSE: They aren't. [*She turns to* TAIG.]

MATTI: And these are not my knickers. [*She pulls them off and hurls them at* TAIG.] Will you make sure of that?

TAIG: I will.

ROSE: What am I to do?

[MATTI *looks threateningly at* ROSE *and goes rigid.*]

TAIG: Give Matti her shawl.

[MATTI *wraps the shawl around her.* ROSE *sits when* MATTI *walks off to upstage left, and stands there with her back to them.* TAIG *is looking into the middle distance.*]

MATTI: Dirt! [*Pulls the shawl around her.*] Nothing but dirt.

ROSE: I've been so wrong.

MATTI: Bastards.

TAIG: They say the guilt accrues not over what you've done, but what you have not done. I wanted someone out of this whole hellhole of a life to be with always. We make it up as we go along, and it's always for the first time. She taught me that.

MATTI: [*Sitting with her back to them on edge of bed.*] Why cannot someone help me? It is infuriating. [ROSE *looks from* TAIG *to* MATTI, *but* MATTI *has her back to her and* TAIG *is looking straight ahead.*]

ROSE: Oh Matti.

MATTI: I've seen all this before. Now it's all the one moment. [*She kicks floor with heel.*]

ROSE: I'm sorry.

MATTI: [*Jerking her head backwards.*] Why didn't this happen to you? [ROSE *utterly lost.*]

TAIG: Maybe we carry the seeds of our distress. Somewhere within us. Maybe.

ROSE: Matti. [*No reply.*]

TAIG: She doesn't hear you – don't you understand? It's one cell at a time, and in that cell 1953 is living, then it's gone, the next cell is 1972, then it's gone. How can you think about what's not there any longer? But the fact that you've forgotten something doesn't matter in the long run – she's taught me that too.

ROSE: I'm sure somewhere inside her head she knows you are there.

TAIG: I wonder.

MATTI: Something is eating away at me! [*She stands and confronts* ROSE.] I'd have given my life to have known one clear day, do you understand?

ROSE: Yes.

MATTI: [*Continuing on towards her chair.*] He tells me I'm going to die.

ROSE: [*Looks at* TAIG, *then at* MATTI.] Did he say that?

MATTI: Oh yes. It's awful then – isn't it?

ROSE: [*Unsure.*] It's dreadful.

MATTI: [*To* ROSE.] And how soon will I die?

TAIG: Matti.

MATTI: Who is speaking to you? [*Back to* ROSE.] I suppose that was a party I never attended. With you looking down out of your window at me in the car. Wondering what I was at. With that fellow.

ROSE: He was a doctor.

MATTI: He was an idiot in leather trousers and you were always at the window. And I was on the train, and though I was carrying a lot of things I didn't put them down but walked up and down looking for my seat. But they all seemed to be facing the wrong way. Then at last . . . [*She looks at* TAIG.] . . . I found you where I had left you.

TAIG: Yes, I remember.

MATTI: [*Now she fixes* TAIG *with the same stare she first gave* ROSE; *then suddenly she breaks the stare to speak to* ROSE, *in an almost ironic tone.*] Outside the house is a problem. Inside a total mystery. [*Pause.*] I was at my mother's yesterday. [*Pause.* ROSE *looks to* TAIG *who accepts everything as normal.*] It was pleasant enough, and then it became intolerable. [*She *becomes authoritative.*] Let them come back and find the sons and daughters they left behind them. [*She looks away, then repeats her direct gaze at* ROSE.] My mother looked just like you.

ROSE: And you always looked like our father.

MATTI: Is that what's wrong? [*She hauls her chair nearer to* ROSE, *sits, then moves it again even nearer, and speaks. She is oblivious of* TAIG]. I can't write a thing. Not a thing. And do you know why? The reason is in here. [*She pats her pocket.*] See! [*She lifts out top of notebook, then conceals it again.*] This is one leg that won't grow back again. [*She lifts out her notebook, hands it to* ROSE.] Read what's written there.

ROSE: [*Reads.*] Matti Foley.

MATTI: That's it. [*She takes back the notebook and sits closer to* ROSE.] I used to sit by you. [*Pause.*] No one will ever know who I was.

TAIG: We will Matti.

MATTI: Who are you to speak! [*Sharp screech.*] You don't know me. I only pretend to know you. Will you please explain to him? [*She takes* ROSE's *hand.*] You are my sister.

ROSE: You mustn't speak to him like that.

MATTI: [*She flings* ROSE's *hand away and starts climbing out of her chair and screams.*] Why are we so many?
[*Immediately a song starts – Jacque Brel's version of Edith Piaf's "Don't Leave Me" sung in French ("Ne me quitte pas").*]

1. *Immediately* NURSE *and* MALE NURSE *enter and begin to move the bed from its current position – parallel to back on stage right – to a new position with the head against the back wall on stage left. The old clothes are put aside, and crisp new sheets and bedspread – all white – are put on to the new hospital bed. This is done very properly.*

2. ROSE *gets up and kisses* MATTI*'s cheeks and leaves through flat 2, stage right. That flat goes to white. She takes the chair with her.*
3. TAIG *begins to fill a little case with* MATTI*'s things. Having*

filled the case he puts it standing by MATTI – *her eyes are on him, not blaming him, just following him after* ROSE *departs. He then takes her armchair and moves it off stage. Then he returns for the table, and does the same. Then* NURSE, *who has begun to dress* MATTI *in a white nightdress, hands him the coloured shawl.* TAIG *takes it and leaves through flat 3, stage right, quite smartly. The flat turns to white.*

4. MATTI *stands until* NURSE *has dressed her in a nightdress. Then she is led over to the bed, and climbs slavishly in.*

5. MALE NURSE *retains one green chair for beside the bed and brings the others out by flat 4, stage left.*

6. NURSE *tightens the sheets in around the bed on the right hand side, while* MALE NURSE *tightens the sheets on the left hand side. They work in complete unison.*

7. *All the various moves should have ended by completion of song. Both nurses exit through flat 4, stage left.*

8. MATTI*'s face is left looking forward into the auditorium, unseeing.*

[*Enter* MRS P *in a dressing gown, with socks and boots. She passes right across the stage and goes out through flat 1, stage right. Then reappears. Head in, withdrawn, then body in. She lights a cigarette and, brandishing it dangerously, approaches the bed.*]

MRS P: Don't I know you pet?
MATTI: I'm sorry – I don't know anyone here.
MRS P: [*Sits.*] Oh I know you – I never forget a face. I'm blessed that way. Well don't fret pet. [*She points towards the auditorium.*] They are madder out there than they are in here. [*She pulls on the cigarette, looks at* MATTI.]
MRS P: Don't you remember me?

MATTI: [*With great dignity.*] I'm afraid I don't know anyone here.

MRS P: [*Inaudible hum is switched off.*] Is there hurt in the memory? [*No reply.*] Was it the nerves? [*No reply.*] Oh well. You find all types here. Those outside are afraid of us. Would you believe it? What's the point is being serious, I ask you. Once you're dead you're serious forever. The psychiatric patient frightens them, did you know that? [*No reply.*] Would you like a smoke? [*She proffers a cigarette and* MATTI *takes a pull, then another, and* MRS P *withdraws it, taps the ash on the floor under the chair, and kicks it backward with her foot.*] I could swear you're the wild spit of someone I knew. [*She laughs.*] We can laugh at ourselves – isn't that right? [*She finishes the cigarette and stamps on it and kicks the butt back under the seat.*] The west of Ireland is a strange place. [*She gets to her feet.*] There's one thing about the dead – the one good thing – and I'll say no more pet: they fertilize the earth. Where my man is, there's a spot of fuchsia now. The poor thing – he could never make a hand of the new money. If he was here – [*She points at* MATTI.] – he'd know the lady that was in it. Isn't that right? [*No reply.*] Well I must be off on my travels – maybe not as far as I'd like – [*She moves off a little.*] – but you have to keep on the move. Else the ticker might play up. [*She stops.*] I'll bring you sweets. Cheery-bye. [*She steps out through flat 3, stage left. The flat turns to white.* MATTI *lies down in the bed. Through a flat on the right come* JOEJOE *and* MR RODGERS *talking.*]

MR RODGERS: I spent a summer pulling beet in Fife.

JOEJOE: And one and seven for a hundred yards.

MR RODGERS: I worked the hammer and the butterfly.

JOEJOE: In Connick outside Inverness.

MR RODGERS: The Polacks banked the face off at the top . . .

JOEJOE: They should not have done that.

MR RODGERS: No, they should have left a vacancy. Then the gas built up.

JOEJOE: These things will happen.

MR RODGERS: Aye.

JOEJOE: Oh a fast race of tepid people.

MR RODGERS: And in winter shuttering above in Oban.

[*They pass out through flat 4, stage left.* MATTI *sits up and looks after them but the flat does not turn to white. While she is watching this,* TAIG *enters through flat 1, stage left. He stands there watching her.*]

TAIG: Matti. Matti. [*Slowly she turns her head.*] Matti. [*He moves over to the bed and takes her hand. She watches her hand in his. He kisses it. She watches. He lifts her other hand and kisses it.*] Matti, I love you. I can't tell you how much I miss you. It's raw and painful and I can't tell you anymore. I think I see you on the street. [*Pause.*] Walking up to me, about to recognize me. The beautiful woman. Walking to meet you. The great warmth of your recognition. But then the face disappears into someone else's face. [*Pause.*] You cross over at the back of a crowded bar. I think I hear you upstairs – but it's not you. I'm no one now. Because I only exist if you remember me. I have no other existence. [*Pause.*] My jealousy was only a want for simplicity. [*Pause.*] I'm sorry you had to come in here. You should be in a different place, I know – you are sane as I am. You've just broken a leg – that's all. But I couldn't bear it any longer. The money was gone. [*Pause.*] I could kill myself for the way I treated you. [*Pause.*] And it's not just the good moments that come back. I loved you always. [*Pause.*] God, how I miss you Matti. [*Pause.*] There's no fun anymore.

[*Enter* NURSE *through flat 4, stage left.*]

NURSE: We must be going now Mr Foley. I'm sure Mrs Foley is thinking of other things.

TAIG: Of what other things?

NURSE: Of sleep for one.

TAIG: Is it that time already?

NURSE: Yes, it flies, doesn't it?

TAIG: Yes, it does. [*He lets go of* MATTI *and slowly stands.*] Goodbye Matti – I'll see you first thing tomorrow.

NURSE: Say goodbye Mrs Foley. [*She begins tucking the blankets in.*] Good night Mr Foley – go quiet if you will.

[MATTI *looks after him.*]

TAIG: Goodnight. [*He steps through flat 1, stage right, and it turns to white.* NURSE *lifts the chair and brings it out through flat 4, then re-enters. She goes round each flat checking that they are all straight. She touches each one as* MATTI *watches. Then with one last look around* NURSE *exits through flat 4, stage left, and the flat turns to white.*]

[MATTI *goes into a foetal position. A spotlight hovers over her bed. The rain begins as at the beginning of the play. As the rain begins, the spotlight over the bed starts to increase. As it does, another spotlight starts increasing stage right.* TAIG *is standing in the second spotlight.* MATTI *turns in the bed, lifts her head up, and looks to where* TAIG *is. But already his spotlight has begun to dissolve. She returns to a foetal shape.*]

[*Darkness.*]

[*The rain continues a little while.*]

END

Blood Wedding

Adapted by Dermot Healy from the original 1933 play by Federico García Lorca. First performed in June 1989 by the Seven Woods Theatre Company, Sligo, at the Hawk's Well Theatre, Sligo. Directed and designed by Frank Conway.

CAST

THE BRIDEGROOM	
THE MOTHER	
THE NEIGHBOUR	
THE MOTHER-IN-LAW	
THE WIFE OF LEONARDO	
LEONARDO	
GIRLS	
THE SERVANT	a woman
THE FATHER OF THE BRIDE	
THE BRIDE	
YOUNG MEN	
WOODCUTTERS	
THE MOON	
DEATH	as a beggar woman
A LITTLE GIRL	

ACT I
SCENE 1

Room painted yellow.

BRIDEGROOM: [*Entering.*] Mother.
MOTHER: What?
BRIDEGROOM: I'm going.
MOTHER: Where pray?
BRIDEGROOM: To the fields. [*He starts to go.*]
MOTHER: Hold your horses.
BRIDEGROOM: Do you want something?
MOTHER: I want you to eat your breakfast.
BRIDEGROOM: Don't fret. I'll eat grapes. Give us the knife.
MOTHER: What for?
BRIDEGROOM: [*Laughing.*] To cut the eyes out of the potatoes. What else?
MOTHER: [*Muttering as she looks.*] The scian, the scian . . . damn the same knives and the good-for-nothing who invented them.
BRIDEGROOM: Leave it.
MOTHER: And shotguns . . . and pistols . . . and even the tiniest knife . . . and pikes and pitchforks.
BRIDEGROOM: I hear you.
MOTHER: Every last thing that can cut into a man's body. A beautiful man, the fullness of life, who goes out to the fields or tends to his crops, because they are his. Nobody else's. Inherited by him.
BRIDEGROOM: Quit it. [*Lowering his head.*]
MOTHER: And that same man doesn't come back. Or if he does it's for cowslip to bind his wound, or a plateful of rock salt to stop the swelling. While you carry a knife on your body how can I forget the hurt of the memory? It's beyond me why I keep this serpent here inside the chest. [*She takes a knife from a kitchen chest.*]
BRIDEGROOM: Have you finished?

MOTHER: If I lived to be a hundred, I'd speak of nothing else. First your father – he had the scent of carnation – who I enjoyed for three short years. Then your brother. Is it fair? Is it possible that a scut of a thing like a knife or a pistol put an end to a man who's a bull? I'll not be quiet. Never! The months pass and despair picks at my eyes, even at the very roots of my hair.

BRIDEGROOM: Are you going to stop!

MOTHER: No. I won't stop! Who can bring your father back? Or your brother. And then there's the jail. What is the jail? They eat there, they smoke there, they play instruments there. My dead men are smothered by weeds, wordless, turning to dust. My two men who were two geraniums. And the murderers sit in jail, not a hate wrong with them, looking at the mountains.

BRIDEGROOM: [*Forcefully.*] Do you want me to kill them?

MOTHER: No. If I go on like this it's because . . . But . . . How can I stop myself if I have to watch you walk out that door? What can I say? I don't like you to carry a knife. It's just that . . . I wish you wouldn't go out to them fields.

BRIDEGROOM: [*Laughing.*] Oh now!

MOTHER: It'd suit me better if you were a woman. You wouldn't be going to the sheugh and I wouldn't be tormented. Instead the two of us could embroider hankies and little woollen dogs.

BRIDEGROOM: [*He puts his arm around his mother and laughs.*] What if I were to take you with me and set you up between the drills?

MOTHER: What would an old scourge like me do in the potato fields? Would you sit me under the potato blossoms?

BRIDEGROOM: [*Lifting her in his arms.*] You old lady, you dear old lady, you dear old little lady.

MOTHER: Your father used to take me there. He came of good stock. That was good blood. Your grandfather left a son standing on every corner. Oh yes, that's what I like. Men to be men and wheat to be wheat.

BRIDEGROOM: And what about my mother?

MOTHER: You, what?

BRIDEGROOM: I'll not ask you again.

MOTHER [*Serious.*] Oh aye.

BRIDEGROOM: So you're against it?

MOTHER: No.

BRIDEGROOM: What then?

MOTHER: I'm at sea. It's so sudden. It's taken the wind out of me. I know the girl is good. She is, isn't she? Well-behaved. Well-got. Hardworking. Bakes her bread and sews her skirts and minds her own business. But even so when I say her name it's as if someone stood on my grave.

BRIDEGROOM: Don't be soft.

MOTHER: I'm not soft. But you're leaving me alone. And you are all that's left to me now and I'll be sorry to see you go.

BRIDEGROOM: But you could come with us.

MOTHER: No. I can't leave your father and brother by themselves in this place. I have to visit the graves every morning, and if I leave, one of the Felixes could die, one of that family of murderers, and they'll bury him next to mine. I won't stand for that. Not on your life. I'll dig them up with my very nails and by myself. I'll break them asunder against the wall.

BRIDEGROOM: We're back there again.

MOTHER: I can't help myself. [*Pause.*] Bear with me. [*Pause.*] How long have you been seeing her?

BRIDEGROOM: Three full years, and now I've bought the farm.

MOTHER: Three years. She used to walk out with another lad, didn't she?

BRIDEGROOM: Not that I've heard. I don't think so. Girls have to study well who they intend to marry.

MOTHER: True. I didn't look at another. I looked at your father and when they killed him I looked at the wall in front of me. One woman to one man, that's how it should be.

BRIDEGROOM: My girl is good.

MOTHER: I didn't say otherwise. All the same, I'd like to have known the cut of her mother.

BRIDEGROOM: What does it matter now?

MOTHER: [*Looking at him.*] Son.

BRIDEGROOM: What do you want?

MOTHER: You're right. It's all in the past. When do you want me to see her?

BRIDEGROOM: [*Happily.*] Would Sunday do?

MOTHER: [*Seriously.*] I'll take her the brass earrings, they go back a long way, and you can buy her . . .

BRIDEGROOM: You know more about these things.

MOTHER: You can buy her some fancy stockings and find yourself two suits . . . No! Three suits. I've only got the one of you.

BRIDEGROOM: I'm going. I'll call on her tomorrow.

MOTHER: Yes, yes, and see if you can make me happy with six grandchildren – no seven, or eight, or as many as you want – seeing as your father didn't live to give them to me.

BRIDEGROOM: The first born will be for you.

MOTHER: Yes, but let them be girls. Because I want to embroider and make lace and be at peace.

BRIDEGROOM: I'm sure you'll take to my bride.

MOTHER: I will. [*She starts to kiss him but changes her mind.*] Go on. You are gone beyond kisses. Save them for your wife. [*Pause. In an aside.*] When she is your wife.

BRIDEGROOM: I'm going.

MOTHER: Turn the soil by the old mill – you've been neglecting it.

BRIDEGROOM: I will, I'm glad we understand each other.

MOTHER: God spare you.

[*The* BRIDEGROOM *leaves. The* MOTHER *remains seated. She keeps her back to the door. A* NEIGHBOUR *woman appears with a handkerchief over her head. She stands by the door.*]

NEIGHBOUR: How are you?

MOTHER: No loss on me.

NEIGHBOUR: I came down to go as far as the shop and so

I stopped in to see you. We live an unearthly distance from each other.

MOTHER: It's twenty good years since I stood at the top of the street.

NEIGHBOUR: You look well.

MOTHER: Do you think so?

NEIGHBOUR: These things will happen. Two days ago they brought my neighbour's son home . . . Both arms were cut clean off him by the machine. [*She sits down.*]

MOTHER: Felim?

NEIGHBOUR: The same. There you have him. You are better off dead. I often think your lad and mine are better off where they are – sleeping and resting without a chance of being crippled.

MOTHER: Quit it. It's all in your head. There's no comfort in such talk.

NEIGHBOUR: [*Sighing.*] Aye.

MOTHER: [*Sighing.*] Aye.

[*Pause.*]

NEIGHBOUR: How is your lad?

MOTHER: He's gone out.

NEIGHBOUR: He came into the farm at last.

MOTHER: He was lucky.

NEIGHBOUR: Next thing he'll be spoken for.

MOTHER: [*As though reminded of something she draws her chair near the neighbour.*] Tell me.

NEIGHBOUR: [*In a confidential manner.*] Yes. What is it?

MOTHER: Do you know my son's sweetheart?

NEIGHBOUR: A decent girl.

MOTHER: Yes, but . . .

NEIGHBOUR: Oh but there's no one can say they really know her. She lives alone with the father – out there – in the back of beyond. It's near fifteen mile from the nearest house. But she's decent, mark my words. And given to isolation.

MOTHER: And the mother?

NEIGHBOUR: I'm sorry. I meant no harm – but it's true. Now

as to whether she was decent or not, that's another thing, that wasn't mentioned. She had airs.

MOTHER: Off you go again.

NEIGHBOUR: It was you that asked me.

MOTHER: I wish the same pair had never been heard of – mother or daughter. Dead or alive. If you but name them they sting like thistles.

NEIGHBOUR: You're right. Your son is dear to you.

MOTHER: He is. That's why I watch out for him. They tell me the girl had another sweetheart in her day.

NEIGHBOUR: She must have been all of fifteen. He got married two years ago now – to a close cousin of hers in fact. No one will remember their engagement – it's too far back.

MOTHER: How come you remember?

NEIGHBOUR: You have a mouth on you.

MOTHER: A body likes to know the things that will hurt them. Who was the lad?

NEIGHBOUR: Leonardo.

MOTHER: Leonardo who?

NEIGHBOUR: Leonardo Felix. One of the Felix family.

MOTHER: The Felixes!

NEIGHBOUR: Yes, but woman dear how can Leonardo be to blame for anything? He was eight years old when these things happened.

MOTHER: I know. But when I hear that name – Felix – it gives me a turn. My heart stops. [*Muttering.*] Felix – that name fills my mouth with slime. [*She spits.*] And I have to spit. I have to spit for fear I'd be poisoned.

NEIGHBOUR: Easy now. What good does it do you?

MOTHER: None. But it sickens me still the same.

NEIGHBOUR: You mustn't stand in the way of your son's happiness. Tell him nothing. You are an old woman. So am I. You and me – we have a secret.

MOTHER: I won't say a word.

NEIGHBOUR: [*Kissing her.*] Not a solitary word.

MOTHER: [*Calmly.*] The things a body does.

NEIGHBOUR: I'm away. My crowd will be in soon from the

fields.

MOTHER: Have you ever known such hot weather?

NEIGHBOUR: The children are black with the sun from taking water out to the men. Goodbye, woman.

MOTHER: Goodbye.

[*Exit* NEIGHBOUR.]

[*The* MOTHER *starts towards the door at the left. Half-way there she stops and slowly crosses herself.*]

[*Curtain.*]

SCENE 2

A room painted rose, with copperware and bunches of common flowers. In the centre of the room is a table with a tablecloth. It is morning. Leonardo's MOTHER-IN-LAW *sits in one corner holding a child in her arms and rocking it. His* WIFE *is in the other corner darning socks.*

MOTHER-IN-LAW:

Lullaby, my precious,
Lullaby, sweet child
Once there was a great horse
Come from the far wild.

He went unto deep water
But would not venture in,
The black water under the branches
Only frightened him.

The trees cast their shadow,
The black stream ran
Till all its waves collected
In one song at the dam.

Who can say, my precious,
What the shadowy water feels,
As he swings his long tail, in his green room,

Underneath the roof of trees.
WIFE: [*Softly.*]
Sleep, carnation, sleep
The horse shies at the stream . . .
MOTHER-IN-LAW:
Dream, my rose, dream
The horse has begun to weep.

His poor hooves are bleeding,
His mane is frozen tight,
Deep inside his lonesome eyes
A silver dagger catches light.

Oh down he went to the river
Right to the river he ran,
But his blood flew thick and fast
Faster than black water can.
WIFE:
Sleep, carnation, sleep
The horse shies at the stream . . .
MOTHER-IN-LAW:
Dream, my rose, dream,
The horse has begun to weep.
WIFE:
He will not touch the water,
Not one hair of him he'll wet,
He will not dip his silver nose in
Though he streams with sweat.

So, to the hard cold mountains,
He whinnies out his dread,
How his parched throat is dry
How the black stream is dead.

Ah-ha for the great stallion
Who didn't drink from the deep;

Ah-ha for the snow-horse of the morning
His wound will make him weep.

MOTHER-IN-LAW:
Don't come in! Stop outside!
Fasten each window catch
With a branch of dreams
And a dreaming branch.

WIFE:
My bairn sleeps.

MOTHER-IN-LAW:
My bairn is mellow.

WIFE:
Look horse
At my bairn's soft pillow.

MOTHER-IN-LAW:
His bed is iron.

WIFE:
His quilt is fine.

MOTHER-IN-LAW:
Lullaby,
My bairn divine.

WIFE:
Ah-ha, for the great stallion
Who didn't drink from the deep . . .

MOTHER-IN-LAW:
Don't come near!
Don't you come in!
Take yourself
To the far mountain.

Search the darkness.
And find the glen.
There your mare is.
In the grey glen.

WIFE: [*Looking.*]
My bairn sleeps.

MOTHER-IN-LAW:

My bairn is mellow.

WIFE:

Sleep, carnation, sleep
The horse shies at the stream.

MOTHER-IN-LAW:

Dream, my rose, dream
The horse begins to weep . . .

[*She carries the child out.* LEONARDO *enters.*]

LEONARDO: Where's the bairn?

WIFE: He's dead to the world.

LEONARDO: He wasn't himself yesterday. He cried during the night.

WIFE: And today he's good as gold. And what about you? Did you go to the blacksmiths?

LEONARDO: I'm just from there. You wouldn't credit it. He's spent the best part of two months putting new shoes on the horse, and off they come, regular as clockwork. I'm sure the beast tears them off on the stones.

WIFE: Could it be because you're never off his back.

LEONARDO: No, I hardly ever ride him.

WIFE: The neighbours say they saw you yesterday the other side of the flat lands.

LEONARDO: Do they now. Who said that?

WIFE: The women who gather mussels. I was taken aback, I can tell you. Was it you?

LEONARDO: How would it be me? What would I be doing over there among the snipe grass?

WIFE: That's what I said. But the horse was half-dead from sweating.

LEONARDO: Did you see him?

WIFE: No, but my mother did.

LEONARDO: Did she now. Is she with the baby?

WIFE: She is. Do you want a drink of lemonade?

LEONARDO: Aye, and with the water cold.

WIFE: Why did you not eat?

LEONARDO: I was with the dealing men. They always keep

a body.

WIFE: [*Making the drink, very tenderly.*] Did they pay anyway decent?

LEONARDO: Middling.

WIFE: I need a new dress. The baby needs a cap with ribbons.

LEONARDO: [*Getting up.*] I'm going below to see him.

WIFE: Go easy. He's asleep.

MOTHER-IN-LAW: [*Entering.*] Who's been racing the horse like that? He's down there with the eyes bulging out of his head. Not a whisper out of him. Like he'd been driven back from the ends of the earth.

LEONARDO: Me, I have.

MOTHER-IN-LAW: Oh excuse me. He's your horse.

WIFE: [*Timidly.*] He was with the dealing men.

MOTHER-IN-LAW: The animal can burst for all I care. [*She sits down. Pause.*]

WIFE: How is your drink? Is it cool enough?

LEONARDO: Yes.

WIFE: Are you aware that they are asking for my cousin's hand?

LEONARDO: When?

WIFE: Tomorrow. The wedding will be before the month is out. I hope we'll be asked.

LEONARDO: [*Seriously.*] I wouldn't count on it.

MOTHER-IN-LAW: His mother I believe, was not very happy with the match.

LEONARDO: She might have reason to be. That one needs careful handling.

WIFE: You shouldn't think bad things about a good girl.

MOTHER-IN-LAW: He means more than he's letting on. Did he not tell you? Do you not know? He courted her for three years.

LEONARDO: But I left her. [*To his* WIFE.] Are you going to cry now? [*He brusquely pulls her hands away from her face.*] Stop it! [*They put their arms around each other.*] Let's go and look at the bairn.

[*They go out.*]

[*A girl appears. She is happy. She enters running.*]

GIRL: Mrs.

MOTHER-IN-LAW: What is it?

GIRL: The groom came to the shop and bought the best of everything they had.

MOTHER-IN-LAW: Was he by himself?

GIRL: No. With the mother. She's serious. A tall, severe lady. But very grand.

MOTHER-IN-LAW: They're not short.

GIRL: And they bought these fancy open-work stockings! You should have seen them. Such stockings! The stockings a woman dreams of. [*She points to her ankle.*] Look: a swallow here! [*She points to her calf.*] A ship here. [*She points to her thigh.*] And here – a rose!

MOTHER-IN-LAW: Shame on you girl!

GIRL: A perfect rose with all its seeds on a stem! Oh, and all in silk!

MOTHER-IN-LAW: Two fortunes are being joined.

[LEONARDO *and his* WIFE *enter.*]

GIRL: I came to tell you what they bought!

LEONARDO: [*Loudly.*] We don't want to know.

WIFE: Leave her be.

MOTHER-IN-LAW: Leonardo, there's no call to act like that.

GIRL: Please excuse me. [*She leaves crying.*]

MOTHER-IN-LAW: Why do you constantly have to get on the wrong side of people?

LEONARDO: Keep your opinions to yourself. [*He sits down.*]

MOTHER-IN-LAW: Very well.

[*Pause.*]

WIFE: [*To* LEONARDO.] What's the matter with you? What madness is boiling away inside your head? Tell me! Don't leave me like this, knowing nothing . . .

LEONARDO: Stop it!

WIFE: No, I want you to look at me and tell me.

LEONARDO: Leave me alone.

[*He gets up.*]

WIFE: Where are you going, love?

LEONARDO: [*Sharply.*] Can't you shut up!

MOTHER-IN-LAW: [*Forcefully, to her daughter.*] Leave it! [LEONARDO *goes.*] The baby!

[*She goes out and reappears with the child in her arms. The* WIFE *has remained standing, motionless.*]

His poor hooves are bleeding
His mane is frozen tight
Deep inside his lonesome eyes
A silver dagger catches light.

Down he went to the river
Right to the river he ran
There his blood flew thick and fast
Faster than black water can.

WIFE:
[*Turning slowly, as if in a dream.*]
Sleep, carnation, sleep
For the horse shies at the stream.

MOTHER-IN-LAW:
Dream, my rose, dream
The horse has begun to weep . . .

WIFE:
Lullaby, my sweet bairn.

MOTHER-IN-LAW:
Ah-ha for the great stallion
Who didn't drink from the deep.

WIFE:
Don't come near
Don't come in
Take yourself
To the far-off mountain

Ah-ha for the snow-horse of the morning
His wound will make him weep.

MOTHER-IN-LAW:

[*Weeping.*]
My bairn is mellow.
WIFE:
My bairn sleeps.
MOTHER-IN-LAW:
Sleep, carnation, sleep
The horse shies at the stream.
WIFE:
Dream, my rose, dream
For the horse has begun to weep.
[*Curtain.*]

SCENE 3

Interior of the cave where the BRIDE *lives. At the back is a cross of large rose-coloured flowers. The round doors have lace curtains with rose-coloured ribbons. On the walls, made of a white and hard material, are spread fans, blue jars and small mirrors.*

SERVANT: Come on in. [*She is very affable, and hypocritically deferential. The* BRIDEGROOM *and his* MOTHER *enter. The* MOTHER *is dressed in a black shawl and wears a black veil. The* BRIDEGROOM *wears black corduroy and a great gold chain.*] Would you like to take a chair? They'll be right with you. [*She goes out. The* MOTHER *and the* BRIDEGROOM *sit stiff as statues. A long pause.*]
MOTHER: Are you wearing your watch?
BRIDEGROOM: I am. [*He takes it out and looks at it.*]
MOTHER: We'd better get back in good time. These people live in the back of beyond.
BRIDEGROOM: The land's good.
MOTHER: Aye, but far too isolated. A four-hour journey and not one house to be seen, not even a tree.
BRIDEGROOM: This is the hungry land of the snipe grass.
MOTHER: Your father would have covered it with trees.
BRIDEGROOM: Without water?

MOTHER: He'd have found it. In the three years we were married he set ten apple trees. [*Remembering.*] Three yew trees by the mill, a whole wheatfield and a plant called Jupiter which had bright red flowers. But it dried up.

[*Pause.*]

BRIDEGROOM: She must be dressing herself.

[*The* FATHER OF THE BRIDE *enters. He is old with shining white hair and bowed head. The* MOTHER *and the* BRIDEGROOM *rise. They shake hands in silence.*]

FATHER: Your journey took a while?

MOTHER: Four hours.

[They sit down.]

FATHER: You must have come the long way round.

MOTHER: I'm too far gone for the uncertain ground by the river.

BRIDEGROOM: It makes her giddy.

[*Pause.*]

FATHER: A fair crop of flax this year.

MOTHER: Oh, very good.

FATHER: In my day this land would not grow even flax. We've had to be hard on it, even make the soil weep, before it would deign to give us something useful.

MOTHER: But now it does. Don't fret. I didn't come this far to ask you for anything.

FATHER: You are a sight better off than me. [*Smiling.*] Your farm is worth its weight in gold. Each young shoot means a silver coin. I'm only sorry that our farms – don't get me wrong – are separated. I like everything together. There's one thorn in my heart, and that's the wee orchard stuck in between my fields. And they won't part with it for love or money.

BRIDEGROOM: These things will happen.

FATHER: If we could only put twenty teams of oxen to draw your acres to here! And have them all on the hillside together! That would be something out of this world.

MOTHER: But why?

FATHER: Because what's mine is hers and what's yours is his.

That's why, certainly. Oh dear. To see them all together! That would put a spring to my step.

BRIDEGROOM: And it would mean less hardship.

MOTHER: When I die, you can sell over there and buy here next to his.

FATHER: Sell is it? Sell! Not on your life! Buy, my good woman, buy every last thing. If I'd sons I'd have bought the whole of the mountain right up to the very stream above. It's not good land, but then again it's not bad land. Strong hands can work wonders. And since you won't find a soul in these parts, there's no one to steal your crops and you can sleep easy. [*Pause.*]

MOTHER: You know why I've come.

FATHER: I do.

MOTHER: So?

FATHER: I'm all for it. They know what they're doing.

MOTHER: My son has plenty, and he knows what to do with it.

FATHER: The same for my daughter.

MOTHER: My lad is handsome. He's never known a woman. His good name is cleaner than a sheet spread in the sun.

FATHER: And what can I say of my daughter? She's baking bread at three by the light of the morning star. She doesn't talk much; she's soft as wool; she likes to embroider all manner of fancy work; she can cut a strong piece of twine with her teeth.

MOTHER: God bless their house.

FATHER: God bless it.

[*The* SERVANT *appears with two trays. One with glasses and the other with sweets. Waits.*]

MOTHER: [*To the son.*] When would you like the wedding to be?

BRIDEGROOM: Next Thursday.

FATHER: To the very day she will be twenty-two-years old.

MOTHER: Twenty-two! That's the age my son would have been if he were still alive. He'd be here today, warm, his own man, if men hadn't invented knives.

FATHER: You mustn't dwell on that.

MOTHER: Every minute of every day. [*She stands. She proffers her hand.*]

FATHER: Thursday then. [*He proffers his hand. They shake hands.*] The bride and groom and us two – we'll go to church by carriage. It's a long road from here. The guests will come by cart, and by horse.

MOTHER: Agreed.

[*The* SERVANT *passes through.*]

FATHER: Tell her we're ready. [*To the mother.*] I'll be very happy if you take to her.

[*The* BRIDE *appears. Her hands at her side in a modest pose, her head bowed. Nod to* BRIDE.]

MOTHER: Come to me. Are you happy?

BRIDE: Yes Ma'am.

FATHER: You mustn't be so serious. In no time she will be your mother.

BRIDE: I'm happy. I said "yes" because I wanted to.

MOTHER: I'm sure. [*She takes her by the chin.*] Look at me.

FATHER: She's the spit of my wife in every way.

MOTHER: Is she now? What a lovely expression! You know what getting married means girl?

BRIDE: [*Seriously.*] I do.

MOTHER: A man, a few children, and after that, a wall that's two foot thick.

BRIDEGROOM: Who'd want for anything else?

MOTHER: No one. Except that you stay alive. That's all – that you should 1ive, and live long at that.

BRIDE: I know my duty.

MOTHER: I brought you some presents.

BRIDE: Thank you.

FATHER: Will you have something?

MOTHER: Not for me. [*To the* BRIDEGROOM.] Will you?

BRIDEGROOM: Yes. Thank you. [*He takes a sweet. The* BRIDE *takes another.*]

FATHER: [*To the* BRIDEGROOM] Whiskey?

MOTHER: He doesn't touch it.

FATHER: Good for him.

[*Pause. They are all standing.*]

BRIDEGROOM: I'll be down tomorrow.

BRIDE: At what time?

BRIDEGROOM: Round five.

BRIDE: I'll be expecting you.

BRIDEGROOM: When I leave your side I am not myself. I feel a terrible emptiness and a kind of lump in the throat.

BRIDE: When you are my husband you won't have it any more.

BRIDEGROOM: That's what I keep telling myself.

MOTHER: It's time we went. The sun won't wait on man or beast. [*To the* FATHER.] Is that everything then?

FATHER: Yes.

[*They shake hands.*]

MOTHER: [*To the* SERVANT.] Goodbye woman.

SERVANT: God go with you.

[*The* MOTHER *kisses the* BRIDE *and they leave in silence.*]

MOTHER: [*At the door.*] Goodbye, daughter.

[*The* BRIDE *answers with her hand.*]

FATHER: I'll step outside with you.

[*They leave.*]

SERVANT: I'm dying to see the presents.

BRIDE: [*Sharply.*] Well you can't.

SERVANT: Oh go on. Show them to me.

BRIDE: I don't want to.

SERVANT: Just the stocking then.

BRIDE: I said no.

SERVANT: They say they're very fancy. Please girl.

BRIDE: I said no and I mean no.

SERVANT: For God's sake. Suit yourself. It's as if you had no wish to get married.

[*The* BRIDE *bites her own hand in anger.*]

BRIDE: Oh!

SERVANT: Girl! Girl! What's the matter with you? Are you sorry to be saying goodbye to the life of a queen? Don't be bitter. You have no call. None in the wide world. Let me see the presents now. [*She takes hold of the box.*]

BRIDE: [*Gripping her by the wrists.*] Let go.

SERVANT: God almighty.

BRIDE: Let go I said.

SERVANT: You're stronger than any man.

BRIDE: Haven't I done a man's work? I wish I was one.

SERVANT: Don't talk like that.

BRIDE: Shut up, I said. Can we talk about something else?

[*The light begins to fade. A long pause.*]

SERVANT: Did you hear a horse last night?

BRIDE: What time?

SERVANT: About three.

BRIDE: It must have been a stray – from the wild ponies.

SERVANT: No. It had a rider.

BRIDE: How do you know?

SERVANT: Because I saw him. He was standing by your window. It gave me a terrible fright.

BRIDE: Oh it was probably my young man. He comes round sometimes at that hour.

SERVANT: No.

BRIDE: You saw who it was?

SERVANT: Yes.

BRIDE: Who was it?

SERVANT: It was Leonardo.

BRIDE: [*Strongly.*] I don't believe you. That's a lie. Liar! Why should he come here?

SERVANT: He was here.

BRIDE: Shut your face! Shut up! Shut up.

[*The sound of a horse is heard.*]

SERVANT: [*At the window.*] Now look! Come here! Was that him or not?

[*Quick curtain.*]

ACT II
SCENE 4

The entrance hall to the BRIDE*'s house. A large door in the background. Night. The* BRIDE *enters wearing a white ruffle with lots of lace and embroidered edgings, and a white bodice. Her arms* *are bare. The* SERVANT *is similarly dressed.*

SERVANT: I'll finish your hair out here.
BRIDE: No one can stay inside in this heat.
SERVANT: In this weather it isn't cool even at dawn.
[*The* BRIDE *sits down on a low chair and looks at herself in a small hand-mirror. The* SERVANT *combs her hair.*]
BRIDE: My mam came from a place where there was no end of trees. It was fertile country.
SERVANT: And she was so content!
BRIDE: But she wasted away here.
SERVANT: These things will happen.
BRIDE: Like we're all wasting away here. These very walls throw the heat out at us. Hey! Don't pull so hard.
SERVANT: It's to fix this strand better. I want it down over your forehead. [*The* BRIDE *looks at herself in the mirror.*] You look beautiful. [*She kisses her with feeling.*]
BRIDE: [*Seriously.*] Just comb my hair, please.
SERVANT: You're the lucky girl . . . [*Combing.*] . . . to be able to put your arms round a man. Oh. To kiss him. To feel his weight.
BRIDE: Stop it.
SERVANT: But the best part is when you wake up to find him there beside you. To feel him there at your side. And he strokes your shoulders with his breath – light as a nightingale's feather.
BRIDE: [*Forcefully.*] Will you quit?
SERVANT: But girl! What is a wedding? A wedding is that and nothing more. Never mind your sweet cake. Forget your bouquet of flowers. A wedding is a shining bed and the man and the woman.
BRIDE: Don't talk about it.
SERVANT: Oh, it's weakening. And plenty of fun too.
BRIDE: And plenty of bitterness after.
SERVANT: I'm going to put the orange blossom from here to here, so that the wreath will be at its best. [*She tries on sprigs*

of orange blossom.]

BRIDE: [*Looking at herself in the mirror.*] Give it to me. [*She takes the orange blossom wreath, looks at it, and lets her head fall dejectedly.*]

SERVANT: Now what's the matter?

BRIDE: Leave me alone.

SERVANT: This is not the time to be feeling sorry for yourself. [*Encouragingly.*] Give me the orange blossom. [*The* BRIDE *throws the wreath away.*] Girl! You'll bring yourself bad luck throwing the flowers on the floor like that. Look at me! Don't you want to get married? Tell me. There's still time for you to change your mind.

[*The* BRIDE *rises.*]

BRIDE: Those are dark clouds. A cold wind cuts through me. Is there a soul hasn't known it?

SERVANT: Do you love this sweetheart of yours?

BRIDE: I love him.

SERVANT: Of course you do.

BRIDE: But it's a very big step.

SERVANT: It has to be taken.

BRIDE: I gave my word.

SERVANT: I'll fix the wreath.

BRIDE: [*She sits down.*] Hurry, they should be here by now.

SERVANT: They've been on that road at least two hours.

BRIDE: Is it far from here to the church?

SERVANT: Five miles by the stream. Twice that by the road.

[*The* BRIDE *gets up and the* SERVANT *is excited as she looks her over.*]

Awake, oh bride, awaken,
On this your wedding day!
May the rivers of the world
Bear your bridal-wreath away.

BRIDE: Oh now [*Smiling.*] Don't.

SERVANT: [*Kissing her with feeling and dancing round her.*]

Awake to the fresh bouquet of the flowering laurel
Awake under the flowering branch of the laurel tree . . .

[*A loud knocking is heard.*]

BRIDE: Open the door! That must be the first of the guests.

[*The* SERVANT *opens the door.*]

SERVANT: [*Startled.*] You!

LEONARDO: Who else? Good morning.

SERVANT: You are the very first!

LEONARDO: Was I not asked?

SERVANT: Yes.

LEONARDO: Well then I'm here.

SERVANT: Where's your wife?

LEONARDO: I came by horse. She's coming by road.

SERVANT: You saw the others?

LEONARDO: I rode past them.

SERVANT: You'll be the death of that poor beast – you'll ride him into the ground.

LEONARDO: If he dies, he dies.

[*A pause.*]

SERVANT: Sit down. There's no one here yet.

LEONARDO: Where is the Bride?

SERVANT: I'm just about to dress her.

LEONARDO: The bride – I suppose she's happy?

SERVANT: [*Changing the subject.*] How's the baby?

LEONARDO: The baby?

SERVANT: Your little son.

LEONARDO: [*Recalling as if in a dream.*] Ah!

SERVANT: Are they taking him?

LEONARDO: No.

[*Pause. Voices sing distantly.*]

VOICES:

Awake, oh bride, awaken
On this your wedding day.

LEONARDO:

Awake, oh bride, awaken
On this her wedding day . . .

SERVANT: It's the guests. They are still some way off.

LEONARDO: [*Getting up.*] I suppose the bride will be wearing a fair wreath of flowers? But it shouldn't be so big. Something smaller would suit her. Has the groom brought the orange blossom she must wear on her heart?

BRIDE: [*She appears still in petticoats with the wreath of flowers in place.*] He brought it.

SERVANT: [*Strongly.*] Don't appear like that.

BRIDE: What does it matter? [*Seriously.*] Why do you want to know if they brought the orange blossom? What are you trying to imply?

LEONARDO: Oh nothing. [*Moving closer.*] You know me – I meant nothing. But tell me. What was I to you back then? Open up your memory, travel back. Wasn't it because two head of cattle and a ruin of a cottage meant little to you. That's the barb!

BRIDE: Why did you come here?

LEONARDO: To see your wedding.

BRIDE: As I saw yours.

LEORARDO: Oh you fixed that, didn't you? You arranged that with your own two hands. Well, your crowd can kill me, but they can't spit on me. Now silver money, shine as it may, can often spit.

BRIDE: You're a liar.

LEORARDO: I don't want to speak out. The blood is up in me and my shouts would worry the furthest hills.

BRIDE: Mine would be louder.

SERVANT: This talk must stop! You mustn't talk about what's over and done with. [*The* SERVANT *looks anxiously toward the door.*]

BRIDE: She's right. I shouldn't even pass you the time of day. But it makes my blood boil that you should have the nerve to come here and watch me and gloat over my wedding and make these insinuations about the orange blossoms. Go out and wait for your wife at the door.

LEONARDO: Can we not talk – you and me?

BRIDE: [*Angrily.*] No. You can't talk.

LEONARDO: From the day of my wedding, I've thought night and day about whose fault it was. Was it you – was it me? And I find a fault that eats the old one up. Then that's followed by another fault, and another. And still another. There's always someone to blame.

BRIDE: A man with a horse looks good. He knows lots of things that can turn a girl's head when she's stuck out in the back of beyond. But I've got my pride. Which is why I'm getting married. And I'll shut myself in with my husband and then I'll have to love him above everything.

LEONARDO: Pride will get you nowhere!

BRIDE: Don't come next or near me!

LEONARDO: To burn with desire and hide it, is the worst punishment we could put ourselves through. What use was pride to me, not seeing you and knowing you were lying awake night after night? It was no use. It only drove me mad and brought the fire down on top of me. You think that time heals, and walls conceal? Well, it's not true. It's gone too deep inside us. There isn't anything anyone can do to change that.

BRIDE: I don't hear you, I don't hear your voice. It's as if I'd drunk a bottle of brandy and fallen asleep under a quilt of roses. And it drags me along, and I know I'm drowning – but I still go on.

SERVANT: [*Seizing* LEONARDO *by the lapels.*] You should leave here. Now!

LEONARDO: It's the last chance I've got to talk to her. At least grant me that. There's nothing to be afraid of.

BRIDE: And I know I'm mad and I know my heart is rotten with yearning, yet here I am – soothed by the sound of his voice, by even the sight of his arms moving.

LEONARDO: I would not have been able to live with myself if I hadn't told you these things. What's done is done. I got married. Now you get married.

SERVANT: She will!

VOICES: [*Getting nearer.*]
Awake, oh bride, awaken
On this your wedding day . . .

BRIDE: Awake, oh bride, awaken. [*She runs to her room.*]

SERVANT: The guests are here. [*To* LEONARDO.] Don't go

near her again.

LEONARDO: You needn't fret. I've had my say. [*He goes out stage left. It starts to get light.*]

FIRST GIRL: [*Entering.*]
Awake, oh bride, awaken
On this her wedding day
May her balcony be strewn with flowers,
And dancing start and music play.

VOICES:
Bride, awaken!

SERVANT:
[*Creating enthusiasm.*]
Awake to the green bouquet of love in flowers
Awake under the flowering branch of the laurel.

SECOND GIRL:
[*Entering.*]
Awake!
Her long hair covers her throat
White as snow is her petticoat.
Her leather boots have silver thread.
And Jasmine crowns her head.

SERVANT:
Oh shepherdess
The moon's undressed.

FIRST GIRL:
Oh handsome dove
Leave your hat in the olive grove.

FIRST YOUNG MAN:
[*Entering, holding his hat on high.*]
Bride awaken!
Across the fields
The guests now thread,
With trays of dahlias
And trays of blessed bread.

VOICES:
Bride awaken!

SECOND GIRL:

The bride
Puts on her floral wreath.
The groom
Ties golden ribbons underneath.

SERVANT:
Under the orange tree
The bride will not sleep.

THIRD GIRL:
[*Entering.*]
Under the vine
His love gifts keep.
[*Three guests come in.*]

FIRST YOUNG MAN:
Oh dove awaken!
After the shadowy bells of night
The clear bell of dawn is shaken

SECOND YOUNG MAN:
The bride, the snow bride
A maiden now
Tomorrow a spouse.

FIRST GIRL:
Dark girl
Come on down
In your train of silk
And trailing gown.

SECOND YOUNG MAN:
Little dark one
Come on down
Less the morning freeze
The dew to the ground

FIRST YOUNG MAN:
Awake, wife, awaken
Orange blossom is shaken
Into the breeze.

SERVANT:
A tree I would embroider
With scarlet ribbons tied

On every one a cupid
And "Long Live" to the bride.

VOICES:
Bride awaken!

FIRST YOUNG MAN:
On this your wedding day.

SECOND YOUNG MAN:
On this her wedding day
She's lovely we will see
A true flower of the mountain
A worthy captain's fancy!

FATHER:
[*Entering.*]
A captain's fancy
The groom will wed
With cattle to carry off his treasure
The groom is captain at their head.

THIRD GIRL:
The groom is a flower of gold
He steps through blossoms on the road.

SERVANT:
Oh lucky girl.

SECOND YOUNG MAN:
Bride, awaken.

SERVANT:
Oh, lovely bride!

FIRST GIRL:
Through the window
Hear the wedding shout!

SECOND GIRL:
Let the bride appear.

FIRST GIRL:
Come out! Come out!

SERVANT:
Let the bell ring
Let the bells ring clear!

FIRST YOUNG MAN:

For she comes! It's her!
The bride is here!

SERVANT:
Like a great bull
The wedding begins to stir.

[*The* BRIDE *comes in. She wears a jet black dress in the style of the 1900s. With a bust and a long train of pleated gauze and heavy lace. On her hair, which is brushed across her forehead, she wears a wreath of orange blossom. Guitars start. The girls kiss the* BRIDE.]

THIRD GIRL: What perfume have you got in your hair?

BRIDE: [*Laughing.*] None.

SECOND GIRL: [*Looking at her dress.*] The material is gorgeous. It would cost the earth today.

FIRST YOUNG MAN: Here's the bridegroom!

BRIDEGROOM: You're all welcome.

FIRST GIRL: [*Placing a flower behind his ear.*] The groom is a flower of gold.

SECOND GIRL: One eye is joyful, one eye is bold.

[*The* BRIDEGROOM *goes over to the* BRIDE.]

BRIDE: Why those pair of shoes?

BRIDEGROOM: They looked more cheerful than the black ones.

WIFE: [*Entering and kissing the* BRIDE.] Congratulations.

[*They all speak excitedly.*]

LEONARDO:
[*Entering like someone performing a duty.*]
On your wedding day
We give you this wreath.

WIFE:
The happy fields will breathe
The dew from your hair.

MOTHER: [*To the* FATHER.] Who invited these people?

FATHER: They are family too. Today's a day for forgiveness.

MOTHER: I will allow it but I won't forget it.

BRIDEGROOM: With that wreath, you are a joy to behold.

BRIDE: Can we go to the church now?

BRIDEGROOM: Why the hurry?

BRIDE: Because I want to be your wife as soon as I can. Because I want to be alone with you. Because I don't want to hear any voice but yours.

BRIDEGROOM: That's what I want too.

BRIDE: And not to see any eyes but yours. And to have you squeeze me so hard that, even if my mother were to call me from the dead. I couldn't pull myself away from you.

BRIDEGROOM: My arms are strong. I'll squeeze you for forty years without stopping.

BRIDE: [*Dramatically taking his arm.*] For always.

FATHER: Let's be quick. Bring the ponies and the carts. The sun is up.

MOTHER: Go carefully! I couldn't face it if anything went wrong.

[*The great door backstage opens.*]

SERVANT:

When you leave your house
Oh maiden white
You're like a distant star
That just caught light.

FIRST GIRL:

Pure her body
Innocent your dress
Leaving home
Bride to be blessed.

[*They start leaving.*]

SECOND GIRL:

Leaving your house
To accept his hand.

SERVANT:

The bright breeze
Blows flowers across the sand.

THIRD GIRL:

Oh maiden white . . .

SERVANT:

And dark winds are the lace
Of her mantilla.
[*They leave. Guitars, castanets and tambourines are heard.* LEONARDO *and his* WIFE *are left together alone.*]

WIFE: Can we go now?

LEONARDO: To where?

WIFE: To the church. And not by horse. You'll come with me.

LEONARDO: In the cart?

WIFE: How else?

LEONARDO: I'm not a man to go by cart.

WIFE: And I'm not a woman will attend a wedding without her husband. I can't take this any longer.

LEONARDO: Neither can I.

WIFE: Why are you looking at me like that? A barb in each eye!

LEONARDO: We'll go.

WIFE: Don't think I don't know what's happening. But that doesn't stop me thinking and I don't want to think. One thing though I do know. I've already been set aside. But I have a son. And another on the way. That's how things are. My mother's fate was the same. But I won't be moved from my place at your side.

VOICES:
[*Outside.*]
When you leave your house
For the church a blessing
Remember you leave
Like a bright star shining!

WIFE:
[*Weeping.*]
Remember you leave
A bright star shining . . .
That's the way I went from my home. A poor idiot. The whole world was before me. They could have told me black was white. Stuffed the whole countryside into my mouth. It made no difference to me.

LEONARDO: [*Getting up.*] We'll go.

WIFE: But you go with me!

LEONARDO: Yes. [*Pause.*] Can we go then? [*They depart.*]
VOICES:
When you leave your house
For the church's blessing
Remember you leave
Like a bright star shining.
[*Slow curtain.*]

SCENE 5

Outside the BRIDE's *cave. Blend of white, grey and cold blue. Large cactus trees. Shadowy and silver tones. Table and chairs the colour of tan biscuits. Everything like a landscape in popular ceramics.*

SERVANT: [*Arranging glasses on a table.*]
Turning,
The wheel turning,
And the water churning.
On their wedding night
May the branches part
For the moon to dart
Across her white balcony.

[*In a loud voice.*] Put out the table cloths!
Singing,
The bride and the groom singing
And the water churning;
On their wedding night.
May the frost glitter
And the almonds bitter
Become sweet honey.

[*In a loud voice.*] Get the wine ready!

[*In a poetic tone.*]
Lovely lass

Loveliest of all
Hear the river churning
On your wedding night
Tuck your skirts in
Slip under his wing
And don't ever leave him.
You have a dove for a husband
His breast is a firebrand
And the fields wait the flood
Of freshly spilt blood.
Turning!
The wheel was turning
And the water churning
On your wedding night
May water catch light.

MOTHER: [*Entering.*] At last.

FATHER: Are we the first?

SERVANT: No. A while back Leonardo got here with his wife. It would break your heart. They must have drove like demons. The wife was white as a sheet. They looked as if they had come by horse.

FATHER: He's out for trouble. There's bad blood there.

MOTHER: What did you expect? Don't you know the class of person you're dealing with? It's there all down through the piece. The bad blood began with his great-grandfather, who started the killing and it went on through the whole bad breed of them. They smile at you one minute, yes, the next they'd knife you in the back.

FATHER: Can we leave it at that?

SERVANT: How can she leave it?

MOTHER: It hurts me to the very tips of my veins. I have only to look into the face of one of them hypocrites to see the hand that killed one of mine. Do you see me? Do I seem mad to you? Well I'm not mad enough to scream out what my heart demands. There's a scream here in my heart that's always standing tiptoe and I can hardly keep it and hide it among these shawls. It makes me sick, you know? They've taken my dead from me and I have to be silent. And because of that some people criticise a person. [*She removes her shawl.*] You brought it up and I had to speak out. And today even more so. Because from today out I'm to be left alone in my own house.

FATHER: But not forever.

MOTHER: That's my hope; grandchildren.

[*They sit down.*]

FATHER: I want them to have many. This land needs hands that will work for free. You have to wage a constant battle against the weeds, the thistles, with the rocks that come from God knows where. And we must keep the work within the family. It's the family must punish and master. They're the ones to make the seed take. Many sons are needed.

MOTHER: And some daughters. Men are like the wind. It's in their nature to take up arms. Girls never go into the street.

FATHER: [*Happily.*] I think they'll have both.

MOTHER: My son will ride her well. He's of good seed. His father could have had no end of sons by me.

FATHER: I'd like to see it all happen in a single day – that straight away they would be granted two or three sons.

MOTHER: But it's not like that, is it? It takes forever. That's why it's so terrible to see your blood spilt on the ground. A fountain spurts for a minute that cost us years. When I got to my son, he was lying in the middle of the road, and I dipped my hands in his blood and licked them clean with my tongue. Because it was blood. You would not understand that. I'd make a shrine of glass and topaz to keep the earth that was steeped in that blood.

FATHER: We have something to live for now. My daughter is wide-hipped and your son is sound.

MOTHER: That's my hope; grandchildren.

[*They rise.*]

FATHER: Get the trays of bread ready.

SERVANT: They're all set.

WIFE: [*Entering.*] The best of luck for the future!

MOTHER: I thank you.

LEONARDO: Is there going to be a session?
FATHER: A small one. The people are short on time.
SERVANT: Here they are!

[*Guests begin entering in happy groups. The* BRIDE *and* BRIDEGROOM *enter arm-in-arm.* LEONARDO *leaves.*]

BRIDEGROOM: I never saw such a crowd at a wedding.
BRIDE: [*Darkly.*] Never.
FATHER: It was grand.
MOTHER: Relations I never thought to see, came.
BRIDEGROOM: People who never stood outside of their house!
MOTHER: Your father sowed that seed. You'll reap the benefit.
BRIDEGROOM: And cousins of mine I'd never met.
MOTHER: All my people from the sea.
BRIDEGROOM: [*Happily.*] They were wary of the ponies.

[*They talk.*]

MOTHER: [*To the* BRIDE.] What are you thinking of?
BRIDE: I'm thinking of nothing.
MOTHER: Your blessings seem a burden. [*Guitars are heard.*]
BRIDE: They weigh like lead.
MOTHER: [*Sternly.*] Well they shouldn't. You should be as light as a dove.
BRIDE: Are you staying the night?
MOTHER: No. There's not a soul in my house.
BRIDE: You should stay.
FATHER: [*To the* MOTHER.] They are making up a dance. The crowd from the sea know their steps.

[LEONARDO *enters and sits down. His* WIFE *stands stiffly behind him.*]

MOTHER: They are my dead husband's cousins. They can stiffen up flint when it comes to dancing.
FATHER: It does my heart good to see them. It makes a change about this house! [*He leaves.*]
BRIDEGROOM: [*To the* BRIDE.] Did you like the orange blossom?
BRIDE: [*Looking at him fixedly.*] Yes.

BRIDEGROOM: They're all made of wax. They'll last forever. I'd 1ove to have seen them all over your dress.

BRIDE: There was no call for that!

[LEONARDO *goes off to the right.*]

FIRST GIRL: We'll take your wedding pins out.

BRIDE: [*To the* BRIDEGROOM.] I'll just be a minute.

WIFE: I hope you'll be content with my cousin!

BRIDEGROOM: I'm sure I will.

WIFE: The pair of you here; never going out; building a home, wanting for nothing. I wish I lived as out of the way as this.

BRIDEGROOM: Why don't you buy your own few acres? The mountain's cheap and it suits the rearing of children.

WIFE: We haven't a penny. And the way we're going!

BRIDEGROOM: Your husband is a good worker.

WIFE: Yes, but he's a fly-by-night. He'll never settle. If it's not one thing, it's the other. He's not steady in himself.

SERVANT: Won't you have something? I'll wrap some wine-cakes for your mother. I know she likes them.

BRIDEGROOM: Give her three dozen.

WIFE: No, not at all. Half-a-dozen will do.

BRIDEGROOM: It's only once in a blue moon.

WIFE: [*To the* SERVANT.] Where's Leonardo?

SERVANT: I haven't laid eyes on him.

BRIDEGROOM: He must be with your relations.

WIFE: I'll go and look. [*She leaves.*]

SERVANT: [*Looking at the dance.*] They can fairly move on their feet. It's beautiful.

BRIDEGROOM: Why aren't you dancing?

SERVANT: There's no one to dance with the like of me.

[*Two girls pass across the background; during the entire scene there will be fast interplay of figures.*]

BRIDEGROOM: [*Happy.*] That's because they're not wise. Lively petite women like you can easily outstep the young ladies.

SERVANT: You're a caution. Another flirt! A whole family of flirts! Men amongst men. When I was child I mind to see your grandfather's wedding. What a man! As if a mountain was getting married.

BRIDEGROOM: I'm not as tall.

SERVANT: Oh, but the same twinkle in the eye. Where's your lady?

BRIDEGROOM: Taking off her head gear.

SERVANT: Now listen. For the middle of the night – since I don't expect you'll be sleeping – I've left some ham and some tall glasses of old wine on the bottom shelf of the cupboard. Just in case the hunger comes on you.

BRIDEGROOM: [*Smiling.*] I won't have the need of it in the middle of the night.

SERVANT: [*Teasing.*] If you don't, your wife might have a craving, so to speak. [*She goes out.*]

FIRST YOUNG MAN: [*Entering.*] You'll have one drink with us.

BRIDEGROOM: I'm waiting for my wife.

SECOND YOUNG MAN: Won't you have her all to yourself in the small hours!

FIRST YOUNG MAN: When it's best.

SECOND YOUNG MAN: Only for a minute!

BRIDEGROOM: Alright – let's go.

[*They leave. Sounds of excitement. The* BRIDE *appears. From the opposite side,* TWO GIRLS *run to meet her.*]

FIRST GIRL: Who did you throw the bouquet to? Me or her?

BRIDE: I don't remember.

FIRST GIRL: You gave it to me right here. To me.

SECOND GIRL: To me. You threw it to me at the altar.

BRIDE: [*Uneasy, with a sense of great inner conflict.*] I don't remember.

FIRST GIRL: I wish you . . .

BRIDE: [*Interrupting.*] And I don't care. I've other things to think of.

SECOND GIRL: Begging your pardon.

[LEONARDO *crosses back stage.*]

BRIDE: [*She sees* LEONARDO.] And it's an unsettling time.

FIRST GIRL: We are not to know.

BRIDE: You'll know soon enough. It's not easy taking this step.
FIRST GIRL: Have we upset you?
BRIDE: No. I'm sorry.
SECOND GIRL: Don't mention it. But the two bouquets will bring us good luck in marriage, won't they?
BRIDE: Yes, both of them.
FIRST GIRL: Now we'll have to wait and see which one of us gets married first.
BRIDE: Is your need so great?
SECOND GIRL: [*Coyly.*] Yes.
BRIDE: But why?
FIRST GIRL: Well . . . [*Embracing the* SECOND GIRL *they run away.*]

[*The* BRIDEGROOM *enters slowly and embraces the* BRIDE *from behind.*]

BRIDE: Don't touch me!
BRIDEGROOM: You're not frightened of me?
BRIDE: Oh, it's you!
BRIDEGROOM: Who else did you think it was? [*Pause.*] Me or your father?
BRIDE: That's true.
BRIDEGROOM: Though your father would have squeezed you more gently.
BRIDE: [*Darkly.*] Of course.
BRIDEGROOM: Because he's getting on. [*He embraces her strongly and a little roughly.*]
BRIDE: [*Curtly.*] Let go of me!
BRIDEGROOM: But why?
BRIDE: Well . . . the others. They might see us.

[*The* SERVANT *crosses backstage again without looking at the* BRIDE *or the* BRIDEGROOM.]

BRIDEGROOM: So what? We're man and wife now.
BRIDE: But let me be . . . for the moment.
BRIDEGROOM: What's the matter? You look frightened.
BRIDE: It's nothing. Don't go!
WIFE: Did my fellow come through here?
BRIDEGROOM: No.

WIFE: I've looked just about everywhere and the horse isn't in the stable.

BRIDEGROOM: [*Happily.*] He's probably gone for a gallop.

[*The* WIFE *leaves, disturbed. The* SERVANT *enters.*]

SERVANT: Aren't you pleased with your reception?

BRIDEGROOM: I wish it was over. The bride is a little tired.

SERVANT: Are you serious child?

BRIDE: It's as if someone stood on my grave.

SERVANT: A bride from the hills has to have gumption. [*To the* BRIDEGROOM.] You're the only one can cure her, now she is yours. [*She runs out.*]

BRIDEGROOM: [*Embracing her.*] Let's have a slide across the boards. [*He kisses her.*]

BRIDE: No. I want to lie down on the bed.

BRIDEGROOM: I'll lie with you.

BRIDE: You won't. With all those people here! No! What would they think? Let me by myself for a while.

BRIDEGROOM: If that's what you want. But I hope you won't be like this tonight.

BRIDE: [*At the door.*] I'll be better tonight. I promise.

BRIDEGROOM: Good, that's what I want to hear.

[*The* MOTHER *enters.*]

MOTHER: Son.

BRIDEGROOM: Where've you been?

MOTHER: In the middle of all that rí-rá. Are you happy?

BRIDEGROOM: Yes.

MOTHER: Where is your wife?

BRIDEGROOM: Having a lie down. It's seemingly a bad day for brides.

MOTHER: A bad day? The only good day in my opinion. For me it was like coming into my own. [*The* SERVANT *enters and goes towards the* BRIDE'*s chamber.*] Like the breaking up of new earth. The planting of new trees.

BRIDEGROOM: Are you thinking of going?

MOTHER: Yes. My place is at home.

BRIDEGROOM: You'll be alone.

MOTHER: I'm never alone. My mind is constantly active what with men and fights.

BRIDEGROOM: But with fights that are fights no longer.

[*The* SERVANT *enters quickly; she runs off via the backstage area.*]

MOTHER: The whole thing is a struggle.

BRIDEGROOM: I'll always do as you say.

MOTHER: Try to be loving towards your wife then, and if she's acting touchy or you find her uppity, give her a hug so that it hurts her a little. Yes, a strong squeeze, a bite, and then a soft kiss. Not to taunt her, mind. But just she'll know that you are the man, the master, the one who gives the orders. That's what I learnt from your father. And because he's not here to guide you, in his place I must teach you to be strong.

BRIDEGROOM: I'll always obey you.

FATHER: [*Entering.*] Where's my lassie?

BRIDEGROOM: She's inside.

[*The* FATHER *goes to look for her.*]

FIRST GIRL: Let's have the bride and groom. We're going to dance a set.

FIRST YOUNG MAN: [*To the* BRIDEGROOM.] And you're going to lead us.

FATHER: [*Entering.*] She isn't there.

BRIDEGROOM: No?

FATHER: She must have gone up to her balcony!

BRIDEGROOM: I'll go and see. [*He goes out.*]

[*A lot of noise and playing of guitars.*]

FIRST GIRL: They're starting! [*She leaves.*]

BRIDEGROOM: [*Entering.*] She's not there either!

MOTHER: [*Uneasily.*] No?

FATHER: Where can she have got to?

SERVANT: [*Entering.*] The girl, where is she?

MOTHER: [*Sombrely.*] This we don't know.

[*The* BRIDEGROOM *goes out. Three guests enter.*]

FATHER: [*Dramatically.*] But isn't she out on the floor?

SERVANT: She's not at the dance.

FATHER: [*Strongly.*] There are so many people there. Go and look!

SERVANT: I've looked already.

FATHER: Then where is she?

BRIDEGROOM: [*Entering.*] There's no sign of her. Anywhere.

MOTHER: [*To the* FATHER.] What is happening? Where is your daughter?

[LEONARDO*'s* WIFE *enters.*]

WIFE: They're gone! They're gone, they're gone. They've run away! Her and Leonardo! On the horse. With her arms around him. They rode off like a bolt out of hell.

FATHER: It's not true! Not my daughter!

MOTHER: Yes, your daughter! Your daughter. The fruit of a wicked mother and him, him too; curse him!

BRIDEGROOM: [*Entering.*] We'll go after them! Who's got a horse?

MOTHER: Who's got a horse? Now! Who's got a horse for my son? I'll give him every last thing I have. My eyes, my tongue, even.

VOICE: I'm with you!

MOTHER: [*To her son.*] Go! Get after them! [*He leaves with two young men.*] No – don't go, don't go! Those people kill quickly. They show no mercy . . . but yes! Go on! I'll follow.

FATHER: It can't be my daughter. Perhaps she's thrown herself into the water.

MOTHER: Only decent women throw themselves into the water. Not that bitch. But now she's my son's wife. Two tribes! Now there are two tribes here! [*They all enter.*] My family and yours. All of you must go. Shake the dust from your heels. Let's see you help my son. [*The people split into two groups.*] He's got family; his cousins from the coast and all those from inland. Go out from here! Search all the roads. Search everywhere. Don't leave a stone unturned, the hour of blood has come again. Two tribes! You with yours, me with mine. After them! After them!

[*Curtain.*]

ACT III

SCENE 6

A forest. It is night time. Great damp tree trunks. A dank dreary atmosphere. Two violins are heard. Three WOODCUTTERS *appear.*

FIRST WOODCUTTER: Any word?
SECOND WOODCUTTER: No. They've the entire country haunted.
THIRD WOODCUTTER: They'll have them soon.
SECOND WOODCUTTER: Whist!
THIRD WOODCUTTER: What?
SECOND WOODCUTTER: They seem to be closing in on all sides at once.
FIRST WOODCUTTER: Wait till the moon rises, then they'll see them.
SECOND WOODCUTTER: They should let them be.
FIRST WOODCUTTER: The world is wide.
SECOND WOODCUTTER: True.
FIRST WOODCUTTER: There's room for all of us.
THIRD WOODCUTTER: It's the nature of the beast. They were right to run away.
FIRST WOODCUTTER: They were only fooling themselves. In the long run, blood was stronger.
THIRD WOODCUTTER: The blood!
FIRST WOODCUTTER: You have to follow the way of the blood.
SECOND WOODCUTTER: True. But the earth will get drunk on blood that sees the light of day.
FIRST WOODCUTTER: What of it? Better to be dead and drained of blood than alive and the blood rotting in your veins.
THIRD WOODCUTTER: Whist!
FIRST WOODCUTTER: Why? Did you hear something?
THIRD WOODCUTTER: I can hear the crickets, the frogs, the night lying in wait.
FIRST WOODCUTTER: But no word of the horse.

THIRD WOODCUTTER: No.

FIRST WOODCUTTER: Now he'll be loving her.

SECOND WOODCUTTER: Her body for him, his body for her.

THIRD WOODCUTTER: They'll get them and they'll kill them.

FIRST WOODCUTTER: But they'll have mingled their blood by then. They'll be like two empty jars, like two dry sheughs.

SECOND WOODCUTTER: The clouds are with them. Maybe the moon won't shine through.

THIRD WOODCUTTER: Moon or no moon, the bridegroom will find them, find them and cut them down. I saw him leave. Like a raging star. His face the colour of ash. That man marked by the fate of his tribe.

FIRST WOODCUTTER: His tribe of dead men stretched in the middle of the street.

SECOND WOODCUTTER: These things will happen.

THIRD WOODCUTTER: Do you think they will break through the cordon?

SECOND WOODCUTTER: They'll have their work cut out. There are knives, and more knives, and shotguns for ten miles around.

THIRD WOODCUTTER: He has a mighty pony.

SECOND WOODCUTTER: But he's carrying a lady.

FIRST WOODCUTTER: And there's the tree at last!

SECOND WOODCUTTER: A tree with forty branches. We'll have it cut in no time.

THIRD WOODCUTTER: Then the moon will see its way. Let's hurry.

[*To the left shines a path of bright light.*]

FIRST WOODCUTTER:

Oh rising moon!
Moon on the great leaves.

SECOND WOODCUTTER:

Smother the blood with jasmine.

FIRST WOODCUTTER:

Oh lonesome moon! Moon on the great leaves.

SECOND WOODCUTTER:

Silver on the bride's face.

THIRD WOODCUTTER:

Oh demon moon!
Leave for their love a branch in shadow.

FIRST WOODCUTTER:

Oh grieving moon!
Leave for their love a branch in shadow!

[*They leave.*]

[*The* MOON *enters through the brightness on stage left. The* MOON *is a young woodcutter with a white face. The stage takes on an intense glow.*]

MOON:

Round swan in the river
Dome of the cathedral,
False dawn amongst the leaves
Am I; they'll not escape!
Who is hiding? Who is sobbing?
In the blackthorn of the valley
The moon ordains a knife
Abandoned in the air.
To lie in wait
And long to be the ache of blood.
Let me come in! I come frozen
Onto walls and windowpanes
Open roofs and hearts
Where I may warm myself!
I'm cold! My ashes
Of slumbering metal
Seek the plume of fire
Through mountains and through streets,
But the snow bears me
On its freckled back,
And water drags me under
Till I'm hard and cold

In pools. But tonight red blood
Will gush though my cheeks
And through the rushes that cluster
At the wide feet of the wind.
Let there be no shadow, no dark nest
Where they may hide!
Oh let me enter a breast
Where I can warm myself!
A heart for me!
Warm, that will spill
Over the craters of my chest;
Let me come in, oh let me! [*To the branches.*]
I want no shadows. My beams
Must stab into every nook!
Even among the dark stems
Let there be a telling gleam of light,
For tonight rich blood
Will gush through my cheeks
And through the rushes that cluster
At the wide feet of the wind
Who is hiding? Out, I say!
No! No! They will not get away!
For I will make the horse catch light
With a lather bright as diamond.

[*The* MOON *goes away among the tree trunks, and the stage returns to its dark lighting. An old* BEGGAR WOMAN *appears completely wrapped in thin dark green cloth. She is barefoot. Her face can barely be seen among the folds. She is, perhaps,* DEATH.]

BEGGAR WOMAN:

The moon goes as they appear.
But they won't get beyond here
The river's whisper
And the whispering trees will drown
The severed flights of their screams.
It has to be here, and soon. I'm tired.
White linen spread, and coffins aired,

All lie in wait on bedroom floors.
No bird walk now! And may the breeze
Collecting their shrieks in her skirt,
Fly them over the black tops of trees
Or bury them in soft dirt.
[*Impatiently.*]
Oh the moon, that moon!
[*The* MOON *appears. The intense blue glow returns.*]

MOON: They come. Some through the gully, and the others along the river. I will light up the stones. Is there something you need?

BEGGAR WOMAN: Not a thing.

MOON: The wind is up, and double-edged.

BEGGAR WOMAN: Light the waistcoat, and open the buttons; the knives will know their own way after that.

MOON:
Oh but let them die slowly! So the blood
May whistle softly between my fingers.
See how my pale valleys are wakening
With longing for this fountain and its terrifying jets.

BEGGAR WOMAN: They must not get beyond the sheugh. Quiet!

MOON: Here they come! [*He goes. The stage is now dark.*]

BEGGAR WOMAN: Quick! Tons of light! Do you hear me? They must not escape no matter what!

[*The* BRIDEGROOM *and the* FIRST YOUNG MAN *appear. The* BEGGAR WOMAN *is seated and covers herself with her cloak.*]

BRIDEGROOM: This way.

FIRST YOUNG MAN: You won't find them.

BRIDEGROOM: [*Forcefully.*] I'll find them.

FIRST YOUNG MAN: Suppose they've taken another way?

BRIDEGROOM: No. A moment ago I heard the clatter of hooves.

FIRST YOUNG MAN: It might have been another horse.

BRIDEGROOM: [*Intensely.*] There is no other horse. There's only the one horse in the whole wide world and it's this one.

Have you got that? If you're going to come with me, then come with me and stay quiet!

FIRST YOUNG MAN: It's just that I wanted to . . .

BRIDEGROOM: Stay quiet I say! I'm sure to find them here. You see this arm? Well that's not my arm. It's my brother's arm and my father's arm and the arm of my dead family. You understand? It has such strength that it could tear yon tree up by the roots if that was called for. Let's away quickly from here. I can feel the clenched teeth of all my loved ones gnawing me so that I can't get my breath.

BEGGAR WOMAN: Ahh!

FIRST YOUNG MAN: Did you hear that?

BRIDEGROOM: You go that way and circle back.

FIRST YOUNG MAN: This is a hunt.

BRIDEGROOM: This is a hunt. The greatest hunt of them all.

[*The* FIRST YOUNG MAN *goes. The* BRIDEGROOM *goes quickly to the left and stumbles upon the* BEGGAR WOMAN, DEATH.]

BEGGAR WOMAN: Oh!

BRIDEGROOM: What do you want?

BEGGAR WOMAN: I'm miserable.

BRIDEGROOM: Where are you for?

BEGGAR WOMAN: [*Whingeing.*] Towards beyond . . . It's a fair distance.

BRIDEGROOM: Where are you from?

BEGGAR WOMAN: From beyond . . . It's a fair distance.

BRIDEGROOM: Did you happen on a man and a woman galloping past on a horse?

BEGGAR WOMAN: [*Wakening.*] Let me see . . . [*She looks at him.*] Such a nice young boy [She rises.] And all the nicer when sleeping.

BRIDEGROOM: Tell me, answer! Did you see them?

BEGGAR WOMAN: Wait a minute . . . What broad shoulders! Would you like to rest on them instead of walking about on the soles of your feet which are so small?

BRIDEGROOM: [*Shaking her.*] I asked you if you'd laid eyes on them. Do you hear me? Have they been through here?

BEGGAR WOMAN: [*Strongly.*] No! They haven't come this way, and they haven't gone that way. But they're coming instead by the hill. Can't you hear them?

BRIDEGROOM: No.

BEGGAR WOMAN: Do you know the road?

BRIDEGROOM: I'll take it anyway.

BEGGAR WOMAN: Then I'll come with you. I know this country.

BRIDEGROOM: [*Impatiently.*] Well what's keeping you? Let's go! Which way?

BEGGAR WOMAN: [*Dramatically.*] Follow me!

[*They leave quickly. In the distance, two violins, representing the forest, play. The* WOODCUTTERS *return. They carry axes on their shoulders. They move very slowly.*]

FIRST WOODCUTTER:
Oh rising death!
Death on the great leaves.

SECOND WOODCUTTER:
Don't loosen the jet of blood!

FIRST WOODCUTTER:
Oh lonesome death!
Death on the dry leaves.

THIRD WOODCUTTER:
Don't smother the wedding with flowers.

SECOND WOODCUTTER:
Oh grieving death!
Leave for their love a green branch!

FIRST WOODCUTTER:
Oh demon death!
Leave for their love a green branch!

[*They go out while they are speaking.* LEONARDO *and the* BRIDE *appear.*]

LEONARDO: Listen!

BRIDE: I'll go on by myself from here. You turn back! I want you to turn back!

LEONARDO: Listen I said!

BRIDE:

With your teeth, with your hands, anyway you can
Release my pure throat
From the metal of this chain
And let me live unremembered
Here in my house under the ground
And if you won't kill me
And you'd step on a small snake
Place in these bride's hands
The barrel of your shotgun.
Oh what grief, what fire,
Sweeps upward through my head!
What glass splinters are on my tongue!

LEONARDO: There's no going back, now; that's it. They are not too far behind us and you are coming with me.

BRIDE: Then it will have to be by force.

LEONARDO:
By force? Who was it
Was first down the stairs?

BRIDE: Me.

LEONARDO:
Who was it put
A fresh saddle on the horse?

BRIDE: Me. It's true.

LEONARDO:
Whose hands
Strapped spurs to the horse?

BRIDE:
The same hands that are yours!
That when they see you want
To slash through the blue branches
And sunder your murmuring veins.
I love you! I love you! But leave me!
If only I could kill you
I'd slip a shroud around you
With edgings of violet.
Oh what grief, what fire,

Sweeps upward through my head.
LEONARDO:
What splinters of glass are on my tongue,
Because I wanted to forget you
I put a wall of stone
Between your house and mine
It's the truth. Do you remember?
And when I saw you beyond me
I threw sand in my eyes
But I'd get on the horse
And the horse would go to your door
And when you threw your bouquet
It made my blood run black
And our dream smothered me.
My flesh was flayed by deadly weeds
But I'm not the fault
The fault is in the earth
And in the scent that carries
From your breasts and hair.
BRIDE:
Why blame me? I don't want
To share your bed or your table,
Yet there's not a minute of each day,
When I don't want to be with you
You drag me down and I come under
And you tell me to go back
And I follow on regardless
Like blown grass-seed.
I've left a decent man
And all his people, yes,
In the middle of my wedding
Still wearing my bridal veil.
But the punishment will fall on you
And I don't want that to happen
So leave me here! You go on!
There is none left to defend you.
LEONARDO:

Birds, of first light,
Stir in the trees.
The tired night dies
On the edge of stone.
Let's hide in a dark corner
Where I can always love you.
For to me, the people mean nothing,
Nor the bile they pour on us.
[*He embraces her strongly.*]

BRIDE:
And I'll sleep at your feet
And keep watch over your dreams.
Without a stitch, looking over the fields
[*Powerfully.*] As if I were a bitch!
Because that's what I am! Oh I look at you
And your beauty scorches me!

LEONARDO:
Flame is fired by flame.
The same small flame
Can eat two ears of wheat together.
Come with me! [*He pulls her.*]

BRIDE: Where are you taking me?

LEONARDO:
Where they can't go
The men who circle us.
Where I can look at you!

BRIDE:
[*Sarcastically.*] Oh yes, take me from fair to market,
A crying shame to proper women,
So that people can view
My poor wedding sheets flapping
On the breeze, like flags.

LEONARDO:
[*The whole scene is very violent, full of great sensuality.*]
I would leave you too
If I was in my right mind
But I go where you go.

For you it's the same. Try a step! See!
Moonlight has nailed
My waist to your hips.

BRIDE: Listen.

LEONARDO: They are coming.

BRIDE:
Run! Run!
It's proper that I should die here,
My feet in water,
Blackthorn in my hair,
And leaves weeping
For a fallen woman
Still a virgin.

LEONARDO: Stop it! They are coming!

BRIDE: Go now!

LEONARDO:
Quiet! Don't let them hear us!
You go on ahead! First you!
[*The* BRIDE *hesitates.*]

BRIDE: The two of us!

LEONARDO:
[*Embracing her.*]
If that's what you want!
If they part us, it will be
Because I am dead.

BRIDE: Then I am dead too.

[*They leave embracing each other.*]

[*The* MOON *appears slowly. The stage takes on a strong blue glow. The two violins are heard. Suddenly, two long ear piercing screams. The violins stop. With the second scream, the* BEGGAR WOMAN *appears and stands with her back to the audience. She opens her cloak and stands in the centre like a great bird with great wings. The* MOON *stops.*]

[*The curtain comes down in total silence.*]

SCENE 7

A white house with arches and thick walls. To the right and left are white stairs. At the back a great arch and a wall of the same colour. The floor is also brilliant white. The simple house should have the monumental feel of a church. There must not be a single grey, or any shadow, or anything that even creates perspective. TWO GIRLS *dressed in dark blue are winding a skein of wool. They are joined by a* LITTLE GIRL.

FIRST GIRL:
Wool, oh red wool,
What are you making?
SECOND GIRL:
Why, dresses of jasmine
From fine coloured thread.
At four o'clock born
At ten o'clock dead.
A thread of this yarn
Will yoke up your feet
With a special knot
For the bitter wreath.
LITTLE GIRL:
[*Singing.*] Were you at the wedding?
FIRST GIRL: No.
LITTLE GIRL:
I wasn't let go.
What can have happened
In the yard of vine?
What can have happened
In the olive grove?
What really happened
That no one came home?
Were you at the wedding?
SECOND GIRL: We've told you once – no!
LITTLE GIRL: [*Leaving.*] And I wasn't let go.
SECOND GIRL:

Wool, oh red wool,
Of what will you sing?

FIRST GIRL:
Of wounds sealed in wax
With myrtle for pain,
Days, dead to the world,
Nights, watching again.

LITTLE GIRL:
[*At the door.*]
The thread snags
On the sharp crags,
Then suddenly spins
Through all the blue mountains.
And it runs, runs, runs
Until it finally comes
Under the blade of a knife.
And the bread is returned.
[*She leaves.*]

SECOND GIRL:
Wool, oh red wool,
What will you tell?

FIRST GIRL:
That the lover's dumb
The groom is red
On a quiet shore
I saw them spread.
[*She stops and looks at the wool.*]

LITTLE GIRL:
[*Appearing at the doorway.*]
Run, run, run.
The thread runs to here,
All covered in earth
I feel them draw near.
Their bodies gone hard
In sheets white as marble. [*She leaves.*]
[LEONARDO*'s* WIFE *and* MOTHER-IN-LAW *appear.*

They are deeply upset.]

FIRST GIRL: Are they here yet?

MOTHER-IN-LAW: [*Harshly.*] How would we know?

SECOND GIRL: Please tell us about the wedding!

FIRST GIRL: Yes do.

MOTHER-IN-LAW: [*Strongly.*] I'll tell you nothing!

WIFE: I want to go back and find out what happened.

MOTHER-IN-LAW:
[*Sternly.*]
You'll stop in your own house.
Brave and alone in your house.
To grow senile and weep
But the door kept shut
Not a soul. Living or dead.
The windows boarded up
And let rain and night
Fall on bitter weeds.

WIFE: What can have happened?

MOTHER-IN-LAW:
It doesn't concern you.
You'll wear black.
Your children are your children.
That's an end of it. On your bed
Make a cross of ash
Where his pillow was [*They go out.*]

BEGGAR WOMAN:
[*At the door.*] Can you spare a crust of bread, little girls?

LITTLE GIRL: [*Following her in.*] Go away!
[*The girls huddle together.*]

BEGGAR WOMAN: But why?

LITTLE GIRL: Because you whinge, that's why. Go away!

FIRST GIRL: Don't be cheeky!

BEGGAR WOMAN: I could have asked for her eyes! A cloud of birds is following me. Would you like one?

LITTLE GIRL: I want my mammy!

SECOND GIRL: [*To the* BEGGAR WOMAN.] Don't pass any

remarks on her.

FIRST GIRL: Did you come the road by the sheugh?

BEGGAR WOMAN: That's the very way I came!

FIRST GIRL: [*Timidly.*] Then, can I ask you something?

BEGGAR WOMAN:

I saw them; they'll be here soon; two wild springs
Quiet at last among the great stones
Two men at the feet of a horse
Two men dead in a grand night.
[*With pleasure.*] Dead, yes, dead.

FIRST GIRL: Be quiet, old crone, be quiet!

BEGGAR WOMAN:

Crushed flowers for eyes, and their teeth
Two fistfuls of rock hard snow
Two of them down, and the bride comes here
With their blood on her skirt and hair
Covered by two sheets, the two come
Borne on the shoulders of two young men
That's the story; no more, no less. And only proper.
Over the golden flower, dirty sand.

[*She leaves. The* GIRLS *bow their heads and start to go out rhythmically.*]

FIRST GIRL:

Dirty sand.

SECOND GIRL:

Over the golden flower.

LITTLE GIRL:

Over the golden flower
They bring the dead from the sheugh.
The one nut brown.
Nut brown the other
Flying shadow of the nightingale mourns
Over the golden flower!

[*She leaves. The stage is bare. The* MOTHER *and the* NEIGHBOUR WOMAN *come on. The* NEIGHBOUR *is weeping.*]

MOTHER: Whist!

NEIGHBOUR: For the life of me I can't.

MOTHER: Hold your whist I said. [*At the door.*] Is there anyone home? [*She puts her hands to her forehead.*] My son by right should have answered me. But by now my son is an armful of withered flowers. By now my son is a voice fast fading beyond the mountains. [*With rage to the* NEIGHBOUR.] Will you shut up! I want no whingeing in this house. Your tears are tears only from the eyes – that's nothing. Mine will come, when I'm alone. From the soles of my feet, from my roots. Yes. And they'll burn brighter than blood.

NEIGHBOUR: You shouldn't stop here. You should come to our house.

MOTHER: This is my rightful place. Here! At peace. They are all dead now. Come midnight, I'll sleep and sleep without fear of a gun or a knife. Other mothers will go to their windows, lashed by rain, to watch for the faces of their sons. Not me! From a dream I'll make a marble dove to fly camellias of frost to the graveyard. No, not a graveyard, not a graveyard; but a bed of earth to shelter them and rock them to sleep in the beyond. [*To the* NEIGHBOUR.] Take your hands from your face. There are bad days ahead. And I don't want to see a soul. Only the earth and me. My grief and me. And these four walls. Ay-y-y. Oh-a-y-ay. [*She sits overcome.*]

NEIGHBOUR: Have pity on yourself.

MOTHER: [*Smoothing her hair back.*] I must put a face on it. [*She sits.*] The neighbours will be here and I wouldn't give them the satisfaction of seeing me so poor. So poor! A woman without a single son left to hold her lips.

[*The* BRIDE *appears. She is without her wreath of orange blossom and wears a black shawl.*]

NEIGHBOUR: [*Angrily, seeing the* BRIDE.] Where do you think you're going?

BRIDE: I'm coming here as you can see.

MOTHER: [*To the* NEIGHBOUR.] Who is that woman?

NEIGHBOUR: Don't you know her?

MOTHER: That's why I'm asking. Because I don't want to know her. If I did I'd sink my teeth into her neck. You serpent! You snake out of hell! [*She moves threateningly towards the* BRIDE, *then stops. To the* NEIGHBOUR.] You see her? There she is – her ladyship – and if she isn't crying! And while I stand here calmly. I don't know what's come over me. Maybe I didn't love my son at all! But what about his good name? Hah! Where is his good name now? Where is it? Where is it? [*She strikes the* BRIDE *who falls to the ground.*]

NEIGHBOUR: In the name of God! [*She tries to separate them.*]

BRIDE: [*To the* NEIGHBOUR.] Let her. I came for her to kill me so I could join them. [*To the* MOTHER.] But not with her hands. With grappling hooks, with a sickle, and with such force that they'll break on my bones. Let her! Let her go on. I want her to know that I'm clean. I may be a lunatic, but they can bury me and not a single man will have seen himself in the whiteness of my breasts.

MOTHER: Shut up! Go to hell! What does that matter to me?

BRIDE: It matters because I ran away with the other one. I ran away. [*With anguish.*] You would have gone too. I was a woman mad with desire, full of sickness inside and out, and your son was a wee drop of water from which I wanted children, land and health; but the other one was a dark river, in full spate, swollen with branches, that carried me the rustle of its reeds. It was weakening. And I was going with your son, who was a child of spring water and the other one sent hundreds of birds that sat on my path and left white frost on my wounds, the wounds of a shrivelled woman, this girl who was touched by fire. I didn't want to, believe me! I didn't want to! Your son was my ambition, and I did not betray him. But the other one's arm dragged out of me; dragged me along like the pull of the sea, like the butt of an ass, and he would have dragged me always, always, always – even if I were an old hag and all your son's sons had tried to hold me back by the scruff of the neck!

[*A* NEIGHBOUR *enters.*]

MOTHER: So she's not to blame! And I'm not to blame! [*Sarcastically.*] Then who's to blame? Not this delicate, useless, restless woman. And what does she do? She flings aside her wreath of orange blossom, and goes looking to climb into the half of a bed warmed by another woman!

BRIDE: Never mind! Listen! Have your revenge on me: Here I am! Look how soft my throat is; you would think less of snipping a dahlia in your garden. But wait, not yet. I'm pure, as clean as a newborn baby girl. And strong enough to prove it! Light the fire. We'll put our hands into the flames: you for the sake of the good name of your son, and I for my body. You'll see: you'll be the first to withdraw.

[Another NEIGHBOUR enters.]

MOTHER: I don't give a curse for your good name! Do you think your death matters to me? What does a dead virgin matter to me! Blessed be the wheat fields, for my sons lie beneath them; blessed be the rain, for it wets the face of the dead; blessed be God for he lays us to rest by each other's side.

[*Another* NEIGHBOUR *enters.*]

BRIDE: Let me weep with you.

MOTHER: Weep if you must. But weep by the door.

[*The* LITTLE GIRL *enters. The* BRIDE *remains by the door. The* MOTHER *stands in the centre of the stage.*]

WIFE:

[*Entering, moving stage left.*]

He was a lovely horseman,
Now he's a hidden heap of snow
Carved at fairs and mountains
And in the arms of women.
Now, the black moss of night
Crowns his temple.

MOTHER:

Sunflower to your mother,
Mirror of the earth.
Let them fix to your breast
A cross of bitter rosebay;
A sheet to cover you
Of brilliant silk;
And water cup its grief

Between your quiet hands.
WIFE:
Oh four good lads
Come with tired shoulders!
BRIDE:
Oh four gallants
Carry death through the air!
MOTHER: Neighbours.
LITTLE GIRL: Here they come.
MOTHER:
Always the same,
The cross, the cross.
WOMEN:
Sweet nails,
Sweet cross,
Sweet name
Of Jesus.
BRIDE:
May the cross protect the dead and the living.
MOTHER:
Neighbours, with a knife,
With a little knife,
On a day ordained, between the hours of two and three,
Two men of love killed each other.
With a knife,
With a little knife,
That scarcely fits into the hand,
But slips clean
Through the astounded flesh,
And then only stops at the place,
Where trembles, entangled,
The dark root of a scream.
BRIDE:
And this is a knife,
A little knife,
Which scarcely fits into the hand;

Fish without fish scales, fish out of water,
So that on the day ordained, between the hour of two and three,
With this knife
Two men are left hard
With yellow lips.

MOTHER:

And scarcely fits into the hand
But slips cold
Through the astounded flesh,
And only stops there, at the place
Where trembles, entangled,
The dark root of a scream.

END

On Broken Wings

First performed in Ennis, Co. Clare, in January 1992 by Theatre Omnibus, Ennis. Directed by Dermot Healy.

CAST

OLD MAN	Timothy
MOTHER	Wami
FATHER	Wadi
TIMOTHY	Younger versions of the OLD MAN
WALTZERS	In masks
POTATO HEADS	In masks
WOMAN	
MAN	
MANGAN	
AMERICAN HEADS	In masks
BIG WOMAN	
ROSIE	
FIFTIES HEADS	In masks
BARWOMAN	
SKELETON	
TESSIE	
BERNIE	

Playwright's Note

The play takes its title from a popular song of the 1930s, a period in which some of the scenes are set. It opens in contemporary Ireland with an old masked figure – Timothy Lavell – seated by the hearth of a cottage on the Mullet peninsula.

The fireplace opens and in strides his mother, father, and himself as a young boy. We follow in Act I scenes from Timothy's childhood, including his trip by boat to Scotland, and his sojourn there potato-picking. The life is rough and picturesque. He returns to find his mother has died. He works at wall building with his father for a period, then leaves home again.

In Act II we follow Timothy Lavell's life in America. He finds work as an elevator man, and encounters many races and creeds. His experiences, his failed love affair, his hallucinations, and his fears are explored. Eventually he returns to Ireland.

He takes up residence again in the cottage where he was born, without electricity, with neighbours who are the children of the neighbours his dead parents knew. He sits by the hearth like his father and mother before him. The fireplace closes as neighbours leave.

He is back as he was at the beginning of the play. It's a simple story told in a visual style with masks used to portray the many characters and the ageing process. Humour and pathos and fatalism are the main ingredients of Timothy Lavell's life. He is a stubborn survivor of another age.

—Dermot Healy, "Playwright's Note," original programme for the Theatre Omnibus production of *On Broken Wings*, 1992

Style: A community play in two acts for three performers and various other players, using sound, masks and puppets.

Set: A fireplace which turns into a bar; the gable of a house which turns into a sail of a ship; a projection screen, a single iron bed, and three chairs.

ACT I
SCENE 1
By the Fire Place

A large empty fireplace sits centre stage in a dark room. Area behind empty except for a suitcase placed in the distance. A sugan chair sits to stage right of the fireplace. Three kitchen chairs downstage right. A sail pegged to the ground makes a gable wall stage left. An OLD MAN *in a grey gabardine coat, baseball cap, and white runners stands in front of the fireplace. His hands are shoved into the pockets of his coat. He has an enormous facemask and a hump. There is the sound of wind outside. A white light shines through the sail, which flutters slightly in the wind. The* OLD MAN *looks at the wall. Then he bends down and turns on a yellow moon of light in the fireplace.*

OLD MAN: Still alive, I think.

[*Pause.*]

OLD MAN: Not now. Once awood. Not now. No, thank you.

[*Then he goes silent again and listens attentively.*]

OLD MAN: I'll sit myself down I think, thank you.

[*He steps back and sits down, arthritically, in the sugan chair.*]

OLD MAN: Going up.

[*Beams of light go everywhere. He studies the fire and flicks his finger.*]

OLD MAN: I'll take off my coat now, thank you.

[*He gives a nod of his head. Stands. He takes off his gabardine coat. Places it on the back of the chair. Sits.*]

OLD MAN: That's it. Now the boots. [*He begins unlacing his boots.*] There we are. Everything neat and tidy. Everything in its place.

[*He puts white runners away.*]

OLD MAN: Wonderful. [*Pause.*] Wonderful and tidy.

[*Considers the fire a moment. Puts out a hand and feels round the space. A rustling noise starts in behind him.*]

OLD MAN: Between three and seven is the worst for this kind of thing.

[*Rustling noise starts again. Immediately the* OLD MAN *looks up.*]

OLD MAN: Hallo!

[*The rustling is not repeated.*]

OLD MAN: Oi! [*Pause.*] Hallo! Is that you Tessie?

[*He stares at the place where the rustling was.*]

OLD MAN: You'll get that, you'll get that between three and seven. The whole planet is on the move. [*Looks at the audience.*] Not that you are expected to know. They say they tell you everything. Indeed they don't. [*Pause.*] Poor Bernie. Poor Bernie Coleman.

[*He whistles to the dog. He looks back into the fire.*]

OLD MAN: That is what you get when you haven't the light.

[*He looks closer into the fire.*]

OLD MAN: Frogs' eyes. [*Pause.*]

OLD MAN: A long twilight, all manner of bastes, and every last one of them middling and nasty.

[*He prods the fire which grows brighter. Settles. Puts one foot out before the fire.*]

OLD MAN: Hmmm, Wadi.

[*Puts second foot out before the fire.*]

OLD MAN: Hmmm, Wami.

[*Another rustling starts behind him. He lifts his head and listens.*]

OLD MAN: Hallo?

[*The rustling is repeated.*]

OLD MAN: Oi! [*Pause.*] What is he trying to convey to me?
[*Then slowly he gets up mumbling. With one-two-three movements of stick, toe, and heel, he pauses; another three steps, then pauses. He begins moving slowly away from the spot where the noise was. He turns suddenly, and retraces his steps. Stands at the spot.*]

OLD MAN: Oi!
[*He gets onto his knees.*]

OLD MAN: Cl! Cl! [*He calls the dog.*]
Pish! Wish! Pish Wish! [*He calls the cat.*]

OLD MAN: You'll get that between three and seven.
[*Behind him the tumult begins. He stays on his knees and watches the fireplace. Wind has started in the chimney.*]

SCENE 2
Studies

The two sides of the fireplace come apart like a theatre curtain. In strides MOTHER *with a huge face and a small hump. She begins sweeping. In strides* FATHER, *large hump, in leather waistcoat and cap. In comes* TIMOTHY *with no hump.*

FATHER: Were you born in a field? [TIMOTHY *closes fireplace.*] Right, gossoon! [FATHER *rubs his hands with pleasure.*] Oi! Hee-hee! [*Pause.*] Ya boy ya! [*Pause. Finds lad following him again.*] Stop where you are! [*Approaches* MOTHER.] Ho-ho, Wami! [FATHER *lifts up a copybook, reads the question and holds copybook behind his back.*] How long is the mare?

TIMOTHY: Eleven months.

FATHER: Is that all?
[*The young* TIMOTHY *takes off walking followed by his* FATHER.]

TIMOTHY: Twelve months if she's auld. Eleven months if she's working.

FATHER: The duck?

TIMOTHY: A month.

FATHER: The goose?

TIMOTHY: A month.
FATHER: And the dog?
TIMOTHY: Three months. Nine days coming, nine days on, nine days going.
[*They stop, and face each other. Then make two circles.*]
FATHER: What goes round the house and round the house? And sits at the door all night long?
TIMOTHY: The broom.
MOTHER: Isn't he good?
FATHER: Round the wood and round the wood and never touches the wood?
TIMOTHY: A penknife in a man's pocket?
[*They stop and face each other. Complete one circle.*]
FATHER: Over the water and under the water and never touches the water?
TIMOTHY: An egg in a duck's arse.
[*They come to a stop looking away from each other.*]
MOTHER: Oh wonders.
FATHER: Plain common sense. [FATHER *and* TIMOTHY *face each other.*] The cow?
TIMOTHY: Nine months!
[FATHER *looks away.*]
MOTHER: Isn't he a dote.
FATHER: I'll catch him yet.
MOTHER: He's well fit for you.
FATHER: [*He fires the questions straight at* TIMOTHY *without moving.*] The hare?
MOTHER: Three weeks.
FATHER: What's going on?
MOTHER: Sorry.
FATHER: I'll have to look that up. [*He brandishes copybook.*] The goat?
[*Silence.*]
TIMOTHY: The goat?
FATHER: The very fellow.
TIMOTHY: The goat.
FATHER: That's the very man we're discussing.

[MOTHER *stops her work to urge on her* TIMOTHY. FATHER *looks away happy that he has outwitted the lad.* MOTHER *lifts three fingers.*]
TIMOTHY: Three months.
FATHER: [*Immediately, spinning on his heels.*] The whale?
TIMOTHY: The whale?
FATHER: The whale, aye.
TIMOTHY: The whale.
FATHER: That shook you, sunflower.
TIMOTHY: It's a hard one.
FATHER: Keep looking at me.
TIMOTHY: I know the elephant.
FATHER: But the elephant won't do.
TIMOTHY: No.
FATHER: No.
[*The* FATHER *does a jig of celebration.*]
FATHER: The whale got the scholar, Wami!
MOTHER: That it did.
FATHER: The whale got Timothy.

SCENE 3
Poor Bernie Coleman

MOTHER, FATHER *and* TIMOTHY. *They look around them. And slowly start sewing.*

MOTHER: I suppose you saw the same people.
FATHER: The same people are everywhere.
MOTHER: Aye.
FATHER: Aye.
MOTHER: It would make you wonder.
FATHER: It would.
MOTHER: It would make you think.
[*They stop sewing a moment and think. Pause.*]
FATHER: Well, Bernie Coleman was there as was Tessie Carey.
MOTHER: Poor Tessie Carey. And the King?
FATHER: Aye, the King was there.

MOTHER: It couldn't go on without him.
FATHER: It could not.
MOTHER: Isn't life delectable?
FATHER: It is. Right enough. Aye.
MOTHER: And we're sitting here.
FATHER: Right as rain.
MOTHER: It would make you wonder.
FATHER: When you think of it.

[*They stop sewing a moment and think. Pause.*]

MOTHER: You wouldn't want to be doing it too often.
FATHER: You would not.
MOTHER: You'd go odd.
FATHER: It's not certain.
MOTHER: There's people.
FATHER: There is.
MOTHER: And then there's Bernie Coleman.
FATHER: Bernie Coleman and Tessie Carey.
MOTHER: The poor souls.

[*They stop knitting.*]

ALL: Oh Rosie!

[*Then start knitting again.*]

FATHER: He's a long time at that article.
MOTHER: Are you near finished, sunflower?
TIMOTHY: I am, Wadi.
FATHER: You have to be fairly tidy with a hump.
MOTHER: Trotting but you have.
FATHER: One wrong move and ha-ha!
MOTHER: That's right.
FATHER: Before you know it it's down at your feet. Oh yes.
MOTHER: That's right.
FATHER: That's right surely. Down round your feet.
MOTHER: Say no more, you'll only make him nervous.
FATHER: Why doesn't he try it on?

[*All sewing stops.* TIMOTHY *stands and hands the cushion to his* MOTHER. MOTHER *takes it and gives it a good beating. She hands it to* FATHER *who gives it a good beating. Meanwhile* MOTHER *opens* TIMOTHY*'s shirt. She* *takes a bag from* FATHER *and shoves it down the back of* TIMOTHY*'s shirt. She tidies his hump.* TIMOTHY *stands back to model his hump. Walks one way, then walks the other.*]

FATHER: That's the very job.

MOTHER: And the beauty is he made it all by himself.

FATHER: He did.

MOTHER: There's some people can turn their hand to anything.

FATHER: Will you look at the cut of him.

MOTHER: It'll be hard to talk to him now.

[*They form a line, one behind the other, displaying their humps.*]

MOTHER: Jimmy!

[FATHER *fetches bell.* MOTHER *drops to knees; reluctantly* FATHER *and* TIMOTHY *do the same.*]

SCENE 4
Prayers

She blesses her lips and chest with fingertips five times. FATHER *blesses himself with a broad gesture of sweeping fingers.* TIMOTHY *blesses himself on the edge of his forehead.* MOTHER *cranks the air in front of her.* FATHER *slowly does the same.* TIMOTHY *does a quick crank.* FATHER *immediately slouches into the chair, head bowed.* MOTHER, *keeping upright, puts her hands in front of her face.* TIMOTHY, *cherub-like, joins his hands on his chest.*

MOTHER: Tie my leg to your father's.

TIMOTHY: I will, Wami.

FATHER: And tie it good and strong.

TIMOTHY: I will Wadi.

MOTHER: And then give us a good scalding.

TIMOTHY: I will Wami.

FATHER: Beat us and don't spare us.

TIMOTHY: I will, Wadi.

MOTHER: The rod.

FATHER: The hazel.

MOTHER: The sally.

FATHER: Oh the stick!
MOTHER: And always do what your father says.
TIMOTHY: I will Wami.
FATHER: And make a mint.
TIMOTHY: I will Wadi.
MOTHER and FATHER: So we can all live in the lap of luxury.
TIMOTHY: Tra-la.
FATHER: May the wind from the North-West never blow.
MOTHER: The scour not strike the hens.
TIMOTHY: And that we all be redeemed.
MOTHER: Oh aren't we blessed in Timothy.
FATHER: Blessed is not the word.
MOTHER: Nor our reason thereof to know.
TIMOTHY: I want a baby.
MOTHER: [*Hands round her face.*] I don't want a baby.
FATHER: [*Slouching down.*] Ham, butter and eggs.
TIMOTHY: I want a baby.
MOTHER: I don't want a baby.
FATHER: Ham, butter and eggs.

[*On the command from* MOTHER *all look up. She begins a sonorous Gregorian chant. Sings verse watched by them, then back to final prayer.*]

TIMOTHY: [*Fast.*] I want a baby.
MOTHER: [*Fast.*] I don't want a baby.
FATHER: [*Fast.*] Ham, butter and eggs.

[*In a hurry, all three crank the air, bless themselves five times as before, then come to their feet and dust their knees madly.*]

MOTHER: Doesn't it do your heart good!
FATHER: It'd give you an appetite.
MOTHER: It would lift you.

[*The fireplace again begins to open. The family shove back the chairs against the walls.*]

SCENE 5

The Waltzers

The waltzing neighbours enter dancing through the fireplace. The waltz is old time, to the beat of one-two-three, one-two-three, with no music. The beat is supplied by FATHER *on the seat of his chair,* MOTHER *with a wooden spoon, and* TIMOTHY *orchestrating with his hands. The waltzers all wear identical masks, caps, leather-backed waistcoats, scarves, booties, and boots, and they look towards the audience for the opening note. When the note comes they sweep forward and backward across the space – sprightly, old-fashioned, and rather severe. When the dance is nearly over, they all part for* MOTHER *to dance with* FATHER *in silence – a stiff parental dance with certain flourishes and decorative sidesteps. And then* MOTHER *calls* TIMOTHY *down and dances a few steps with him – a mother-and-son dance that is very plain when they are together. Suddenly, they let go of each other and do some set dance-style sidekicks; the neighbours join in for a few moments. Then, slightly ashamed of themselves, they start waltzing again. The neighbours dance out into the wings in couples.* FATHER, MOTHER *and* TIMOTHY *continue with the beat for some time, improvising new sounds, and with a final crazy solo from* FATHER.

MOTHER: You'd wonder about some people.
FATHER: You would.
MOTHER: Did you see the face on that one, Teasy Gaynor?
FATHER: I did.
MOTHER: Lord, but it's a crime.
FATHER: Now Dorothy! Ahmmm, ahmmm, Dorothy.
[*The three sit round the fire with their legs stretched out. Then* MOTHER *moves her stool stage right. The other pair edge their stools after her. She moves a little more. They do too.*]
TIMOTHY: Hmmm, Wami. [*Now* FATHER *edges his chair a little stage left. The other pair edge their stools after him. He moves a little more. They do too.*] Hmmm, Wadi.
[*All three tighten in together. All stretch their hands in front of the fire. Suddenly* TIMOTHY *throws something over his*

shoulder. All turn, look over their shoulders tiredly at the noise, and sigh.]

ALL: [*Sighing.*] Ahh! [*Then look back to the fire.*]

[FATHER *is well into the grate, slouching with hands stretched out.* MOTHER *further back, hands open on her knees.* TIMOTHY *with his hands open in front of his face.*]

ALL: [*A sound of pure relaxation, reaching quaint sounds of ecstasy, and the family spill onto the ground lazily.*] Hmmm. Hmmm. Hmmm.

FATHER: Is that you Dorothy?

MOTHER: Oh Jimmy Lavell.

[TIMOTHY *gets up and coughs loudly.*]

TIMOTHY: Pollanbaid.

FATHER: [*Angrily.*] Hmmmmmmm.

MOTHER: [*Angrily.*] Ohhhh.

FATHER: Ahmmm!

MOTHER: Ah.

SCENE 6

Cleaning Up the House

MOTHER *and* FATHER *begin to rise guiltily and lift the chairs and stack them.*

MOTHER: Isn't it terrible when you think about it. [*All freeze and think.*] And you know I'm awful sorry to say it, but the chairs suddenly weigh so heavy.

FATHER: Chairs are always heavy.

MOTHER: That may well be.

FATHER: And each chair is a different weight, although some are the same, or nearly the same, isn't that it sunflower?

TIMOTHY: Yes Wadi.

MOTHER: "Yes Wadi," how often have I heard that phrase? [*She begins to sweep the space.*] But the broom is light.

FATHER: I'm sure it is.

MOTHER: The broom is light.

FATHER: What do you smell?

TIMOTHY: I can smell nothing.
FATHER: Try again.
TIMOTHY: Salt.
FATHER: Soot. Can't you smell soot? Go over there and put your head up the chimney. Now what do you smell?
TIMOTHY: Soot.
FATHER: And what does it smell like? I'll tell you what soot smells like – it smells like work. Work and more work. Isn't that right Dorothy? [*Slowly she brooms the space without answering.*] Is there no end in sight?
MOTHER: [*As she keeps sweeping.*] None.
FATHER: Nothing but work.
MOTHER: That's right.
FATHER: Are we there yet?
TIMOTHY: I can't say.
FATHER: And now?
MOTHER: Well?
FATHER: Well?
TIMOTHY: No sign yet.
[TIMOTHY *takes the moon from fireplace and puts it into his case.*]
MOTHER: What's happening?
FATHER: I don't know.
MOTHER: Well don't just stand there.
FATHER: What can I do?
MOTHER: If you don't look out he'll be gone over the sea.
FATHER: Come down son, or you'll fall.
MOTHER: Catch him or he's gone to Scotland.
FATHER: Timothy!
MOTHER: Now do you see!
FATHER: Timothy.
MOTHER: Timothy.

SCENE 7

The Journey to Scotland

A foghorn sounds. Waves on the sea. Onto the deck of the ship come some travelling people, wearing red POTATO HEADS. *All of the other passengers have grey, downcast* POTATO HEADS. *They all carry sacks, each containing a lit moon. In rhythm, they all move. The travellers go sideways, like pendulums.* TIMOTHY *goes backwards and forwards. The movements grow exaggerated, from small to large. And on the seventh beat each move reaches its climax and they all freeze for a moment. Then the movements alternate.* TIMOTHY *goes sideways, they go backwards-and-forwards, again building up over seven beats. At each climax one of the crowd shrieks like a seagull. Then the movements start again. After the fourth shriek these exact movements begin to break down. Each red traveller gets his movements mixed up and as he does so groans "Ohhhhhhh!" The others follow suit. The redheads walk sick passengers to and fro, commiserating with them, while the sick feel their way around in a kind of blind man's bluff. One sick man goes to hurl himself into the sea with a roar. The others stop him. He is offered a potato to eat; he attempts to jump again at the mere sight of it.* TIMOTHY *puts his hands over his eyes. They stop the sick passenger from jumping over again.* TIMOTHY *looks out. The movements around him are chaotic. Then one of the crowd blows a whistle. Everyone freezes. He blows the whistle again. Each group sits down on benches opposite each other, murmuring.*

They are now on a train.

LEAD VOICE: Dedum.
ALL: Dedum! Dedum!
LEAD VOICE: Dedum! Dedum! Dedum!
ALL: Dedum.
LEAD VOICE: Deum Dedao.
ALL: Lumen de luminae.
LEAD VOICE: Deum Verum.
ALL: In Unum Vero.
LEAD VOICE: Deum Dedao.

ALL: Lumen de luminae.
LEAD VOICE: Deum Verum.
ALL: In Unum Vero.
LEAD VOICE: Dedum!
ALL: Dedum! Dedum!
LEAD VOICE: Dedum!
ALL: Dedum! Dedum!

[*And so the train leaves the station.* TIMOTHY *watches, listens, shifts his head constantly. He looks around while the others, sitting very upright, sing the train song. The "Dedums" reach their loudest point as one figure conducts the orchestra of travellers in a chorus of different train sounds. Slowly, in a whisper, the train enters the station. It shudders to a stop. The "Dedums" go to a whisper and get slower. At a given moment they all blow out breezily through their lips. The travellers vibrate in their seats and then all of them climb out. They gather in a line with their sacks on their backs. Awkwardly,* TIMOTHY *climbs out alongside them and finds himself at the end of the queue, his case at his feet.*]

TIMOTHY: Dedum! [*But no one answers.*] Dedum! Dedum!

[*They all turn around and look at him. Then he goes quiet. And he crosses himself with a broad wave of sweeping fingers like his father before him.*]

SCENE 8
In the Bothy

Lights come up full. The POTATO HEADS *stand ready at intervals. They are old hands.* TIMOTHY *watches them. It is quiet. They look towards the audience. They start exhorting each other and clapping their hands, spitting like Trojans. They roll up their sleeves and brace themselves.* TIMOTHY *does an exaggerated* version *of everything he sees, snapping his case open and closed. Then everyone drops to their hunkers and begins to move forward, filling their bags.*

WOMAN: Oh! Ho-ho-ho-ho! I nair saw the lykes.

MAN: It'll not be long now afore we're there.

[*They move forward towards the centre. Filling and then emptying, and then filling again. The* WOMAN *gets up and looks at the others.*]

WOMAN: Hiy yee, gi'a a moo on! Hi ye, gi'a moo on. Iss nee a' hume ye'air noo.

[*Then she goes to her knees collecting and chewing.*]

TIMOTHY: What's she saying?

MAN: She says that there is no use in fussing. No use in fussing.

[*They work on a while.*]

WOMAN: I nair sin tay noo sooch tattyhokers i'day field O'Ayershare.

TIMOTHY: What did she say?

MAN: She says that you should never cross The Red Mangans.

[*They work on.*]

WOMAN: The dearth o' Eerelan' a'ha heer ta mah discredit. Twould shame a lady. Twould.

[TIMOTHY *looks at the man for an explanation.*]

MAN: She says that it's two hundred and fifteen sweet Irish miles from Belmullet town to Kinnegad.

TIMOTHY: Ask her how long is the whale.

MAN: How long is the whale?

[*No answer.*]

TIMOTHY: Ask her again.

MAN: How long is the whale?

WOMAN: Are ou talkin ta may? Ay swar his talkin ta may. It's nay gude ya talkin ta may, mun. I canna say ha lang the weenee'd sit inis Mama's gut. I ken how lang my bairn he stopped in mine, and das enuf.

[TIMOTHY *looks at him.*]

MAN: It's certain as there is a sky in the heavens that all of our hearts will be broken one day.

[*They reach the end of the line. All stand and cough and cough.*]

SCENE 9

The Inoculation

TIMOTHY *snaps his case shut. The* POTATO HEADS *fall into line with their sacks on their backs, looking dizzy and downhearted. The* MAN *seats himself at a table, stage right. He rings a small bell.*

MAN: Timothy Lavell! [TIMOTHY *moves forward.*] You have to have your inoculation.
TIMOTHY: And what about my wages?
MAN: Indeed, you have to have the inoculation.
TIMOTHY: And what about my wages?
MAN: First the jab.
WOMAN: Then the money.
MAN: That's the way it is. [TIMOTHY *plants his case on the ground.*] Take off your shirt. [TIMOTHY *takes off his shirt.*] And your trousers.
TIMOTHY: You want me to take off my trousers?
MAN: I do.
TIMOTHY: I never knew about this when I was leaving Ireland.
MAN: That's the way.
TIMOTHY: Why do you want me to take off my trousers?
MAN: We need to see your ding-dong.
WOMAN: That's nice, that's lovely. [*And she gives a sudden screech of laughter. And then, when the men look at her, she pats her chest.*] It's my heart, I took a twinge during the night.
MAN: Your trousers.
TIMOTHY: It's not fair.
WOMAN: Who said it would be?
TIMOTHY: I'm cold.
WOMAN: It's always colder in someone else's house.
[*Behind them the queue of people agree with this. A snort of assent goes up, much nodding. The* MAN *rings the bell.*]
MAN: I can't stay here all day.
TIMOTHY: I demand to see someone in higher authority.
MAN: There's no higher you can go than me.
WOMAN: He's the boss, worse luck. The best thing you can do

is hoist your arse in his direction.

[*The* MAN *lifts out a syringe and sprays it. He holds it and smiles at it.*]

TIMOTHY: I don't know. [TIMOTHY *bends over with his head bowed to the audience. The queue of potato pickers and the* MAN *and* WOMAN *clap as if he were taking a bow. He bows left and right to thunderous applause. And suddenly to his bewilderment he is injected from behind.*] Wadi!

[TIMOTHY *opens his case and takes out the moon. He picks a spot as the others lie down. He lies down and curls up for sleep beside his moon. The lights go lower. The space fills with groans and sneezes. Then at one particular groan everyone turns one way while* TIMOTHY *turns the other. A moment later they all turn the other way and again* TIMOTHY *turns the opposite direction. A light catches all the* POTATO HEADS *as if they were laid in drills. Each person's head is lying on a moon.*]

SCENE 10
Sleep

WOMAN: Are you there?

TIMOTHY: Yes.

WOMAN: Tell us what you see?

TIMOTHY: Why I see a small room with a dresser, the sea, hens and things. Potatoes are flowering.

MAN: Leave the spuds out of it, if you would.

TIMOTHY: Bernie Coleman's there, as is Tessie Carey. My father is shoeing a horse and someone is dead in the next parish.

WOMAN: [*Ironically.*] Wonderful.

MAN: [*Ironically.*] They're kept busy in your place.

TIMOTHY: You're right.

MAN: The days are lengthening where you are now.

TIMOTHY: They are.

MAN: I'd as soon be there as here.

WOMAN: Lord above, but they killed poor Gaynor for no

reason in the earthly.

[*A loud cheer is heard.*]

TIMOTHY: Who's that?

WOMAN: Them's the tinkers.

MAN: The Red Mangans.

VOICE: [*Off.*] Come out you long fucker you, and I'll show you. [*Then there is the sound of someone urinating in the dark.*]

WOMAN: The bladders that some people have. Isn't it dreadful to think that the human body could contain such a wealth of urine.

MAN: Especially on a Saturday night.

WOMAN: What are we but animals.

MAN: Aye. There's a power of piss on a Saturday.

WOMAN: Tell us more.

MAN: There is no more to tell only sleep. Sleep is when you are out working for the stranger. The man that can do without sleep hasn't woken up yet. In my sleep I pick acres and acres for a man I've never laid my eyes upon.

WOMAN: That's right.

MAN: Acres and acres.

WOMAN: Oh I know.

MAN: For the stranger. And then I find that what I'm picking are not spuds at all.

WOMAN: No?

MAN: No.

[*Silence.*]

TIMOTHY: So what are they?

MAN: I'd rather not say.

WOMAN: I understand.

MAN: That's right. Now I'm not saying that someone I know won't turn up in my sleep, I'm not saying that. [*Pause.*] I'm not saying that.

TIMOTHY: No.

WOMAN: Indeed you're not.

MAN: I'm not.

WOMAN: You're not.

MAN: I'm not saying that.

SLEEPER: You're not.
MAN: [*Sleepily.*] I'm not.
WOMAN: You're not.
[*Pause.*]
MAN: I'm not saying that.
SLEEPER: You're not saying that.
[*Lights going down.*]
MAN: I'm not.
WOMAN: You're not.
MAN: I'm not.
WOMAN: You're not.
[*Silence.*]
MAN: I'm not saying that. [*Silence.*] They were goat droppings in fact. Black lads everywhere I looked. And I wouldn't mind, but whatever the story was, I had to lift every last one. Now I ask you. Oh but this is it. Certainly. No rest for the wicked. All go. That's what it means – out working for the stranger. That's what those words mean. Hardship. Aptly named. Hard-ship. Oh yes. And there's no harder taskmaster in this world than the human mind, especially when it's your own. There's no end to the villainy you'll set yourself. The first hours asleep bent double collecting Kerr's Pinks in a field like no field I ever saw. And then when I shoulda been dreaming of the ladies look what happens – I'm off down the King's Highway gathering goat marbles.
[*Silence. Darkness.*]

SCENE 11
The Nightmare

TIMOTHY *screams in the dark.*

TIMOTHY: I thought I was falling into to the sea.
[*Little pinpoints of light from small flashlights occur here and there as the sleepers speak.*]
MAN: You're not.
TIMOTHY: I'm not.

WOMAN: You're not.
TIMOTHY: I'm not.
SLEEPERS: You're not.
TIMOTHY: I'm not.
MAN: Poll an tsagairt.
WOMAN: Pollawadra.
TIMOTHY: Pollawain.
MAN: Pollanbradain.
WOMAN: Pollanponee.
TIMOTHY: Pollantowen.
MAN: Pollbrisheach.
WOMAN: Pollglass.
TIMOTHY: Polldorcach.
MAN: Gortnatsuil.
WOMAN: The field of eyes.
TIMOTHY: The field of eyes.

[*In the dark, little lights twitch on and off. Then it all goes dark.*]

SCENE 12
The Deadman's Breakfast

VOICE: Ga up ta fook ta work ya wee miserable hures.

MANGAN: Shut your gob ya Scottish shite. [*A moan of dissent goes up. The* POTATO HEADS *gather for breakfast mumbling to each other by a long narrow table. Enter the* WOMAN *with the bucket of porridge. Each person has a tin bowl in front of them. The* WOMAN *very carefully pours a glutinous portion of porridge into each bowl.*] You have to be careful with the drink first thing in the morning. God bless us, you could go blind.

MAN: Were you ever in Oxford on a Sunday morning? That's one cold spot after you're driven out of the hostel.

MANGAN: And Southampton, God Bless us. Don't forget Southampton.

WOMAN: And how can I – isn't that where the Health Board buried poor Gaynor. He caught his death there in the Easter snow.

MAN: Sweet God.

[*The* WOMAN *pours out the porridge in front of a man who is seated by the table with his eyes closed, steady as a rock.*]

WOMAN: Hi! There's your breakfast. [*She goes onto the next man, but the other fellow does not budge.*] Hi you, eat your breakfast! [*But he makes no move. She tips him very lightly with her finger and he drops dead. He lies flat on the floor. Everything stops. The people stand and look down at him.*]

MANGAN: He's dead. Just like that.

MAN: I thought he did not look well.

WOMAN: Did anyone know him?

MANGAN: Not at all, the poor cratur could be anybody.

[*They look at him lying there then sit back down to eat. The* WOMAN *pushes the deadman's bowl of porridge in front of the next man*, MANGAN. *He pushes it away. She pushes it back in front him again.*]

MANGAN: [*Pushing it away.*] That's the deadman's breakfast.

WOMAN: He didn't touch it. [*She pushes it back in front of him again.*]

MANGAN: I'll eat no porridge belonging to a deadman as sure as I'm a Mangan. [*He pushes it away again.*]

WOMAN: If you don't eat it, you'll get nothing.

MANGAN: [*Roaring.*] I'll eat no porridge belonging to a deadman. [*And he stands facing her.*]

TIMOTHY: I'll eat it.

[*Everyone stops and turns to look at him.*]

WOMAN: There you are, he'll eat it. [*She moves the dead man's porridge along in front of* TIMOTHY. *The lad raises his spoon to his lips.*]

MANGAN: I never thought I'd live to see the day. That a living man would eat a deadman's breakfast. [TIMOTHY *hesitates.*] That's right, fill your gob you stunted whore. May the lumps in that porridge snag on your windpipe – that's right, and turn to stone in your gullet. You're one sorry fucker. But don't let me stop you. [*He spits on the ground. He strides to the door and raises his arm in the gesture of a curse.*] I'll eat no breakfast alongside some sham would eat the bit intended for a deadman!

[TIMOTHY *looks nervously about him.*]

MAN: [*Whispers.*] You shouldn't do it. [TIMOTHY *halts with the spoon to his lips.*] It's the principle of the thing, you see. [*All wait to see what will happen.*]

TIMOTHY: I'll eat no deadman's porridge. [TIMOTHY *pushes the bowl away.*]

MANGAN: Good man, good man – I knew you were dacent.

TIMOTHY: I'll eat no breakfast belonging to a deadman.

[*A roar of approval goes up. Then everyone freezes. They tie the sacks of spuds to their backs, and the moons light up in the sacks. They all stand on a ridge of skyline.*]

SCENE 13

Where's Wami?

The wind is blowing the sail of the gable. TIMOTHY *strides by, with a hump on his back, and enters the kitchen.* FATHER, *now an old man with a huge hump, is seated by the empty fireplace.* TIMOTHY *takes his moon from his suitcase and places it in the fireplace. They look at each other.*

FATHER: Oh!

TIMOTHY: Oh! [TIMOTHY *lifts out a wad of money. Places it on the table.*]

FATHER: Oh!

TIMOTHY: Aye!

FATHER: Um!

TIMOTHY: Aw.

FATHER: Ah-ha.

TIMOTHY: Oh.

FATHER: Hm. Hm.

TIMOTHY: Ha.

FATHER: Very good. Very good. Very good. Very good.

[*Pause.*]

TIMOTHY: Where's Wami? [*The* FATHER *points overhead with*

his index finger. Both look up. Then they look at each other.] Oh!

FATHER: Aye!

[TIMOTHY *sits by the fireplace. They sit there a long time looking into the fire. Then they look at each other, then look back at the fire.* TIMOTHY *throws a sod on to the fire. Silence. They sit there looking into the fire. Then* MOTHER *enters unnoticed by the two men. She stands alone, stage left.*]

MOTHER:

[*Sings.*]
On broken wings
No bird can fly
And broken promises
Means love must fade away and die.

TIMOTHY, FATHER AND MOTHER:

I trusted you,
You can't be true,
My love no longer sings . . .

MOTHER:

Its wings are broken too.
[MOTHER *leaves.*]

TIMOTHY and FATHER:

I trusted you,
You can't be true,
My heart no longer sings,
Its wings are broken too.
[*They sit there.*]

SCENE 14
Building the Wall

FATHER *is building a wall at the corner downstage right.* TIMOTHY *is carrying turf to him from the stack. The turf is heavy.* TIMOTHY *places it beside* FATHER.

TIMOTHY: Oha.

FATHER: Agh. Aghhh. Agh. [FATHER *selects one sod, puts it in place, and then studies the wall. He lifts another.* TIMOTHY *returns with second load.*]

TIMOTHY: Oha.

FATHER: Agh. Aghhh. Agh. [*The* FATHER *selects one, puts it in place, and then studies the wall. He lifts another.* TIMOTHY *returns with third load.*]

TIMOTHY: Oha.

FATHER: Agh. Aghh. Agh.

[TIMOTHY *walks into house and lifts his case. He stops and looks at his* FATHER. FATHER *continues to work. He takes the moon from the fireplace and puts it in his case.*]

TIMOTHY: Oha.

FATHER: Agh. Aghhh. Agh.

[TIMOTHY *moves on a little with his case and looks back.* FATHER *continues to build.*]

TIMOTHY: Oha.

FATHER: Agh. Aghhh. Agh. [TIMOTHY, *his hump larger, walks off carrying his case.* FATHER *works on.*] Agh. Aghhh. Agh. [*He selects the last piece of turf.*] Agh. Aghhh. Agh. [*He looks behind him for more turf but sees none; he straightens up slowly and looks off into the distance after* TIMOTHY.]

ACT II
SCENE 15
Pushing Your Bed through New York

Just an open space with the sail at the back – a screen onto which images can be projected. An exotic bird screams as if in a zoo or jungle. The bird repeats its scream. Lights come up a little. The bird screams again. TIMOTHY *pushes his small bed onstage. His case sits on it. He goes in one direction, swings bed around grandly, and returns pushing the bed like a trolley.* AMERICAN HEADS *join him on stage and go past him in a constant traffic to-and-fro. He pushes his bed around some more. Stops.* AMERICAN HEADS *gather round.* TIMOTHY *sits on the bed stage right. Light goes down. The bird screams.* TIMOTHY *takes the moon from his suitcase and hangs it on the head of the bed. He lies down and sits bolt upright listening to the sound of some traditional reels by*

Michael Coleman.

AMERICAN HEADS: Oh Rosie!
[*The sounds of traffic grows deafening.* TIMOTHY *pushes his single bed a little further into the corner. Sits on it. His case sits in front of him. Traffic stops. He hears a rustle in the far corner. Nothing. Then the bird screams.*]
VOICE: [*Off.*] God damn it Sara-Jane! [*He sits there on the bed. Dawn light comes up a little. He puts the moon back in the suitcase. He pushes the bed off. Sets out with his case.*]

SCENE 16
The Big Woman

TIMOTHY *is met by a* BIG WOMAN. *She is carrying a clothes hanger from which hangs a blue uniform. She directs him to put it on by holding it up against herself and then placing a porter's cap on his head. He dresses in the blue uniform with the woman's help. She pats him on the head. Takes out part of his hump and places it in his belly. She stands in a certain place admiring him. Then directs him to stand beside her. This is the elevator space. He is afraid of going in there. He goes in tentatively looking round him. She salutes. He salutes. She directs him to pull the gates behind him. He does. She presses a button. He falls forward. First floor – a far-off sound of geese. He falls backward. Second floor – mumbo-jumbo from films. In fright he holds her. They ascend swaying between floors in the elevator. Behind him in the sail/screen the floors go by. Then with a shudder the elevator come to a stop. An eerie silence.* TIMOTHY *is dizzy. The* BIG WOMAN *waits. Then he does what she is waiting for – opens the gates. She salutes. He salutes.*

TIMOTHY: Going up!
[AMERICAN HEADS *appear. He salutes each one. They all cram into the elevator until it is packed. All of them are grunting wildly till they enter. Then all conversation stops.* TIMOTHY *presses the button. He is in command.*] Going down! [*All sway silently as they descend. Each floor has a different sound. That*

increases and diminishes as we reach them and pass them by. First the sound of a spaceship. Then, on the fifth floor, gunfire. The fourth floor, Calypso music. Then the elevator shudders to a stop. Some AMERICAN HEADS *get off. They begin grunting wildly. He salutes them. Closes gates.*] Going down! [*At the third floor we hear a hymn. On the second floor, Hollywood sounds. The first floor is the sound of geese. Then the elevator shudders to a stop.* AMERICAN HEADS *talk wildly once they get out.*]

SCENE 17
A Date

TIMOTHY *sits on his bed shining his shoes. He has developed a small belly. He is humming the tune of* "On Broken Wings." *There's a knock of a heel on the floor.*

TIMOTHY: [*Coughs.*] Ka-ka-ka-ah-ka.

[ROSIE *enters dressed in the regalia of the 1930s. She has a tall hat with feathers on it, high heels, and a huge handbag.*]

ROSIE: My mother says you can come down to watch the television if you like.

TIMOTHY: I'm grand here. The television only makes me dizzy.

ROSIE: The television only makes him dizzy.

TIMOTHY: That's right.

[*Pause.*]

ROSIE: So where is home?

TIMOTHY: Somewhere else.

ROSIE: And then?

TIMOTHY: Ham, butter, and eggs. [*He taps his foot. She answers with a tap of heel and toe.*] Ham, butter, and eggs.

ROSIE: Ham, butter, sausages, and rashers.

TIMOTHY: Ham, butter. and eggs. Ham, butter. and eggs.

ROSIE: Ham, butter, and sausages and rashers.

TIMOTHY: Ham, butter, and eggs. Ham, butter, and eggs.

[*Pause.* ROSIE *sits on the only chair. He makes his foot stop quiet.*] Quack!

ROSIE: Quack!

[*Pause and silence.*]

TIMOTHY: What colour was your kitchen at home?

ROSIE: Peach. And yours?

TIMOTHY: Battleship grey, canary yellow, and chocolate brown.

ROSIE: Lord. [*Pause.*] Quack!

TIMOTHY: Quack!

ROSIE: Quack-quack!

TIMOTHY: Quack. [*Pause.*] And then I'd like you to take your clothes off.

ROSIE: Certainly. When I get my breath back.

TIMOTHY: I took my clothes off in Scotland. In Scotland, in the potato fields.

ROSIE: Did you indeed?

TIMOTHY: Certainly, every last stitch.

ROSIE: But you're better now?

TIMOTHY: I am, thanks be to God.

[*She lights a cigarette. Pause.*]

ROSIE: I was down in Memphis with Sara-Jane.

TIMOTHY: I didn't know Sara-Jane was down in Memphis.

ROSIE: I saw her every other day.

TIMOTHY: What was she doing down there?

ROSIE: I don't know. But you see I was in Memphis with Sara-Jane. For two whole years. Then I was in Boston and got to know everyone. Do you see all the friends I have? [*Pause.*] I have friends everywhere and you have no one. [*She puts out the cigarette.*]

TIMOTHY: Of course I don't expect you to take off everything.

ROSIE: Just the odd garter.

TIMOTHY: Oh!

ROSIE: And the slip.

TIMOTHY: Oh!

ROSIE: And the petticoat.

TIMOTHY: That would do, thank you. That would be very

convincing.
ROSIE: It would?
TIMOTHY: America.
ROSIE: Ah. America.
TIMOTHY: America. [*Nodding.*]
ROSIE: Then there's Russia.
TIMOTHY: Whisper.
[*She stands. He stands. She holds out her elbow.*]
ROSIE: That was kind of nice.

SCENE 18
The Film

ROSIE *and* TIMOTHY *sit centre stage, facing backstage as if they were at the cinema. Lights out. The screen lights up. A fiddle sounds to signal the opening of the show. They sway to the music. A brush appears hesitantly on the screen. Then it begins to paint flowers all over the screen. Two voices: both voices are pre-taped. The voices are recognisably* TIMOTHY*'s and* ROSIE*'s, but blurred and cracked as in an old soundtrack.*

LADY: I love walking the streets of Boston.
SIR: Lord above, I never.
[ROSIE *claps.*]
LADY: Like the cat I want to talk but know I shouldn't.
SIR: I'm never done talking myself though I regret all I say, even the good things, never mind the bad.
LADY: It would be alright if I was another.
SIR: Once they know who you are, you are who you are for good.
LADY: And when you tell the story of your life, you're lost in every direction.
SIR: That's right. You've given it all away.
LADY: And then there's no way back.
SIR: It's too late entirely.
[*They come to a stop.* TIMOTHY *gets up. A thunderclap.*

Pause.]

TIMOTHY: I want to go to the toilet.

ROSIE: Ah don't.

[*Voices continue.*]

SIR: I forgot something important, whatever it was, it was on the tip of my tongue. And now it's gone.

LADY: The same thing is always happening me.

SIR: And now it's gone.

LADY: I'll forgive you, Sir. I'll forgive you for what you can't remember, but what will I do with the things you can't forget?

[*They touch foreheads. Pause.*]

SIR: A stocking.

LADY: A shoe.

SIR: Oh!

ROSIE: Oh the poor fellow is love sick, God help him.

SIR: Oh.

[*Pause.*]

LADY: What's wrong?

SIR: I'm not well.

LADY: Will I lie down beside you? Would that make you better?

SIR: It might.

[TIMOTHY *puts his arm around* ROSIE. *Pinches her; a squeal from* ROSIE.]

LADY: [*The sound of a kiss.*] Are we getting older?

ROSIE: Indeed we are Mrs.

SIR: I think so. [*Pause.*] I love you.

LADY: And I love you, but . . .

SIR: Yes?

LADY: But . . .

[*The show comes to an end.* ROSIE *claps. Music stops.*]

ROSIE: It's not over, is it?

TIMOTHY: I think so.

ROSIE: What happens next?

TIMOTHY: You'll have to wait and see.

ROSIE: I'd like to see them happy. Everybody should have somebody when you come to think about it. [*Pause.*] But that was very nice, wasn't it?

TIMOTHY: Yes. I was as happy as I am now because I was then.

ROSIE: But no matter, what matter. [*Short pause.*] I have to go.

TIMOTHY: Yes.

[ROSIE *leaves slowly.* TIMOTHY *closes his case. He looks after her retreating figure. Raises a hand in farewell.*] Quack! [*Pause.*] Quack! [TIMOTHY *puts on his jacket and cap and looks in the mirror.*]

SCENE 19
Meeting Your Double

Absolute silence. TIMOTHY *is standing by the side of his bed looking stage right after* ROSIE. *Enter stage left* TIMOTHY*'s exact double with his back to* TIMOTHY. TIMOTHY *turns. He sees the figure the same size as himself with his back to him.* TIMOTHY *makes a small grunt of fear.*

TIMOTHY: Oh! [*Fearfully. The other figure does not move.* TIMOTHY *moves a little towards him.* TIMOTHY's *double turns around.*] Oh! [*Very frightened.* TIMOTHY *turns away wringing his hands. His double steps backward one step.* TIMOTHY *turns. The figure is still there.*] Oh! [*Fearfully,* TIMOTHY *turns away again and lies on the bed. He looks again and then buries his head under the pillow on the bed. His double moves further away stage left.* TIMOTHY *steals a look.*] Oh! [*Despairingly,* TIMOTHY *buries his head again. The figure moves away soundlessly.* TIMOTHY *looks up slowly and sees no one there. Immediately he blesses himself.*] May the North-West wind never blow. The chicken not get the scour. And we all be redeemed. [*He looks up to see if the figure is still there.* TIMOTHY *rises, blesses himself, and walks over to where the figure had stood. As he faces stage left, his double reappears stage right behind* TIMOTHY *and sits on the bed.* TIMOTHY *stands for a moment, relieved, looking stage left. He then turns and sees his double seated on the bed, exactly where he always sits, watching him.* TIMOTHY *screams.*] Ah!

Ah! Ah! [TIMOTHY *turns away. The figure on the bed moves away soundlessly.* TIMOTHY *looks again. Sees the empty bed. He approaches, wringing his hands. He sits where his double sat a moment before. Softly.*] Wadi? Wadi? [*Pause.*] Am I the right way up, Wadi? [TIMOTHY *puts on a middle-aged mask. Takes up his position in the elevator space.*] Going Up! [*Travels up alone in his cell. Wringing his hands and muttering. He presses the button and ascends through sounds that become increasingly frantic. First floor – geese. Second floor – Hollywood voices. Third floor – a hymn. He opens the gate.*] Going Up! [FIFTIES HEADS *enter, grunting wildly.*] Going Up! [*Fourth floor – a police siren. Fifth floor – Donald Duck squawks. Sixth floor – a swallow chirping. Seventh floor – the eerie sound of the first man on the moon. Eighth floor – a sound of explosions. Ninth floor – Verdi's "Chorus of the Hebrew Slaves." On arrival, the* FIFTIES HEADS *enter the doubles bar. The* BARWOMAN *directs them to tables.*]

SCENE 20
It's Tuesday

One light shows ROSIE *centre stage.* TIMOTHY *appears in silhouette behind the screen. A small step dance is heard off-stage.* ROSIE *listens. The small shuffle of heel and toe is heard again. She moves a little towards it. Stops. The shuffle sound comes again.* ROSIE *moves forward and listens. She gives a hard knocking of her feet in return. A small step off-stage. More hard knocking of heel and toe from her. She stop and, listens. Silence.* ROSIE *gives a small shuffle. Silence.*

TIMOTHY: [*Off.*] It's Tuesday.

[*Pause.*]

ROSIE: I know what day of the week it is, thank you. [*She does not move. His steps go around the stage. She follows the sound turning on her feet. He goes right round her again. She follows his every move. He stops.*]

TIMOTHY: Don't you want to know what happens?

ROSIE: No.

TIMOTHY: Why?

ROSIE: Aren't we grand as we are? [*Pause.*] Sometimes I think we are better off not knowing. [*In the dark he completes another circle. She follows him with her eyes.*] You've got to stop tormenting me.

[*Pause. He starts to go round her again.*]

TIMOTHY: [*Sings.*] Will you marry me? [*Pause.*] Will you marry me? Marry me? Marry me?

ROSIE: [*Sings.*] I'll marry you. [*Pause.*] I'll marry you. Marry you. Marry you. On the day of judgement.

[*Pause.*]

TIMOTHY: [*Normal.*] On the day of judgement.

ROSIE: [*Sings.*] I'll marry you. Marry you. Marry you. On the day of judgement. [*Silence. She sees and hears him begin to circle the stage again. The sound of his feet grows frantic.*]

TIMOTHY: [*Quick prayer.*] I want a baby.

WOMAN: [*Quick prayer.*] I don't want a baby.

[*He goes round again.*]

TIMOTHY: [*Quicker.*] I want a baby.

WOMAN: [*Quicker.*] I don't want a baby.

[*Silence.*]

TIMOTHY: [*Frantically.*] Ham, butter, and eggs.

ROSIE [*Reasonably.*] Ham, butter, and sausages and rashers.

[*Pause. His steps start again.*]

TIMOTHY: I beg of you.

ROSIE: Don't talk like that.

TIMOTHY: What do I have to do?

ROSIE: I don't know.

[*His steps stop. Everything goes silent.*]

SCENE 21

The Doubles Bar

The FIFTIES HEADS *are seated at their tables. The* BARWOMAN *distributes a mirror to each of them, which they look into with self-adoration.* TIMOTHY *enters the bar.*

TIMOTHY: Where am I?
BARWOMAN: You're in the Doubles Bar.
[TIMOTHY *moves among the tables, peering at the heads. They ignore him.*]
TIMOTHY: Excuse me, excuse me. Thanks awfully. That'll do nicely. [*Sits at table.*]
BARWOMAN: What can I get you?
TIMOTHY: [*Loudly.*] Give us a small one.
BARWOMAN: Say please.
TIMOTHY: Please.
BARWOMAN: Sure thing. [*The* BARWOMAN *wipes a small gold-rimmed mirror and hands it to* TIMOTHY. TIMOTHY *leaves it face down on the table then lifts it up and looks into it.*]
TIMOTHY: Oh Lord!
FIFTIES HEADS: Oh Rosie! [TIMOTHY *replaces mirror.*]
BARWOMAN: One of those days, ain't it? I don't feel so well myself.
TIMOTHY: That's right.
[BARWOMAN *approaches table.*]
BARWOMAN: Do you want another?
TIMOTHY: Give us a large one. [TIMOTHY *looks in large mirror.*] Oh Lord!
FIFTIES HEADS: Oh Rosie!
[BARWOMAN *takes mirror from* TIMOTHY *and looks into it.*]
BARWOMAN: Seems okay to me Mick.
TIMOTHY: I crashed no car in Croom.
BARWOMAN: [*Holding up the mirror.*] You want to watch that. It gets you pretty bad sometimes.
TIMOTHY: I will, thank you.
BARWOMAN: Just tell the folks I said hello.
TIMOTHY: I will. [*Nodding nervously. He moves shakily on his feet towards centre stage. Walks to the front of the stage, close to audience. He steadies himself against anything he can find.*] I

just came round to ask you one more time. [*He appeals to the* FIFTIES HEADS. *Each turns away and leaves, one by one, as he approaches them.*] No, No, don't tell me. I don't want to know. [TIMOTHY *changes his mask for a huge* OLD MAN*'s mask. He picks up his suitcase and returns to the elevator.*]

SCENE 22:
Meeting the Skeleton

TIMOTHY *is in the elevator.*

TIMOTHY: Going up! [*Slowly making his way across the space is an abnormally tall* SKELETON. *He is too tall to get into the elevator. He lifts off his head and hands it to* TIMOTHY. *Now he fits into the elevator. With* TIMOTHY *holding the* SKELETON*'s head, and the* SKELETON *holding* TIMOTHY*'s case, they ascend. They move between floors for a long time. The sound of the sea is heard. A boat engine. The sound of gulls, then more gulls, and the sound of surf. They shudder to a stop eventually. The wind is blowing. They stand there a moment. The* SKELETON *puts down* TIMOTHY*'s case.* TIMOTHY *hands him his head. The* SKELETON *puts on his head.* TIMOTHY *lifts his case. The* SKELETON *walks off slowly. At last* TIMOTHY *lifts his case. The sail is moved back into position of gable. The fireplace is wheeled on. A gale of wind sounds. When the fireplace is put back into position, the mirror is placed on the fireplace and the sail is again erected at the gable end. The space fills with wind.* TIMOTHY *opens his case, takes out the moon and places it in the fireplace.*]

SCENE 23
Wadi's Death

TIMOTHY *enters the kitchen.*

TIMOTHY: [*Shouts.*] Wadi! [*Leaves down case. Shouting and searching.*] Wadi! [*He walks out to the front.*] Wadi!

[*A woman appears.*]

TESSIE: Timothy?

TIMOTHY: Tessie?

TESSIE: Aye.

[*Pause.*]

TIMOTHY: Where's Wadi? [*She points upward. He looks up. Sits on a kitchen chair with* TESSIE *opposite him on a chair. Sings.*]

On broken wings
No bird can fly . . .

TESSIE: [*Sings.*]

And broken promises
Mean love must fade and die.

BOTH:

I trusted you.
You can't be true
My heart no longer sings
Its wings are broken too.

[*They sit there. The fire lights up. He stirs it.*]

TIMOTHY: You look to me like a sensible woman.

TESSIE: You look good, Timothy Lavell.

TIMOTHY: I'd like to be alone now, thank you.

TESSIE: And why wouldn't you. It's a long winter.

[*But* TESSIE *does not move. Lights dim.*]

SCENE 24
Home

TIMOTHY *is sitting in a baseball cap as before.* TESSIE *has relaxed into her chair. He spits happily.*

TESSIE: It's desperate weather.

TIMOTHY: It is.

TESSIE: The wind from the east would kill you.

TIMOTHY: It would.

TESSIE: It's winter here.

TIMOTHY: It's winter everywhere.
TESSIE: But the days are lengthening.
TIMOTHY: They are. They are.
[*Pause.*]
TESSIE: And was the yank in love while he was abroad?
TIMOTHY: He was. I had a girl back then.
TESSIE: It happens the best of us.
TIMOTHY: It does. [*Pause.*] She was sturdy.
TESSIE: And you left her there.
TIMOTHY: I did.
TESSIE: And now you're back.
TIMOTHY: I am.
TESSIE: Isn't life terrible?
TIMOTHY: It is.
TESSIE: Now for you.
[*Pause. Light change. Time passing.*]
TIMOTHY: But I hope to see her again.
[TESSIE *nods.*]
TIMOTHY: The air is thin in America [*Pause.*] So I've got the thin blood now.
TESSIE: So you have, and why wouldn't you.
[*Pause.*]
TIMOTHY: We built walls and then I found myself in Wall Street. [*He spits.*]
TESSIE: The Russians have a woman who is a hundred and six.
TIMOTHY: They should send her to the moon.
TESSIE: It's a mystery.
TIMOTHY: It is. And so is the Parthenon.
TESSIE: That would be a wall in Greece.
TIMOTHY: It was once upon a time. But not any longer. They have one in America now. Yes. Getty came and took each stone across by plane and built her again in Washington Free State. The Parthenon.
TESSIE: Now.
TIMOTHY: I saw it seven times. Seven times. [*He spits.*]
[*Light change. Passing time.*]

TESSIE: Will there be rain?
TIMOTHY: Ask the radio.
TESSIE: Will there be wind?
TIMOTHY: There's always wind. There's even wind in the Bronx.
TESSIE: I'm sorry to hear that.
[*Pause.*]
TIMOTHY: Courage! Courage!
TESSIE: What?
TIMOTHY: A dying man told me that. Courage! he said to me. Courage!
[*Pause. Light comes down till only the moon in the fireplace glows. They move in closer.*]

SCENE 25
Last Days

The fire is lit low.

TIMOTHY: Come in Bernie.
[BERNIE *enters stage left.*]
TESSIE: In this world you can choke eating a sweet.
BERNIE: Yiz.
TIMOTHY: And it might be the only sweet in the house.
TESSIE: The wind is turning.
BERNIE: Yiz.
TESSIE: You should put a cap on that chimney.
BERNIE: Yiz.
TESSIE: The draught is something terrible. I can find it up my skirt. You'd get your death. [*Pause.*] I told this man here he should get the electricity in.
BERNIE: Yiz. Oh yiz.
TESSIE: Do you know what it is? The light? The electric light? It's the light from heaven. When I step into my mobile all I have to do is reach out my hand and I can tell where I am.
BERNIE: Yiz.

TESSIE: Oh but some people.
TIMOTHY: Haven't I the fire?
TESSIE: Happy Christmas.
TIMOTHY: Many happy returns. [*Pause.*] I saw things.
TESSIE: And the sea is still coming in and out.
[*Pause.*]
ALL TOGETHER: Oh Rosie.
[BERNIE *moves off to the left. The other two follow him.* TESSIE *edges to the right. The other two follow her. Then all three tighten in round* TIMOTHY. *They sit there a moment. The wind in the chimney starts. It grows fierce. The gable sail shakes.* TESSIE *gets up and shakes hands with* TIMOTHY. BERNIE *gets up and shakes hands with* TIMOTHY. BERNIE *swings open the fireplace and the two enter it. Then the fireplace swings shut.*]

SCENE 26
The Fireplace

TIMOTHY *is kneeling barefoot where he was before, when we left him at the end of the first scene. Something rustles. He edges forward on his knees. Something rustles to his left.*

TIMOTHY: Oi! [*Nothing.*] Come out whoever you are! [*Wind hits the gable wall.*] You'll get that. [*Pause.*] You'll get that between three and seven. [*Wind strikes it again. A white light reaches through the gable sail hitting him. Then it passes.*] Between three and seven is the worst for this kind of thing. [*Pause.*] That's it now, thank you. [*Pause.*] Immmm Wadi. [*Pause.*] Immmm Wami. [*The draught in the chimney grows. The gable grows white again. It passes. The rustling starts again.*] Oi! [*He gets up slowly. Looks towards where the rustling was.*] I'll sit down again, thank you. [*He sits again.*] That's what you get when you haven't the light. [*He begins to sway gently in his seat.*] All manner of beasts. [*He continues to sway looking into the fire.*] Going up! [*He stops swaying. Pause.*] Quack!

[TIMOTHY *begins swaying in the chair again. The wind in the chimney dies.*] Quack!
[TIMOTHY *turns off the yellow moon of light in the fireplace.*]

END

On the Ramparts

First performed by the Drogheda Youth Theatre at the Droichead Arts Centre, Drogheda, in 1994. Directed by Dermot Healy.

CAST

FIGURE 1	female
FIGURE 2	male
FIGURE 3	female
GUIDE	
JIMMY	
LOUISE	
CAVAN	
MAGELLA	
AMANDA	
MARY ANNE	
DRUMMERS	
A FIFE PLAYER	
NUN	
PRIEST	
SHARON	
MUSICIAN	plays Irish horn or didgeridoo

SCENE 1

Darkness. A single light, needle-like, strikes the floor stage right. It jumps a fraction forward, grows in intensity, and then wanes. Indian bells sound, then the sound of rain, and finally the single beat of a stick on wood. As the first light wanes, small lights gradually come up over FIGURE 1 *(female),* FIGURE 2 *(male) and* FIGURE 3 *(female). They are situated stage left, in a half-circle, with* FIGURE 1 *separated somewhat from the other two. The three figures wear flat masks with minimal features and large mouth openings. They are seated in three stone-coloured partitions. They cannot see each other. They all wear black. At an appropriate moment, after a beat of stick on wood,* FIGURE 1 *moves her foot,* FIGURE 2 *moves his arm, and* FIGURE 3 *moves her head. Silence.* FIGURE 1 *and* FIGURE 2 *raise their arms onto their laps.*

FIGURE 1: Is he there?

[FIGURE 3 *knocks on partition separating her from* FIGURE 2. *She knocks again.* FIGURE 2 *does not move.*]

FIGURE 3: Still away unfortunately.

FIGURE 1: Not there.

FIGURE 3: No.

FIGURE 1: Oh. [*They raise their other arms. Incline heads.*] What time are we in?

FIGURE 3: Late spring I think.

FIGURE 1: A while to go yet.

FIGURE 3: Yes.

FIGURE 1: Every year it seems to get longer.

FIGURE 3: I would have liked an opening overhead.

FIGURE 1: Yes.

FIGURE 3: To see the clouds.

FIGURE 1: Yes. [FIGURE 2 *inclines his head.*] See if he's there now.

FIGURE 3: Again?

FIGURE 1: Please.

[FIGURE 3 *knocks once.*]

FIGURE 3: No, nothing.

FIGURE 1: Nobody.

FIGURE 3: No.

FIGURE 1: Oh.

[*A beat of stick on wood.*]

FIGURE 3: There it is again.

FIGURE 1: What?

FIGURE 3: Listen,

FIGURE 1: I'm listening.

FIGURE 3: Did you hear it?

FIGURE 1: No.

FIGURE 3: But you must.

FIGURE 1: No. I was dreaming. I had a dream in which my mother flew. Like a bird. Then she began to fall and I ran to catch her. [*Pause.*] But I couldn't waken up. [*Pause.*] Then there's my nose. My nose runs. It's terrible.

[FIGURE 2 *suddenly jerks his head.*]

FIGURE 2: Where are we?

FIGURE 3: Late spring.

FIGURE 2: I thought so. And the light?

FIGURE 1: Over there – to the right.

FIGURE 2: Yes, I see it. [*Pause.*] So it has not reached you yet?

FIGURE 1: No.

FIGURE 2: My poor lady.

FIGURE 3: It must be awful for you. If you were where I am now, you could, like I can, feel him touch your hair, softly.

[FIGURE 1 *inclines her head forward.* FIGURE 2 *and* FIGURE 3 *inclines their heads towards each other.*]

FIGURE 1: Are you touching her?

FIGURE 2: Yes.

FIGURE 1: Right now?

FIGURE 2: Yes.

FIGURE 1: Where?

FIGURE 2: Her hair.

FIGURE 1: And then?

FIGURE 2: Her cheeks.

FIGURE 1: Her cheeks and her hair?

FIGURE 2: Yes.

FIGURE 1: Oh God. [*Pause. Nobody moves.*] Is he touching you still?

FIGURE 3: Yes.

FIGURE 1: Oh God. [FIGURE 1 *moves her head from side to side.*]

FIGURE 2: One of these days I'll make it across to you.

FIGURE 3: You always say that but never do. [*Pause.*] I don't think it will ever happen.

[FIGURE 1 *goes still.*]

FIGURE 2: Let us begin.

FIGURE 1: Now?

FIGURE 2: Yes.

FIGURE 1: But I'm not ready.

FIGURE 2: It's time.

FIGURE 1: No, not yet.

FIGURE 2: If we wait any longer they'll come.

FIGURE 3: Wait . . . I wish to compose myself.

FIGURE 2: No.

FIGURE 3: A while longer please.

FIGURE 2: Now. [FIGURE 2 *freezes, head forward.* FIGURE 3 *freezes, head forward.*]

FIGURE 1: Can it be over already?

[FIGURE 1 *freezes, head forward.*]

[*Lights down. A tap of the stick on wood, the sound of rain, and the Indian bells.*]

SCENE 2

A radio tuned to RTÉ Radio 1 breaks into the silence. Lights up. Sound grows louder as a crowd of tourists from Drogheda enter the tomb. One fellow in leather gear is carrying the radio. Others wear personal stereos. A GUIDE *leads them into the chamber.*

GUIDE: Will you please, please switch off that radio? [JIMMY *switches off the radio.*] You are now in the innermost chamber where on the morning of the winter solstice a beam of sunlight enters through the roof ledge at the entrance and shines down along the passageway, eventually reaching the recess over there. [*She stands aside reaches up to a switch.*] We can now give you an artificial demonstration of what happens here in the chamber. [*She hits switch, place plunges into darkness.*]

LOUISE: Where the fuck are we?

[*Light comes on, pencil light, stage left. In it stands* CAVAN. CAVAN, *finding himself in the spotlight, immediately makes a grand balletic gesture.*]

MAGELLA: Lovely.

GUIDE: Would you please step out of the light? [*Light now strikes the three figures.* GUIDE *switches it off. Darkness a moment.*]

AMANDA: Jimmy Reynolds, take your hand off my bum.

[*Lights come up.* GUIDE *steps forward.*]

GUIDE: Would you now please follow me.

[*The crowd moves back the way they came in.* LOUISE *goes over and sits on* FIGURE 1*'s knee.* AMANDA *peers into* FIGURE 3*'s eyes.* JIMMY *lies on the ground.* CAVAN *moves stage left and coughs violently.* MAGELLA *and* MARY ANNE *stand centre stage looking round.*]

MAGELLA: That place was weird. [*Pause.*] Hey, Jimmy. Jimmy!

JIMMY: [*Taking off earphones.*] Yeh?

MAGELLA: Give us a fag.

JIMMY: I don't have any. I gave them to Amanda. Amanda, give Magella a fag.

AMANDA: They're all gone. I gave them to Louise.

LOUISE: But I don't smoke.

MARY ANNE: Since when?

LOUISE: Yesterday.

JIMMY: Louise.

LOUISE: Yeh?

JIMMY: What's the name of that dog?

LOUISE: What dog?

JIMMY: The brown fellow.
LOUISE: I don't know that dog.
JIMMY: Yes you do. He hangs out with those guys.
LOUISE: I don't remember. Ask Mary Anne. She knows all about the dogs round Drogheda.
JIMMY: Hey, Mary Anne.
MARY ANNE: Aye?
JIMMY: Have you ever been to the Canaries?
LOUSIE: What do you mean asking her has been to the Canaries?
JIMMY: What's wrong with that?
LOUISE: That's not what you asked me.
MARY ANNE: Why – have you been to the Canaries?
LOUISE: No.
MARY ANNE: Then what's the problem?
LOUISE: The dog.
MARY ANNE: The dog. What dog?
LOUISE: His fucking dog. The one he says hangs around the place.
MARY ANNE: Oh that dog.
JIMMY: You know him?
MARY ANNE: I do. Certainly. That's Buttercup.
JIMMY: Buttercup – there you are, do you see?
LOUISE: See what?
JIMMY: She knows the animal.
LOUISE: What has that got to do with the Canaries?
JIMMY: Fuck all.
MAGELLA: Lovely. [AMANDA *sneezes loudly*.] God bless you.
AMANDA: It's all the fields of rape in the Boyne valley. They have me destroyed.
JIMMY: It's not the fields of rape.
LOUISE: This place makes me want to go to the toilet.
JIMMY: I know what you mean.
MARY ANNE: I know what you mean but the grass is wet.
JIMMY: Oh yeh.

[MAGELLA *tours the space*.]

MAGELLA: I don't know like. I get this weird feeling.

AMANDA: So do I. [*She sniffs loudly.*]

MAGELLA: [*Touching mask of* FIGURE 1.] Do you think could they talk like us?

LOUISE: Why wouldn't they? They were only people like you and me.

JIMMY: Grunt – that's all those fuckers could do.

MARY ANNE: Like that Newcastle band?

LOUISE: What band?

MARY ANNE: You know.

LOUISE: I don't know.

AMANDA: Is it the Bald Scullions?

MARY ANNE: Will you cop yourself on Amanda.

AMANDA: I was only asking.

MARY ANNE: Oh God, what is it. Hey, Cavan. Cavan.

[CAVAN *lifts off his earphones.*]

CAVAN: Ha?

MARY ANNE: Who are those crowd from Newcastle?

CAVAN: The Neanderthals.

MARY ANNE: That's right. The Neanderthals

MAGELLA: Oh Cavan knows everything. Don't you.

JIMMY: Ah Magella, don't start.

MAGELLA: [*Louder.*] Start what?

JIMMY: For fuck sake.

LOUISE: Magella?

MAGELLA: [*Sharply.*] Yes?

LOUISE: Take it easy.

AMANDA: Yes, that's right Magella, take it easy.

MAGELLA: Oh God.

[*Pause.* AMANDA *sneezes furiously.*]

JIMMY: Jesus. That hit me.

AMANDA: [*All serious.*] Do you know that a sneeze hits you at a hundred miles an hour?

JIMMY: I can well believe it.

AMANDA: That's why after you sneeze that you feel so tired.

MAGELLA: [*Walking around.*] I don't know like. I was at home above in the house, feeling low, or something like. You know what I mean? So, no problem, I'm getting out. And wait till

I tell you. When I step outside, who's coming up the street? [*Steps in front of* CAVAN.] Who else but Sharon McEntee. She keeps moving. Like you know Sharon. She's flying. So "Hallo Sharon," I say. And do you know what happened? [*She looks at* CAVAN.] She walked by me as if I didn't exist. Can you believe that? "Sharon," I called after her. But she never turned. Not once. She just went walking on. [*Nobody says anything.*] Isn't that strange?

JIMMY: Yeh, it's fucking bizarre.

MAGELLA: Who's speaking to you?

LOUISE: Ah Magella, don't.

AMANDA: That's right, Magella, don't.

[*The beat of stick on wood.*]

MARY ANNE: Did you hear that?

LOUISE: Hear what?

MARY ANNE: There was something.

LOUISE: I heard nothing.

AMANDA: Neither did I.

MARY ANNE: Well I heard something odd.

LOUISE: Stop that Mary Anne.

MARY ANNE: My father says this place lights up at night.

JIMMY: What does he think it is – Luciano's?

MARY ANNE: Will you be serious?

AMANDA: That's right, will you be serious, Jimmy Reynolds?

JIMMY: So what did it sound like?

MARY ANNE: I don't know.

JIMMY: For fuck sake.

MARY ANNE: I'm telling you.

JIMMY: That's it. [*He jumps to his feet.*]

LOUISE: What?

JIMMY: I'm away out of here.

LOUISE: Yeh, let's split.

AMANDA: Yeh, that's right, let's split.

[MAGELLA *crosses over to* CAVAN.]

MAGELLA: Why do you think Sharon went by me like that?

CAVAN: Look Magella, I can't say.

MAGELLA: Oh can't you?

JIMMY: I said I'm away out of here.
LOUISE: Hey, Magella?
MAGELLA: Yeh?
LOUISE: We're going.
MAGELLA: Well work away.
LOUISE: I said we're going.
MAGELLA: Well go on.
AMANDA: That's nice.
MARY ANNE: She's always like that.
LOUISE: Just leave her.
AMANDA: Yes, just leave her.
MAGELLA: Yeh, what harm. [MAGELLA *sits. The others leave.* CAVAN *stands by.*] Cavan?
CAVAN: Yeh?
MAGELLA: Sit down.
CAVAN: You want me to sit down? [*Sits.*] Now Magella, I'm sitting down.
MAGELLA: Give me your hand.
CAVAN: You want my hand – here's my hand.
MAGELLA: Give me your two hands.
[*Off-stage, a shout comes.*]
LOUISE: Hey, Magella.
MAGELLA: Piss off Louise. [*Pause.*] You know what I think Cavan?
CAVAN: What?
MAGELLA: I think Sharon fancies you, you jammy fucker.
CAVAN: Ha-ha-ha, go on, Magella.
MAGELLA: And she thinks you're after me.
CAVAN: Well I'm not after her.
MAGELLA: Aren't you?
CAVAN: No – I'm not.
MAGELLA: So why were you hanging round Loughlin's yesterday?
CAVAN: I was up there with the lads.
MAGELLA: Sharon was there.
CAVAN: Was she?
MAGELLA: Yes she was.

CAVAN: I suppose she might have been.

MAGELLA: You didn't see her?

CAVAN: I didn't notice her.

MAGELLA: You know what Cavan?

CAVAN: What?

MAGELLA: You're a fucking liar.

CAVAN: Ah Magella.

MAGELLA: Don't "ah Magella" me! Don't give me that crap. I know what you're at. [*Pause.*] She was above with you in McHugh's last night, wasn't she?

CAVAN: I wasn't in McHugh's last night.

MAGELLA: Were you not?

CAVAN: No. I was in McPhail's.

MAGELLA: It must have been your brother.

CAVAN: That's right.

MAGELLA: If I find out it was you I'll break your face, Cavan.

CAVAN: Right Magella.

MAGELLA: You hear me?

CAVAN: I do. [*Pause.*] We better get out of here. [*He coughs violently.*]

MAGELLA: If you let me down I'll strangle you. Your name will be shit round this town, you hear! Next time you come looking for your hole, remember that! [*She turns away from him.*] If Sharon McEntee thinks she'll walk by me without a word the bitch has another think coming.

CAVAN: Okay.

MAGELLA: Okay.

[*Pause. Shout from off-stage.*]

JIMMY: Hey Cavan, what's the story?

CAVAN: Coming Jimmy.

MAGELLA: If you tell anyone what I said . . .

CAVAN: I won't.

MAGELLA: You promise?

CAVAN: I do.

MAGELLA: [*She approaches him flirting.*] Did you know that a baby's larynx is in a different place after it's born, and then it moves slowly for up to two years round the back of your mouth till a chamber is formed – [*She touches his cheek, then his neck.*] – just there, and there – and this chamber is full of echoes – [*She touches his lips.*] – and the larynx sits up in its new position and then you can talk. [*She goes round him tantalizingly.*] That's why – [*She takes his arm.*] – you can't talk after you're born. The larynx is in the wrong place. Did you know that?

CAVAN: No, I did not.

MAGELLA: Well there you are. That's why the human being can talk. We are the only animal in the whole world this happens to. Isn't it marvellous?

CAVAN: Did you hear that on the box?

MAGELLA: I did.

CAVAN: The box is great.

MAGELLA: It is.

CAVAN: Aye.

MAGELLA: I saw what-do-you-call him on the box the other night. That fellow is great. All he has to do is move his face and I'm away.

CAVAN: Aye.

[*They begin to leave space.*]

MAGELLA: Cavan?

CAVAN: Majella.

[*Pause.*]

MAGELLA: Oh never mind.

[*Darkness.*]

SCENE 3

Light strikes floor. Jumps, brightens, wanes. The Indian bell, the sound of rain, the tap of a stick on wood. Lights go up over the three figures. A foot moves, a hand moves, a head moves.

FIGURE 1: Is he there?

[FIGURE 3 *knocks twice on partition.*]

FIGURE 3: Still away unfortunately.

FIGURE 1: Nobody?

FIGURE 3: No.

FIGURE 1: Oh. [*Pause.*] And the time?

FIGURE 3: And the time? Early summer I think.

FIGURE 1: A while to go yet.

FIGURE 3: Yes.

FIGURE 1: It's a long way back.

[*Pause.*]

FIGURE 3: I can smell pine needles.

FIGURE 1: I can smell nothing at all but ash.

FIGURE 3: When they made the niche – [*She taps her mask.*] – in my skull, the last thing I heard were pine needles falling in. They fell in – very green – like rain. [*Pause.*] Then flowers came.

FIGURE 1: [*Painfully.*] Ah.

FIGURE 3: What's wrong?

FIGURE 1: My nose runs. [*Pause.*] See if he's there.

FIGURE 3: Again?

FIGURE 1: Please.

[FIGURE 3 *knocks once on the partition.* FIGURE 2 *stirs.*]

FIGURE 2: I had a terrible dream. And there they were. In their inconsequence. Their pettiness. The living torment me in my sleep.

FIGURE 3: It was only a dream.

FIGURE 2: And always the same voices. The same names. Always the same. [*Pause.*] What time of the year is it?

FIGURE 3: I can smell pine needles.

FIGURE 1: I can smell nothing at all but ash. Ashes, soot.

FIGURE 3: Early summer.

[FIGURE 2 *inclines his head towards* FIGURE 3. FIGURE 3 *inclines her head towards him.* FIGURE 1 *inclines her head forward.*]

FIGURE 1: Is he touching you?

FIGURE 3: Yes.

FIGURE 1: Right now?

FIGURE 3: Yes.

FIGURE 1: Where?

FIGURE 3: My hair.
FIGURE 1: And then?
FIGURE 3: And then?
FIGURE 1: Yes.
FIGURE 3: He stopped.
[*Pause.*]
FIGURE 1: He stopped?
FIGURE 3: Yes.
FIGURE 1: Oh God.
FIGURE 2: Because it's time.
FIGURE 1: Already?
FIGURE 2: Yes.
FIGURE 3: Not yet please.
FIGURE 2: Now, immediately. [*He bows his head, freezes.*]
FIGURE 1: Is he gone?
FIGURE 3: Yes. [FIGURE 3 *bows her head, freezes.*]
FIGURE 1: Oh. [FIGURE 1 *bows her head, freezes.*]
[*Lights down. A stick tap on wood, the sound of rain, and the Indian bells.*]

SCENE 4

The DRUMMERS *start thunderously making their entrance through a door on the right which is held open till all have entered. Taking up position throughout the space they begin the sequence. Low lights flash on and off, but nothing and nobody is made distinct. The pace of the drumming increases. It slows for the playing of "Lillibullero" by the* FIFE PLAYER. *Back to* DRUMMERS. *The sequence travels from one drummer to another. It reaches a climax, then falls. A side door opens, and slowly the entire band exits stage right. They drum a military tap. When door closes, the space immediately goes into a deafening silence and darkness.*

SCENE 5

A pencil light strikes, jumps, brightens, wanes. Indian bell sounds, then the sound of rain, then the tap of a stick on wood. Lights rise over the three figures. A hand moves, a leg moves, then a head.

FIGURE 1: Is he still here? [*Lifts arm. She knocks at the timber partition. She knocks again. He does not move.*]

FIGURE 3: Still away.

FIGURE 1: Nobody there.

FIGURE 3: No.

FIGURE 1: Oi! [*Stretches legs, stretches arms.*] What time of the year are we in?

FIGURE 3: [*Ponders.*] Late summer.

FIGURE 1: Are you where you were before?

FIGURE 3: I am.

FIGURE 1: But there is a little while to go yet?

FIGURE 3: Yes. I wish it did not have to happen all in a single day.

FIGURE 1: Please see if he's there.

FIGURE 3: Now?

FIGURE 1: Yes. [FIGURE 3 *knocks once on partition.*] Is he there?

[*No reply.* FIGURE 2 *inclines his head towards* FIGURE 3. FIGURE 3 *inclines her head towards* FIGURE 2. FIGURE 1 *inclines her head forward.*]

FIGURE 2: Is this your neck?

FIGURE 3: Yes.

FIGURE 2: And this?

FIGURE 3: My breast.

FIGURE 1: Your breast?

FIGURE 3: Yes.

FIGURE 1: He touches your neck and breast?

FIGURE 3: He does.

FIGURE 1: Oh God.

[*Pause.*]

FIGURE 2: Someone comes.

FIGURE 3: Already?

FIGURE 2: Yes. They are nearly among us. [*He bows head, freezes.*]

[FIGURE 3 *bows head, freezes.*]

FIGURE 1: Just one moment longer. Another word. One more word. A single word. [FIGURE 1 *listens to the silence, then she bows head, freezes.*]

[*Lights down. The tap on wood, the sound of rain, the Indian bell.*]

SCENE 6

Into the space comes a NUN *bearing a candle.*

NUN: [*In a whisper.*] Your grace. [*She moves round the space.*] Your grace. [*She lights a further candle and places it in front of* FIGURE 1.]

PRIEST: Yes sister, I'm here. [*A priest, with long hair, appears. He has been lying backstage. He wears the long priestly collar of the seventeenth century.*]

NUN: Father, you frightened me.

PRIEST: I was sleeping.

NUN: But why are you in the dark?

PRIEST: Because these heads terrify me. It is unsettling here. [*Pause.*] I thought I might retire with my books and candle to a hut somewhere in some mountain or wood, not to this godforsaken place.

NUN: They search for you everywhere Father. Not a soul can walk outside their homes but they're questioned. Some say you're in France, others that you've gone to Rome. [*She lights further candle.*]

PRIEST: And here I am in this hole in the earth. While I sleep these figures torment me. Is it not ironic that I should be driven to seek refuge in a pagan site?

NUN: You must eat Father.

PRIEST: I have no appetite.

NUN: It will only be for another few days.

[*He moves towards* FIGURE 2.]

PRIEST: Another few days and I think I will lose my senses.

NUN: The people ask after you constantly.

PRIEST: They do? Sometimes I think the storm will never pass.

Tell me sister, is the wind blowing above?

NUN: The wind blows. The grain has been harvested.

PRIEST: Ah. [*He looks into* FIGURE 2*'s face.*] See the gouged eye, the disembodiment. The sheer lust. [*He goes closer.*] Look at the head. Look at the face. It might as well be my face.

NUN: You must not despair Father.

PRIEST: Why was this place left standing when others are long gone?

NUN: The people are superstitious.

PRIEST: It's good that the people are superstitious. Otherwise I might not be alive. I will leave with you today.

NUN: But Father, the countryside teems with infantry.

PRIEST: I would be with the people. What good is it for me to be here, listening to the incessant whispering – I would rather take my chance among the living.

NUN: If that is your wish, Father.

PRIEST: It is.

NUN: Maybe your grace is overwrought?

PRIEST: I am over-nourished and sad. My belly has grown slack. [*He walks the space in front of the figures.*] I feel I have been in this place before. This cell under the earth. Or maybe it is that I will be here again. [He pauses.] The thoughts I have will not render themselves up as words. [*He blows out candle in front of* FIGURE 1.] Last night in my sleep I dreamed that this tomb was being flooded. The waters of the Boyne were pouring down through the entrance. And I could not wake. [*He walks the space holding candle.*] And when I did wake, it was as if something terrible had happened. It was as if I no longer had a physical presence. My body had been taken from me. [*He lifts his chalice from its place.*] And still there I was – a poor human breathing faintly in the dark.

NUN: You frighten me, Father.

PRIEST: I'm sorry. I'm frightening myself. [*He kneels behind him, she kneels.*] Give me strength against despair. Pity us who are driven into the dark. Light up the way I implore you.

NUN: Amen.

[*They rise, bearing candles they leave. She goes on ahead. He*

waits a moment in the space. Then blows his candle out.]
[*Darkness.*]

SCENE 7

A pencil light darts forward, jumps, brightens, wanes. The Indian bells sound, then the sound of rain, then a single tap on wood. A hand moves, a leg moves, a head moves.

FIGURE 1: Is he still here?
FIGURE 3: [*Knocks once on the partition.* FIGURE 2 *does not move.*] Still away.
FIGURE 1: What time of the year is it?
FIGURE 3: Autumn, I think.
FIGURE 1: A little way to go yet.
FIGURE 3: Yes.
FIGURE 1: See if he's there.
FIGURE 3: So soon?
FIGURE 1: Yes.
FIGURE 2: I'm here.
FIGURE 1: I can't see you.
FIGURE 2: Just try.
FIGURE 1: I can't.
FIGURE 2: Look up. Look up. Look up high. Do you see me now?
[FIGURE 1 *looks up.*]
FIGURE 1: No.
FIGURE 2: My poor lady.
[*Silence.*]
FIGURE 1: Is he touching you?
FIGURE 3: No.
[*Pause.*]
FIGURE 1: Now?
FIGURE 3: No.
FIGURE 1: Oh. [*Pause.*] Are you touching him?
FIGURE 3: Yes.

FIGURE 1: Right now?
FIGURE 3: Yes.
FIGURE 1: Oh God.
[*Silence. The sound of rain ceases.*]
FIGURE 3: I think it's over already.
FIGURE 1: Already?
FIGURE 3: Yes. [*She immediately stiffens.*]
[FIGURE 1 *stiffens in her turn.* FIGURE 2 *moves frantically.*]
FIGURE 2: Where is the light? [*Silence.*] Has it reached you yet? [*He stiffens.*]
[*Lights down. The tap on wood, the rain, the Indian bells. Darkness.*]

SCENE 8

SHARON *stands stage right, smoking. She's wearing a baseball cap, white runners, and black skintight tights.* CAVAN *enters.*

SHARON: What kept you?
CAVAN: I had a problem with the bike.
SHARON: Oh excuse me. You bring me all the way out here, and then keep me waiting for over an hour?
CAVAN: Look, I'm sorry Sharon.
SHARON: Why couldn't we just meet in town?
CAVAN: There would be no problem with that whatsoever.
SHARON: So why here?
CAVAN: I thought it would be romantic.
SHARON: Don't go all soft on me, Cavan.
CAVAN: Correct me if I'm wrong, but wouldn't you say it's real, like, Pink Floyd territory, like, you know?
[*Pause. She sneezes.*]
SHARON: So what do we do now?
CAVAN: We could sit. [*They sit.*] Look at the lovely ducks.
SHARON: Wise up.
CAVAN: I was only joking. [*Pause.*] Do you see over there?
SHARON: Aye?

CAVAN: That stretch of river.

SHARON: Yeh?

CAVAN: That's where King William fought.

SHARON: What's this – a history lesson?

CAVAN: I just thought you'd like to know.

SHARON: Cavan, what's wrong with you?

CAVAN: I don't know. [*He takes off his boots.*] You know how it is. [*He looks around him.*].

[*Pause.*]

SHARON: Well?

[*He looks round him some more, then gives her a quick peck on the cheek.*]

CAVAN: You have lovely hair.

SHARON: [*Ironically.*] Ah Jiminy.

CAVAN: Are you taking the piss out of me?

SHARON: Sure I wouldn't do that to you . . .

CAVAN: There was an awful fucking crash last night at the new bridge.

SHARON: Oh yeh?

CAVAN: I swear. There was this lorry, like, and it jack-knifed and there was this Merc coming from Belfast, oh he was booting it in style, and then some fucker in a Fiat wouldn't you know, pulls up right in front of the lorry. Well he put the foot down on the brake and fuck me. Fuck me pink. The lorry jack-knifes across the road and straight into the Merc. There was blood and glass everywhere. The guy from Belfast was fairly shook. And do you know what?

SHARON: What?

CAVAN: The fucker in the Fiat just drove off as if nothing had happened.

SHARON: And someone stole their knickers off the nun's washing line.

CAVAN: What did you say?

SHARON: Nothing.

CAVAN: Jesus Sharon. You have a terrible mind.

[*Pause.*]

SHARON: Did you ever try to imagine your mother and father

at it?

CAVAN: I did not.

SHARON: Why not?

CAVAN: Jesus. You can't be thinking things like that.

SHARON: Well I do. Everywhere I go I look at people, like in the supermarket when they're paying me at the till, and I think how what must it be like for them. And I try to imagine them at it. You know Wobbler Daley and his wife. Now try to imagine her climbing up on him.

CAVAN: Jesus Christ.

SHARON: You can't. [*He shakes his head*]. I can. [*Pause.*] You're shocked.

CAVAN: I am.

SHARON: I often frighten myself with the things I think of.

CAVAN: You're making me lightheaded. [*Pause.*] I didn't know women thought like that.

SHARON: Oh but they do. All the time. You can take it from me. [*He looks round him again.*] Cavan, what are you looking at?

CAVAN: I don't know, just looking. [*Enter* MARY ANNE, LOUISE, AMANDA, JIMMY.] Oh Jesus.

JIMMY: Good man, Cavan.

CAVAN: Jimmy.

MARY ANNE: How are you Cavan?

CAVAN: Mary Anne.

LOUISE: Sharon.

SHARON: Hallo.

AMANDA: Hello Sharon.

JIMMY: So what's the story?

CAVAN: Ah you know yourself.

LOUISE: I do.

JIMMY: That's the way.

CAVAN: Yeh.

JIMMY: I love the ramparts. I always loved a walk on the ramparts. Did you Louise?

LOUISE: Yeh.

AMANDA: So did I.

JIMMY: Of course you have to be careful. You could get carried away.

MARY ANNE: Is that what happened you?

JIMMY: Go away you slapper. [*They move around annoyingly.*] Were you ever in Crete Sharon?

SHARON: No?

JIMMY: Crete is class. There's nothing like sitting out on the beach drinking Chilean wine.

LOUISE: I prefer Corfu.

MARY ANNE: Give me Skerries any day.

AMANDA: I like Balbriggan, except for the wasps.

JIMMY: What?

AMANDA: Well you see we were in the caravan, and in through the door came the wasps, thousands of them, oh there were queen bees, and king bees, and every kind of bees, and we were destroyed. I came out all in a rash. I was out like that. That's right.

MARY ANNE: I never heard of anyone went on their holidays to Balbriggan.

AMANDA: Well we did, so there.

JIMMY: Well that's that. I suppose we should be going.

CAVAN: See you Jimmy.

JIMMY: Good man Cavan.

LOUISE: See you Sharon.

SHARON: See you.

MARY ANNE: Ta-ra. [*Touches* CAVAN*'s head.*] Ta-ra. [*Touches* SHARON*'s head.*]

AMANDA: Ta-ra. Ta-ra.

MARY ANNE: Oh Cavan?

CAVAN: Yeh?

MARY ANNE: You didn't happen to see Magella?

AMANDA: Yes, that's right, Cavan, did you see Magella?

CAVAN: No.

MARY ANNE: Are you sure?

CAVAN: Yes, I'm sure, Mary Anne.

MARY ANNE: Well it's just that I thought you might have, like.

AMANDA: That's right.

CAVAN: Well I didn't.

MARY ANNE: No.

[*They stand there.*]

SHARON: Is there anything else?

MARY ANNE: Oh sorry Sharon, I suppose we should be going.

AMANDA: It's such a lovely day.

SHARON: Beautiful.

JIMMY: What are youse thinking of doing after?

CAVAN: We're going bungee-jumping Jimmy.

JIMMY: Ha-ha.

MARY ANNE: Well, if you see Magella will you tell her we were looking for her?

CAVAN: Yeh we will.

MARY ANNE: Thanks Cavan, you're a pet.

SHARON: Isn't he but.

MARY ANNE: Oh Sharon, you're a scream. Well ta-ra.

AMANDA: Ta-ra.

LOUISE: Bye.

JIMMY: Nice one Cavan [*Gives the thumb.*] See you Sharon.

[*They leave. The pair sit in silence.*]

SHARON: Did you ever dream of flying Cavan?

CAVAN: What?

SHARON: I mean did you ever take off in your sleep?

CAVAN: Not that I can remember.

SHARON: Well if you did, that's your subconscious thinking of sex.

CAVAN: Is that so.

SHARON: So they say.

CAVAN: And do you dream of flying?

SHARON: Me. Oh yeh. But it's not me that's flying. It's me mother.

CAVAN: Jesus, Sharon.

SHARON: It's true. My mother takes off like a bird and goes thrashing round the sky.

CAVAN: Dear God.

SHARON: And just as she's about to fall I wake up. Just as I'm rushing to save her I wake. [*Pause.*] You should meet my

mother sometime. [*Pause.*] Cavan – what do you like in a woman?
CAVAN: Oh I don't know.
SHARON: Try, just for me.
CAVAN: Well, I like it if she laughs a lot.
SHARON: That's not what I'm talking about. I'm talking about her body.
CAVAN: Oh.
SHARON: Yes.
CAVAN: Her body.
SHARON: Yes, her body.
CAVAN: I like nice hands.
SHARON: You can do better than that.
CAVAN: Hair, I like long hair.
SHARON: And?
CAVAN: Ah you know.
SHARON: You're fierce innocent.
CAVAN: So what do you like in a man?
SHARON: Do you really want to know? [*Pause.*] I like a nice, round, solid, firm bum.
CAVAN: Oh.
SHARON: Something to hold onto – don't you know – in the dark. [*Pause.*] What does Magella like in a man?
CAVAN: How would I know?
SHARON: Ah Cavan. You never asked her.
CAVAN: No.
SHARON: Maybe I should ask her myself.
[*Pause.*]
CAVAN: I think we better go on.
SHARON: So soon?
CAVAN: Yeh.
[*She moves on a little.*]
SHARON: I'll go on first. You stay there a while.
CAVAN: Okay.
[*She moves further on.*]
SHARON: See you Cavan.
CAVAN: See you Sharon.

[*She leaves.* CAVAN *stays in position. He looks after her. Lights down slowly.*]

SCENE 9

Tinkle of Indian bells, then the sound of rain, followed by the beat on wood. The needle light appears, jumps, brightens, wanes. Lights gradually up on the three figures. A leg moves, a hand moves, a head moves.

FIGURE 1: Is he there? [*Knocks quickly.*] Still away. Nobody.
FIGURE 3: Nothing.
FIGURE 1: Oh.
FIGURE 3: I know.
[*Pause.*]
FIGURE 1: Try again.
FIGURE 3: So soon?
FIGURE 1: Yes.
FIGURE 3: [*Knocking quickly.*] No, nothing.
FIGURE 1: The whole thing is a mystery.
FIGURE 3: I wouldn't dwell on it.
[*Pause.*]
FIGURE 1: Is he gone forever?
FIGURE 3: I don't know.
FIGURE 2: [*Without moving.*] Has the light reached you yet?
FIGURE 1: No.
FIGURE 2: Ah my poor lady.
[*Pause.*]
FIGURE 1: Is he touching you?
FIGURE 3: No.
FIGURE 1: Are you touching him?
FIGURE 3: No.
FIGURE 1: You do not touch each other?
FIGURE 3: No.
FIGURE 1: Oh God.
FIGURE 3: It's time.
FIGURE 1: Already?

FIGURE 3: Yes.
FIGURE 1: Just us two?
FIGURE 3: Yes.
FIGURE 1: Without him?
FIGURE 3: He has already begun.
FIGURE 1: Ah.
[*Silence. Lights Down.*]

SCENE 10

MAGELLA *stands stage right, looking off.*

MAGELLA: Sharon McEntee. [*Silence.*] Sharon McEntee, I know you're in there. I want to speak to you. Do you hear me? [*Pause.*] I'm going to stay here till you come out – even if that means staying here all fucking night – do you hear me – all fucking night! [*Pause.*] Who do you think you are! [*Aside.*] Bitch! [*She paces space.*] I know what's going on. Do you think I came down with the last shower of rain? [*Screams.*] Sharon!
[LOUISE *appears.*]
LOUISE: Magella.
MAGELLA: Piss off Louise.
LOUISE: You're making a fool of yourself.
MAGELLA: What do I care.
LOUISE: The whole street can hear you.
MAGELLA: Well let them.
LOUISE: He's not worth it.
MAGELLA: Who said he was?
LOUISE: No man is.
MAGELLA: Oh you'd know, wouldn't you? Well listen, I don't give a damn about him. It's me I'm thinking about.
LOUISE: Then leave it.
MAGELLA: No.
LOUISE: Please Magella.
MAGELLA: Sharon! [*She screams.*] Sharon!
[SHARON *steps out. Silence a moment.*]

SHARON: It's all right Louise you can go.

[LOUISE *looks at both of them then goes.*]

SHARON: Hallo Magella.

MAGELLA: What's going on between you and Cavan?

SHARON: Nothing.

MAGELLA: Nothing?

SHARON: No, nothing.

MAGELLA: Are you sure?

SHARON: I am.

[*Pause.*]

MAGELLA: Did he ever touch you?

SHARON: No.

MAGELLA: Are you sure?

SHARON: Yes.

MAGELLA: Never?

SHARON: He kissed me once.

MAGELLA: Where?

SHARON: On the cheek.

MAGELLA: He kissed you on the cheek?

SHARON: Yes.

MAGELLA: Oh God. [*Silence.*] But that's all?

SHARON: Yes.

MAGELLA: And did you love him?

SHARON: A little.

MAGELLA: Oh God. [*Silence.*] Will you promise me something?

SHARON: If I can.

MAGELLA: Will you promise me . . .

SHARON: Yes?

MAGELLA: Will you promise me you'll leave him alone?

SHARON: I can't.

MAGELLA: Sharon, please.

SHARON: I can't promise you.

[*Silence.*]

MAGELLA: This is terrible.

SHARON: I'm sorry. [*Silence.*] What do we do now?

MAGELLA: I want you to stay there. Right there, do you hear?

SHARON: I hear you.

MAGELLA: Don't move.

SHARON: I won't.

[MAGELLA *leaves the space.* SHARON *stands mid-stage, unmoving.*]

MAGELLA: [*Off-stage.*] Cavan! [MAGELLA *walks on.* CAVAN *follows.*]

CAVAN: Sharon.

SHARON: Cavan.

MAGELLA: I told him you wanted to see him.

SHARON: Why?

MAGELLA: Just because.

SHARON: Because what?

MAGELLA: I want him to choose between us. Because I want to know.

SHARON: Why can't you leave things as they are?

MAGELLA: You might be able to live like that, but I can't.

SHARON: Well, see if he's there.

MAGELLA: Cavan! [*No reply.*] I wouldn't be surprised if he's took off.

SHARON: Try again.

MAGELLA: Cavan! [CAVAN *returns.*] Well?

CAVAN: Whenever I stand in a toilet I get filled with sorrow and regret.

MAGELLA: For fuck sake.

CAVAN: But it's true. I hear voices when I go to the toilet.

SHARON: What sort of voices?

CAVAN: Ordinary voices, yeh they're ordinary voices, whispering things, whispering names like: "Is that you Charlie! Charlie! Philip! Philip, come here! Sidney! Sidney! Spare the rod!" [*Silence.*]

MAGELLA: That's brutal, Cavan.

CAVAN: It is. The whole thing is a mystery.

SHARON: I wouldn't dwell on it.

[*Pause.*]

MAGELLA: Well.

CAVAN: I can't. [MAGELLA *goes to her knees and hammers floor with her fists.*] Magella.

MAGELLA: Don't you speak to me, do you hear! I don't want to hear you say another word.

[*He looks at* SHARON. *She looks away.* MAGELLA *stands. The three stand there,* SHARON *stage right,* CAVAN *centre stage,* MAGELLA *stage left.*]

CAVAN: It's getting late.

MAGELLA: The winter is coming.

SHARON: It is.

MAGELLA: It's going to piss from the heavens.

CAVAN: It's time we went inside.

SHARON: Do we have to?

CAVAN: No.

SHARON: Well let's stay a moment longer, okay?

MAGELLA: Okay, just a moment longer.

CAVAN: Sure.

[*The three of them stand there. The lights come down. Three musicians move mid-stage and look towards the light. The musicians move back to their seats. The three figures move slightly; then an arm moves, a leg moves, a head. The light on them comes up slowly, and they lift their heads towards it. The three figures now lift up three large mirrors. The light grows in intensity. The mirrors flash the light at the audience. When the light is at its fullest, a* MUSICIAN *plays two minutes on the Irish horn or didgeridoo. At end of the blast of music the lights goes off. The three candles continue to burn. There is whispering and stirring amongst the three figures. Then slowly each of them lifts off their mask, leans forward, and blows out the candles. Darkness. The tap of a stick on wood, the sound of rain, the Indian bell.*]

END

Last Night's Fun

First performed in Ennis, Co. Clare, in February 1996 by Theatre Omnibus, Ennis. Directed by Dermot Healy.

CAST

GLORIA	a housewife
DECLAN McINERNEY	Gloria's husband
MOTHER	Declan's mother, Maggie

Set: Minimal in all aspects. Two apartments, one large, one small, with an illusory wall between the two spaces acting as both a door and a mirror. The large room is referred to in the text as Room 1, and the small room as Room 2. In Room 1, extreme stage right, is a bed that closes up against the wall and becomes another mirror. Downstage of Room 1 is a table, and a cooker sits at the side of the bed. Its cooking rings are musical. Also a cupboard containing cutlery, plates and various musical instruments. Room 1 also contains a variety of domestic appliances that turn into musical instruments, e.g. pots and pans, etc., which are all roped together and operate via an overhead pulley. One chair, referred to in the text as the Weeping Chair, sits stage left in the front Room 1. Room 2, the "granny flat," contains MOTHER*'s armchair, a tall ashtray, and an imitation window that can be moved round the walls like a picture. A small radio sits on the floor by the armchair. In each room various objects hang overhead: in Room 1, a clothes hanger; in Room 2, a handbag, a hat, etc.*

Style: No character looks at the other except where there are explicit directions to do so. The action takes place simultaneously in both rooms. All movements are choreographed by sound. Audience participation may or may not take place. Workshops prior to performance would allow a group of five or six performers to sit among the audience. These performers may be conducted from the stage to play various instruments at particular moments, giving single notes, melodies and discordant tunes. In the absence of audience participation, allowance has been made for the actors themselves to create the same musical text on stage. Therefore, what instruments the performers in the audience might use must be duplicated on stage, whether hanging from wire or elsewhere, and played accordingly. So the text contains possibilities for audience participation or its alternative. This means any tune or note in the text where audience participation is expected to occur is repeated on stage. The text should be read with this in mind. All the characters appear as musical notes and announce themselves through certain instruments.

ACT I

A faraway funeral dirge is heard on the radio in the darkness. As lights come up on Room 2, MOTHER *is in her chair, with her back to the audience listening. Lights up on Room 1.* GLORIA *is lying on the bed in a blue dress, dreaming. Music ends.* MOTHER *turns off her radio, shrugs her shoulders, and settles. Silence. Off-stage,* DECLAN *clears his throat and bangs a gong.* MOTHER *rises off her chair a fraction then sits again.* GLORIA *looks up immediately. She rings her Indian bell in reply. Then she dutifully climbs out and sits on the edge of the bed, with her head in her hands and her bell at the ready.* DECLAN *clears his throat again, and sounds the gong.* GLORIA *replies with Indian bells and* MOTHER *moves in consternation.*

MOTHER: [*Shouts.*] Alright, I hear you. [MOTHER *blows whistle in late reply. Both women move simultaneously towards the partition as if it were a mirror.* MOTHER *in bed coat,* GLORIA *in her blue dress.* MOTHER *makes precise movements, while* GLORIA*'s movements are bouncier. They face each other directly through the illusionary mirror and put on their make-up.* MOTHER *looks at* GLORIA, *a younger version of herself.*]

GLORIA: Good morning Mrs McInerney. [*Happily.*]

MOTHER: Good morning to you, Mrs McInerney. [*Tiredly.*] [GLORIA *turns her mouth into a smile with a sweep of lipstick.* MOTHER *starts to put make-up on her face, turning her lips and eyebrows downwards.* GLORIA *touches a lash of her eyes.* MOTHER *corrects her.* GLORIA *does the movement differently,* MOTHER *nods. Off-stage* DECLAN *coughs. Now* GLORIA *and* MOTHER *face each other completely.* GLORIA *looks forward at the reflection of her eyes.* MOTHER *does the same.* DECLAN *coughs. They look closely into each other's eyes, then they freeze a moment.*] You look just like I did.

GLORIA: Thank you mom.

MOTHER: It's nothing to be thankful for. [MOTHER *indicates a further secret.* MOTHER *faces audience.*] They leave you, you know. [DECLAN *leans his head in further.*] They get up and go and that's the end of it and you never see them again. [*Immediately they click off the lights, put back their make-up kits, and* GLORIA *backs off.* MOTHER *heads back to her chair assuming a weary posture, and sits with her back to audience as before. Meanwhile,* GLORIA *puts on her slippers and awaits the gong with her Indian bells cocked.* DECLAN *coughs, bangs the gong;* GLORIA *rings her bell; and* MOTHER *blows her whistle. This is done three times. Then* GLORIA *sits herself in the weeping chair, does sad finger-movements;* DECLAN *puts the gong away in his briefcase and bangs it closed. At this signal she leaps to her feet and awaits him on her toes with an extraordinary smile.* DECLAN *enters* MOTHER*'s room. He is wearing a black suit with no tie over long johns.*]

DECLAN: Mother. [*He bows.*]

MOTHER: Aye Declan. [*She remains seated.*] So what's the word?

DECLAN: Nocturnal? [*About to go on.*]

MOTHER: No. [DECLAN *stops and turns.*] Not at all.

DECLAN: [*He rotates his finger in the air.*] Uncanny?

MOTHER: That's it. It's uncanny. The older you get the more like him you become. On you go.

[*He steps into Room 1 through the mirror partition.*]

DECLAN: Gloria.

GLORIA: Honeybun! [GLORIA *does a great leap in the air to greet him.*] *Then they both look in different directions and hurry off there. He drops his briefcase with a bang. Meanwhile, she slips the sheet off the bed, cracks it in the air, while he dusts his suit jacket with a flourish and hangs it up overhead. As she settles the sheet on the table, he opens his briefcase, takes out the gong, and taps it softly – which is the signal for* GLORIA *to speak.*] What is it?

DECLAN: It's the nights.

GLORIA: Ah.

DECLAN: The days are bad enough. I can take the days, but

the nights, the nights are the worst. [DECLAN *puts the gong on the stool.* GLORIA *taps the cooker in reply.*] That's right. [GLORIA *shakes a pan of peas.*] That's right, that's right. [*He stands a moment pondering, and making circles in the air.* GLORIA *hits a blue pot.*] There are quite a few missing consonants you know. [*She lifts the bed up.*] Quite a few, you understand. [GLORIA *gives three taps.*] And I don't like saying this.

GLORIA: No?

DECLAN: I don't.

GLORIA: Then don't.

DECLAN: [*Bewildered.*] What key are we in?

GLORIA: [*Pause.*] I don't know.

DECLAN: You don't.

GLORIA: No.

DECLAN: There it is again – that infernal negative. That word "no." [*Strikes gong.*] And worse is "don't" . . . [*Strikes gong.*] . . . and then there's "do." [*Strikes gong and puts it down on table.*] Oh yes, Oh yes, there's always "do." [MOTHER *shakes her rattle and both look at her.*] And it's worse than "don't," Gloria.

GLORIA: So I've heard.

DECLAN: [*He takes off his trousers as he speaks.*] But you know what I believe – well I'm inclined to think, but of course I'd never say it, not a whisper, but as a matter of fact – I'm sure that Audrey is, I'm certain, it's apparent to everyone, that Audrey is back on the drugs.

GLORIA: Oh.

DECLAN: [*Lifts hand for iron.*] And Muriel too.

[MOTHER *rings her bells impatiently and both look at her. During the above exchange* DECLAN *takes off his trousers, shakes them once, twice, and then lays them on table. And while he irons his suit very methodically on the table,* GLORIA *checks that everything is ready. He is in long johns.*]

GLORIA: I was thinking of getting a bigger fridge.

DECLAN: No, don't do that. [*Bang of iron.*] *She throws down a corkscrew. She hits the blue pot, hits the plates twice, and then hits the top of the blue pot. She repeats these actions.*] What's wrong with an old fridge? [*Bang of iron.*] The old fridge is too small. [GLORIA *hits the top of the blue pot, the plates, and the side of the blue pot twice.*] The new fridge will be too loud. [GLORIA *taps the side of the blue pot and hits the notes C and B on the musical cooker*]. Yes, that's right. [GLORIA *bangs plates and rattles wood.*] No, I don't mean that. That's not what I meant at all. [GLORIA *taps cooker and pots, and taps a bottle of wine with the corkscrew.*] That's it. You see I don't like the sound those freezers make. Dum! Dum! It's not right. [*Pause.*]

GLORIA: It's better than living in London.

DECLAN: Maybe. [*Pause. He goes over and tests the pulley rope.*]

GLORIA: Are you anxious?

DECLAN: No.

GLORIA: Are you under pressure?

DECLAN: Not at all. [*Pause.*] It's just that I'm qualitatively distinct.

GLORIA: No, you're not.

[*Pause.*]

DECLAN: [*Bangs iron.*] For a moment there I thought I was.

GLORIA: [*Pause.*] Is it the hardware?

DECLAN: Maybe. Anyway they're only words. Only words, Gloria. [*He waves his finger in the air.*]

[*They look at each other and smile. She hands him the wine bottle. He tries to pull the cork – a series of sounds emanate from the audience – he gives up on the cork. The audience sounds stop. He leans in and offers the bottle to* MOTHER. MOTHER *waves a negative hand in the air. He hands the bottle to* GLORIA. *Audience sounds start again. Eventually she pulls the cork out.* MOTHER *blows on her whistle. Audience sounds stop. This is the signal for* MOTHER *to rise, and she enters through the mirror in the partition.* DECLAN *is hanging up his trousers very correctly while* GLORIA *is busy in the kitchen.* MOTHER *enters with the same high step as her son through the partition.*]

MOTHER: I missed the deaths.

DECLAN: You did.

MOTHER: I did. I missed the deaths. I was too late. I'd just switched the transistor on and they were gone. All I could hear was that other fellow whose voice I don't like – whatever you call him, spouting more misery.

DECLAN: You'll hear it on the nine o'clock.

MOTHER: By then it'll be too late. They'll all be gone whoever they were. To hell, no doubt, where all the quality go. [*Pause.*] And how was your day?

DECLAN: Night Mother.

MOTHER: Night then.

DECLAN: Wonderful.

MOTHER: I'm glad to hear it. Us two dolls were above in Nelly's. Then we went to Freddie's.

DECLAN: Freddie's? Who's Freddie?

MOTHER: Ah now. [GLORIA *chortles.*] That'd be telling. [MOTHER *chortles.*]. He's a new class of a man in town. Where was I? Had a sup there and a chat and what-have-you. And on then to John's.

DECLAN: Is that so.

MOTHER: After that we stopped in to see Josie.

DECLAN: Did you.

MOTHER: And then we came home. [*She goes to sit in the weeping chair.*]

DECLAN: Don't sit there Mother.

MOTHER: Why?

DECLAN: You won't like it.

MOTHER: Why?

DECLAN: It only upsets you.

MOTHER: [*Studies chair.*] If you say so.

[*They watch her every move as she leaves the room and when she turns to look at them they look away.* MOTHER *exits mournfully. She sits in her chair with her back to the audience. She rattles her ash tray and lights a cigarette, which is the signal for them to begin next rapid exchange. During this exchange* GLORIA *starts preliminary cooking,* DECLAN *sets the table, and* MOTHER *smokes. Polite musical notes are exchanged that grow increasingly frantic.*]

DECLAN: The boss was in.

GLORIA: He was?

DECLAN: Indeed he was. [*Plate.*]

GLORIA: And did you speak? [*Taps musical cooker.*]

DECLAN: "Good night McInerney," he said, and "How are we?" "We are fine, sir," I said. "Tip-top, dandy." [*She bangs plates.*] "No anxiety?" he asked. "None," I said. "Good McInerney, very good."

GLORIA: And that was all?

DECLAN: That was it. [*Gloria shakes peas.*] Except I saw him look at Audrey most peculiarly. [*He waves his finger in the air as usual.*] And then he stopped at Muriel's desk and said "And how is our in-tray today, Miss Currid?" [GLORIA *bangs plates.*] "How is our in-tray today?" And do you know what she said? [*Pause.*] She said . . .

GLORIA: Yes?

DECLAN: She said . . . [*Pause.*]

GLORIA: Yes? [*Taps plates.*]

DECLAN: She said . . .

GLORIA: Yes? [*Adjusts hair.*]

DECLAN: "Do you believe your own propaganda, Mr Jenkins?"

GLORIA: She did not. [*Taps music.*]

DECLAN: She did.

GLORIA: And he said?

DECLAN: "What do you mean Miss Currid. What exactly do you mean?" [*He taps spoons.*]

GLORIA: Go on.

DECLAN: And she said, "Well look outside sir, it's nights, Mr Jenkins. Nights. [*He taps spoons.*] And he said nothing, not a word, he just passed right on through. [*Pause as he politely taps gong.*] Gloria, Gloria, time to tidy, Gloria. [*He watches her. She advances to pull the pulley, stands beside it, then suddenly she hauls all the pots and pans overhead. Meanwhile, next door,* MOTHER *rings her bell. The pots shake to and fro;* DECLAN *listens. Next-door, the pots sound is a cue for* MOTHER *to rise and dress for dinner. As she does so, she tinkles the bell and ashtray. MOTHER puts on her hat and fur coat, and waits for exchange next-door to end.* DECLAN *taps a spoon.*] What key are we in?

GLORIA: C?

DECLAN: Ah-ha! [*He shakes his head. Taps spoon.*] And now?

GLORIA: D?

DECLAN: No Gloria. [*Places spoon.*] We were in D and now we're in C.

GLORIA: We are?

DECLAN: [*Places spoon with a triumphant tap.*] We were.

GLORIA: Oh.

DECLAN: Yes. [*Finger in air.*] Perfect, Gloria.

MOTHER: [*Shouts.*] Are we going to get a bite to eat in this kip or not?

DECLAN: Coming Mother. [*He places plates on the table and nods to the audience who commence meal-setting sounds. Meanwhile,* GLORIA *tinkers with a love theme as she plays music on the cooker, one-two-three, me-him-her, in rhythm with his movements. The sequence is brought to a halt when* GLORIA *bangs a pot on the line. The bang stops the audience sounds. Silence.* DECLAN *runs a stick over the assorted pots overhead.* GLORIA *follows him. The sequence ends when* DECLAN *gives three bangs on the best-sounding overhead pot. This is the signal for* MOTHER *to blow on her whistle.*]

MOTHER: I thought you'd never call. [*She enters.* DECLAN *and* GLORIA *enter with a new wild flurry.* MOTHER *waits patiently, listening. Meanwhile,* DECLAN *corrects some of the overhead pots and pans, waving his finger to* GLORIA, *while she answers from the cooker.*]

DECLAN: Now that's not right. Not quite correct. [*Tap.*] Yes that's better. [*Tap.*] Now see. [MOTHER *listens until* GLORIA *stops the chaos with four strikes on wood.*]

MOTHER: How long must this go on, I ask myself.

[*All turn and look at each other, then head off in their various directions, which in fact may take some time until they find their orientation. Eventually* MOTHER *seats herself at the table. He sits.* GLORIA *offers wine to* MOTHER. *Hands over glass.*] No, thank you. I always maintain you should never take a drink till the news is over. [GLORIA *returns with a pot of hard beans which she spills into vessel. She returns to the cooker. He lifts out a mouth organ, plays a short tune while* GLORIA *looks at him and* MOTHER *looks away.* MOTHER *raises a hand to stop him playing.*] I do not know why we have to listen to that confounded instrument.

GLORIA: Well I like it.

MOTHER: So did we all, once upon a time.

[GLORIA *sits.* DECLAN *gives out spoons, then plates. They exchange plates and tap them to find what note they're in. Eventually each of them finds their own plate.* DECLAN *gives the opening note on a tuning fork, and they all start eating. The audience contribute an ensemble of bizarre sounds. As they eat, each sound is magnified, and the eating builds to a crescendo.*]

DECLAN: Stop! [*Raising hand to audience. All sound stops, including that from the audience.* MOTHER *and* GLORIA *look at* DECLAN *in wide-eyed astonishment.*] The potatoes are lovely.

GLORIA: Are they?

DECLAN: I think so.

MOTHER: May we return to our culinary efforts?

DECLAN: You may.

[*They all return to eating in their own particular style.* MOTHER *beats out a rhythmic sound and she is accompanied by her section of the audience; then* GLORIA, and *she is accompanied by her section; then* DECLAN, *and he is accompanied by his section. The whole thing works up to a wild climax, and then there are three endings: first,* GLORIA *finishes her meal, and the others continue; then* MOTHER *ends hers; finally, they wait on* DECLAN *to finish but he goes on accompanied by his section of the audience.* GLORIA *and* MOTHER *stare at* DECLAN*; he stops, but his section of the audience continues to play. He signals for them to stop. They* *stop. A single sound continues.* DECLAN *stands up. The single sound stops.* DECLAN *sits.*] There's nothing like a cup of tea.

MOTHER: So what are we having for dinner?

[GLORIA *belches. Then silence. The three of them sit like an orchestra that has just finished playing a symphony, with their hands on their stomachs, full.* DECLAN *taps the table with his tuning fork, signalling that conversation may begin.*] Gloria?

GLORIA: Mum?

MOTHER: Would you have pig in England?

GLORIA: Pig?

DECLAN: Pork, Mother.

MOTHER: Pork, then, if you must. Would you have pork?

GLORIA: Oh yes, sometimes.

MOTHER: And sprouts, would you have sprouts?

GLORIA: Yes Mum.

DECLAN: Of course she'd have sprouts.

MOTHER: But the Eskimos loved deer. Morning, noon and night. [*Pause.*] And there's a thing I love best of all, there's an item, the turnip, the plain turnip, would you have it?

GLORIA: Perhaps not.

MOTHER: There's a hypnotist just moved in down the street.

GLORIA: Now.

MOTHER: He can cure anything. Everything under the sun. He learned it in Korea off a guru where he was learning kung fu. The wife does tai chi and the children are in St Brigid's. And Nelly, thank God, is on the mend. [*He turns away.*] Now listen – listen here – all he has to do is look into your eyes. And you'll stop whatever you're at. Declan.

DECLAN: Mother.

MOTHER: You should go to him.

DECLAN: Why should I go to him? There's nothing wrong with me.

MOTHER: Then why are you walking about the house at all hours?

DECLAN: Thinking.

MOTHER: Thinking of what?

DECLAN: Just thinking.

MOTHER: Well I went to him, a Mr Godfrey – Geoffrey Godfrey – yesterday, yesterday it was. The back room was lit up like a shrine and you left your shoes at the door. I'd been to see Nelly and I thought why not. It was Nelly put it into my head. So there I was and I heard from your father. [*He stands.*] He told me there's promotion coming your way.

DECLAN: Is that so.

MOTHER: Certainly. But you must – must – come in the front door. Do you understand – the front door.

DECLAN: Yes Mother.

MOTHER: Whatever you do you must come in the front door. "He must straighten his back," your father said, "Tell him he must straighten his back." So there. [DECLAN *lifts a newspaper from the drawer, looks in the mirror, and straightens his back. Puts the newspaper under arm.*] So you're off to the toilet.

DECLAN: I am.

GLORIA: Declan likes to read in the toilet.

MOTHER: [*Bitterly.*] So did his father.

[DECLAN *steps through the mirror in the partition, walks into the other room.* MOTHER *holds out her plate.* DECLAN *holds out his newspaper.* GLORIA *holds out the teapot. They all break into song.]*

ALL: Oh . . . .

Oh the song of the toilet.
Oh the song of the toilet.
Oh the song of the toilet.
And the world beyond this one.

[DECLAN *sits into the armchair, furls open the newspaper with his back to the audience, and reads intently. He studies the crossword.* GLORIA *pours water from a jug into another vessel.* MOTHER *taps it underneath with a spoon, producing an upward sound.*]

DECLAN: What's another word for dispute?

GLORIA: How many letters?

DECLAN: Nine.

GLORIA: Have you got any?

DECLAN: No.

GLORIA: Oh.

[*The women fill a second vessel and* DECLAN *begins cursing.*]

DECLAN: Anything?

GLORIA: No.

DECLAN: Oh.

[*The ladies fill a third vessel.* DECLAN *keeps cursing.*]

MOTHER: Yes, so did his father. [DECLAN *stops mumbling and listens.*] He'd be off to the toilet with the newspapers once upon a time. Whatever he could lay his hands on and he'd be off. A great reader was his father. [DECLAN *recommences mumbling.*] Then this malady set in. [*Mumble.*] He was perplexed. [*Louder mumble.*] Some aberration, you see, my dear. [*Mumble.*] Then along came the day when he left the newspapers behind. He knew all they had to say. He went to the toilet alone. That's a bad sign.

GLORIA: It is?

MOTHER: It is. Always make sure that fellow of yours brings a book.

GLORIA: I will.

MOTHER: Or at least a magazine. Anything.

GLORIA: Yes Mum. [GLORIA *gets up to go. Mumbling rises.* MOTHER *calls her back with a stern finger.* DECLAN *stops mumbling and cursing and inclines his head to listen.*]

MOTHER: They go out through that door and they never come back. [*Stern whisper.*] You mark my words.

GLORIA: Don't say that Mum.

MOTHER: His father was sitting there in that chair. [*She points to weeping chair.*] And he says to me, "Maggie," he says, "I'll go down to see Mickey Foran, it's time I was off to a neighbour's house." A neighbour's house. [DECLAN *recommences mumbling and cursing.*] What does that mean, daughter? [*The ladies rise.* GLORIA *holds a bucket.* MOTHER *empties the three vessels into the bucket, tapping each as before with a spoon, getting a downward sound.* DECLAN *mumbles and curses loudly and, moves uncomfortably on the toilet.* MOTHER *puts a finger in her ear.*] I have a tick in my ear I think. [GLORIA *bangs the bucket lid.* DECLAN *rises and looks back into armchair to study its contents, folds his newspaper, and prepares to return.*]. I'll go next door and write a letter maybe. Who knows? [*She finds herself facing her son on his return through the partition mirror. They look at each other.*] Oh dear.

DECLAN: Mother?

[GLORIA *bangs bucket on floor.*]

MOTHER: I often think the wrong things without meaning to.

DECLAN: It'll pass. [DECLAN *steps aside.* MOTHER *enters Room 2. He enters Room 1. Single bell from audience. He stands perplexed.* MOTHER *stands perplexed.* GLORIA *stands perplexed.*] That was them.

GLORIA: The bells?

DECLAN: Yes.

GLORIA: Again?

DECLAN: Yes.

MOTHER: [*In Room 2.*] There are no bells.

DECLAN: I hear them.

MOTHER: There are no bells. It's extraordinary. Your father once heard a mouth organ that wasn't there either. That was when it started. [*Looking into Room 1.*] Above in the Yukon. [*Back into Room 2.*] I loved it there. [*Moves on into Room 2.*]. The Yukon was grand except for the mouth organ. [DECLAN *tidies plates,* GLORIA *collects her make-up and stool, and* MOTHER *takes off her hat and coat.* GLORIA *takes off her smiling face and she makes up her night face.*] Declan.

DECLAN: Yes Mother.

MOTHER: Come in and move the window.

DECLAN: Yes, Mother. [*He moves window.*] Is that alright?

MOTHER: A bit more to the right. [*He moves window.*] A little bit more. [*He moves window.*] That'll do nicely. [MOTHER *moves her chair to face the window. She sits, then leaps up, looks into Room 2 and blows her whistle.*] Someone has been using my telephone. There are numbers here on my bill I never ever heard of. [MOTHER *goes back to her armchair and begins muttering.* DECLAN, *in turn, begins muttering.* GLORIA *continues to put on make-up in front of the mirror. Lights in both rooms dim imperceptibly. Muttering stops.* MOTHER *taps the radio. After the same mournful dirge, we hear the death notices.* MOTHER *lifts her handbag and takes out a small white purse. She then takes out her nail varnish, and lights up a cigarette.*]

ANNOUNCER: The family of Willie Farrelly wish you to pray for the repose of their husband and father who departed this world, this morning, the 15th of November, at Our Lady's. [*Pause.*] Mary O'Sullivan, late of Harmony Hill, at St John's. The remains will be removed to Our Lady of Lourdes, this evening, 7 o'clock. [GLORIA *sits by the mirror and watches* MOTHER *carefully.*] Paddy Geraghty, Ballinfull, Maugherow, aged 92, who died peacefully in his sleep, at his residence. Mourned by his sisters Beezie, Mary and Nelly. The funeral mass will take place tomorrow at 11 o'clock in St Johns, followed by the burial in Maugherow Cemetery. [GLORIA *watches* MOTHER.] Joe Brady, Milk Harbour, this afternoon, suddenly. May God have mercy on his soul. The removal will take place tomorrow at 6.30 to St Daphne's Church, Grange. Miss Annie Flynn, late of Tubber, died after a long illness at her residence in Long Island, New York, on December 10th. Her relatives wish to thank all those who called to give their condolences. May she Rest in Peace. [GLORIA *freezes.*] Gerry Gray, 17, of Ballintogher, who was killed in a car crash this evening. Funeral arrangements have yet to be made. Please pray for us in our bereavement. [*The funeral dirge comes on again, and smoke spirals up from* MOTHER. *She taps the ash carefully into the standing ashtray. Funeral dirge ends.*]

[MOTHER *puts out a hand, taps radio. Sound ends. Silence.*]

MOTHER: That's that, I suppose.

DECLAN: [*Shouts.*] You should be saying your prayers, Mother.

MOTHER: [*Shouts.*] So should we all.

DECLAN: At least I have nothing to be ashamed of.

GLORIA: Yes you have.

DECLAN: What!

MOTHER: You tell him Gloria.

DECLAN: Youse are all turning against me again. [*He races into Room 2 and begins weeping.*]

MOTHER: What's wrong with you?

DECLAN: I don't know.

MOTHER: Go back into your own room and go to bed.

DECLAN: Alright.

[*Meanwhile,* GLORIA *whips off her blue dress. She is wearing a black body stocking with a cluster of sequins on it.* DECLAN *lets down the bed, whips the sheet off the table, and unfurls it over the bed. He takes hold of pulley rope.* GLORIA *skips into bed.* DECLAN *pulls the rope and the pots collapse.* MOTHER *jumps up and during her speech she moves to the window, turns her chair, and ends up facing audience.*]

MOTHER: Will you stop that racket! [*She mumbles incoherently.*] Is that all you can think about? Have you no shame? [*Mumbles more.*]

GLORIA: But Mum, we're enjoying last night's fun.

MOTHER: Well could ye not wait till I'd gone asleep at least. Oh no. [*More mumbles.*] This is it. This is it, you see.

DECLAN: Go down and pay the girls, Mother.

MOTHER: What? What are you saying? Fiend! You fiend out of hell. [*She sits.* DECLAN *takes out the mouth organ and plays a love tune.*] Not the blasted mouth organ. [*He plays on.*] Will you stop it. [*He stops playing.*]

GLORIA: But Mum, I like the mouth organ.

MOTHER: Well, I prefer the gong.

GLORIA: And I like the mouth organ.

MOTHER: Yes, but see where it gets you. [*She snorts devilishly.*] Yes, see where it gets you. I've heard all that before. [MOTHER *mumbles.* DECLAN *gets into bed beside* GLORIA. *He continues playing, coming in and out of the main love theme. He lifts his hands and conducts the audience, who join in with going-to-bed sounds. He stops the audience after a short time but he continues to play on.* GLORIA *falls asleep.* MOTHER *falls asleep.* DECLAN *plays on some more. Stops. Silence. Pause.*]

DECLAN: Are you asleep Gloria? [*Silence.*] Good. [*Pause.*] Are you asleep mother? [*Silence.*] Good. [*Pause.*] I was thinking of Muriel again, because you see it's Muriel takes the drugs now. [*Silence, and then he begins to conduct a conversation with* GLORIA *as if she was answering him.*] And Audrey's at them too. [*Silence.*] No, not me. Muriel does. Not me, I said. Not us. Not these days, no. That's right. Just Muriel and the rest of them. I see her at her desk and she's not there. They're all away. That's right. That's right. That's right. Could we afford that? Because there's quite a few missing vowels you know. By the way, who is this Freddie? [*Silence.*] I said who is this fellow Freddie? [*Silence.*]

GLORIA: I'd be glad Mr McInerney if you'd step out of the way.

DECLAN: I will.

GLORIA: And I'm not going to climb up there with you no matter what you say.

DECLAN: You don't have to.

GLORIA: Good.

MOTHER: That will be two and six, Mr McInerney, Mr Declan McInerney, thank you.

[DECLAN *lies down.*]

GLORIA: We can't do that out here.

DECLAN: Do what?

GLORIA: You know what I mean.

DECLAN: But I didn't do anything.

GLORIA: Stop it I said.

DECLAN: But Gloria.

GLORIA: Declan! In front of everyone!

DECLAN: What?

GLORIA: Put that away – immediately.

DECLAN: Ah now look.

GLORIA: Can you not see where we are?

DECLAN: No, where are we?

GLORIA: My God, in a hotel foyer. Are you mad? [*She hides beneath sheet.*] Don't move or they'll see us.

DECLAN: Gloria?

GLORIA: Declan.

DECLAN: Will you be coming out soon?

GLORIA: Are they gone?

DECLAN: Who?

GLORIA: The bus queue.

DECLAN: [*He looks around.*] Yeh.

GLORIA: Are you sure?

DECLAN: I'm certain. [*Pause.*] Honestly, they're gone. [*Pause.*] I swear there is not a soul.

GLORIA: How could you ask me do that and everyone looking?

DECLAN: Sorry about that.

GLORIA: And so you should be. Now how do we get out of here? Well?

DECLAN: I'm thinking.

GLORIA: Is that all you can say? We can't lie naked here much longer. [*Whispers.*] Where are my knickers?

DECLAN: They're on you.

GLORIA: [*Shrill whisper.*] No they're not. You took them. Now you can go and get them back.

DECLAN: Right now?

GLORIA: Yes.

DECLAN: Okay. [*He steals out of the bed. Stands by the table, wondering. The rhythm of the following exchange gets faster and faster as he puts on his suit.*]

GLORIA: Did you find them?

DECLAN: [*Putting on trousers.*] I'm looking.

GLORIA: Be quick!

MOTHER: Declan – Declan McInerney.

DECLAN: Yes Mother.

MOTHER: I'm not your Mother you fool. You must be dreaming. I'm your wife. And I want you to get back into bed beside me immediately.

DECLAN: I'm coming.

MOTHER: You're letting the draught in.
DECLAN: Just a minute.
MOTHER: What are you doing?
DECLAN: I'm fixing this bloody thing.
MOTHER: Why did we have to come up here of all places? Why?
DECLAN: [*Putting on coat.*] I don't know.
GLORIA: My knickers, Declan, or I'm never speaking to you again.
MOTHER: To the Yukon of all places.
GLORIA: My knickers.
MOTHER: The Yukon by God. [*Lifts briefcase.*]
GLORIA: And everyone looking.
MOTHER: I want to go home.
DECLAN: What key are we in? [*Lifts gong.*]
MOTHER: I said I want to go home.
DECLAN: We will.
MOTHER: But first.
DECLAN: [*Puts case on table.*] Yes?
GLORIA: The Manager is coming.
MOTHER: Get back in here beside me.
GLORIA: The Manager is coming I said.
MOTHER: What are you doing?
GLORIA: My knickers Declan.
MOTHER: Get back in, I said.
[*He strikes gong.* MOTHER *starts awake.* GLORIA *wakes. Both ladies look at him.*]
GLORIA: Declan – are you alright?
DECLAN: Perfect.
MOTHER: Ask him what is he doing out at this unearthly hour of the night.
DECLAN: I was looking for something.
GLORIA: What are you doing dressed?
[*He lifts his finger in the air.*]
DECLAN: Am I on nights or am I on days?
GLORIA: Your nights are over.

MOTHER: You're on days.

DECLAN: Are you sure?

GLORIA: Yes.

DECLAN: Oh.

GLORIA: Come to bed Declan.

DECLAN: I will. [*Tick-tocks from one person starts.*] The clock is dripping into the sink. Can you hear the ticks? [*The tick-tocks start getting stronger and stronger.* GLORIA *is lying down and* DECLAN *is standing up facing the audience. More members of the audience join in.* DECLAN *stops the audience with a wave of his hand.*] The shop is in rag order. I say the shop is in rag order.

GLORIA: Well it's not my fault.

DECLAN: [*Shouts.*] Is it raining?

MOTHER: [*Shouts.*] Call in the dog and see if he's wet.

DECLAN: Yes, that's right, that's right. [*Ticking starts again, grows louder.*] Stop! [*Ticking stops. He climbs into bed. Immediate darkness.*]

[*In the dark the gong sounds, then the Indian bells, and then the whistle. Again the gong, and finally the Indian bells.*]

[*End of* ACT 1.]

ACT 2

Darkness. The whistle blows from MOTHER*'s room. Lights up on Room 1 and 2.* MOTHER *is seated, back to audience, in her armchair, as before. There is no reply from Room 1.* MOTHER *mumbles to herself. In Room 1* GLORIA *and* DECLAN *are in bed under the sheet. The couple move together in bed to the left.* MOTHER *whistles again. A small tinkle on the Indian bells in reply from* GLORIA. *The couple move to the right.* MOTHER *awaits a reply from* DECLAN. *None comes. She curses.* MOTHER *rises. Gets up with hat, coat, and bag.* GLORIA *and* DECLAN *move again to the left, then to the right.* MOTHER *mumbles* *harshly, then steps into Room 1.* GLORIA *and* DECLAN *are lying haphazardly across the bed.* MOTHER *studies them. Raises her shoulders. She pulls the pulley sharply.*

DECLAN: [*Raises his head sharply.*] Hallo.
MOTHER: Time to get up.
DECLAN: Hmmm. [*Lays his head down again.*]
MOTHER: Declan.
DECLAN: Hmm.
MOTHER: Declan McInerney.
DECLAN: Yes.
MOTHER: Get up.
DECLAN: [*Raises up his head.*] Why?
MOTHER: You're on days.
DECLAN: I'm on nights. [*Down goes his head.*]
[*She pulls pulley.*]
MOTHER: You're on days.
DECLAN: [*Up head.*] No I'm not. [*Down head.*]
MOTHER: Get up.
DECLAN: I can't.
MOTHER: You get up now Declan McInerney.
DECLAN: I can't. I want more sleep. I need to sleep more.
MOTHER: It's past eight.
DECLAN: [*Looks up.*] What key are we in?
MOTHER: I said it's past eight.
DECLAN: [*Drops head.*] I don't care. [*Lifts head.*] Go down and pay the girls.
MOTHER: What?
DECLAN: I said go down and pay the girls.
MOTHER: What?
DECLAN: I said go down and pay the girls. [*Drops head.*]
MOTHER: What are you talking about?
DECLAN: Never mind. I'm staying here.
[MOTHER *pulls the pulley.*]
MOTHER: Declan!
DECLAN: No.
MOTHER: Please.

DECLAN: I can't.

MOTHER: You mean you won't. If you weren't trudging round the house at all hours this wouldn't happen. Get up.

DECLAN: No. I'm staying here with Gloria.

MOTHER: Well do as you please. [*She moves forward.*]

DECLAN: I will.

MOTHER: And you won't go in the front door.

DECLAN: [*Up head.*] No. [*Down head.*]

MOTHER: Even though your father told you.

DECLAN: [*Up head.*] Yes.

MOTHER: Well it's a shame. A crying shame.

DECLAN: [*Down head.*] Hmm.

MOTHER: Hmmm! [*Pause.*] Gloria. [*Sharply.*]

GLORIA: [*Lifts head.*] Yes Mum.

MOTHER: Will you tell honeybuns that if he does not get up this very minute I'm going to sit in the weeping chair.

GLORIA: Declan.

DECLAN: Yes. [*Tiredly.*]

GLORIA: You heard what Mum said.

MOTHER: I said I'm going straight across to that chair.

DECLAN: Don't do that Mother. [*Lifts head.*]

MOTHER: I will. [*The both look at her, sheet to their chins, as she advances towards chair.*] I'm there. [*Pause.*] I said I'm there. And I'm going to sit down. [*Pause.*] You don't care for me at all.

GLORIA: Yes, we do.

MOTHER: You'll be sorry when I'm gone.

DECLAN: I know.

MOTHER: Well have it your own way. [*She sits in the weeping chair. She gives a few heart-felt tears. Moans. Goes into an extraordinary lament.* GLORIA *and* DECLAN *look over the sheet at her. Then* MOTHER *stands.*]

DECLAN: Are you back to yourself?

MOTHER: I am, but no thanks to you. [*They look at her as she goes. She turns, and they look away.* MOTHER *re-enters Room 2. Sher taps her musical ashtray, which is a signal for* GLORIA *and* DECLAN *to lie down again. They make assorted love and sleep sounds. Audience joins in with small snatches of love sounds.* MOTHER, *mumbling to herself, takes off her hat, hangs it overhead, then hangs bag, and is about to put her coat away when she hears love sounds from the sleepers next door.* MOTHER *blows whistle quite severely.* GLORIA *jumps up and tiredly sits on the bottom of the bed.* MOTHER *rings her bell.* GLORIA *gets out of bed and* DECLAN *immediately returns to sleep, making snoring sounds.* GLORIA *stands askance, her hands on back of* MOTHER'*s chair, listening to him do assorted moans.*]

GLORIA: Declan! [DECLAN *does not heed her and continues sleeping.*] Declan!

DECLAN: What?

GLORIA: The bed. [*She points. Reluctantly he gets up, mumbling, and lifts the bed to the wall. He looks into the mirror.*]

MOTHER: Declan.

DECLAN: What?

GLORIA: The window. [DECLAN *goes into Room 2 and moves the window for* MOTHER *as she turns she her chair to face the stage left wall.*]

MOTHER: More. [DECLAN *moves the window.*] More.

DECLAN: Will that do?

MOTHER: [*Glances out window.*] Yes.

DECLAN: Will there be anything else Mother?

MOTHER: No thank you. [DECLAN *returns to Room 1.* GLORIA *directs him to be ready to pull the pulley, while she goes over to the weeping chair.* GLORIA *wrings her hands in sorrow.* MOTHER *sits in her armchair.* DECLAN *pulls the overhead pulley, and both women leap up and advance to the partition mirror to put make-up on. Meanwhile,* DECLAN *throws the sheet over the table, making cursing sounds as he does so.*] Good afternoon to you, Mrs McInerney.

GLORIA: And good afternoon to you, Mrs McInerney.

MOTHER: What's wrong with him?

DECLAN: I'm sick.

MOTHER: Sick, is it? [*Does her lips.*] Is the frontal lobes? [*Does *her eyes.*] The lack of serotonin?

DECLAN: Pardon?

MOTHER: Has he worms? [GLORIA *laughs.* MOTHER *laughs.* DECLAN *imitates her laugh. He flicks the sheet harshly, cursing.*] Have you worms? [*Laughs.*] Is it the memory again? [*Laughs. Both women look into each other's eyes, then* MOTHER *goes to her chair, while* GLORIA *goes to the mirror and gets ready to commence exercise. Audience commence low weeping through otherworldly sounds. Meanwhile,* DECLAN *goes quickly to the weeping chair, and wonders about it – it's like stepping into cold water in the middle of winter. Eventually he sits for a quick moment, gives a yelp of pain, and begins a period of pretend crying. With each cry from him,* GLORIA *does a step. Then freezes when he stops.* DECLAN *notices this. He does three long weeping stretches and two short ones, and each time* GLORIA *stops. Then* DECLAN *coughs. This is a signal for* MOTHER *to begin singing.* MOTHER *rises and breaks into a jocular children's song, which stops* GLORIA *exercising and stops* DECLAN *mourning. They listen to her, while she sings looking out the window.*]

Demi Carney
Went to Blarney
On a pony and trap,
He stopped the once
He stopped the twice

AUDIENCE JOIN IN:

And I don't know
What comes after that.

ALL:

And I don't know
What comes after that.

[DECLAN *immediately starts weeping again as before.* GLORIA *continues in front of the mirror with a series of exercises, ballet-style, in time to his weeping.* DECLAN *takes note of this again. When he stops weeping for a moment, she stops; when he continues, she goes on. He starts, then stops, leaving her in awkward position. He gives a few moans, and she moves. A further moan; another movement. A screech. She lands upright. A further screech, and a pirouette.* DECLAN *coughs and* MOTHER *sings.*]

MOTHER:

Mary Sherry
Lost her berry
And her father's name was Pat,
They lived on treacle
And hogweed beevil

AUDIENCE SING:

But I don't know
What comes after that.

ALL:

But I don't know
What comes after that.

[DECLAN *gives a few more moans,* GLORIA *dances to them. He goes to her but she is unaware of his presence. He lifts his leg in the air to accompany her dance. But* GLORIA *goes the other way. He tries a high step. She goes up on ballet toes. He tries to do a step with her by the mirror, twice. They stand back to back.*]

GLORIA: Oh Freddie.

[*He stops dance.*]

DECLAN: Freddie? Freddie! Who the hell is Freddie?

[GLORIA *stops, caught out, and does not know what to say. She lifts her tick-tock clock.*]

GLORIA: [*Tick.*]

DECLAN: Don't give me that — I distinctly heard you say the name Freddie.

GLORIA: [*Tock.*]

DECLAN: Yes you did.

GLORIA: [*Tick.*]

DECLAN: You did!

[*She drops her tick-tock. Turns around.*]

GLORIA: Argument.

DECLAN: What?

GLORIA: Nine letters.

DECLAN: What?

GLORIA: Dispute.

DECLAN: [*Finger in air.*] Am I on nights or am I on days?

GLORIA: Days.

DECLAN: And what key are we in.

GLORIA: C?

DECLAN: C sharp. [*Shouts.*]

GLORIA: I was doing nothing wrong, honestly.

[MOTHER *shakes her rattle next door. They look at her. Immediately all three walk off in various directions –* MOTHER *up and down her room, then into their room while they patrol Room 1. They all meet in front of the mirror.* MOTHER *re-enters Room 2 and sits.* DECLAN *and* GLORIA *watch her until she sits down, then they start their argument again.*]

DECLAN: [*Angry.*] Ahhhhhh.

GLORIA: [*Pleading.*] Ahhhh.

DECLAN: [*Low, dismissive.*] Ohdedo.

GLORIA: Ohdo.

DECLAN: [*Goes to strangle her.*] Ohnono.

GLORIA: Oh!

DECLAN: [*Roars.*] Agh! [DECLAN *rushes away, finds the gong and strikes it.* GLORIA *tinkles her bells. He strikes the gong. She answers with her bells. He strikes the gong. She answers with her bells. And then there is a sharp blast from next door on the whistle from* MOTHER. DECLAN *rushes into Room 2.*] Who's talking to you? Hah?

MOTHER: What would your father say if he heard you talking to me like that?

DECLAN: My father is dead.

MOTHER: No, he's not.

DECLAN: He is.

[*Meanwhile* GLORIA *goes to her hunkers, stage right front, with her hands around her ears.*]

MOTHER: No, he's not.

DECLAN: Yes he is.

MOTHER: Oh my God.

DECLAN: What's wrong now.

MOTHER: There's something else you might like to know.
DECLAN: What?
MOTHER: You have his feet. How awful.
DECLAN: I have his feet.
MOTHER: That's right, God help you.

[DECLAN *re-enters Room 1. He stands speechless. He beats out angry sounds on the overhead pots, manically. The audience joins in, and with assorted sounds the whole thing builds up to a crescendo.* DECLAN *rushes downstage, holds up the gong to stop the audience.*]

DECLAN: No! [*Gong.*] Do! [*Gong.*] Don't! [*Gong.*] No! [*Gong.*] Do! [*Gong.*] Don't! [*Gong.*] No! Do! Don't! [*He walks over to the weeping chair, and stands with one hand on back of it.*] No!
GLORIA: Do!
MOTHER: Don't.
DECLAN: Do.
MOTHER: No.
GLORIA: Don't!

[DECLAN *stands stage left behind the weeping chair and throws his hands in the air, exasperated and a little crazy.* GLORIA *is situated in a crouch stage right front. She watches him a while. Then she taps the Indian bells. He looks at her, she looks at him, and he looks away.* GLORIA *is bewildered. She moves towards him. Again she rings her Indian bells. No reply from* DECLAN. *She goes behind him. Rings bells. He looks away. Next door,* MOTHER *smokes. Saddened,* GLORIA *leans up and plays a little love symphony on the overhead pots and pans.* DECLAN *listens, turns to watch.* GLORIA *looks towards him, but he turns away. Another tune. The same again. Another tune. The same again. He looks away.* GLORIA *goes to the cooker. Plays three short musical love sequences, but he still refuses her. Silence.* GLORIA *strikes a wooden mallet.*]

MOTHER: Is he sulking?
GLORIA: [*Tick. Pause.*]
MOTHER: I thought so?
GLORIA: [*Tick.*]
MOTHER: [*Rises and looks into Room 1.*] What's going on in

here? [MOTHER *starts to pace Room 2 up and down, while next-door* GLORIA *goes down and up tapping her kitchen utensils.* DECLAN *stands by the weeping chair looking away but answering* MOTHER*'s complaints with wild jeers as she paces Room 2.*] If he had not been born in that godforsaken place none of this would have happened. [*He jeers.*] Will you stop that! [MOTHER *carries on pacing as before.*] I should have known, I should have known in the first place. [*Finger in air. Walking up* and *down room.*] But that's what comes from marrying into Longford. [*Jeer from him.*] Stop that! Stop it, I say. [*Off again pacing.*] Him and his sweet van. Off to the Yukon with a Longford man. That bloody place. That blasted creature and his mouth organ. What got into me I'll never know. [*She bears up.* DECLAN *hums.* MOTHER *enters Room 1.*] Stop that. Stop that dreadful humming and listen to me. [GLORIA *strikes the wooden mallet twice.*] This is your Mother speaking. [*Pause.*] How long are you going to keep up this business? [*Silence.*] Do you hear me? [*Pause.* DECLAN *hums on.* MOTHER *raps a saucepan on the line.* GLORIA *strikes a pot on the line.* DECLAN *makes a bird-noise.*] Now you be good, Declan McInerney.

GLORIA: Declan, I can't go on like this.

DECLAN: [*Lunatic roar.*] Hahahow.

GLORIA: I'm sorry for what I done – [*He looks at her.*] – whatever it was. [*He looks away.*]

MOTHER: What did you do?

GLORIA: Nothing.

MOTHER: Are you listening?

DECLAN: Hahaha.

GLORIA: It was nothing, nothing at all. [*She tinkles her bell behind him.*] He won't speak to me. [*She sits in weeping chair.*] It's dreadful. [GLORIA *weeps quietly.* DECLAN *makes crazy sounds.*]

MOTHER: Will you stop that nonsense immediately? Come here to me! [DECLAN *faces her mid-stage behind* GLORIA.] Look what you've done to that poor English girl. Oh you unfortunate! [GLORIA *rises.*] If you had gone to work none of this would have happened. [*Pause.*] What is to become of us? [DECLAN *heads towards the mirror. He hums.*] By the way are we going to get fed today? [*The two women walk off in various directions while he patrols the mirror area.* MOTHER *eventually finds herself seated as before at the table, then* GLORIA *arrives with three plates, and eventually and reluctantly* DECLAN *seats himself. They eat in silence. Not a sound.*]

GLORIA: Declan.

[*He gets up and stands.*]

MOTHER: Now Declan dear we will not persist with this . . . this idiocy, will we? [*Pause.*] Is it the itch?

DECLAN: No.

GLORIA: Is it the nights?

MOTHER: Is it the days? [*Pause.*] Tell me Declan, did you do your business today?

DECLAN: I'm turning into someone else.

MOTHER: Who?

DECLAN: That fucker Freddie.

MOTHER: And whose fault is that, pray?

[DECLAN *lets an almighty roar, breaks into a mirthless laugh, and suddenly* GLORIA *strikes his gong. They each look at the other.*]

DECLAN: You hit my gong.

GLORIA: I did.

[*This silences him.*]

DECLAN: But that's my gong.

GLORIA: That's right. [*She hands him his gong. Each of three look at each other and start moving around.* MOTHER *returns to her window.*]

MOTHER: [*Moves window to the front, looks out.*] The weather's improving thanks be to God.

[*Everything, it would appear, is back to normal.*]

DECLAN: Ha-Ha. [DECLAN *tidies up the plates. He watches* GLORIA *in wonder, as she takes her blue dress and puts it on. As the women dress, the audience participants play assorted sounds.* GLORIA *puts on a see-through raincoat with* DECLAN *trying to help.* GLORIA *steps towards the partition, and looks back at* DECLAN. *He raises his hand in the air, the sounds stop from audience, and* GLORIA *turns away and steps into Room 2.*]

GLORIA: Are you ready mum?

MOTHER: Why yes, Gloria. [MOTHER *takes her arm.*] And where are we for today?

GLORIA: Shall we go see Mr Godfrey? [*They exit.*]

MOTHER: Geoffrey Godfrey?

GLORIA: Yes.

MOTHER: That would be wonderful. Just wonderful. And certain people can do whatever they like – isn't that right?

GLORIA: Yes Mum.

[DECLAN *covers his head with the sheet. Lights come up very low and* GLORIA *and* MOTHER *enter. Suddenly a whistle blows from next door in Room 2. The Indian bells sound in Room 1. The sounds are repeated – whistle, then Indian bell.* DECLAN *is sitting in the weeping chair with his head covered by the sheet.* GLORIA *stands behind him in her raincoat.* MOTHER *is back in her armchair.*]

DECLAN: Who's Freddie? [GLORIA *quietly taps a pot overhead.*] Freddie Jones by God.

[*She quietly taps pots.*] He's a what? [DECLAN *lifts his head from under the sheet.* GLORIA *taps the pots again.*] An apothecary. What's that? [GLORIA *taps the pots again.*] Oh I see. [GLORIA *taps the pots.*] But why did you . . . why did you say his . . . And I didn't . . . Because of that, you see . . . I thought he was the other fellow . . . And it wasn't the right fellow . . . and I didn't . . . [GLORIA *gives light taps along the line of pots in answer to speech above. Then she strikes two pots.*] Oh. [*Strikes another.*] I see. [*Strikes another quietly.*] Sorry about that, I hope you can forgive me. [*He jumps up, drops the sheet, and hops over in his old exuberant manner while* GLORIA *watches him. He grabs the gong and is about to strike it.*]

GLORIA: No. [DECLAN *points at a pot overhead, ready to strike it.*] No.

[*He goes to strike another saucepan.* GLORIA *shakes her head negatively. Cooker? No, she shakes her head.* DECLAN *does not know what to do. He turns, and signals to one of the audience participants.*] No. [*He tries another participant. She shakes her head. He's lost.* MOTHER *turns to watch him.* DECLAN *watches* GLORIA. *Then he looks at* MOTHER, *then back to* GLORIA. *Then he marches over and back the front of the stage, thinking. Then it strikes him. He taps his pocket, lifts out the mouth organ and plays a little riff.* GLORIA *nods.*]

MOTHER: Not that blasted mouth organ again.

GLORIA: Mother – stop.

MOTHER: I want the gong.

GLORIA: You can't have the gong. Not anymore.

MOTHER: I said I want the gong. I demand the gong. [*Strikes chair.*]

GLORIA: No.

MOTHER: Is the gong gone?

GLORIA: Yes.

MOTHER: I thought so. [*Pause.*] That's what you get, no thanks. A kick in the arse, that's all. Ha-ha. Hmm. [MOTHER *and* GLORIA *take off their coats and approach each other at the mirror. The audience makes busy sounds.*] I was thinking of getting my hair dyed.

GLORIA: Yes Mum.

MOTHER: Carrot, I think. [GLORIA *returns and both women look at each other for a moment through the partition.*] A wave and a perm would cheer me up.

GLORIA: Yes Mum.

MOTHER: I'll have a word with Freddie.

DECLAN: Hah? [*Both women look at him.*] Oh that's right, that's right.

[GLORIA *gets her stool and sits by the mirror.* DECLAN *sits by the table.* MOTHER *sits in her armchair.*]

GLORIA: I'm stuck now for anything to say. [*Pause.*] What do we do now I ask myself? Be silent, I suppose, be quiet for a time. [DECLAN *and* GLORIA *look at each other. Then they look away, look at each other again, then look away again.*] I came back because there was no place else to go. If I could have found someplace else I'd be there now. I could be in Herefordshire, mind. I could be. But I'm not. You think of that. [*Pause.*] You think of that.

MOTHER: Or the Yukon.

GLORIA: Yes Mum.

MOTHER: I loved it there. The Yukon was grand except for the mouth organ. [DECLAN *plays four riffs on the mouth organ.* MOTHER *taps her radio and turns it on. She starts to smoke another cigarette, then switches the radio off. Silence.*] I missed the deaths again. That's the second time in two days.

DECLAN: You'll get it on the nine o'clock.

MOTHER: By then it'll be too late.

DECLAN: You should take up line dancing, Mother.

MOTHER: I will in my hole.

DECLAN: That's nice talk.

MOTHER: There wasn't much chat out of you a while back. [DECLAN *lets down the bed.* GLORIA *takes the sheet off the weeping chair, undresses, and gets into bed.*]

DECLAN: Oh that's true.

MOTHER: Then his father bought this television. "Maggie," he says, "look at that". But I said it was a daft auld thing. I didn't want it. And then I did, of course. What night is tonight?

DECLAN: Friday.

MOTHER: Friday already?

DECLAN: Yes Mother.

MOTHER: We saw John.

DECLAN: You did.

MOTHER: We did. He went by on a bike. [*She cackles wickedly.*] [DECLAN *plays the mouth organ as he goes to drop down the pots. The lights dim imperceptively.* GLORIA *is in bed.* DECLAN *stands by the pulley.*] No!

GLORIA: Do!

MOTHER: Don't. [DECLAN *softly lets the rope go down halfway.*] You're learning.

DECLAN: [*He lets the pots sit quietly onto the floor.*] I am.

MOTHER: About time. [MOTHER *turns her chair and window to face audience. Sits with a sigh.*]

GLORIA: We had great fun tonight, hadn't we?

DECLAN: We had.

GLORIA: Now come to bed.

MOTHER: And keep him in it if you can. We'll be long enough in the boneyard.

[*The lights dim.* DECLAN *gets into bed. He lifts his hand. The audience participants do assorted nightmare sounds.* DECLAN *looks too and fro.* GLORIA *falls asleep.* MOTHER *falls asleep.* DECLAN *stays sitting up. He stops the audience with a finger to his lips.* DECLAN *plays on the mouth organ.*]

DECLAN: Are you asleep Gloria? [*Pause.*] Good. Are you asleep Mother? [*Pause.*] Good. [*Pause.*] I wonder what Muriel is at now?

GLORIA: Stop Declan.

DECLAN: What?

GLORIA: I can't climb up there.

MOTHER: What got into your head that you took us out to this godforsaken spot?

GLORIA: I'll fall.

MOTHER: It's dreadful.

GLORIA: Pitiful!

MOTHER: Woeful!

GLORIA: Awful.

MOTHER: You're right. It's awful to see what we're reduced to.

[*Pause.* DECLAN *gets out, tidies the sheet over* GLORIA, *and puts his gong in his briefcase.*]

GLORIA: I can't go on any further so don't ask me.

DECLAN: I won't.

[*Pause.*]

GLORIA: Oh Declan.

MOTHER: What is that you're doing Declan?

GLORIA: I can't look down.

MOTHER: Oh God.

GLORIA: Oh dear.

MOTHER: Out here of all places.

GLORIA: There's no bottom.
MOTHER: We'll be destroyed.
GLORIA: Please. I'll fall. [*Pause.*] Wake me Declan.
MOTHER: Don't leave me.
GLORIA: Wake me Declan, please.
MOTHER: Don't go!
GLORIA: Wake me!

[*Pause.* MOTHER *gets up out of her armchair. Heads directly into Room 1 and across to their bed. Climbs into bed beside* GLORIA. DECLAN *watches in consternation.*]

GLORIA: Declan!
MOTHER: Declan!
GLORIA: Declan!
MOTHER: Declan!
GLORIA: Declan!
MOTHER: Declan!

[*Silence.* DECLAN *gets up, walks over, and takes* MOTHER*'s arm.* MOTHER *gets out of bed and follows him.*]

DECLAN: Maggie. [*Pause.*] Maggie, you're in the wrong bed. Come Maggie.
MOTHER: Is that you?
DECLAN: Yes.
MOTHER: Are you in heaven?
DECLAN: Not yet.
MOTHER: But you're getting there?
DECLAN: I am.
MOTHER: Good. I'm glad for you. [*Pause.*] You're getting older.
DECLAN: A little.
MOTHER: It suits you.
DECLAN: Thank you. [*He sits her in armchair.*] Are you alright now?
MOTHER: Fine. Fine. [*Pause.*] And you'll stay?
DECLAN: I will. [*He leaves her. Enters Room 1. Clears throat.*] Gloria. Gloria?
GLORIA: Yes, What time is it?
DECLAN: It's two.
GLORIA: I thought so, will you be coming back to bed soon?

DECLAN: Yes.

GLORIA: I dreamed I was in a coffin. [*Pause.*] And I couldn't wake. I knew everything that was happening but I couldn't wake.

DECLAN: I know.

GLORIA: And I called to you but I couldn't reach you.

DECLAN: I heard you.

GLORIA: You did.

DECLAN: Yes.

GLORIA: In the dream you didn't.

DECLAN: But it's over now.

GLORIA: Are you sure?

DECLAN: Yes.

GLORIA: I'm glad – come in soon.

DECLAN: I will.

GLORIA: I miss you beside me.

DECLAN: Just a minute. [*He stands with one hand on table. Drops the briefcase on table.*]

[MOTHER *looks from her chair, looks around.*]

MOTHER: Are you out of bed again? And that poor English girl, and she has very good manners, I'll say that for her, but . . .

DECLAN: Good night Mother.

MOTHER: Oh yes. Good night you. [*Pause. Lights down.* DECLAN *gets into bed.* GLORIA *sits up.*] Could we have the gong again for old time's sake?

GLORIA: No Mother.

MOTHER: No gong?

GLORIA: No.

MOTHER: I thought so – the gong is gone.

GLORIA: Yes.

MOTHER: Oh well, it was good fun while it lasted. [DECLAN *and the audience play a celebration.* DECLAN *waves to stop the audience.*] Is tomorrow nights or days?

DECLAN: Nights I think.

GLORIA: Yes, that's right.

MOTHER: Can it be nights again already?

DECLAN: So it seems.

[*Their three faces look at the audience. Small sounds from audience participants as the lights come down. The sounds stop. In the darkness* we hear MOTHER*'s whistle,* GLORIA*'s Indian bell and, lastly, a small blow on the mouth organ.*]

END

The Music Box

First performed at the Peacock Theatre, Dublin, on 24 January 1998. *The Music Box* – a.k.a. *Boxes* – formed part of a trilogy of short plays entitled *Swans, Boots, and Boxes*, written by Eugene McCabe, Éilís Ní Dhuibhne, and Dermot Healy respectively. The extant script is a second draft dated "4 November 1997," and is described by the author as "A Prose Treatment of a Play."

CAST

Jack Straw

A YOUTH
A PEDDLER
A WASHERWOMAN
THE KING
THE KING'S COURTIERS
A TORTURER

SCENE 1

There is a great summer storm on the path that leads into the high forest below the mountain. Lightning strikes everywhere.

A youth comes running down the path. He is being hurled to and fro by the storm.

The eye of the storm opens.

He falls prostrate. He's terrified. He crouches down under the blanket he carries over his shoulders. It's red on one side and green on the other.

The storm finishes suddenly with a click.

He sits up, peers out from under his blanket, ducks a last wind that shoots across from the trees, covers himself, looks out again.

It's over.

He looks round him with wonder and fear.

SCENE 2

A peddler, with a stick over his shoulder, from which an onion sack hangs with a box in it, approaches whistling.

Good day, says the lad.

The peddler gets a shock.

Good day, yourself, says the peddler with surprise. I thought I was by myself. How did you get there?

I'm hiding.

Hiding from what? he asks suspiciously. Is there someone else here?

No.

Then what are you hiding from?

The storm.

Storm? Storm! He gives a bitter laugh. Hah-hah-hah! What storm?

But you must have seen it.

I did not.

There was lightning.

I saw no lightning. And neither did you.

I did.

You did not.

But you must have felt the winds. Terrible winds.

No. There was no wind, says the peddler. And I don't want to hear another word about storms.

There was a storm.

Go long out of that – ha-ha-ha! – sure there was no storm.

There was, said the youth, a few moments ago.

There was no storm, says the peddler angrily.

There was.

Don't be a cry baby, said the peddler, and get up out of that. That was no storm.

No?

No, he says with great finality.

Alright, if you say so, said the lad and he rose.

SCENE 3

They sit on the rocks. The peddler leaves down his stick and his bag very gently.

What are you doing out here anyway?

Living, says the lad. And running.

Bedad. Living all by yourself.

That's right.

And running.

That too.

So there you are.

That's me.

Indeedy. That's you.

It is.

Well now. And this is me.

The peddler checks the box is in the bag. He looks in at the box, wets a finger and taps the box.

That's mine, he says.

I know that, says the lad.

Well you can never be too careful. Indeedy. Do you own anything?

No.

A man that does not own anything is a danger, says the peddler. He's a threat. He is, indeedy.

Well I have my blanket.

That will do, I suppose.

But the peddler is still wary of him.

SCENE 4

Is the war over, asks the lad.

What war?

The war.

That war.

Yes.

That war finished years ago.

Oh. And is there another one going on?

Not that I know of.

You see, says the lad—

The peddler holds his hand in front of the youth's face.

Stop, says the peddler. You can tell me your story later.

He stands.

You'll have to excuse me, says the peddler, for I have to go to the toilet.

He hides his bag behind a bush and heads off into the trees. The lad whistles a ditty, he looks at the peddler's bag, rises, looks round him, takes a step towards it, stops, goes on, listens, opens the bag, wets his finger, taps the box, shyly opens the lid a fraction and the storm blows quietly. He ducks. Fearfully he closes it again. He puts it away quickly, looks around him and sits again. Then all of a sudden from another direction the sound of a great sea washes in. Gravel slides to and fro. Mountainous waves break.

Then the sea stops with a click.

SCENE 5

A woman approaches. She has a thorn umbrella with the spokes showing. She has a box in a straw bag.

Good day, says the lad.

You gave me a turn, she says, and puts a hand to her heart.

Did you hear that?

Hear what.

The sea.

I heard no sea.

But I heard it.

Don't be daft. The sea is miles away. Miles and miles.

I tell you I heard it.

You heard nothing – do you hear me? Nothing.

But I did.

Stop, she shouts.

There were great waves.

Stop I say!

She waves a finger angrily at him.

Mighty waves, he shouts back.

Keep your voice down, she says, looking behind her.

I heard a sea breaking, he whispers.

No you didn't, she whispers back, coming closer to him.

I did, he whispers even softer.

No, she says opening her lips into a wide "O." She comes closer again. No, she repeats.

Alright then, he says.

Dearie dearie me, she says. What we have to learn.

SCENE 6

She sits by the lad with the umbrella open over them. The bag with the box in it sits by her side.

Me old segocia, she says. I didn't expect to see anyone in these parts, she says.

I'm waiting for the peddler.

But there is no peddler.

He's gone over there.

Is he now.

He is.

Is he bedad.

Yes.

If you say so.

I do.

Well let's wait and see this peddler.

That's fine by me.

Is it now? I'm glad to hear it. You're a proper scald, she says. Do you know what I think?

What do you think?

I think you're not right in the head.

That's not a nice thing to say to me, he says.

Oh, and she chuckles.

The peddler that was here before you said that he couldn't hear the storm.

Did he now.

Then you come along and you say you didn't hear the sea.

Well I didn't, says she. And I don't want to hear another word about it. Do you hear me?

I do, he says sadly.

SCENE 7

And where is your peddler?

He's gone to the toilet.

Oh.

He's away a long time.

Well I can't help that.

Hm!

He looks at her.

Have you far to go?

Enough to be doing me. And you?

Well, he says, it's a long story. You see—

Oh dearie, she says.

She stands.

Is something wrong? he asks.

It just came over me. I think I'll be off to the toilet myself.

She hides her bag behind a log. She heads off into the woods.

He whistles a ditty then reaches over and lifts the box out of her bag. Opens the lid a fraction for a second and the sea laps quietly. He closes it immediately. He takes the peddler's box out, looks behind him, opens it an even smaller fraction than before and the quiet winds blow. He closes it quickly. He holds both boxes in his hands. Then he puts the storm box belonging to the peddler into her bag and the sea box of the woman into the onion bag on the stick. He has just put them away and sat back on his blanket when the peddler returns.

The peddler goes over and checks his stick and bag, looks at the lad, grunts, comes over to the lad and sits.

He smiles at the lad.

The lad looks away.

What's up now?

I don't want to talk to you, says the lad.

And why is that?

Because no-one believes me.

Well that's a terror.

Not even you.

No.

And the last woman who sat where you are now said you were never here at all.

Did she now.

She did.

And where is the lady that said I didn't exist.

She's gone to the toilet.

That was me went to the toilet ya madman.

Well she wanted to go as well.

Did she indeedy.

She did.

Oh-ho-ho, says the peddler. It's a popular sport.

So it appears.

I'll tell you what I'll do, says the peddler. Just to be fair. I'll stop here a bit till she comes back.

That's up to you.

The peddler pulls a snot from his nose. He claps his knees and gets up and takes a long look back at the way he's come. Then he sits again.

She's away a long time, says the peddler ironically.

So were you.

But I came back.

So will she.

When?

After you have gone.

You're making her up.

I'm not.

Because you want me to go. Do you want me to go?

I don't care.

God, but you're hard pleased. Well then I'm off. I can't be spending all day taking to his grumpiness.

He gets to his feet. Takes up his stick.

Moves a little. Looks back.

Are you sure you want me to go?

I don't care.

Suit yourself.

The peddler goes a bit further. Then he looks back again.

Are you certain sure?

I am.

Ha! says the peddler. Now if anyone asks after me, you didn't see me right?

Right, says the lad.

Right, says the peddler with ferocity.

He goes.

SCENE 8

The woman immediately appears, goes over and checks her basket and the box in it, then she hoists her umbrella and trots over, basket in hand, and sits by the lad.

Any sign of your peddler?

He came and he went.

Is that so, she says without believing him.

But I didn't see him. You didn't see him?

No.

He took off without you knowing?

That's right.

So he didn't exist.

No.

Ah I thought so.

And neither do you I think.

Me?

Yes.

But I'm here beside you.

Not for long.

True.

They sit there a while without speaking. She is a little alarmed.

Do you say so, says the woman suddenly.

I didn't say anything.

You didn't?

No.

Oh.

They sit a while longer. She grows impatient, gets up and looks back the way she'd come.

Well, I suppose if your peddler is gone there's not much sense in me stopping here.

No.

You're right.

She takes her bag and brolly.

I'm going now.

Alright.

Now if anyone asks after me—

I'll tell them I didn't see you.

That's right, she says suspiciously. Tell them you didn't see me.

I will.

She moves off a space. Turns.

How did you know to say that?

He told me.

Who? The peddler?

Yes.

She goes a bit further.

Turns.

But he doesn't exist.

No, says the lad. But then, neither do you.

Dearie me, she says and leaves.

SCENE 9

This is a strange place, says the lad. What you see in front of your face is not there. So the people you meet do not exist. Neither Mister Indeedy or Mrs Dearie. Nor Mrs Dearie or Mister Indeedy. Not one of them. And what you hear is not heard by anyone else. Oh not at all. Neither storm nor sea. I don't know. And when you want to tell your story to someone they get up and go off to the toilet. That's the truth. And then—

No, he says.

It grows louder.

That's not music.

It comes closer.

No doubt about it, says the lad, that's not music.

It comes closer.

No, he says, covering his ears.

Then he throws the blanket round his head and sits.

SCENE 10

The King and his courtiers enter with great fanfare. Underneath the blanket the lad's head moves to and fro. The King is carrying another box much like the others. He closes it and the music stops. Halt! says the King.

He studies the figure under the blanket. Signals the torturer who approaches the figure with sword in hand, leans over, and whips the blanket off the lad.

Rise to the King! shouts the torturer.

Good man, says the King.

Your honour, says the lad.

Why had your head covered?

Just because.

Did you not like the music?

I didn't hear it, says the lad.

You didn't hear it?

No.

How come?

It's better that way.

I don't understand.

Neither do I, your honour.

The King is astonished.

He puts the box to the boy's ear, opens the lid and this symphony blares out.

He snaps the lid shut.

Now did you hear it?

No.

What! You did not hear music?

No.

The King puts the box to the lad's ear again, opens the lid, out blares the music, then he snaps it shut.

And did you hear that?

No, your honour. You just thought I did.

I just thought you did. The King strides about, flapping his robe. The others follow suit, weaving about in puzzlement and obsequiousness. I just thought you did, says the King. What does that mean?

The parade stops.

I know not, your Highness, says one courtier.

Neither do I, says another.

Torture him, says the torturer.

Hold it there, torturer, says the King, just hold it there.

He approaches the lad.

Do you hear me, boy! says the King, you're not deaf are you?

No.

So what do you mean?

It means I thought I heard a storm and I thought I heard

a sea then I thought I heard music but I didn't really. You just thought I did.

Aha, said the King.

The King ponders the lad.

If you didn't hear the music – he twirls his moustache and goes up on his toes in the manner of a great interrogator – did you happen – he gives a grandiose wave of his arm and flutters his fingers – to see a peddler?

I did and I didn't.

You did and you didn't.

That's right.

This is extraordinary, says the King to a courtier. He did and he didn't.

He did, says the courtier, and he didn't.

He speaks in riddles this one, says the King.

He does.

He does.

The King strides about deep in thought.

And – he twirls his moustache and goes up on his toes – a washerwoman, did she – he gives a grandiose wave and flutters his fingers – perchance pass by?

She did and she didn't.

She did and she didn't, repeats the King.

That's right.

Oh dear, says the King, there it is again. He turns to his courtiers. She did and she didn't. This is a great puzzle, says the King.

A very great puzzle, nods a courtier.

A conundrum, says a courtier.

Torture him, says the torturer.

The courtiers shout their approval.

Hold it there, torturer, says the King.

The courtiers show their disapproval of the torturer.

Let's not be hasty, says the King.

SCENE 11

The King approaches the lad.

What is your name, asks the King.

Jack Straw, says the lad.

Well now Jack Straw, listen to me a while. This peddler and this washerwoman who of course you never met – or did you – well no matter – what is the point – we will not go into all that again – no – where was I?

Where was he? asks one courtier of the others.

Where was the King, shouts the torturer with ferocity.

The courtiers try to remember.

You were speaking, says the lad . . .

Yes? says the King.

. . . Of some peddler and washerwoman.

Oh yes, says the King. How well you should remember – but we won't go into that – no – I have it now – that's who I was speaking of – that dreadful twosome you never met – or did you – hah? – strange – strange – now what – yes?

He looks around him lost again.

The peddler and the washerwoman, says the lad.

Ah yes Jack Straw, says the King grandly. The very ones. Now let me tell you this. Those pair are both thieves.

Thieves?

Thieves of the highest order.

Oh.

They stole my storm. My daddy's storm.

They did not.

They did. And then they stole my sea.

That's bad.

My mammy's sea. And the people are very angry.

The lad nods and thinks to himself.

Very angry indeed, the King says.

The lad looks straight ahead.

So can you help me? asks the King.

The boy stays silent.

I can offer you a handsome reward.

The boy stays silent.

All I need to know is in which direction they've gone, then we can follow them.

There's no need, says the lad, and he sits. They'll be back.

How do you now?

I know.

He knows, says the King.

The courtiers nod.

He knows, says the King with satisfaction to his courtiers who bow grandly and congratulate each other.

SCENE 12

The King sits and his retinue sits.

The King places the music box between him and the lad.

They are away a long time, says the King.

So they were before, your honour, says the lad.

No more riddles if you please, says the King.

The King and his retinue grow impatient.

They wait a while longer.

It's terrible, says the King, this silence.

His retinue nods. The lad nods. The King nods. The King hoists a finger. All stop nodding.

The King pulls the music box closer to him.

They took the box I kept the storm in while I was at the toilet, explains the King.

They did, agrees a courtier.

That happens, says the lad.

And they took the sea box while I was looking for the storm box.

Terrible, says a courtier.

Terrible out, your honour, says the lad.

The King pulls the music box closer to him.

Now all I have is the music, says the King.

They sit in silence.

In the distance the peddler is heard shouting. His roars

grow louder.

Hide! Hide! says the lad.

The King and his retinue in one sweep disappear and hide.

Where are you, you bugger you? shouts the peddler. You gimp! You imp out of hell.

Over here, says the lad.

The peddler appears.

You there!

Yes, says the lad.

Did you lay a hand on my belongings?

I did, says the lad, and I did not.

Cut out the buckin' nonsense, says the peddler. Or I'll make mincemeat of you.

There's no need to curse.

Oh God in heaven help me. He beats his head with his knuckles. This is not happening. This is not happening at all.

He turns on the lad and shows him his fist.

Are you telling me lies?

Not at all.

I lost my storm, says the peddler.

I thought there was no storm.

None of that now, shouts the peddler, none of that smart stuff. He is about to strike the lad when the next thing the washerwoman screams from afar.

When I get you, she says, I'll tan your hide. Where are you, you devil?

Over here, says the lad.

She approaches him swinging her brolly.

Who are you? she asks, confronting the peddler.

I'm the peddler. And who are you?

The washerwoman.

They are thrown off balance. They look at each, then at the lad.

And I didn't see either of you, he says.

Shut up you! shouts the washerwoman. You stole my sea.

I did not, say the lad. He did.

What, shouts the peddler, it was him stole my storm.

I did not, says the lad, she did.

I did not, says she.

Anyway, says the lad, I thought there was no storm and no sea.

Never mind that, screeches the washerwoman.

I'll break every bone in his body, says the peddler.

SCENE 13

Look, says the washerwoman, what I found in my bag, and she takes out the storm box.

And buckin' look, says the peddler, what I found in mine, and he takes out the sea box.

They both open the lids a fraction. The sea pounds and the storms blow. They snap the lids shut and confront each other.

Hell and high water, says she, that's mine.

You crone, says he, you took that box from me.

That's mine, says she.

That's mine, says he.

He whips his stick in the air and points it at her. She freezes.

Can't you see, she says, it was that lad there that fooled us.

Him? He looks at the lad. Ya blaggard!

Ya thief! she shouts.

They are both about to turn on the lad when the King, followed by his retinue, appears.

Ah japers, says the peddler.

Dearie me, says the washerwoman.

The courtiers surround them.

Good day, says the King.

Good day your honour, they both say in unison.

I'll have those articles back, says the King.

Quite right too, says the peddler.

Indeed, says the washerwoman, and you're welcome.

One courtier takes one box and another courtier takes the other and the two boxes are handed to the King.

And I hope you haven't broken them, says the King. I just hope you haven't broken them.

Oh no, your honour, says the peddler.
Cross my heart, says the washerwoman.

SCENE 14

The King opens the storm box and the place is swept by storms. He closes it. Then he opens the sea box and the place is swept by sea sounds. He closes it.

He nods.

You're lucky.

Yes, your honour, they say in unison.

Very lucky, says the King.

We are, says the peddler.

We are, says the washerwoman.

Are they not lucky? the King asks the courtiers.

They all nod. The King lifts a finger in the air. The nodding stops.

Can I go now? asks the peddler.

Can I go now? asks the washerwoman.

No, says the King.

It's not my fault your honour, says the peddler in a wheedling voice.

And it's not mine either, says the washerwoman adamantly.

You see that lad there must have stolen my box from me, says the peddler, and put it in her bag.

And he stole mine from me and put it in his bag.

And who stole them in the first place? Hah! says the King.

Hah! says the torturer.

You both stole them from me, says the King.

Oh, says the peddler.

I had forgotten about that, says the washerwoman.

Well it wouldn't have happened, says the lad, if you all had not gone to the toilet.

That's true, said the King.

The peddler nods. The washerwoman nods. The retinue nod. Everyone goes into a frenzy of nodding.

Stop, says the King, you're making me dizzy.

The nodding stops.

So what's to be done? says the King.

SCENE 15

Everyone walks about considering what is to be done. The peddler secretly shakes his fist at the lad. The washerwoman surreptitiously shakes an angry finger in his face. Then she bows obsequiously to the King.

The King stops.

All stop.

Well says the King, has anyone any ideas?

The torturer raises a hand.

Excuse me, say the torturer.

Not you torturer, says the King.

Aw, he says.

Then the peddler summons up an idea. He tips his cap.

Ahem, he says.

Yes, says the King.

The best thing I think you could do, your honour, says the peddler – after due consideration of course – and after looking at all the alternatives – with due regard to the necessities, etc. – yes indeedy, yes – the best thing you could do is let us go.

I concur with that, says the washerwoman.

Concur? asks the King. Concur! What is she talking about?

A courtier rises his hands in bafflement in the air.

The torturer makes a face and taps his head.

What are you talking about? the King asks her.

I agree, says the washerwoman timidly, with him.

Ah, says the King. You agree with that infidel over there.

I do.

Well I don't, says the King.

Neither do I either, says the washerwoman.

So what do we do? he asks.

Torture them, says the torturer.

The courtiers call for blood.

Hold it there torturer, says the King.

The courtiers turn on the torturer.
Silence, says the King.

SCENE 16

What do you say? the King asks the lad. I will leave the final judgment to you.

The lad bows. Then he walks to and fro. The lad considers the peddler.

Mr Indeedy, he says.

Mr Indeedy indeed, says the peddler, and he grins idiotically, then stops. Are you talking to me?

I am. You told me that the war was over.

But it is, says the peddler.

No, it's not, says the lad. It's only beginning.

Now he considers the washerwoman.

Mrs Dearie, he says. You told me that I wasn't right in the head.

I did to my shame.

She waves her hands. But I was only joking.

He considers them both. They bow their heads and shake their shoulders.

You were the first human beings I'd seen in seven years since I fled as a lad into the forest and the mountains.

Have pity, says the peddler.

Do, says she, please.

Is the war still on? he asks the peddler.

If you say so.

I do.

Then it is.

Am I mad? he asks the washerwoman.

No, she says.

But you said I was.

I was wrong.

So now you're sorry.

Yes! says the peddler quickly.

Yes! says the washerwoman, angry that the peddler got in

before her.

I don't know, says the lad.

The peddler goes to his knees.

Then the washerwoman goes to her knees.

I don't know, says the lad.

Have pity! cries the peddler.

Have pity! says the washerwoman.

I don't know, says the lad. He stops a moment to consider. Maybe I should go to the toilet.

Oh don't do that, says the peddler.

No I beg you, says the washerwoman, or something terrible might happen.

You think so? says the lad, and he ponders them both.

SCENE 17

Could I have the lend of your box, your honour, says the lad to the King.

Why certainly, says the King.

The lad takes the box with a bow. He strolls to and fro in front of the peddler and washerwoman.

Now, he says, I want you to listen.

I'm listening, says the peddler.

I want you to listen hard, says the lad.

I'm listening hard, says the washerwoman and she squeezes her eyes closed and listens.

The lad opens the box and music bursts forth. He closes the box. He gives it back to the King. The King indicates with a nod that the lad may continue with his interrogation. The lad bows.

Did you hear music? the lad asks the peddler.

The peddler looks at the lad, then at the woman, then at the courtiers, smiles, then the King, smiles, then for a long time without smiling at the torturer who is on the verge of speaking, then back at the lad.

Ah that's a difficult question.

It is?

Yes, very difficult.

It's a very good question, I think, says the King.

Yes it is, says the retinue together in a chorus.

The peddler smiles idiotically.

Oh I know it's a very good question, but, you see – he throws the palms of his hands up in front of him as if to say it was all beyond him – but you see it's difficult to say.

Well try.

The peddler raises his shoulders.

Yes? asks the lad.

Ah . . . the peddler looks at the washerwoman.

Well? asks the lad.

Ah . . . the peddler looks at the torturer who raises a finger as if to speak.

Excuse me, says the torturer.

Quiet! says the King.

Aw, says the torturer.

Continue, says the King.

Well? asks the lad.

Ah . . .

Did you hear music? asks the lad.

I don't know, says the peddler and he stops smiling.

SCENE 18

The lad turns to the washerwoman.

And did you hear music? he asks her.

Oh dearie me, she says.

Well?

I'm not sure.

You're not sure.

No, she says.

She now looks at everyone, face by face, then back to him. She puts a finger to her cheek and ponders the question. She looks at the peddler and he looks at her earnestly.

I think . . .

Yes, says the lad.

Yes, says the peddler.

Yes, says the King.

I think . . .

Go on, says the peddler.

She shakes her head.

It's just that . . .

Yes, says the lad.

She looks at the peddler again.

Ask him, she says pointing at the peddler.

Ask me, says the offended peddler, ask me is it!

Yes, ask him, she says.

But he already has, says the peddler angrily.

Ask him again, she says.

This is not fair, says the peddler.

Why? asks the King.

Because, your honour, my life depends upon my answer.

That's true, says the torturer.

It is, says the King.

Very true, says the courtiers.

And it's very hard to hear music, says the peddler sadly to the courtiers, when your life is at stake.

It is, says the washerwoman. I'll grant you that.

It's very simple, says the lad, did you hear music or not?

Well . . .

Yes?

It depends, says the peddler.

It depends on what?

On whether . . .

Yes?

On whether you heard it, says the peddler.

That's right, says the washerwoman eagerly. That's right!

You see, says the peddler, if you heard it then so did I.

And so did I, the washerwoman says happily. If you heard the music then so did I – I heard it clear as day.

And if I didn't?

They hesitate a moment.

Then neither did I, says the washerwoman adamantly, and she shakes her head.

That's right, said the peddler. Neither did I.

Not a sound, says the washerwoman. Not a beep.

Nothing, says the peddler. Not a peep.

I see, he says.

SCENE 19

They watch him carefully as he steps to and fro. He takes the music box from the King again, bows, opens it, a sudden snatch of music erupts, he snaps the box closed, looks at them, they look at him with mouths open about to agree or disagree, the lad himself pretends to ponder whether he heard music or not, they are tortured waiting, then he continues on his walk, stops near the King, lifts the box to the King's ear, opens it, the King listens, the music soars, the lad closes the box again, returns it to the King, bows, looks at them, they look at him, he heads off again, they look at the King for guidance, they look after the lad.

He stops. He turns to the King.

Did you perchance hear music? your honour, he asks.

Me?

Yes.

Ah, must I tell? says the King.

It would be best, says the lad.

Pray tell me why.

Because.

But I was enjoying this.

Put them out of their misery, says the lad.

That's right, says the torturer.

Well now, says the King. The question is—

Did you hear music?

Ah! Did I hear music? he says pondering.

Yes? says the wide-eyed peddler.

Yes? says the washerwoman eagerly.

They watch the King as he thinks over the question. He holds a hand to his forehead. He raises his face skyward.

Did I hear music? he says.

Did you? calls the peddler frantically.

Did I? the King asks himself.

He touches his forehead.

I did, says the King.

So did I, shouts the peddler happily.

So did I, says the washerwoman, clapping her hands.

I did, says the King, and I didn't.

Ah japers, says the peddler.

Ah dearie dearie me, says the washerwoman.

SCENE 20

The lad turns to them.

So was there a storm?

There was, I think, says the peddler with uncertainty.

Was there a sea?

There was, says the washerwoman very slowly.

I see, he says.

The peddler and the washerwoman stand there, mouths opens, wondering what will happen next and afraid of having given the wrong answers. The lad turns away from them.

So was there music? asks the lad with his back to them.

They hesitate. He turns.

Was there music? he repeats.

There was indeed, says the torturer.

What did he say? shouts the King.

Everyone turns to the torturer.

Excuse me, he asks, did I say the wrong thing?

You almighty fool, says the King.

But . . . says the torturer.

You idiot, says the King.

But I heard it, your Highness.

No you didn't, says the King.

I'm lost, says the peddler.

So am I, says the washerwoman.

What's wrong with you, you blithering fool, says the King.

I . . . the torturer stammers.

Let them go, says the lad.

The retinue blame one another. Shouting and arguing starts. The place is in chaos.

Let them go, shouts the lad again because it was like no one had heard him the first time.

Quiet! You heard him, says the King. Let them go.

SCENE 21

Oh blessings on you, Jack Straw, says the washerwoman.

My heartfelt thanks, says the peddler.

They rise bowing and scraping. They kiss his hands.

Take this mirror, says the washerwoman, as a token.

He takes the mirror.

But don't look into it, she says quickly.

And what use is a mirror to him that he can't look into, asks the King.

It will keep him from growing old, she says.

And what happened to you?

To my great sorrow I looked into it.

Oh.

Take this stick, says the peddler. And if you strap it to your back you can fly to eternity.

No, says the lad, you own that stick.

But I'm giving it to you.

If you gave it to me, you'd own nothing.

True.

And the man that owns nothing is a threat.

The peddler raises a finger.

Ah very good! he says.

Keep your mirror and your stick, he says, I have no need of them.

The lad picks up his blanket.

Come back with me to the palace, says the King.

No, says the lad. I will remain here.

Running, nods the peddler.

That's right, agrees the lad.

But I could give you anything, says the King.

Then tell me this – is the war truly over?

It is, says the King.

The one I fled from? asks the lad.

The one you fled from, says the King nodding.

It's over?

It is.

Then I have only one request, says the lad.

Whatever you ask for, says the King.

Play those boxes for me. I'd like to hear them.

Then you shall.

The King places the three boxes at intervals along the ground. A courtier stands by each box. The torturer sits to listen. The peddler and the washerwoman sit. The King sits. The lad sits.

The King signals like a conductor.

The lids of all three boxes are thrown fully open. The courtiers sit. The sea and the storm and the music pour forth. All gather in pace together. One by one they stop, the music last of all, in darkness.

END

Mr Staines

First performed 21 September 1999 at the Samuel Beckett Theatre, Dublin, by Pan Pan Theatre Company, Dublin. Directed by Gavin Quinn and designed by Aedín Cosgrove.

CAST

STAINES
GLORIA
McGREGOR
THE MANAGER
MOTHER

Set: Two beams whose bottoms rest stage left and stage right and which rise till their tops pass each other in a high V overhead near centre. They are held together by ropes, which are looped overhead and then tied to two posts on stage left and right. A small writing table, two small chairs, and one large chair. A prayer spot in front stage left.

ACT I

Area in darkness. Sudden beam of light from spot one on Mister STAINES. STAINES *is sitting with his eyes closed, half-dressed, sleeping, in a wooden armchair, jacket on back of chair, legs crossed, very dandyish, facing the audience. He has a cloth to his chin. He goes into a little frenzy. He opens his eyes. He registers the light, clamps his hands on the armrest, looks overhead to the lighting box, but sees nothing. Looks to the wings, but sees nothing. Hand to his forehead he looks down at the audience. Nothing. So he lies back.*

GLORIA: [*Off-stage.*] You're on.
STAINES: I'm what?
GLORIA: [*Off-stage.*] You're on.
STAINES: Christ! Not again.
GLORIA: I'm afraid so.
STAINES: Why does this always happen? [STAINES *jumps to his feet, smiles an actorly false smile, stands, and opens arms to begin a great speech.*] I . . . I came down Forty-Second Street with this chap Dodo in my wake. Winter of 19 and 82. Then he told me his scandalous—
GLORIA: [*Off-stage.*] No.
STAINES: Right. Dear God. [*New pose.*] Earwigger I said, what is the score my valiant lad, as we climbed down hill, down ravine, clambering perches above the enemy.
GLORIA: [*Off-stage.*] No.
STAINES: No?
GLORIA: [*Off-stage.*] No.

STAINES: Got you. [*Adopts further pose and begins again.*] Gabriella, I said, longingly . . .

GLORIA: No.

[*He violently throws the cloth to the floor.]*

STAINES: Well balls. Always the same shagging story. [*He gives a kick at nothing. No reply. He begins dressing.*] Are we in the round?

GLORIA: [*Off-stage.*] The square.

STAINES: Back to the square. This is preposterous. Where are the documents? The damn documents? [*Immediately spot 2 comes on. A man,* McGREGOR, *walks on stage left, gives* STAINES *a small fright, nods at* STAINES, *throws a sharp glance at the auditorium, pauses a beat, and with a rather false smile, scurries off.* STAINES *rises and looks after him. Quite composed.*] Well that was brief. One could hardly call that an appearance. Could we have that again pray? [*Silence.*] Hey.

GLORIA: Yes?

STAINES: Not you – him.

McGREGOR: [*Off-stage.*] Me?

STAINES: Yes.

[McGREGOR *returns.*]

McGREGOR: Excuse me?

STAINES: What's happening?

McGREGOR: I don't know.

STAINES: Have we started?

McGREGOR: I don't know that either.

STAINES: Well I have it on good authority that we have begun. [*Putting on his shirt.*]

McGREGOR: Is that so.

STAINES: But whether to believe it or not is another thing. Could be a jaunt to nowhere.

McGREGOR: You're right.

STAINES: Where are you going?

McGREGOR: I was on my way . . . to my mother's.

STAINES: [*He looks at him questioningly.*] To your mother's?

McGREGOR: Yes.

STAINES: [*Pondering the man.*] What text is this? [*Studies him intimately.*] This goes where? [*Lifts the chair and places it next to table.*] Here you think? [McGREGOR *nods.*] Good. [*Comes back and winks at* McGREGOR.] What next I wonder?

McGREGOR: [*Winking back.*] I couldn't say.

STAINES: Well we're not where I thought we were. Not the Americas. Not Nance. Someplace parochial, I would think. The parish of nod. Will you do up my buttons? [McGREGOR *begins doing up the buttons of his shirt.*] I am happy to see you have achieved a persona.

McGREGOR: Thank you.

STAINES: Let's hope it will improve upon acquaintanceship. We all need to improve upon acquaintanceship because you see . . . [*Searches.*]

MOTHER: We are never alone.

STAINES: Oh yes – quite! – we are never alone. [*Silence.*] Do you know that one?

McGREGOR: I'm afraid not. [*Steps back.*]

STAINES: Are you sure you don't know that one?

McGREGOR: I'm certain.

STAINES: What a pity.

McGREGOR: How does it go?

STAINES: How does it go – well now – first we must establish our whereabouts. That's essential. [*He clears throat, tours the space and begins growing theatrical and animated.*] For you may be sure that we are never alone. The lighting man is in his box. Up among the steel blues. The fag topped, the torch glowing. A moral man, one with whom one must not trifle. Of course for him there is no true night or true day. Yes. And let us not overlook the Manager – he too will make an appearance. Sadly, yes. And let us not forget the girl in the foyer. At this moment the girl in the foyer is counting the takings after stowing away the sweets. The . . . [*He grows puzzled.*] . . . the man on the door is resting. The . . .

GLORIA: [*Off-stage.*] The women in the wings wait to come on.

STAINES: Of course. [*Clicks fingers.*]

McGREGOR: Excuse me.

STAINES: And certainly, certainly, I have not forgotten you. I must not forget my colleague.

McGREGOR: I'll be off.

STAINES: But I'm trying.

McGREGOR: You see I go most evenings at this time.

STAINES: That's a different story, do you understand? I don't know that one.

McGREGOR: No?

STAINES: And I'm trying very hard.

McGREGOR: It's not easy.

STAINES: Indeed. [*Growing animated to his task.*] It's not easy. Not easy. Yes I understand – it's not easy for my colleague. [*Tips* McGREGOR's *shoulder asking him to concur.*] Tonight his prison door swung quietly open. [*Spins* McGREGOR.] Its newly-oiled hinges concurring. The trajectory – do you see the trajectory? – leads to escape. [*He points to the audience.*] There are socks and well-shined shoes left at the door.

McGREGOR: [*Tentatively.*] Goodbye.

STAINES: [*Nodding.*] Yes indeed, "Goodbye," someone calls. "Goodbye Mac," someone calls from another cell. Goodbye. The other doors give as if by magic. A car with a full tank stands at the main gate of Mountjoy. The car door is ajar as if the Minister of Prisons were expected to emerge. At the wheel is a chauffeur in a shining white suit. He is ready to spirit my colleague to freedom.

McGREGOR: I think you have the wrong man.

STAINES: [*He clicks his fingers.*] But the chauffeur says no, I have the right man. [*Thinks.*] Privately the chauffeur dreams of the total annihilation of the human species. But he will wait. [*He waits.*]

McGREGOR: [*Tentatively.*] I am honoured.

STAINES: Indeed. [*Nods in agreement with the improvisation.*] I am honoured, says the chauffeur. Because his duty, this wonderful night, is to free his passenger, my colleague, a friend, into my care. I ask you. Can the chauffeur fight off this evilness that has taken root in his being?

McGREGOR: [*Taking interest.*] I doubt it.

STAINES: Which can bestir the evilness that lies at rest in me.

McGREGOR: Oh.

STAINES: In you. [*Gestures towards the audience.*] In all of us. [*He stops, puzzled.*] I repeat in all of us. [*Waits.*]

McGREGOR: [*Wondering.*] You might be right.

STAINES: [*Raises voice.*] I repeat in all of us.

McGREGOR: I say there, you might be right.

STAINES: [*Losing place.*] God Almighty.

MOTHER: [*Off-stage.*] Where is the man I can tell my story to?

STAINES: Indeed – will there ever be another?

McGREGOR: As I was saying, I go most nights at this time.

STAINES: To the mother's.

McGREGOR: You find that entertaining?

STAINES: Not at all.

McGREGOR: It amuses you? [*Growing angrier.*]

STAINES: You've got me wrong. You are imagining things.

McGREGOR: Is that right.

STAINES: What I mean is . . .

McGREGOR: Be that as it may. It's a class of a low day.

[McGREGOR *exits stage right.*]

STAINES: I see. [*He looks after him towards the wings.*] This is very nice I must say. Kneeling light please. [*Nothing happens.*] Prayer spot please. [*His kneeling light comes on stage left front.*] I am obliged. [*He walks over and kneels.*] Here we go again. His passenger, the prisoner, my colleague, a friend. No Dodo. No Gabriella. No. Only moi. [*He prostrates himself.*] Thank you. [*He rises.*]

[McGREGOR *enters stage right with a briefcase and different jacket.*]

STAINES: What now!

McGREGOR: Could you sign here please?

STAINES: Not again.

McGREGOR: I'm afraid so. You want the documents, you sign for the documents.

STAINES: I see.

[McGREGOR *opens the briefcase, extracts a text and pen, goes to the table and sits in a clerkish manner.*]

McGREGOR: Please sit.

STAINES: Certainly.

McGREGOR: Sign just there.

STAINES: For you – anything. [STAINES *sighs.* McGREGOR *snaps the briefcase shut. The two sit with nothing to say.*]

GLORIA: [*Off-stage.*] I was expecting a lady.

STAINES: Oh yes. That's right. I was expecting a lady, but the sight of anyone is encouraging. Don't get me wrong. And you have your little briefcase. Your little briefcase. It is uncanny. That too is encouraging. You have come perhaps to enlighten us?

McGREGOR: I was sent for by the management . . .

STAINES: Not by me . . .

McGREGOR: By someone . . .

STAINES: And I was expecting a female. [*He stands.*] You are, I take it, standing in for the lady?

McGREGOR: You have the wrong man. That business is not for me.

STAINES: We all say that at the beginning in this house. It is understandable. But in one brain cell God labours on. [*He tours the space.*] The cell is only one of the many where sits that rare thing ticking away – the . . .

GLORIA: [*Off-Stage.*] The void.

STAINES: The very thing. I had forgotten. How careless of me. Indeed the void, which in time, I assure you, will be filled.

McGREGOR: By what?

STAINES: Indeed, by what. [*He stands puzzled by lack of text.*]

McGREGOR: And how is Mister Jones?

STAINES: [*Lost.*] Ahem?

McGREGOR: And Gerty?

STAINES: [*In wonder.*] Gerty by God!

McGREGOR: And Geoffrey?

STAINES: Geoffrey is it?

McGREGOR: Geoffrey it is. [*Pause.*] All well?

STAINES: [*Clears throat.*] Uhh. Yes. [*Very uncertainly.*] I believe they are all well. [*Pretending knowledge.*] Doing fine, thank you.

McGREGOR: I believe Sam took bad putting down the fire.

The wind got him. I was not to know, was I?

STAINES: No, not at all.

McGREGOR: [*Very emotionally.*] It broke me.

STAINES: I thank you. Very good. [*Turns to the audience.*] He is emotionally upset. He has woken from a bad dream. And yet he is to be humoured. [*Turns to* McGREGOR.] I say, perhaps you should scale down the emotional side. You know what I mean?

McGREGOR: [*Quietly.*] It broke me.

STAINES: Not so bad.

McGREGOR: You like it.

STAINES: I do.

McGREGOR: [*Quieter still.*] It broke me.

STAINES: Fine. Now as to our friends, if we have any? How can one tell in the dark – and with these lights – but let's assume we have some friends. They sit there facing you. [*He gestures to the audience.*] I pray you, kneel before them.

McGREGOR: No.

STAINES: You will kneel to the third party in time, never fear.

McGREGOR: Never. They are not of my concern.

STAINES: They will be when you think you are alone. That is the first step. The first on the gradient. And I wish to state now, before anything else happens, before we get carried away, that you are never alone.

[*A long silence.*]

GLORIA: A long silence.

STAINES: Right.

McGREGOR: Certainly.

STAINES: You got that?

McGREGOR: I have.

[*Enter the* MANAGER *with a picnic basket, golf putter, radio and assorted papers. He walks sharply across the space if there was no one else present. Stops. Looks at his files to see if they are open. He trundles by* STAINES *and* McGREGOR, *doffs his coat, very precisely, on back of chair, stands a moment.*]

STAINES: Did you see that?

McGREGOR: I did.

STAINES: He just walked by me.
McGREGOR: He did.
[*The* MANAGER *tries all three chairs, picks one, then sits at small portable writing desk. Begins placing everything in perfect order.*]
STAINES: A Manager by God.
McGREGOR: Is that what it is?
STAINES: Of all blooming things.
McGREGOR: Bless us . . . he knows how to make himself at home.
STAINES: Of course he was promised. [*They view him.*] Hark at the superstition. The want for order. The . . .
McGREGOR: The . . .
STAINES: The . . .!
McGREGOR: The bellicosity!
STAINES: Right! [*Affirming with disbelief.*] Bellicosity. [*The* MANAGER *gets up and, hand above the eyes, views the lighting.*] It's bad luck when one of those boys appear you know.
McGREGOR: You don't like it.
STAINES: I don't like it. What follows is never nice.
[*The* MANAGER *returns, sits with a priestly supplication, buries himself in words.*]
McGREGOR: Where is the pain?
STAINES: Just a moment. [*He checks his body. Simultaneously the* MANAGER *checks his body.*]
McGREGOR: I ask you again. Where is the pain?
STAINES: Pain? What pain?
McGREGOR: The painful silence, which for you, must forever be filled.
[*The* MANAGER *returns to his writing.*]
STAINES: What are you talking about?
McGREGOR: Lie down, why don't you?
STAINES: Have you taken leave of your senses?
McGREGOR: Is it the heart?
STAINES: My heart is going round perfectly well, thank you.
McGREGOR: Is it the lungs?

STAINES: Stop the nonsense. I am not given to improvisation.

McGREGOR: And I will not be chained by dogma. Or fettered by fate.

STAINES: La-de-da!

McGREGOR: Why does silence threaten you?

STAINES: Sit down.

McGREGOR: I am seated. [*Sitting down by the* MANAGER.]

STAINES: So am I. [*Sitting down by the* MANAGER. MANAGER *stands, straightens his back, does a few shoulder-turns, neck-straightenings, puffs out air, then sits. Pause.*] This is much better, is it not? The three of us here comfy in the house. The evening before us. And all recrimination done with.

McGREGOR: After the initial compromise. [*Sadly.*] It's downhill all the way. [*Pause. The* MANAGER *hits a radio knob. Blast of pop music. Turns it off.*] Where are we?

STAINES: Lost again, I should think. [*He leans over, lifts a page at the* MANAGER*'s desk, glances at it, the* MANAGER *give him deadly look, turns sharply violent, and* STAINES *returns it.*]

McGREGOR: Any joy?

STAINES: I believe we are in a square of sorts.

McGREGOR: Mountjoy?

STAINES: Sadly this is not Mountjoy.

McGREGOR: No?

STAINES: No.

McGREGOR: Ah well. I could have sworn we were in Mountjoy a while back. I'm sure I heard mention of Mountjoy Square.

STAINES: No. Not a dickey bird.

McGREGOR: What square then?

STAINES: The possibilities are endless.

McGREGOR: I thought as much. Always with you at the beginning it appears that the possibilities are endless, then slowly the limitations appear. [*Pause.*]

STAINES: [*To the audience.*] A few minutes ago he did not know me.

McGREGOR: [*To the audience.*] What did he say?

STAINES: Is all this really happening?

McGREGOR: I have seen all this happen before.

STAINES: God almighty! It is the nature of things that they resemble something else. It's down to the state of mind. But I guarantee you, when you have been here some time you will know that this is not the Bois de Bologne, nor Mountjoy, and even if it was it would soon not be.

McGREGOR: The Bois de Bologne?

STAINES: Yes. [*Nostalgically.*] All of a sudden the leaves fell.

McGREGOR: I was afraid of this.

STAINES: Never fear. Your moment will come. And remember, we have the Manager on board.

McGREGOR: Him?

STAINES: The very man.

[*They study him. He has a glass of wine before him.*]

McGREGOR: He's supping.

STAINES: In silence.

McGREGOR: In silence, supping.

[*The* MANAGER *studies them, then works on.*]

STAINES: And should the Manager fail us, well then the ladies will support us.

McGREGOR: The ladies?

STAINES: Why yes, the ladies.

McGREGOR: And where are they?

STAINES: Where do you expect? They wait in the wings. And then you'll ask me why. And I will answer patiently – they wait till the time is right. You ask me – why? And I will reply – because of us, what else. They wait to see how we get on. And do they come on? Well sometimes they feel it is not advantageous to appear. On certain nights they do not appear at all. And who could blame them. When they are in good spirits of course they come on first and we wait in the wings.

McGREGOR: But either way the documents remain the same?

STAINES: Let's say with some minor adjustments the documents remain the same.

McGREGOR: And do we get to meet the ladies?

STAINES: This is impossible.

McGREGOR: It's not possible?

STAINES: Why do you ask me these things? [*Sharply.*] I thought that was cut. [*To himself.*] I was certain that was cut. But no. [*To himself.*] Of course – [*To* McGREGOR.] – it's possible. [*He sits.*] It depends.

McGREGOR: On what?

STAINES: Line!

GLORIA: On the day we went bathing in Uttoxeter.

[*Both* STAINES *and the* MANAGER *look towards* GLORIA *in the wings with astonishment.*]

STAINES: [*In consternation he rises.*] What?

GLORIA: On how muffled the drum is.

STAINES: This is preposterous.

MOTHER: [*Off-stage.*] On something that might happen during the performance.

STAINES: Thank you. There you have it. It depends on something that might happen during the performance. Something we might say or do.

McGREGOR: Ha! I don't believe you.

STAINES: Why?

McGREGOR: You got a cue. I could have sworn you got a cue. Yes, you got a cue.

STAINES: And what is wrong with that? Is the cue not infinitely human? Is the cue not something we should be eternally grateful for?

McGREGOR: I got on without cues all my life.

STAINES: You smug fellow. One day you'll be grateful for the whisper. The aside, the . . . hint.

McGREGOR: [*Acting.*] Never!

STAINES: You should be grateful – when I go to my knees I'm grateful.

McGREGOR: [*Loping away.*] To whom?

STAINES: To whom? To what? Where are we? Because! You bat out of hell.

McGREGOR: Be nice now.

STAINES: How long do I have to put up with this?

[*The* MANAGER *rises.*]

McGREGOR: I don't know.
STAINES: How long do I have to put up with this?
McGREGOR: I don't know.
STAINES: Me neither.
McGREGOR: So?
STAINES: You will learn to be grateful to the others, to those beyond, to those out there.
McGREGOR: Women or men?
STAINES: Does it matter? [*He watches the audience. The* MANAGER *watches the audience.*] I can't tell because of the lights. The lights blind one. They blind a body. [STAINES *and* McGREGOR *stand staring at the audience.*] Sometimes you can tell by the laughter.
McGREGOR: I see.

[*The* MANAGER *stands stage left.*]

STAINES: For the woman laughs at our condition; the man laughs because he is part of it.
GLORIA: Ha-ha.
McGREGOR: Ha-ha.
STAINES: Restrain yourself. [*He looks to the wings.*]
McGREGOR: So this is a comedy.
STAINES: Who said that? [*Looking away.*]
McGREGOR: I did.
STAINES: I know that.
McGREGOR: Oh.
STAINES: [*Searching.*] But who said what?
McGREGOR: [*Playful.*] It was me.

[MANAGER *goes to and fro between them working out his plot.*]

STAINES: [*Slightly playful and looking in different directions.*] You?
McGREGOR: [*Enjoying himself.*] Me.
STAINES: You said this was a comedy? [*Turning angry and advancing at him.*]

[*The* MANAGER *stops, concentrates.*]

McGREGOR: [*Backing off.*] Yes.
STAINES: [*Advances.*] You said that?

[*The* MANAGER *moves on.*]

McGREGOR: [*Backing off.*] Yes.

STAINES: You . . .

McGREGOR: Excuse me, where are we?

STAINES: [*Stops.*] What?

[*The* MANAGER *stops, returns to his desk, and goes backwards through his manuscript reading.*]

McGREGOR: I asked you where are we?

STAINES: Let's go back a bit.

McGREGOR: Okay. [*They step back a bit, one after the other, over old routes they've taken earlier. On the way* McGREGOR *takes up his briefcase. The* MANAGER *hesitates at a certain page in the text. They stop.*]

McGREGOR: Are we perchance back in the Bois de Bologne?

STAINES: No.

McGREGOR: Ah. And not a word about Uttoxeter?

STAINES: Not a dickey bird.

McGREGOR: I thought so. [*They move forward a bit. They stop. Wondering.*] Always with you at the beginning it appears the possibilities are endless, then slowly the limitations appear.

STAINES: [*In pain.*] No, I say. Not that either.

[*They move on through earlier permutations.*]

McGREGOR: Are we there?

STAINES: [*As they go.*] Yes. Nearly.

McGREGOR: Did I hear mention of Mountjoy?

STAINES: You did not.

[*They go a bit further backwards.*]

McGREGOR: Now?

STAINES: Further.

[*On they go.* STAINES *stops, holds up a hand, then* McGREGOR *stops. They take up positions they had when earlier* McGREGOR *said "So this is a comedy?"* STAINES *signals* McGREGOR *to start.*]

McGREGOR: [*Tentatively.*] So this a comedy?

STAINES: [*Very seriously.*] Who said that?

McGREGOR: I did.

STAINES: [*More seriously.*] I know that.

McGREGOR: Oh.

STAINES: But who said what?

[McGREGOR *uncertain whether to continue as it might provoke more anger.*]

McGREGOR: It was . . .. [*He gestures "where are we," and looks round with wonder.*] And then I said excuse me, where are we?

[STAINES *waits a moment, then nods.*]

STAINES: I think we are in your room. In happier times.

GLORIA: [*Off-stage.*] What happy times . . .

McGREGOR: . . . are you referring to?

GLORIA: What a laugh!

McGREGOR: Oh. I knew it. [*Nervously.*] It was going to be a right laugh.

STAINES: Don't listen to her.

McGREGOR: You do.

STAINES: But sometimes she can lead you astray. [*Considers.*] You can tell gender equally well from tears.

McGREGOR: But tonight we can tell by the laugh.

STAINES: How do you know?

McGREGOR: [*Puzzled.*] I'm certain I acquired the knowledge recently.

STAINES: Not from me you didn't.

McGREGOR: Oh a chap happened by with the news.

STAINES: What? Did I hear correctly?

McGREGOR: You did.

[*Pause. They watch each other carefully.*]

STAINES: I repeat – as I said earlier – tonight we can expect the laughter of contempt or sympathy. It makes no difference in the long run. The two conditions are interchangeable.

McGREGOR: But if there are no women out there . . .?

STAINES: Well then we can sit back and enjoy the laughter of conspiracy. This auditorium will fill with the waft of old prick.

McGREGOR: How awful. Dreadful. Some sad night then we may find ourselves before an audience of men.

STAINES: Never. Before that eventuality the women in the

wings will save us.
McGREGOR: Are you very sure of that?
STAINES: I am positively certain.
McGREGOR: But we may have already entered the conspiracy. Down there, there may be none but men.
STAINES: I tell you this in confidence. There is always the possibility of one woman, who because of things in the outside world has been held up.
McGREGOR: She is on her way?
STAINES: She has turned the corner.
McGREGOR: She's through the door.
STAINES: She has taken her seat.
[*They both listen.*]
McGREGOR: She's very quiet tonight.
STAINES: She's settling herself.
[*They listen again.*]
McGREGOR: I . . .
STAINES: Sh!
[They listen.]
McGREGOR: Not a thing.
STAINES: Not a whimper. Not yet. But she'll come.
McGREGOR: You reckon?
STAINES: I do.
McGREGOR: So – let me see if I have got this right – our rightful agenda is that single lady?
STAINES: Yes.
McGREGOR: [*Brightening up.*] Ah.
STAINES: You are glad of that?
McGREGOR: I am.
STAINES: Now do you see how easy it is to be grateful? When I go to my knees. I'm grateful. I get this spiritual—
McGREGOR: Don't say that word.
STAINES: Which word?
McGREGOR: That word you just said.
STAINES: Spiritual?
McGREGOR: You've just said it again. Do you hear me – don't

say that word.[*Anger.*] That word is banned.

STAINES: I only said—

McGREGOR: [*Enraged.*] Banned you hear?

STAINES: I hear you. But this is ridiculous. It's ridiculous. I say, it's ridiculous. You can't stop me saying what I want to do. At the end of the day—

McGREGOR: [*Backing off.*] No.

STAINES: No what?

McGREGOR: No. [*In pain.*] Oh, oh, oh.

STAINES: What's wrong now?

McGREGOR: Don't say those words either, ever.

STAINES: What words?

McGREGOR: What you just said.

STAINES: I said that at the end of the day—

McGREGOR: You've just said them again. They're banned also, you hear me! They are banned.

STAINES: Jesus Christ. Can we say any fucking thing? [*Lights dim considerably.* STAINES *speaks to the overhead lights man.*] I beg your pardon. [*Lights come up a little.*] Dreadfully sorry. [*Lights go back to normal.*]

McGREGOR: [*Walks over to the* MANAGER.] Excuse me, sir. [*Very courteous.*] Are those words he said not banned? [*The* MANAGER *lifts his head from his task, which at the moment is playing cards. He nods.*] You see. He nods. The manager nods.

STAINES: [*To the lighting man overhead.*] Prayer spot please. [*Prayer spot comes on.*] Thank you, very kind. [*He kneels and prostrates himself.*] That fucking . . . [*Whispers.*] . . . cunt over there. [*Mumbles.*] Yes, yes. It began with who and what and Uttoxeter. Contained. Cannot. Blasted Managers. All again me. Yes. Yes. [*A few seconds silence.*] Thank you. [*He comes to his knees.*]

[*The two stand a moment in silence.*]

McGREGOR: [*Apologetically.*] What we need is a diversion.

STAINES: All we have been given is these four walls.

McGREGOR: All I can see is three. Or less than that. At a touch. [*He walks across space to blank side wall.*] Where do these steps lead to?

STAINES: [*Baffled.*] I have no idea.

McGREGOR: Okay, got you. Can we return to the subject of the ladies?

STAINES: If you must.

McGREGOR: What happens if we find ourselves before an audience of women? Do we continue?

STAINES: From somewhere. [*Tiredly.*] We wait . . . [*Exhausted.*] For a man.

McGREGOR: As previously we waited for a woman.

STAINES: Yes. [*Exhausted.*] Yes. [*Slumps down in the chair by the* MANAGER.]

McGREGOR: So that's the story.

STAINES: [*Eyes closed.*] That is – [*Slowly.*] – the condition.

McGREGOR: Ah. [*Pause.* McGREGOR *counts the permutations on his fingers.*] So we wait and see the gender of each audience?

STAINES: [*Eyes closed.*] That is correct.

[*The* MANAGER, *only once, with his arm outstretched, strokes* STAINES*'s head. Withdraws it just as suddenly.*]

McGREGOR: And they always come, Mister Staines?

STAINES: I'm tired of this.

McGREGOR: And they always come?

STAINES: Oh eventually, yes.

McGREGOR: You know what that means, don't you?

STAINES: [*Opening eyes.*] No.

McGREGOR: It means we shall never see the women in the wings. You lied to me. It's all a prevarication.

[STAINES *rises. Comes forward slowly. Looks into* McGREGOR*'s eyes.*]

STAINES: If you don't stop I'll give you one! You hear!

McGREGOR: Are you threatening me?

STAINES: However did you get that into your head? [*Backing off as if the threat never happened.*] All I can say, is that on the nights they appear, the ladies, arguing in the same manner as us, will have to go through the whole range of phenomena we have encountered, and perhaps understand no more than we do. It will not be the same for them as it was for us, yet it cannot be all that different.

[McGREGOR *retreats from him to extreme stage left.*]

McGREGOR: [*Sadly.*] And I thought this was an entertainment.

STAINES: Depends, depends.

McGREGOR: I, for one, was looking forward to meeting them.

STAINES: [*He considers this.*] Perhaps you will.

McGREGOR: Sometimes you can tell by the laughter, you said. Well I've heard none, Mister Staines.

[*The* MANAGER *laughs in derision.*]

STAINES: I'm sure I heard a laugh just then Mister McGregor.

McGREGOR: With resignation I say I didn't.

STAINES: Surely there was something? I say in hope.

McGREGOR: No, I answer, with greater resignation than before . . .

STAINES: Ah, I mutter, forlornly.

McGREGOR: Oh, I say, hopelessly.

STAINES: Have patience, my friend, I add.

McGREGOR: There's only one thing to do, I say again, with optimism. Call on the women in the wings.

STAINES: If you bring on the women before they're ready, I reply, it will lead to tragedy.

McGREGOR: Is that the one?

STAINES: Aye.

McGREGOR: But something you must admit has already gone badly wrong.

STAINES: I detect a maudlin spirit. [*Puts hand to his heart.*] Oh, excuse me, a maudlin goblin at work. Although I should add there are familiar airs and graces about the thing, you know. Familiar airs and graces which I can't at the moment . . . place. Tell me this Mister McGregor, before you go.

McGREGOR: Was I going somewhere?

STAINES: Oh yes.

McGREGOR: Strange.

STAINES: You said to me: where do those steps lead to, and I, baffled, said I had no idea.

McGREGOR: Did I say steps?

STAINES: Indeed you did.

McGREGOR: Strange.

STAINES: [*To himself.*] Steps you said.

McGREGOR: And I said "where do they lead to?"

STAINES: You did.

McGREGOR: Now. Imagine that. Steps I said. [*He goes back to the place where the imaginary steps are.*] They certainly go to a great height.

STAINES: [*Joining him.*] They do.

McGREGOR: Hundreds.

STAINES: [*Humouring him.*] Thousands.

McGREGOR: Hallo! [*He calls again up the steps that don't exist.*] Hallo. [*No reply. They look at each other very carefully, wondering which of them is madder. Whispering.*] I think there's no one at home.

STAINES: I'm afraid you're right.

McGREGOR: It would appear so.

STAINES: [*Whispering. He again looks overhead.*] Yes. The place is deserted. Since yesteryear. [*Now back to normality.*] So tell me McGregor.

McGREGOR: Yes sir.

STAINES: Were you ever in oblivion?

McGREGOR: Only the once. [*Pause.*] And I didn't like it. [*Pause.*] And I believe it's starting again. Another class of a low day. The whole sad business all over.

STAINES: Are we reduced to this?

GLORIA: [*Off-stage.*]You should have looked after me when you had me. [*A long silence.*] You should have looked after me when you had me.

STAINES: [*He speaks curtly.*] "You should have looked after me when you had me." Do you know that one?

McGREGOR: No.

STAINES: I think you do.

McGREGOR: I don't know what you are talking about. To what tryst are you referring?

STAINES: But you see I was expecting a lady.

McGREGOR: Well that's hard luck.

STAINES: Alright. [*He turns to* McGREGOR *with great earnestness and pain.*] You should have looked after me when you had me.

McGREGOR: Hah?

[*A long silence. The* MANAGER *looks to the wings. Nervously the men look from one to another, waiting on the other to begin.*]

STAINES: Line!

McGREGOR: Silence as they say . . .

STAINES: Line.

McGREGOR: Nothing but silence.

STAINES: I was expecting this. All evening people have been speaking out of turn. Tell me this, McGregor, what are the conventions?

McGREGOR: Me not know.

STAINES: [*Theatrically.*] What splendid things have been forgot?

McGREGOR: Each one unique . . .

STAINES: Splendidly forgot . . .

McGREGOR: . . . and never equalled. [*Pause.*] A drink perhaps?

STAINES: Once you enter these rooms the only contentment there to be had is in prayer.

McGREGOR: Just the one.

STAINES: Don't play the victim with me. You hear! Have you the documents?

McGREGOR: I have. [*He gets the documents from his briefcase.*]

STAINES: And how are we to know that the documents are in order? For instance, yours could tell a completely different story than mine.

[*They both look at their individual set of documents.*]

McGREGOR: It's better that way.

STAINES: Perhaps you're right. [*He hands the documents to* McGREGOR *who replaces them in the briefcase.*] We are allowing the others get an approximate version of who we are. But let's leave that. Yes. Our purpose will become clear as we proceed. For the time being, let us possess a sense of wonder. A sense of wonder is a prerequisite. Though admittedly, at times we look at the world – at the sea for instance – and find nothing there but the great resounding unseen. [*The* MANAGER *grows distressed.*] Look, McGregor, at the great resounding unseen. [*He looks.*] The second on the grid. In time we will be forgiven. I believe this. For all of us have said things that we later regretted. Regretted. Regretted. [MANAGER *nods vehemently.*] Others have made commitments which they have not fulfilled. Fulfilled. Fulfilled. Think, McGregor, of those grave commitments. You too and the others have passed the sea and seen nothing. Yes my friend, my colleague. Not till later, much later, when well removed from that natural place, did you hear the waves break. What I mean is – our innocence returns to us. For argument's sake, let's say here, in this holy spot.

[*Pause. The* MANAGER *is unhappy. During the above speech he makes a number of distress signals.*]

STAINES: Let us two stand in rapture.

McGREGOR: [*Breaking out of reverie.*] You are in a worse state than I thought you were. [*Pause.*] You have degenerated. [*Pause.*] I thought you might amount to something once.

STAINES: Stay quiet.

McGREGOR: Why?

STAINES: It's useless to talk at this moment.

McGREGOR: It is?

STAINES: [*He checks his watch.*] You see an aeroplane flies overhead at this hour.

McGREGOR: I can't hear it.

STAINES: Spot on!

McGREGOR: Hah?

STAINES: What a disturbance! What a racket!

[*Pause. The* MANAGER *acts more demented.*]

McGREGOR: Is it gone?

STAINES: Yes.

McGREGOR: Good. I can speak now.

STAINES: Aye.

McGREGOR: But what was I going to say?

STAINES: The whole thing is a mystery. Even if we have the

words off by heart we'll never know. Each night is a different night. But at least we are in the best of health. That's something. Except for the fact that my waste pipe is flittered. Flittered I say!

[*The* MANAGER *grows more distressed.*]

McGREGOR: So this is an entertainment.

STAINES: For the moment.

McGREGOR: Good.

STAINES: You welcome this notion?

McGREGOR: I do.

STAINES: I'm glad.

McGREGOR: So am I.

STAINES: A brave concession. Would you care for a stroll? To clear the head? Get the blood flowing?

McGREGOR: Leaving you was the best thing I ever did.

[*At this point the* MANAGER *rises.* STAINES *takes* McGREGOR*'s arm and hurries him along from underneath the yardarm on stage left. As he does, the* MANAGER *behind him undoes a rope, sits down, and the yardarm crashes to the floor with a huge bang. The* MANAGER *idles.*]

McGREGOR: What the hell was that?

STAINES: It appears the yardarm came undone.

McGREGOR: The yardarm! The yardarm!

STAINES: I guess the fixture must have been haphazardly tied.

McGREGOR: I could have been killed.

STAINES: So once again we survived.

McGREGOR: I tell you we could have been killed.

[*The* MANAGER *starts packing up the golf club, the radio, and the papers. He puts the bottle into the picnic basket.*]

STAINES: The man is packing.

McGREGOR: So I see.

STAINES: It must be nearing an end.

McGREGOR: Well pull the shagging curtains.

STAINES: That's not possible.

McGREGOR: Will you pull the curtains and let us get out of here?

STAINES: No.

McGREGOR: Did you not see what happened?

STAINES: I did, the wind must have turned.

McGREGOR: The wind?

STAINES: Yes. I'd hazard a guess – it's gone North-West. [*He steps back for a long look.*]

McGREGOR: And what if the other one comes down? [*He races out from underneath it.*]

STAINES: I can assure you it won't.

McGREGOR: Oh yeah?

STAINES: Believe me, McGregor, it's not due to topple yet. [McGREGOR, *very frightened, goes over and sits by the* MANAGER *who has grown impassive.* McGREGOR *looks at the second beam. Moves his chair closer to the* MANAGER. *Moves chair again. He looks at* STAINES *who is strutting contentedly. He looks at the* MANAGER.]

McGREGOR: Look at him – doesn't take a budge out of him. [*He gets up and goes over and looks at the fallen beam.*] That could have taken off both our heads. [*He walks stage left, looks overhead.*] This is not an entertainment. [STAINES *laughs cruelly.*] And by the way, sex is not a laughing matter.

STAINES: If it's not, you're in trouble.

McGREGOR: I'm in trouble anyway.

STAINES: Never mind. The top of the class is peopled by those who suffer. Suffering, like wonder, is a prerequisite.

GLORIA: [*Off-stage.*] And you had them, when I met you first, in great abundance.

STAINES: Are you back?

McGREGOR: [*Continuing on regardless.*] Back to Mountjoy. Not Mountjoy Square, but to a square, some square, nameless, I was told not so long ago, by a complete stranger. I met this stranger, a man-person, while I was on the way to see my mother. A journey I make most evenings. I could have continued with my troubles but I didn't. We stopped up for a chat and he explained about the women and I explained how Sam had lost the wind putting down a fire. For some reason this stranger took me to be an escaped convict, then he took me to be a lady, and tried to kill me.

STAINES: [*Continuing on regardless.*] Indeed I did. Quite so. For the present we are in the square, but eventually we might end up elsewhere.

McGREGOR: For instance?

STAINES: We might one fine day find ourselves in the round. [*They consider this project. Behind them the* MANAGER *stacks his things away. Gets up and leaves.*]

McGREGOR: The round, by God.

STAINES: Prayer spot, please. [*Prayer spot comes on.*] Will you join me?

McGREGOR: Never.

STAINES: You will in time, never fear. If you want off. [*He kneels.*] Thank you, so kind. [*To the lighting man.*] I am obliged. [*Lights on. He prostrates himself.*] Yes, fulfilled, wonder, Gloria, entertainment for Christ's sake, grave commitments, yes, yes. – [*Light dies on* McGREGOR.] – survived the yardarm once again, thank you, thank you, with great resignation, yours, Joey. [*Light dies. Comes up an instance.* MOTHER *prostrate where* STAINES *was.* GLORIA *standing where* McGREGOR *was. Light dies immediately. Comes back up.* STAINES *where* MOTHER *was.* McGREGOR *where* GLORIA *was.* STAINES *rises. They eye each other.*]

STAINES: I trust you understand that you can't keep that appointment.

McGREGOR: What appointment?

STAINES: With the mother.

McGREGOR: If you say so.

STAINES: I do.

McGREGOR: [*He turns away.*] You think that's funny?

STAINES: Why no.

McGREGOR: And if I were to go, I fancy you will besmirch my character when I'm gone.

STAINES: You have my word.

GLORIA: [*Off-stage.*] I heard that before.

STAINES: I will not speak badly of you.

McGREGOR: No?
STAINES: I promise.
McGREGOR: Indeed. I'm glad to hear it. Well I will definitely speak ill of you. For I woke from a dream and I heard you. I heard you, you hear. I heard what you said about me. Your atrocious voice. Your arrogance. Your contempt. I hear you all the time.
STAINES: That argument is over.
McGREGOR: It's not over. I hear you all the time, you hear? Have you nothing better to do than nattering on about me? Hah? I can assure you that when you are not present, your name never crosses my lips, neither in besmirchment nor praise.
GLORIA: [*Off-stage.*] Liar!
McGREGOR: Cheat!
GLORIA [*Off-stage.*] Gob!
STAINES: Stop it!
GLORIA: Scoundrel! Lecher! Ah . . . .
McGREGOR: Fucker!

[*The lights dip.*]

STAINES: Forgive him. [*To the man in the lighting box.*]
McGREGOR: Who?
STAINES: You.
McGREGOR: It's starting again. The whole sad business all over.

[*The lights dim a little more.*]

STAINES: Say you're sorry.
McGREGOR: I am not sorry. [*Lights dim a little more.*] And I will not go.
STAINES: But I believe you have to meet your esteemed mother.
McGREGOR: It is no longer necessary.
STAINES: A second ago it was.
McGREGOR: But it is no longer.
STAINES: You're learning.
McGREGOR: I'm forgetting.

[*Pause. He sits in the* MANAGER*'s chair.*]

STAINES: And where would you go? [*Peering about him busily.*] Back to that creature I expect.

MANAGER: Certainly.
GLORIA: [*Off-stage.*] I like him because he hates you.
STAINES: Stop it!
McGREGOR: We have spent many pleasant evenings speaking dreadful things about you.
[*Pause.*]
STAINES: When you left the last time I was not well. [*Sadly.*] I was not well at all.
McGREGOR: And for some reason I missed your whine.
[*The lights come up a little.*]
STAINES: You see, the lighting man approves. Now is the moment.
McGREGOR: For what?
STAINES: Why – [*Ponders the reply.*] – to pray.
McGREGOR: I will not pray.
STAINES: Well if you will not pray then how about a speech?
McGREGOR: I'll make no speech.
STAINES: Go on.
McGREGOR: No.
STAINES: But McGregor you were made for the speech. I can feel it in my bones. From the beginning I knew it. The great denouement. You could glide up and down the scales, protest, contain. You could soar.
McGREGOR: Never.
STAINES: But, sir, all evening I have felt a speech coming on. I've seen it in your hesitancies. In the graceful demeanour. As a matter of fact, I think you came close to the preamble a number of times.
McGREGOR: I did?
STAINES: Certainly.
McGREGOR: [*Aside.*] I mourn the ladies.
STAINES: Very Good. [*Silence. Grand gesture.*] I said "Carry on!"
[*Silence.*]
McGREGOR: There is some mention of chip-peas. [*Struggling.*] Ailments of a kind. [*Further struggle.*] And Christians.
STAINES: [*Grand gesture.*] Do carry on.

McGREGOR: [*Grand gesture.*] Do carry on.
STAINES: What are you doing?
McGREGOR: I'm doing nothing.
STAINES: You have so little character you have begun to imitate me. [*Enraged.*] Me, do you hear!
McGREGOR: I hear you.
STAINES: Find you own damn persona if you would be so kind!
McGREGOR: [*Fearfully.*] I will.
STAINES: I have no wish to see my distress mirrored in another.
McGREGOR: Okay.
STAINES: [*He advances threateningly.*] You hear me!
McGREGOR: No.
STAINES: Confounded fool!
McGREGOR: If you lay a finger on me, I'll tell.
STAINES: [*Dropping tone.*] It's uncanny.
McGREGOR: What is uncanny?
STAINES: [*Backing off.*] For a moment there I . . .
McGREGOR: Yes?
STAINES: I . . .
McGREGOR: Yes?
STAINES: [*Shaking his head.*] It's of no importance. It's a part of the past.
McGREGOR: [*Sadly.*] What is?
STAINES: [*He looks at him.*] No. [*With finality turning away.*] No. [*Looking back at him.*] No. [*Losing the script they both stand there, awkwardly.*] Line! [*No answer.*] Line! [*No answer.*] We've been abandoned. [*Pause.*] There's not a soul. [*Pause.*] I might have known. [*Pause.*] Speech.
McGREGOR: No. [*Quietly.* McGREGOR *sits with the briefcase on his lap.*]
STAINES: [*Roars.*] Speech! [McGREGOR *clutching the briefcase shakes his head. Demented,* STAINES *approaches him.*] What are you looking at? [*No response.*] I said what are you looking at?
McGREGOR: I was thinking I'm sorry for you.
STAINES: Hold on, I'll be back in a minute.

[STAINES *looks towards the man in the box. He storms off*

leaving McGREGOR *sitting as before.* McGREGOR *smiles an apologetic smile. The* MANAGER *looks in.*]

McGREGOR: [*Raising a hand.*] Hi Boss! [MANAGER *ducks off.*] Thanks awfully. [McGREGOR *sits waiting, pretending.*] Fuck.

[*The lights come down abruptly a moment later.*]

End of ACT I

ACT II

Women's voices now come from different sides. Lights come up stage right. McGREGOR *is sitting on a chair, alone, briefcase on lap, waiting to begin. He watches the lights come on. Decides to get in character, then checks the pages left on the* MANAGER*'s table.*

McGREGOR: [*Reads.*] I can have ten orgasms at a sitting. [*Drops text.*] Blimey.

[*Returns to his chair.* STAINES *comes on, stands directly in front of him.*] Would you please move?

STAINES: I'm sorry?

McGREGOR: Get out of the way. [*Frantic whisper.*] I can't be seen.

STAINES: By whom?

McGREGOR: The third party.

STAINES: I thought they were not of your concern.

McGREGOR: [*Riled.*] You're blocking me.

STAINES: Oh.

McGREGOR: That was very nice, I must say.

[STAINES *moves off stage left, very slowly.*]

STAINES: Any sign of the other fellow?

McGREGOR: No. [*Pause.*] What were you in the other world?

STAINES: Line!

GLORIA: [*Off-stage.*] I was a spark.

STAINES: I was a spark. And you?

McGREGOR: A humble chippy. [*He rises.*] And that – [*He points at the fallen beam.*] – could have killed me. Here in this . . . [*Pause.*] In this . . .

STAINES: Yes?

MOTHER: [*Off-stage.*] We must restrict ourselves.

STAINES: As I said: for the moment we must restrict ourselves to the square.

McGREGOR: Are there no other options?

STAINES: Well there was talk of a trajectory. In fact it has been mooted by the powers-that-be that a trajectory from here could run down the centre aisle.

McGREGOR: How sad that there is no trajectory. [*Goes centre stage, entranced.*]

STAINES: And then there is the possibility of revolving.

McGREGOR: Cripes!

STAINES: I had the privilege myself in 19 of 82 of seeing the phenomenon in The National Theatre. In that place we would disappear. A wheel would turn, our scene swing out to the East, a light would go with us. A light would come with them, those coming on, those ladies in the wings.

McGREGOR: How sad.

STAINES: There would only be the slight whirr of the hinges concurring.

McGREGOR: How infinitely sad there is no revolving.

STAINES: And then there is the possibility of levels.

McGREGOR: [*Entranced.*] Ah.

STAINES: With different levels we could consider simultaneous action. Two levels I promise you. At a touch, three.

McGREGOR: Thunder berries! What intoxication.

STAINES: Restrain yourself.

McGREGOR: Can another take our place?

STAINES: No. Sorry. You abandoned that privilege when you came on.

McGREGOR: [*Affronted.*] It's not right. [*Whinging.*] It's not right.

STAINES: It's how we survive. In this hall. In this house. In these rooms.

McGREGOR: [*He sits.*] And to think that a moment ago I

was standing up there, surveying the world. [*He falls into a depression.*] I have it!

STAINES: [*To himself.*] Got out of that place. Did. Go down there. Another cut, thank you. Yes. Check with Gloria. Into the hall. "Hall" says I fretfully: have I got that right?

McGREGOR: I said I have it.

STAINES: Pardon?

McGREGOR: How about a curtain?

STAINES: You got it right?

McGREGOR: A curtain!

STAINES: [*Looks at him closely.*] Obviously he expects an answer. [*He turns away.*] Appearances, of course. And reverbs. All that happens is. [*Looks back at* McGREGOR *who is following him.*] A mistake, definitely. Afraid of what? But how-and-ever. [*Returns to normal.*] Excuse me, you were saying?

McGREGOR: How about . . . the possibility . . . of . . . a curtain?

STAINES: We are restrained from the use of a curtain. Since we did not use them in the beginning then we cannot use them now.

McGREGOR: And why did we not use them in the beginning?

STAINES: For fear we might someday find ourselves in the round.

McGREGOR: In the round there is no curtain?

STAINES: No, only in the square.

McGREGOR: But yet, while we are in the square which might bear many distinguished draperies, we are denied the use of a curtain.

STAINES: I'm sorry.

McGREGOR: Could we not have a curtain now and then for a few seconds – just to separate one item from another – to recuperate – to contemplate – to regain oneself?

STAINES: No.

McGREGOR: All I need is a few moments to gather my wits.

STAINES: In the dark and confusion another might take your place.

McGREGOR: No, not true. However did you get that idea?

STAINES: I have my suspicions.

McGREGOR: In the past that might have been true. Yes, I admit it. For all those years I was with you I often imagined I was with someone else.

STAINES: Stop it.

GLORIA: [*Off-stage.*] When you thought I was taking pleasure in your company I was in fact remembering happier times with others.

STAINES: Please. [*He looks from one to the other wildly.*]

McGREGOR: And I think you liked it.

GLORIA: Yes he did.

McGREGOR: Dirty bugger.

GLORIA: Remember the times you interrogated me.

McGREGOR: Aye indeed.

GLORIA: Night after night.

McGREGOR: Wanting to know of all I had ever lain with.

STAINES: Stop!

McGREGOR: Over and over.

GLORIA: The whole sordid details.

McGREGOR: Indeed.

GLORIA: Yes.

McGREGOR: And then it was . . .

GLORIA: . . . where did I go? Where did I go last night?

McGREGOR: And . . .

GLORIA: . . . what was I at? And . . .

McGREGOR: . . . who was I with?

GLORIA: And . . .

McGREGOR: . . . was I standing by myself in the wardrobe?

STAINES: [*To* McGREGOR.] I do not want to hear of this. [*To* GLORIA.] I never entertained that fantasy, I was always only ever with you. In the dark or the light. [*To* McGREGOR.] Perhaps at times, because of your fantasy, I might have imagined someone else with you. I, in fact, may have often tried to become the someone else I imagined . . .

GLORIA: [*Coldly.*] So you say.

STAINES: Your hatred cannot touch me anymore.

McGREGOR: So, no curtain?

STAINES: [*Finally.*] No.

McGREGOR: I thought so. [STAINES *withdraws to a corner.*] Are you upset? [*No reply.*] Are you not talking? [*No reply.*] Would you care to go your prayer spot? [*No reply.*] It might give you some comfort. [STAINES *glares at him.*] I'm only saying. [STAINES *rises.*]

STAINES: I'll . . .

[McGREGOR *backs off, afraid. Just then the* MANAGER *enters laughing to himself at some joke. He carries a parcel of books, a plastic bag, and a hat with fishing hooks. He passes by* STAINES *and sits down. Looks inquisitively at both men, nods, and goes to his manual.*]

STAINES: Did you see that?

McGREGOR: I did.

STAINES: He did it again.

McGREGOR: Now.

STAINES: He just walked by me. [*He looks at* MANAGER.] Quare background, you know. [*Then looks at* McGREGOR.] You know what that means? [McGREGOR *raises his hands and shrugs.*] More melancholy.

McGREGOR: More supping.

STAINES: More banter.

McGREGOR: More barrage.

STAINES: More delusions.

McGREGOR: Speaking of illusions. How about the curtain?

STAINES: No curtain! [*He goes mad a moment.*] Had we the use of a curtain we would not have entered the world we presently find ourselves in. We would avoid continuity. And worse grow used – as we did before – to the habitual rest. Our senses seize up. The jitters accrue. The audience find a route in the dark to escape us. And worse still, and I repeat, worse still . . .

McGREGOR: Yes?

STAINES: . . . we might take refuge in the breaks.

McGREGOR: I would like that.

STAINES: Then we might fear to come back on.

McGREGOR: And is there not the chance – the chance I say

– that one could conceive, say, of the propriety of allowing for a curtain while we are in the square and the absence of a curtain while we are in the round?

STAINES: Mow.

McGREGOR: Mow? What is mow?

STAINES: Excuse me, no.

McGREGOR: [*Strangely triumphant.*] And that's definite?

STAINES: [*Sharply.*] Yes.

McGREGOR: How infinitely sad. [*He stops his strut.*] So though we are in the square we are actually preparing for the round.

STAINES: [*Stops.*] We are making – [*Flourish.*] – allowances for the possibility of the round.

McGREGOR: So we might never be in the round?

STAINES: I did not say that.

McGREGOR: We will never be in the round. We shall never see the trajectory you promised. Nor the revolving stage. There shall never be the three levels, or at a touch, two. How sad. Now I crave the round where we might never be.

STAINES: [*Feints pride.*] That is the condition. [*He takes off.*]

McGREGOR: But worse – [*Takes off after him.*] – we are in fact pretending to be in the round while we are in the square.

STAINES: [*Stops.*] Agh! [To himself.] Ask me arse. [*Realising he has cursed he looks to the lighting box. Lights dim a little.*]

McGREGOR: [*Stops.*] Pardon?

STAINES: [*Screams to himself. Screams to the wings.*] You could put it like that.

McGREGOR: Curse the round. [*They look at each other.*] It does not exist at present! We are not sure it will ever exist. All those nights spent making it up! And because of its possible existence we are denied the square.

STAINES: Sh!

McGREGOR: Another aeroplane?

STAINES: No.

McGREGOR: Then what is the disturbance?

STAINES: You.

McGREGOR: Always the bitter word.

STAINES: [*Looks overhead at the lighting man.*] Sorry.

McGREGOR: That's alright.

STAINES: I was not speaking to you. I was apologising to the man in the box.

McGREGOR: But it was me you insulted.

STAINES: But it was him took umbrage.

[*Lights return to normal.* McGREGOR *goes off and sits by the* MANAGER. *Watches him.* STAINES *sits down in the other chair. The* MANAGER *sups, they watch him, he sups again, content, takes up his pen, ponders, makes a signal, then starts playing solitaire.* McGREGOR *looks at the remaining beam. Moves his chair a little. Looks up at the beam. Moves chair again. The three idle away there waiting for someone to begin.*]

GLORIA: [*Off-stage.*] We imagine there is a curtain.

[*Pause.*]

STAINES: [*He looks toward the voice with irritation.*] Agh. [*Contemplates not going on.*] Look at it like this.

McGREGOR: I will look at it like this. [*Makes posture.*]

STAINES: Hah?

McGREGOR: Alright.

STAINES: Yes, we imagine there is a curtain. The curtain is there when we need it. The curtain is always here. Right now we are behind a curtain. [*He moves along front of stage feeling the curtain.*] See! [McGREGOR *gets up and studies the curtain that is not there.*] Do you see how it ripples? [*He flicks his fingers.*] Ruffles? [McGREGOR *watches him carefully.*] What texture. What weight!

McGREGOR: What colour?

STAINES: You are not convinced? [McGREGOR *shakes his head.*] Then let me put it another way. We shall imagine – but in fact it is true – that the action commenced before the curtain ascended and will continue after the curtain descends. As it will.

McGREGOR: We work then with an imagined curtain.

STAINES: Yes, we work with the possibility of a curtain.

McGREGOR: Which does not exist.

STAINES: But may do so.

McGREGOR: [*Nodding.*] In the square.

STAINES: [*Carefully.*] Yes.

McGREGOR: But not this square.

STAINES: [*Faltering.*] No.

McGREGOR: Because of the round.

STAINES: Yes.

[*Silence.*]

McGREGOR: Curse the round. [McGREGOR *sets off at a fast pace, avoiding the beam overhead and stepping over and back across the fallen one. He looks at the possibility of various exits. Turns to find* STAINES *behind him. Sets off again followed by* STAINES.] I demand a curtain. [*As they move.*]

STAINES: On what grounds? [*As they move.*]

McGREGOR: Because I am allowed to imagine what I will.

STAINES: We are all granted that privilege to a greater or lesser degree.

McGREGOR: [*Stopping mid-stage.*] Then, for me, now, the curtain descends.

[STAINES *stands in wretched awe.* McGREGOR *looks up. He follows the falling curtain that is not there. The* MANAGER, *perplexed, rises and comes over. He too looks at the curtain that is not there.*]

STAINES: It has descended. [*His head falls.*] It is your wish.

McGREGOR: I have commanded the curtain to fall.

STAINES: It has fallen.

McGREGOR: I have closed off the lights.

STAINES: The lights have dimmed. [*The lights dim.*] They are going. [*The lights dim some more.*] Soon they will be gone altogether.

McGREGOR: I demand that the women enter.

STAINES: They are entering.

McGREGOR: [McGREGOR *closes his eyes.*] At my command the women enter. They disperse themselves here and there discussing us. Broad and energetic they are about some business known only to themselves. Their whispers drop to a murmur. Sh! The unmentionable is mentioned. [*The* MANAGER *steps into shadow.*] Now they return to normal aspirations! All are wild to get away! Off to the swings. To the toilets. Listen! There is the soft rustle of skirts behind us. Something even less tangible than that. The old ladies are about the house. Each welcome the glass of soda water for the troubled stomach.

STAINES: They do? [*Disbelieving.*]

McGREGOR: Of course.

STAINES: My.

McGREGOR: Sh!

STAINES: [*Whispers.*] Are they here for the night?

McGREGOR: Sh! They are preparing themselves for other women. [*He turns rigid.*] My senses have turned giddy. [*The* MANAGER *steps out of the shadow at another place.*] The thing was uncertain. Very uncertain. [*The* MANAGER *disappears again.*] Then it turned. It turned to the good. This is a level-headed place. I am at peace.

McGREGOR: You are?

STAINES: I am. Now is the time to go to your knees.

McGREGOR: No, no yet, I beg you. [MANAGER *returns.*] Let me have this unforgettable moment, a moment longer.

STAINES: As you wish.

McGREGOR: Please do not speak. [*Pause. The* MANAGER *looks sternly at* McGREGOR *then at* STAINES.] At this moment – [*Coldly.*] – the void looks into the mirror.

STAINES: Come, come.

McGREGOR: Sh! They have noticed us.

[*Pause.*]

STAINES: What's happening McGregor?

McGREGOR: The Holy Infinite.

[*Long pause.*]

STAINES: [*Gently.*] Are you in prayer?

McGREGOR: God's curse on you. [*Shouts.*] Stay quiet! [*Pause. Sadly.*] They've gone.

[*The* MANAGER *returns to his table. The lights start coming back up a fraction.*]

STAINES: [*Patronisingly.*] And lo and behold you the lights have returned. All is as it was. [McGREGOR *opens his eyes.*] We have our space back.

McGREGOR: Oh no! [*He draws back in horror from* STAINES.]

STAINES: What's wrong?

McGREGOR: [*Drawing back further.*] It's you.

STAINES: Stop this!

McGREGOR: Joey fucking Staines. I knew it. I knew it! This is hell. [*He runs across to the* MANAGER.]

STAINES: Come, come, McGregor.

McGREGOR: When did they let you out?

STAINES: Steady.

McGREGOR: How is Mister Coyle and all the others? Fine? Wilting? Did you get a new car? A convertible? Blimey! [*He barks.*]

[STAINES, *smiling, takes new tack.*]

STAINES: I'm sure you are wondering at the size of my appendage.

McGREGOR: Are you going to show it?

STAINES: I'll not appal you by going into its dimensions.

McGREGOR: The women say it doesn't matter.

STAINES: It's also the same women say it does. [*Pause.*] Indeed I've heard it put rather crudely. [*He goes over and whispers into* McGREGOR*'s ear.*]

McGREGOR: You heard a woman say that!

STAINES: Sadly yes.

McGREGOR: Crickey! Lord above!

STAINES: But my relationships, despite my prowess, have been less then successful. [*He sits.*]

McGREGOR: [*Quickly to himself.*] Thank God. [*Normal voice.*] Oh, of course, I'm sorry to hear that.

STAINES: One lives with it. [*The two sit, then stand, then sit, then stand.*] See what happens when we two men, in a public place, before the eyes of others, offer each other consolation. Let me reassure you McGregor that we have come a long way. Has there ever been a moment when the whole business came to a standstill? [*Pause of enlightenment.*] Here, put your hand down my trousers.

McGREGOR: I will not.

STAINES: Do please.

McGREGOR: No.

STAINES: Then you can see for yourself.

McGREGOR: I don't want to.

STAINES: Just a little feel.

McGREGOR: Keep back. [*Grabbing his briefcase.*]

STAINES: Come on.

McGREGOR: [*To the lighting box.*] Hey.

STAINES: He can't hear you.

McGREGOR: Keep back I say.

STAINES: Oh well, [*Turning away.*] And so we hurtle on through the night.

[*The* MANAGER *quickly rises and goes off stage right.* McGREGOR *looks overhead fearing the beam will fall. The stage is plunged into sudden darkness. A barrage of sound. Lights up.* MOTHER *is standing where* STAINES *was, and the* MANAGER *is back in his chair. Beside him sits* GLORIA *where* McGREGOR *was.*]

MOTHER: Those men were not real to me, I assure you.

GLORIA: Their presence was infinitely superior to yours.

MOTHER: Get up from there!

GLORIA: No.

MOTHER: You trollop.

McGREGOR: [*Off-stage.*] I demand to meet the real men.

GLORIA: I demand to meet the real men.

MOTHER: That unfortunately is not up to me. The men in the wings can only come at a time deemed appropriate by them. [*She studies the* MANAGER *who is working away.*] And for them it will be no different than it was for us. First: we must consider tenderness, not frustration. Security not panic. We must contend with physicality not visions.

GLORIA: I believe the men have been and gone and that you drove them away.

MOTHER: And how could I have done that?

GLORIA: In the dark and confusion while the curtain was drawn.

MOTHER: There is no curtain.

GLORIA: There was.

MOTHER: No, I tell you.

GLORIA: I saw it.

MOTHER: Why do you continuously harp on about the cursed curtain? Why! [MOTHER *screams.*]

STAINES: [*Off-stage.*] Why? [*He screams.*]

GLORIA: [*Very quietly.*] Because the curtain for me is a long uninterrupted sleep. It is when I am closed for business. The shop dark. The corns cut. The line out. The curtain for me is an afternoon by the sea away from it all.

McGREGOR: [*Off-stage.*] It's when the flies stop.

GLORIA: When the flies stop. The chip-peas soak. It is the moment when the man who hurt me most – and who can never make me well – is loved by me again, though I know that ahead of me is the long life without him. Once it was with him, then without. First the hurt, then the without. A bad time. The curtains open wide for all to see. There it was, my misery parading. The joyless hours. The averted eye. The whispers in the queue. And asides. And asides. And I saw him in a dream and approached him. At first he did not know who I was. I said it was me. And he looked at me and said:

McGREGOR: [*Off-stage.*] We will die separately.

GLORIA: We will die separately, he said. And I moved on up the street thinking on what he had said. Separately, he said.

MOTHER: Oh. [*Turns aside ruminating.*] Have I misunderstood her? She has been visited by the ideal. There is no accounting for this. Even if during the act you remain outside observing yourself. Even if the yardarm holds, and the cries of pleasure resemble those of pain.

STAINES: [*Off-stage.*] We have come a long way. [MOTHER *and* GLORIA *remain still as if they have heard nothing. Raises his voice.*] We have come a long way I said.

MOTHER: We have come a long way.

GLORIA: We are not suitable. [*She gets onto her feet.*] We are too volatile. [*Sits again.*] We tried once.

MOTHER: You're depressing.

GLORIA: Do you believe the things we say to each other?

MOTHER: [*Considering this.*] At the time I suppose we do. [*Considering it further.*] But only for the duration.

GLORIA: Is that all?

MOTHER: Unfortunately we said the same things to others in the past, and meant it then, as we mean it now.

GLORIA: But surely the emphasis has changed. Are we not approaching the day of the few words known to us? The three of four words that will not destroy the thing they say.

MOTHER: Perhaps we are. But what are those few words Gloria, that's what I'd like to know.

GLORIA: Indeed. What are they?

MOTHER: Yes, and what do they mean?

GLORIA: Tell me this . . . Mother.

MOTHER: Yes.

GLORIA: Whatever became of self-esteem?

MOTHER: Self-esteem is only fifth on the gradient.

GLORIA: Oh. Is it that far down?

MOTHER: I'm afraid so.

GLORIA: And self-pity?

MOTHER: And self-pity?

GLORIA: Yes?

MOTHER: Why, it does not appear at all. [*Pause.* GLORIA *distressed.*] Never mind, you and me shall for a short time look into the void together.

GLORIA: If God is there, the woman isn't.

MOTHER: Let that pass.

GLORIA: It's not a perspective I can view a great deal of comfort.

MOTHER: Indeed. But let's say, for argument's sake, that between us all is well.

GLORIA: All is not well.

MOTHER: Was all well in the other place?

GLORIA: It had its moments. [*She rises.*]

MOTHER: Permit me to boast.

GLORIA: You are free to boast.

MOTHER: I can at a sitting experience ten to twelve orgasms . . .

GLORIA: Do I have to listen to this?

MOTHER: At a sitting!

GLORIA: I don't believe you.

MOTHER: You may believe it or not – my function is merely to impart the information.

GLORIA: And this you've done. And what in God's name do you be thinking of?

MOTHER: Why I cast my mind forward towards the next orgasm.

GLORIA: Is that the secret?

MOTHER: The trick is to forego self-loathing Gloria. Which I believe is second on the gradient.

GLORIA: Oh.

MOTHER: And third? [*Ruminates.*] To mow. I said to Gertie that thing. There. As a child I was wont. As a girl never. [*Halts, lost.*] Most important thing, my father said, is . . . [*Looks again at the* MANAGER.] Trifles the rest. [*Sees* GLORIA.] And this one. [*Approaches.*] Tell me that word from which memory sends its noise.

GLORIA: [*Not helpful, on guard.*] I have not heard of it.

[*The* MANAGER *stops writing. Ponders.*]

MOTHER: Of course you have. It sounds like bells.

GLORIA: No.

MOTHER: What is it? What is it?

GLORIA: A medley?

MOTHER: My God – [*She says backing away.*] – you are sitting in my chair.

GLORIA: I am? [*Without moving.*]

MOTHER: Yes.

GLORIA: I'm dreadfully sorry, Mother. Dreadfully. Please take it. [*Without moving.*]

MOTHER: No, no I couldn't.

GLORIA: Oh do. [*Without moving.*]

MOTHER: There's no need.

GLORIA: Oh please. [*She remains where she is, staring ahead.*]

MOTHER: If you say so. [*Remains where she is staring ahead.*]

GLORIA: I do.

MOTHER: Thank you, no.

GLORIA: Someone else can take my place.

[*Pause.*]

MOTHER: I believe they already have.

GLORIA: [*She rises.*] Someone younger than me I take it.

MOTHER: Someone different, that's all.

GLORIA: So now I can go home.

MOTHER: And where is home?

GLORIA: Somewhere else. Where there are intervals. Christians. Curtains. Sleep. There is the radio. The possibility of hearing John McCormack sing. A breeze through the window at night from the sea. My rituals. Will o' the wisps. Kittiwakes. [*Pause.*] A dog might bark. [*Pause.*] A man might visit.

MOTHER: What freedoms you possess.

GLORIA: They satisfy me.

MOTHER: So why not move all your material possessions to here – take the whole bloody lot here – then you would be in the same position as at home.

GLORIA: With one immediate difference.

MOTHER: Oh?

GLORIA: At home you would not be there.

MOTHER: So without me you think things would be different?

GLORIA: The obsession would be over.

[*Pause.*]

MOTHER: [*Ironic.*] John McCormack?

GLORIA: Yes.

MOTHER: A breeze at night?

GLORIA: Yes.

[*Pause.*]

MOTHER: [*More Ironic.*]And, I believe, a dog might bark?

GLORIA: Correct.

MOTHER: A man visit? [*With deep contempt.*] A man visit?

GLORIA: Yes.

MOTHER: Do you really think so? Are you so perverse that you would fool yourself again? [*She shakes head violently.*] We are separated from the men.

GLORIA: No.

MOTHER: But you yourself, only a moment ago, said it.

GLORIA: But not for ever.

MOTHER: I'm afraid so. [*They stand a moment. The* MANAGER *rises, crosses the space, re-crosses, making signals, lost. He sits. Gets up, goes over to the prayer spot, checks with the lighting man, checks its dimensions, makes it smaller, gives thumbs up, and returns to his seat.*] Resonance.

GLORIA: Ah.

[*Pause. The* MANAGER *sups.*]

STAINES: [*Off-stage.*] I thought we were friends.

MOTHER: For a while there I thought we were friends. Now all that remains is to ape the condition till the arrival of the men.

GLORIA: I believe they have come and gone.

MOTHER: I would be careful if I was you.

GLORIA: If you were me! [*She looks up, avoids the beam overhead and carries on.*] I doubt that will ever happen.

MOTHER: Wherever you go, wherever you are, I will persist in your consciousness.

GLORIA: In time I'll rid myself of that.

MOTHER: Perhaps.

GLORIA: I did it before.

MOTHER: Did you?

GLORIA: And I'll do it again.

MOTHER: I promise you I will exist more strongly in your head than I do in my own. It is ever so.

GLORIA: Before long you will be part of the past.

MOTHER: I already am. And yet a few seconds ago you needed me.

GLORIA: I panicked.

MOTHER: You'll panic again.

McGREGOR: [*Off-stage.*] Never.

GLORIA: Never. Draw the curtain across my half. I can clear off and you remain. You can speak to me as if I was here and I will answer for a while. And slowly I'll just fade away. No-one will notice. Maybe in the bookshops, or in that bar, the queue, but after a while they will forget. And you can proceed without me, as you care to. I will become an interval in your thoughts. Your bitterness can be given full rein! What do you say! [*The lights go blue.*] Your half of the stage will grow large as the human mind itself.

[*Pause.*]

MOTHER: See how she despises me!

[*Pause.*]

GLORIA: You will arrange for my side of the curtain to fall.

[*The* MANAGER *rises as before to study the phenomenon.*]

MOTHER: [*Tiredly as if she has been through this experience countless times.*] It has fallen.

GLORIA: [*Closing her eyes.*] I am going over to the far side.

MOTHER: Adieu. [*The* MANAGER *steps into the shadows.*]

GLORIA: I am going. The burden of self is too much for one woman to bear.

MOTHER: Adios.

[*Two spots illuminate both of them.*]

GLORIA: Something is wrong.

[*The lights come full up. The* MANAGER *stands under the rope holding second yardarm.*]

MOTHER: Come here!

GLORIA: Quiet!

MOTHER: [*Backing away.*] Come here I say!

GLORIA: No, I beg you – let me have this unforgettable moment a moment longer.

MOTHER: [*Screaming.*] Immediately, or it will be too late.

[GLORIA *rushes over to* MOTHER. *As she arrives, the second yardarm crashes to the floor where* GLORIA *has just been standing. The* MANAGER *sits, sups, uncertain of himself. A crisis strikes him.*]

GLORIA: [*Screams.*] Jesus Christ!

MOTHER: That was close.

GLORIA: What happened?

MOTHER: There was an accident.

GLORIA: An accident!

MOTHER: Yes, with the second yardarm.

GLORIA: The first time I thought maybe. But the second time – no. That was no accident – you knew it would happen.

MOTHER: That's the tragedy. But does it make any difference? [*She looks up at the lighting box.*] Either way it could have killed you.

GLORIA: Christ Almighty.

MOTHER: You were lucky. And as for pretty speech – the speech you should have made long ago – you have overlooked one essential thing. [*She points at the curtain that is not here.*] Both sides of the curtains – the curtain that is not there – work simultaneously.

GLORIA: I was very nearly killed.

MOTHER: So you were.

GLORIA: That beam could have taken my head off.

MOTHER: As I was saying, if your side comes across, so does mine. Perhaps they should act independently of each other. Perhaps. But they are planned to act as one. Of course in the early days the curtains were plagued by unsatisfactory timing. One side crept over before the other had quite begun. One returned without the other having started. Yes. On one side the action finished, while here on the other it continued on.

GLORIA: It continued on.

MOTHER: The heroine was lost. [*The* MANAGER *takes his bag, dons his hat, replaces his hat, looks through sheets of paper, looks under his table, stands, and then sits.* GLORIA *puts her hand in the air.*] Yes Gloria?

GLORIA: Many's the seasoned drama, Madam, that finishes unresolved.

MOTHER: Very good Gloria. Brilliant in f—

GLORIA: Don't say that word!

MOTHER: What word?

GLORIA: That word.

MOTHER: Brilliant?

GLORIA: There you've just said it again. [*Screams.*] Stop it, you hear?

MOTHER: And what would you have me say in its stead?

GLORIA: Anything but it.

MOTHER: How about excellent?

GLORIA: [*Hands to her ears.*] No.

MOTHER: I can't even say excel—

GLORIA: Stop it!

MOTHER: Dear god!

GLORIA: Never say that word, ever.

MOTHER: Well fuck it. [*Lights dim.* MOTHER *looks up to the lighting box.*] Sorry. I said I'm sorry. [*Lights return to normal.*]

MOTHER: And those were not real men.

GLORIA: And what did I see?

MOTHER: You saw a vision.

[*Pause.*]

GLORIA: It will suffice.

[*Pause.*]

McGREGOR: [*Off-stage.*] The burden.

GLORIA: The burden. [*Pause.*] Yes?

McGREGOR: [*Off-stage.*] The burden of self.

GLORIA: The burden of self. [*Pause.*] Yes?

MOTHER: You said something important back there. Indeed you did. I was quite taken aback. You said the burden of self is too much for one woman to bear.

GLORIA: Did I? It seems a long time ago. In the preamble I forgot.

MOTHER: How could you forget something so noble?

GLORIA: I had forgotten. Now I remember.

MOTHER: [*With a sigh.*] I remembered.

GLORIA: [*With a sigh.*] Then oblige me by allowing me to forget it again. [*Pause.*] As I had forgotten him. I had not seen him in the flesh for years, in donkeys, in my day – I had forgotten him. [*The* MANAGER *pauses, listening intently.*] Then in this dream he appears on the street, a distance away from me. How they turn up! Back-as-they-were. Without a-by-your-leave. These familiars. I am on my way to the newsagent's maybe, in a strange town, or to the bakery for a dollop of cream, alas. At first he does not recognise me. But I keep walking towards him, smiling.

[*She stands still, smiling.*]

MOTHER: Go on.

GLORIA: Then he says . . .

MOTHER: Yes.

GLORIA: "We shall die separately." [*The* MANAGER *drops his head.*] And do you know what the strange thing is – he will never know he said those words to me. Isn't that strange.

MOTHER: You should kneel.

GLORIA: No.

MOTHER: [*To the lighting man.*] Prayer spot please. Now, immediately. [*Light comes on prayer spot.*] Thank you. [*She kneels.*] Kneel, I beg you, beside me.

GLORIA: No.

MOTHER: Why do you watch me like that? What are you thinking of?

GLORIA: That in the past you must have done something dreadful wrong. [MOTHER *is stricken. The* MANAGER *listens in pain.*] I will tell them of your violence.

MOTHER: They will not believe you. [MOTHER *is adamant. She gets up.*] I saved your life.

GLORIA: But it was you that threatened it.

[*Pause.*]

MOTHER: I sang for you.

GLORIA: I listened.

[*Pause.*]

MOTHER: Think of all the time lost in getting this far. As far as we got. I could have, for instance, hit it off on a bad note with some other. [*The* MANAGER *returns to his notes.*]

GLORIA: As you did with me.

MOTHER: [*Expansively.*] But we got over that. Look, we are still here.

STAINES: [*Off-stage.*] The tensions increase.

GLORIA: If you had suffered my absence none of this would have happened.

MOTHER: I could have gone on with my life.

GLORIA: But you kept coming back.

McGREGOR: [*Off-stage.*] For more.

GLORIA: And more.

McGREGOR: [*Off-stage.*] And more.

GLORIA: And more.

McGREGOR: [*Off-stage.*] Speaking bad of me.
GLORIA: Then the interrogation.
McGREGOR: [*Off-stage.*] The recriminations.
GLORIA: Smelling the sheets.
McGREGOR: [*Off-stage.*] Yes.
GLORIA: Who was he?
McGREGOR: [*Off-stage.*] Where was I?
GLORIA: Wanting to know all who I had ever lain with.
MOTHER: Stop!
GLORIA: I knew it.
MOTHER: What?
GLORIA: The parallelogram is a myth.
MOTHER: I don't follow you.
GLORIA: We are in a square but we are not allowed the full use of its dimensions.
MOTHER: The absence of a fourth wall – [*She points to the front of stage.*] – is to provide for the third party.
GLORIA: And you tell me self-pity does not appear on the gradient?
MOTHER: No.
GLORIA: A body is not even allowed that.
MOTHER: No.
GLORIA: How sad. [*Pause.*] Soon now the curtain will fall.
MOTHER: There is no curtain.
GLORIA: Bollocks.

[*The lights come down a little. The* MANAGER *rises collects his things and leaves. They do not notice this.*]

MOTHER: See now what you've done.
GLORIA: What have I done?
MOTHER: You have offended the sensibilities of the man in the box.
GLORIA: [*Looking up.*] He too is in a square? Like us?
MOTHER: [*Looking up.*] Yes.
GLORIA: My heart goes out to him.
MOTHER: If you curse again, the man in the box will plunge us into darkness.
GLORIA: I'm sorry. [*Looking up.*] What more can I say? [*The*

lights dim a little more.]

MOTHER: Now you see.

GLORIA: Tell him I'm sorry.

MOTHER: [*Whispers.*] I'm afraid that may not be enough.

GLORIA: [*Whispers.*] And what should I do?

MOTHER: Perhaps you should go to your knees. Come to your knees here beside me.

GLORIA: Never. That is asking too much.

MOTHER: Prayer spot, please. [*It does not come on.*]. Prayers spot please, I beg you. [*It does not come on.*] Just one last time. [*Prayer spot comes on.*] I thank you. [*She goes to her knees.*] Join me.

GLORIA: No.

MOTHER: [*She prostates herself.*] Please.

GLORIA: No.

MOTHER: It will be different this time. Please.

GLORIA: If I must. [*She kneels by* MOTHER.]

[*The place goes into darkness. Pause. Lights come on, but dim.* STAINES *is kneeling where* MOTHER *was and* McGREGOR *is where* GLORIA *was.*]

STAINES: Now pray.

McGREGOR: Sh! Can we not watch the night fall in silence?

STAINES: That is not real night.

McGREGOR: The stars are coming out.

STAINES: Those are not real stars.

McGREGOR: And the ships they are returning.

STAINES: [*Loudly.*] Those are not ships. Those were not real women. And you . . . you! You arrive to a place and expect a curtain because you believe a curtain goes with a square.

McGREGOR: Which they do.

STAINES: You do not accept that the absence of a curtain can still suggest a square.

McGREGOR: You can't have it both ways.

[*The lights dim some more.*]

STAINES: I don't see how that arises.

McGREGOR: Now you say that the absence of a curtain suggests a square – earlier the absence of a curtain presumed the possibility of the round.

STAINES: If we had a curtain, and it was drawn, you could not see the stars.

McGREGOR: So you see – the stars exist. The boats exist. And the night.

STAINES: Fuck the curtain.

McGREGOR: Fuck the curtain surely. [*He rises. Lights dim more.*] Look at the fireflies.

STAINES: What fireflies?

McGREGOR: Why there. [*A firefly appears.*] And there.

STAINES: Those have been concocted by the man in the box. The man you offended.

McGREGOR: It was you asked me to put my hand down your trousers.

STAINES: Never mind that. Look my friend and colleague – there are no fireflies. There are no fireflies. You hear me – none!

McGREGOR: And very beautiful they are too.

STAINES: [*Exasperated.*] There are no fireflies.

McGREGOR: I'm sorry sir. I see fireflies before me. [*Very quietly.*] Soon the flies will stop. The chip-peas soak. The shop will go dark. The toes be clipped. Once it was with her, then without. First the hurt, then the without. A bad time. There it was, my misery parading. The joyless hours. The averted eye. The whispers in the queue. And asides.

STAINES: Line!

McGREGOR: And asides. And cues.

STAINES: Line!

McGREGOR: And I saw her in a dream and approached her. At first I did not recognise her. Then she said it was her. To run into her on a strange street like that! And I looked at her and said . . .

STAINES: Line!

McGREGOR: . . . before I could stop myself . . .

STAINES: Line! For God's sake, take pity.

McGREGOR: . . . we will die separately.

STAINES: Have pity!

[*The* MANAGER *looks in.*]

McGREGOR: I'm sorry. It's not on the gradient.

STAINES: No?

McGREGOR: No.

[*The* MANAGER *leaves.*]

STAINES: [*Quietly.*] Line.

[*Pause.*]

GLORIA: [*Off-stage.*] Curtain.

McGREGOR: Curtain.

STAINES: No curtain! There is no curtain. [McGREGOR *approaches him.*] No curtain you hear! Prayer spot, please. Prayer spot. [*He prostrates himself.*]

McGREGOR: Mister Staines?

STAINES: Yes.

McGREGOR: I'll be on my way now.

STAINES: Fine. [McGREGOR *leaves briskly in the same manner as he came on.*] Dodo, I said, as we came up Forty-Second Street. Winter of 19 and 82. [*Pause.*] With Earwigger along the ravine under the shots. [*Pause.*] Then into the kitchen in Nance. What cuts there were! What scandalous dreams! [*The* MANAGER *appears in the dark, stage right, watching for a moment.*] She nestling her head onto my shoulder. Tired, at the end of her days. Mother I said, is it yourself? And still she bowed her head. But could I? No, too late. [*He looks up.*] Too late, man. [*Closes eyes.*] Wanted to say the word rump, just once, but I couldn't. Nor calf! Not allowed. Local government you see. Well, I had my say, so I might go down the field for a while. Just one prayer I beg you! [*He beseeches the lighting man.*] Nothing but mission boxes. Sins. Curtains. Ghosts. Managers. And a certain lady who will remain nameless. For security reasons. In matters of security, you see. Who comes in some nights. As she was. Is not. Cannot be. And then doesn't leave me, and then does. Well. Left. Not a dickey bird. Serious. [*The* MANAGER *leaves slowly.*] And down it came. Bang down. Just there beyond. [*Opens eyes.*] Bang down! [*He shakes his head.*] Dearie me. [*Looks out.*] And the hole flittered. And the head unwell. Then this crowd. The same

crowd. Gathered. But I said I was having none of it. Mow. [*Takes off his jacket and throws it behind him.*] I thought of writing a reply. But said no. I had my allocation. Thanking you. Ready when you are I said. You hear me? [*Throws himself prostrate.*] Prayer spot I beg you! Please! [*Kneads his head.*] Don't then. Well this is it. No Dodo. No Gabrielle. [*He batters the floor with his fists.*] Just Mac. He has the knack of saying blimey. And all I asked for was a speech. And would he give me that? Not at all. A fucking speech . . . [*Lights fade.*] Ah well, and so we hurtle on through the night.
[*Lights out.*]

END

Men to the Right, Women to the Left

Written by Dermot Healy in collaboration with The Clones Drama Group, Monaghan. First performed at the Abbey Theatre Bar, Dublin, as part of Bealtaine, the Season of Creativity in Older Age, in May 2001. Directed by Dermot Healy. It was broadcast on RTÉ Radio 1 in 2002 (produced by Ann Walsh), and was revived at the Peacock Theatre, Dublin, as part of the 2003 Bealtaine Festival.

CAST

MAN	
WOMAN 1 [W1]	a younger woman
WOMAN 2 [W2]	an older woman

Note: The performers play a variety of characters.

Set: Three chairs. Beside the chair on stage right there is an old pram. From the pram will come odd cries mimed by W1. *A small table and small bed at the back. A pulley rope dangles from above.*

In the far distance the roar of a train.
Darkness on stage.

MAN: Ah Christ. Is that the . . . [*Searching.*] . . . the Ballyhaise?
W2: No.
MAN: Well blast it. Hold it – Clones, hah?
W2: No.
MAN: Well pray tell?
W1: That'd be the 6.15 ta Dundalk, I'd warrant.
MAN: Is that her? Be God!
[*Lights up.* W2 *and* MAN *on their feet, readying themselves. He puts on his cap.* W1 *asleep.*]
W2: No question about it.
MAN: Now. Mother knows. [*He claps his pocket.*] Do you hear that, you?
W2: She's asleep.
[*Claps his other pocket.*]
W1: Fast.
MAN: Oh fast out. [*Claps his head, finds cap.*] How did that get there?
W2: [*Grabbing scarf.*] You see, for my sins, I was born in a railway house.
W1: I was born above a drapers.
MAN: [*Fitting cap.*] You were, God help us.
W2: Me father . . .
MAN: Was a class of a stoker.
W2: And yours?
MAN: A saddler, I believe, and what's wrong with that?
W2: Nottin.
W1: And mine mended tar barrels.
MAN: Oh indeed he did. Isn't it great the way that wee girl can

talk in her sleep. [*Looks at himself in mirror.*] Ah lovely. I don't know where I got it from. Are you right?

W2: Right.

W1: To continue, if I might.

W2: On you go.

W1: When you heard the code of rings you knew a train was due from Clones.

MAN: [*Finger up, knowing a thing or two.*] Or Newbliss.

W2: Maybe Cavan.

W1: Or Drogheda.

MAN: Or – [*Losing the knowledge.*] – where was it . . .

W1: Belcoo?

MAN: The very place, you're right. And . . .

W1: Me mother'd go out . . .

W2: [W2 *advances centre stage.*] And . . .

W1: Open these huge white gates . . .

MAN: She would . . .

W2: And . . .

W1: Then step back.

[W2 *opens arms.* MAN *pulls rope. Train comes closer. With a great roar the train passes.* MAN *lets go rope and the train goes off slowly into the distance.* W2 *and* MAN *return and sit.*]

MAN: Gone, just like that.

W1: It passed so close to the house it was frightening. [*Pause.*] Everything shook.

MAN: Including the bucken bed.

W2: And then you'd know the day was started.

MAN: [*Loud.*] Get up you!

W2: Ah Da.

MAN: Get out of yon bed. Open the damn eyes and tell me this.

W2: Ah God.

MAN: In what county is Birrrrr?

W2: Please Daddy.

MAN: That got ya.

[*He clatters his knee with his cap.* W1 *opens eyes. The dialogue suddenly goes fast like a train.*]

W1: The trains were all right.

MAN: They were.

W1: You could take your bike with you.

W2: You could sleep in one.

MAN: You could.

W2: When I started nursing I'd leave Belfast after having been up all night on duty and it was great to fall asleep on a train. I'd shut me eyes and away with us. A train was better than a bed.

MAN: The chew-chews.

W2: The Great Northern.

MAN: The Great Southern.

W1: The . . .

MAN: The curse of God on them . . .

W1: Ruining a body's sleep . . .

W2: You might wake up anywhere.

MAN: True.

W1: And I often did, God help us.

W2: And we'd go out to meet her and no one there.

W1: And I'd look round me in a strange town not knowing where I was.

MAN: Oh but you knew where you were all right.

W1: Don't start.

MAN: Hooooh! Mr Comfortable, do ya recall him? He wouldn't be far away, would he? Not Mr Comfortable, oh no. With his airs and graces.

W1: Stop it.

MAN: Mr bloody Comfortable. Lie up like. And . . .

W2: Daddy!

MAN: What?

W1: The neighbours. [*She nods towards audience.*]

MAN: Oh. [*Smartens himself.*] Oy yis. Ha-ha-ha. [*Salutes.*] Good morning. [MAN *stands, puts his cap on and turns into the train conductor.*] Come along now.

W2: We're coming.

[*The women rise.*]

MAN: [*Checking watch.*] We're leaving on the hour.

W2: Oh yes, trains. Trains with carriages that were there since

Queen Victoria's time, all red flush padding with loads of buttons and tassels.

MAN: [*Waves a rolled-up newspaper.*] Enniskillen to Sligo!

W1: Mrs Farrell!

W2: Mrs Foley!

MAN: Dreadful morning.

W2: Dreadful.

[W1 *and* W2 *shuffle down aisle dragging heavy bags.*]

MAN: All aboard!

W1: On the narrow gauge from Belturbet to Drumsna.

MAN: Calling all!

W1: And tin hot water bottles under the seats to keep you warm.

MAN: Good morning sir. Good morning madam.

W1: [*Normal.*] Mr McGoldrick. [*Aside.*] It's far from Madam he was born.

W2: [*Smiling.*] Mr McGoldrick.

MAN: [*Lecherous.*] Hallo Sara. [*Father's warning voice.*] Mr McGoldrick. [*Conductor's voice.*] Hallo sir, how do you do. [*Finger to forehead.*] Take your seats now. Take your seats. [*Father whispers.*] Kiss me arse.

W1: Then there was the judge's carriage. [MAN *sits, and opens newspaper.*] Where he'd sit when he'd come to court.

MAN: A tot of sherry, please, McGoldrick. Yes, your honour. No wild animals on the crossing this morning? No, your honour. And smugglers, do we have any smugglers on board? No. Good, good, McGoldrick. [*Conductor, sarcastically.*] Good, good, McGoldrick.

W2: All away!

W1: On the Cavan-Leitrim railway.

MAN: [*Roars standing.*] Stand back now!

W2: Whist!

MAN: [*Back to himself.*] What's wrong?

W2: You'll wake the baby.

MAN: Aw.

[*All sit. He looks into the pram.*]

MAN: For all my sins. Tar barrels, tar barrels, poverty and strawmen. Jump Joe. Jump Joe. Tar barrels, tar barrels, poverty and chocolate.

[*Rocks the pram a little.*]

W2: I can remember being in that cot.

W1: You cannot.

W2: And I remember his nibs going on with the Jump Joes.*

MAN: No.

W1: Yes.

MAN: No one can go back that far.

W2: I can.

W1: She would, she'd go back in here – [*Pointing at her stomach.*] – if she could.

W2: And the cat . . . got in . . . and sat . . . on my mouth.

W1: Get away outta dat.

W2: Did.

MAN: Did not.

W2: I nearly suffocated.

MAN: Do you hear that Gertie?

W1: I did.

MAN: And who was on duty that blessed night?

W2: You.

MAN: Oh.

[*Pause.*]

W2: I heard things as a nurse in Belfast and later in Birmingham that would turn your head. What the doctors told you would sicken you. The things that happen a body are beyond belief.

MAN: True. You have to do a lotta work this side of the grave.

W2: You have.

MAN: And it's the light work does the blooming damage.

W1: Now.

MAN: Take me. [*Both women swing around to look at him.*] I took a clot in my leg cutting a hedge. If I'd been building a wall it wouldn't have happened. But feck it. I have no time for sentiment. It hardens the arteries.

W1: It does.

MAN: And there's no use being serious.

W2: No.

* Jumping up and down in the cot.

MAN: If you're serious you have to call in the long jaws.

W2: The lawyers.

W1: Them's the boys.

MAN: Them's the boys. The bucken long jaws. Get them in and that's . . .

W1: When . . .

W2: The music . . .

W1: Starts.

MAN: Aye!

[*Pause.*]

W2: My father was always thundering. He was strict. The bits he missed my Auntie caught.

MAN: You!

W2: He would fly into a temper. He used roar like an auctioneer.

MAN: [*Loud.*] Get down here! [*She runs to him.*] Put on that fire! [*She ducks down.*] Get back from that window. There's nottin out there for you.

W2: Day in, day out, roaring.

MAN: [*Loud.*] Come over here you. If I get you – I'll . . . I'll . . .

W1: I'll cut the snot of ya.

MAN: Did ya hear that Gertie? Did you hear what the baby said?

W2: I did, God bless us.

MAN: Well the grown-up article. [*Curls index finger menacingly.*] Come over here to me.

W2: No.

MAN: Be Jesus!

W1: I had a father who was quiet.

MAN: [*Quietly.*] I was.

W1: He would not say boo.

MAN: No.

W1: It's my mother was the boss.

W2: Come in that door, you trollop!

W1: She had the sting of the O'Byrne's.

W2: [*Shaking the finger.*] When I get you home!

MAN: [*Roaring.*] I'll . . . I'll . . .

W1: I'll . . .

W2: That's what he was like. I thought all men were like him. I thought when I married that my man would be the same as my father.

MAN: [*Quietly.*] I wasn't.

W2: No.

MAN: I was quiet.

W2: Yes. My man was quiet.

MAN: [*Quietly.*] I was. [*He nods thinking about it.*] Despite myself.

[*Pause. Suddenly all three get up and begin moving.*]

W2: Right?

MAN: Right.

W1: It was an evening in summer and there was great bustle about – Bessie and her piglets nosing around, cows in for milking, and the cows were Sara . . .

W2: Jibber . . .

MAN: Minnie . . .

W2: The Black Lady . . .

W1: And The Brute. He'd lash you with his tail. Then there was Jenny the horse and she was so quiet we used walk in and out under her belly. We need that horse said my mother, like . . .

W2: Like we need a hole in the head.

W1: Because, you see, my father could not stop his damn dayling. Wheeling and dayling.

MAN: I could not.

W1: Would ya . . .

MAN: Take off a tanner?

W1: I would.

MAN: If you'll throw in the calf.

W2: No bucken way.

W1: She has all her faculties.

MAN: She has in her shite.

W2: I'll take three and ten.

MAN: You'll take buck all.

W1: Are you still there?

W2: I am.

MAN: Well clear off. There's a train leaving town at six and you should take it and see the world.

W1: Daft bollax.

MAN: What!

W1: What'd ya say?

W2: What'd ya say to my father?

MAN: Speak up man.

W2: Three bob.

MAN: Did I hear right?

W1: Ya did.

MAN: Done [*He proffers his hand.*]. Good man. [*Gives him the thumbs-up and walks round the beast.*]
[*Swings back into the kitchen.*]

W1: Wheeling and dayling. Anyway, there was food being rationed into buckets for calves, the hens to be locked in for the night, food cooking on the hearth, and there I was, I can see myself, tottering about.

W2: Getting in everyone's way.

W1: I was not.

W2: You were, you scut.

W1: When without warning . . .

MAN: I warned you.

W1: I was unceremoniously lobbed into a tea-chest in a nook beside the parlour door for . . .

W2: Looking for attention.

W1: [*Sits.*] Well I was outraged and roared . . .

W2: [*Sits.*] Like a bull.

W1: And roared.

MAN: Do you hear her?

W2: Take no notice.

W1: But no one took the slightest heed. You see nobody loved me. Not a one in the world. Not a soul in the earthly. Not one in all eternity.

W2: Ah stay quiet.

W1: So I decided I would get even with them. I decided I would do my number two.

MAN: Good God.

W1: I pushed and I shoved till I'm sure I was purple in the face and . . . alas, there my memory ends. [*Goes back to her seat.*] Gone. Just like that. For the life of me I've forgot. But I would not let it be, would I. I would not. Years later I was talking to Aunty Mai. Were you there that day? I asked her.

W2: I was.

W1: And did anything . . . happen?

W2: Nothing happened.

W1: No?

W2: No. You were always tight.

W1: Thank you.

W2: Think nothing of it.

W1: See? That was our crowd. Loved? Hah!

[*Pause.*]

MAN: Since I got auld I never had it so good. And I'll tell you this – I regret nottin. [*Pause. He shakes the pram.*] No, nottin! [*Nods to* W1, *and winks at* W2.] Then there's Gertie. And then there's cajolery.

W1: He's starting.

W2: Oh dear.

MAN: Wasn't there?

W2: Full of cajolery he was.

MAN: Till I got auld. [*Curls index finger and gives loud whisper.*] On the QT one a' de weeman musta slipped something into my tay.

W2: I wish I had.

MAN: Unnoticed by me, pray. And there's no sign since. No. Oh but I would!

W1: [*Whisper.*] Daddy.

MAN: [*Does not hear her.*] Oh yes. I would. Ah-ha.

W1: Daddy!

MAN: Excuse me?

W1: [*Points.*] Stop it.

MAN: [*Raises hand.*] Oh.

[W2 *rises and goes over and taps the* MAN *with her fist on the shoulder, shaping up like a boxer.*]

W2: Take that!

MAN: What now?
W2: C'mon!
MAN: Stop teasing me!
W2: Up with the fists!
MAN: Baby.
W2: C'mon!
MAN: Will you leave me alone.
W2: C'mon, you boy ya!
MAN: Stop it, baby, or I'll tell.
M2: Tell who? [*Thumps him.*] C'mon. Tell who. You'll say nottin. I can best ya.
MAN: Mammy!
M2: You're no good to bawx.
MAN: Stop it, Maggie.
M2: I'll bawx the face of you.
MAN: Will you leave me alone?
M2: You're no good.
[MAN *gets up, runs over and gets something, comes back and swishes something across her face. She recoils.*]
W2: [*Screaming.*] Daddy! Daddy!
MAN: Sh! You'll wake the baby.
W2: Jimmy hit me with the tongs.
W1: Did ya?
MAN: I did.
W2: You should send him to jail.
MAN: It's you are at fault here. [MAN *sits.*] I told ya to stop, baby.
W2: [*Sits.*] I was an awful scourge.
MAN: She was a bucken dread.
[*Pause.*]
W1: My brother said something
MAN: Mumble, mumble . . .
W1: When Granny hit her leg off a post.
W2: [*Screech in pain.*] What are you saying?
MAN: Good enough.
W2: Come again?
MAN: Nufin.

W2: What are you saying?

MAN: Good enough for you Granny.

W2: My God, and me in pain – and is that the sympathy I get.

W1: And he got away with that. And then acoorse the poor cratur did not like fish.

MAN: I did not, no. The smell. I could never like them. No.

W1: I hate people who say, I don't like this, and I don't like that, and I don't like the other.

MAN: I don't care.

W1: Shut up!

MAN: I don't care if you say . . .

WI: Don't try me!

MAN: . . . If you say you hate people who say I don't like this and I don't like that.

W1: Stop it!

MAN: I won't. Because you're only saying the same as me. Isn't that right, Ma?

W2: That's right, son.

MAN: Just because I don't like fish, she doesn't like me.

W2: [*Ma nods in another world.*] Now.

MAN: [*He turns to W1.*] Same as you're saying you don't like me just because I say what I don't like.

W1: [*She tries to puzzle it out.*] I don't know what you're saying.

MAN: It's you, it's you yourself that's always saying that ya don't like this and don't like that, and . . .

W1: You see what I mean. And not only did he not like fish – [*Imitating the mother.*] – but the poor cratur couldn't say the word fish.

MAN: Ah don't bring that up.

W1: I will if I want to.

MAN: Always the bucken same story.

W1: Instead of fish he said . . .

MAN: [*Reluctantly, and sad and ashamed of himself, in that order.*] Shit . . .

W1: And one day Grandda had fish for dinner.

MAN: Very nice too.

W1: And when Mammy came in, me brother said . . .

MAN: Mammy.

W2: Yes.

MAN: Grandda ate two shits for his dinner. Me told nanny me no ate shit.

W2: Good boy, you poor cratur . . .

W1: Said our mother. And he got away with it. [*Imitating the mother.*] The poor cratur got away with anything. That was my brother. He said shit instead of fish, he couldn't talk and couldn't bawx.

[MAN *sits.*]

MAN: [*Older.*] I told ya baby.

W1: I hated him.

MAN: [*Younger.*] I don't care.

[*Pause.*]

W2: Then there was the time he wanted to get out the window on the second storey. I was working in the kitchen when I heard a window being opened. I ran upstairs to the boy's room. I found him, he was sleepwalking and about to go out the window. I grabbed him by the ankle and we collapsed onto the bed. So deep was his sleep he didn't even waken. So I tucked him in and kissed him and left the room. When Daddy got home, he said . . .

MAN: Ya look like a ghost.

W2: I told him what had happened.

MAN: My God.

W2: He went immediately and locked all the windows. The strange thing is . . .

MAN: How did you hear the window being opened from the kitchen?

W2: The bedroom window was so far away there was no way I could have heard it being opened, but hear it I did. Secondly, had it been the sound of him opening the window that I heard, by the time I reached the room he would have been long gone to his reward.

MAN: So what did you hear?

W2: I don't know. My only regret is . . .

MAN: And what is that?

W2: That I didn't let you jump.

MAN: Ah, that's rough.

[W2 *breaks into laughter. Child cries.* MAN *pushes the pram over and back a moment.*]

W2: Tricia was a wee brat. She was always crying. Now don't, I'd say.

W1: [*Sniffs.*]

W2: Always sniffing.

W1: [*Sniffs.*]

MAN: Quiet down there. [*Toward floor.*]

W2: And I'd say, now, don't cry any more.

W1: [*Louder.*] Sniff.

MAN: Stay quiet. [*Toward ceiling.*] I can't hear meself.

W2: And on she'd go. And I'd say Tricia, don't cry anymore and maybe I'll give you . . .

W1: [*Hold sniff.*]

W2: Sweets, I'd say . . .

W1: [*Loud sniff.*]

W2: Or a penny.

W1: [*Stops immediately.*]

W2: [*Rising.*] And she'd stop immediately and so I'd give her a good thump for crying for nothing. And then what would happen?

W1: [*Sniffs.*]

W2: It would start all over again. And it'd go through you. There's nottin worse than a child crying.

MAN: Dear Jesus, you're right there.

W2: I was not allowed tears. [*Ends sniffing.*] No. [*Pause.*] Not by anyone. I hadn't much of a life as a child. I was the eldest girl and there was seven of them. [*Up and away with her.*] And of course because I was the eldest the work fell to me. [*The others lie back scoffing.*]

W1: Hazel!

W2: Do this.

MAN: Hazel!

W2: Do that. I could never get to my granny's because I had to mind them.

MAN/W1: Hazel!

W2: Those ones. [*Points.*] Never got to my granny's once. I used to feed them on everything I could lay my hands on thinking that the more food they got the quicker they'd grow up. And during the Emergency the one'd be staling from the other's plate. [*The others eat away.*] And they ate all before them and never grew. Not that I could see anyway.

MAN/W1: Hazel!

W2: The demands just got worse.

MAN: There's no butter.

W1: No sugar.

W2: Try explaining rationing to them. I was demented. So I'd yell . . .

W1: Hitler'll blow you all to hell in your beds.

MAN: I didn't like the sound of that.

W2: You did not. They were always there, wanting this and wanting that. [*She taps her skull.*] Wanting the other.

W1: Hazel. [*Head down.*] There's a mystery tour at the door.

W2: A what?

W1: A mystery tour.

W2: And who were they? A crowd from the North looking for direction ta the boom town of Clones. They were after meat during the war. What we had they lacked. And what they couldn't buy, they stole . . .

MAN: Good day there. There's childer out front a da house trying to sell us a few hens.

W2: They're what?

MAN: Aye. In exchange for some cheese.

W2: Were you trying to sell our blooming hens?

W1: [*Head down.*] No Hazel.

W2: For feckin cheese?

W1: [*Sobbing.*] No.

W2: And all the time I couldn't think with thinking we would be bombed. Every time ya turned on the radio it was going on. I used terrify myself. I'd lie down in the bed at night and listen. And hear her crying. And downstairs my father telling me mother what would happen. Oh God!!

MAN: [*Quietly.*] Hazel.

W2: [*Terrified.*] Daddy.

MAN: [*Quietly.*] It's all right.

W2: Daddy.

MAN: Sleep now.

W2: And at first light land back again to earth on the godforsaken farm. A bitter reward for a nightmare. We farmed cattle, sheep and pigs. From morning till night. On the go. They did not do a tap, the young ones – maybe they did later, not then. Then there was the kitchen.

MAN/W1: Hazel!

W2: Washing, cleaning, ironing, starching collars, emptying ashes, blackening the range . . .

MAN: Hazel!

W2: And I don't forgive them. [*Pause.*] No.

MAN: There's worse.

W2: No.

W1: Ah, Hazel.

W2: No. I couldn't wait to grow up. [*Pause.*] Never again. I lost my childhood. Because of ye. But I have to say it was great training for the nursing. [*Pause.*] So I upped and went the first chance I had.

W1: I missed you.

MAN: Go then, if you must.

W2: And who's to stop me? I'd done my bit.

MAN: I doubt you'll last the month.

W2: I proved me father wrong. I was gone thirteen year. From day one it was all go in the hospitals in England. You were on call six days a week, twenty-four hours a day. They didn't understand my way of talking.

MAN: Come again?

W2: Was all I heard. And when I got used to one place I was moved off into another dialect.

MAN: Come again?

W2: Doing TB they gave you danger money. I saw many a nurse

get the cough and begin fading. [W1 *bows head.*] And fading. People went to nothing in front of you. Some of the tales the doctors told you, you could not put down on paper. And if you were called out in the middle of the night you might be collected in . . .

W1: A hearse . . .

W2: A lorry, anything, and brought you ya knew not where. And up in the Bronte Country the matron took us out for a drive and hit the wall of the Alhamlia Theatre and she said . . .

W1: If that had been built one foot further back I would have missed it.

W2: And I have to admit I missed home, especially on Sunday mornings when I'd hear the bells.

[*Pause.*]

MAN: There's the geese going over. It's winter.

[*He lifts his hat off his head, waves, replaces it, hums.*]

W1: He might break into "Jerusalem."

MAN: A tight city under siege.

[*Pause.*]

W1: He'd sing "Four and Nine."

W2: I never heard anyone else sing that song.

W1: Then click the clogs. They had leather uppers and wooden soles with steel tips on the heels and toes.

W2: I know.

W1: I know you know.

W2: [*Slight competitiveness.*] Rocks a' Clones made them.

W1: Now.

W2: Rocks it was.

W1: Well the only problem with Rocks' shop . . .

W2: Do tell.

W1: Is that it was not in Clones.

W2: Is that so?

W1: No. It was in Newbliss.

W2: I see.

W1: Yes – you were going to say?

W2: Nottin.

[*Pause.*]

MAN: Curse that bucket.
W2: Go on with it.
MAN: If only I could lift the well and bring it ta the house . . .
W2: My brother would say.
MAN: And then ye's'd have all the water ye want.
W1: And before too many years . . .
W2: His wish came true . . .
W1: We had us a bathroom . . .
W2: With tiles.
MAN: And that was the end of the wash on a Saturday night . . .
W2: Be the fire . . .
MAN: In the big galvanised bath.
W1: And we didn't have to look . . .
W2: Thank God!
W1: Upon . . .
W2: His nibs in the nip . . .
W1: Again.

[W1 *and* W2 *hands to the mouth. Pause.*]

MAN: That's lovely talk.
W1: Well, don't be listening.
MAN: If I was to talk like that I'd be tauld to shut up.
W2: That's women's talk.
MAN: Is that what they call it?
W2: Indeed it is.
W1: So mind your business.
MAN: [*Educated voice.*] Well I'm glad I learned that. Women's talk. Very good. [*Starts to pretend scribbling.*] Thank you Miss Foley. I'll keep a record of that for again, if you don't mind. [*Pen sharply back into top pocket.*] And then I must have a word with the authorities in Cavan town and get it put onto the relevant – ah – curr . . .
W1: Curriculum.
MAN: Thank you, curriculum.
W2: And do I get the job, sir?
MAN: We'll have to see.
W2: Thank you.
MAN: [*Stern nod.*] Next!

[*Pause.*]

W1: Ah we had great nights winding up the brother.

[*Pause.*]

MAN: [*Quietly and aged.*] Hazel?

W2: Yes?

MAN: Are you there?

W2: Yes.

MAN: Good.

[*Pause. Lights down a little and continue to go down.*]

MAN: We'll be destroyed.

W2: I don't mind.

MAN: And tell me this – who is paying for it? Me.

W2: I know.

MAN: Not that bucken crowd. And I went down to the fucking side room of the town hall to help them on voting day. And that's the bucken thanks I get!

W2: But think a' the . . .

MAN: And poles going every which way.

W2: It's your decision.

MAN: And in the wind up we'll be burnt in our beds.

W1: Daddy!

MAN: I'll not take it.

W1: Everyone else is.

MAN: Stay quiet you. I said, I'll not take it.

W1: I'm only saying, all the girls at school say that their parents are getting it in.

MAN: Well let them. I'll not take the light and that's that.

W1: If you don't I'm for London.

MAN: Can I go with ya?

[*Lights suddenly off.*]

W2: Are you right?

MAN: Right.

W2: Well hit the switch.

MAN: What are you saying?

W2: Hit the switch.

MAN: Where is it?

W2: Over there.

MAN: Over there where? Is this the yoke – Jesus? [*The lights suddenly come on. He jumps back. He looks up a long time and shakes his head.*] Bedad. The light from heaven . . .

W1: He called it.

W2: After all his infernal . . .

W1: Arguing.

MAN: My, my . . .

W1: He said.

MAN: Just look at dat.

W1: A bulb in every room and a plug in the kitchen.

MAN: I told ya it'd be fine, and if I told you any different, well, you know yourself . . .

W2: Oh he was happy all right. He's stand outside the shed with a finger to his lips listening to the clatter of the milking machine. The jackass. But it was the light caught me out. I never thought the place looked so dirty. It was a pig sty.

W1: And what about the pot, Mammy?

W2: Yes. And then there was me pot.

W1: In which she used cook the bread on the open fire.

W2: Me three-legged pot.

W1: And now the pot was useless.

W2: But I said I'd not let the pot best me.

W1: I heard her say . . .

W2: Get in there! You see it would not fit into the Stanley oven.

W1: It would not.

W2: No. I tried everything. I thought my baking days were over.

W1: She used try ramming it in . . .

W2: When she thought no-one was looking.

MAN: What are ya at – you'll destroy the bucken oven.

W2: If I'm going to cook . . .

W1: It's in me pot . . .

W2: I'll cook, have ya got that?

MAN: Jesus, some people. What direction is the pub?

W2: So I went to Charlie Flynn, the smith, and had the legs took clean off and then I was able to put it into the oven. And then we had the right bread again. Now.

[*Pause.* MAN *rises, cap onto head, and goes to back.* W2 *rises and goes sit in his chair.*]

W1: I mind to see my father seated under a pruned tree on the crocus slope. He loved to sit out there looking over the fields.

[*He raises his hat.*]

MAN: Always raise your hat to the magpie.

W1: Good afternoon, sir.

[*Dons hat, slowly returns.*]

MAN: Now listen, the back was at me, at me bad. Now take note, I went to the doctor. I'm law-abiding, I am. And do you know what the doctor said to me? Listen to this. This is rare. Note this down. He said as calm and matter-of-fact as if he was sitting there where you are now. He said. We get backache because we only wash the front of the body. Now consider that. Well after he said that I considered him in a new light. Entirely.

[*He returns to his chair. Spreads open his newspaper. Pause.*]

W1: I'll not forget that day.

MAN: [*Reading.*] Trottin but you won't, lochy . . .*

W1: He always called me lochy.

MAN: [*Reading.*] Trottin but you won't, lochy child.

W1: I came down in me jammies and got dressed in front of the oven door.

MAN: Ya did.

W1: And he said . . .

MAN: [*Winding up newspaper.*] You're for the larning.

W1: We took off and a neighbouring man shouted . . .

MAN: For heaven's sake lift your feet and they'll fall be themselves.

W1: I wanted to go back home.

MAN: No, I'm sorry – on!

W1: So I climbed up into the ditch.

MAN: [*Pointing.*] The countryside is looking at you.

W1: I don't care.

MAN: Get down.

W1: No.

MAN: Bridget!

* Indeed you will not, love.

W1: So my father got me aunt to take me.

MAN: On you go.

W1: Please.

W2: No.

W1: Eventually my aunt landed me sister and me at the door of the school and off she went and this huge female in black and smelling of coco shooed us into a room full of boys and girls. [W1 *sits, head down, shyly.*]

W2: [*Shaking hand in front of her.*] C'mon, shh, shhh, inside, inside, Jacinta Murray! Norah Bell!

W1: I had on a dress with blue dots and a huge collar which I kept to my face the whole day while I cried.

W2: Sit straight.

W1: Who is that, pray?

W2: My first day I arrived to school on my brother's back.

MAN: [*Rises.*] Get up, Rosie.

W2: He carried me the whole one and a half mile.

MAN: And we're coming here to there and over Beecher's on Mr What.

W2: And I suppose if he hadn't a-carried me I would'n've gone. But he said . . .

MAN: I'll look after ya.

W2: [*Rises.*] And he did.

MAN: No bother.

W2: Then he landed me at the door.

W1: And that was . . .

W2: The beginning of my downfall. [*All three stand.*] I wore a dress with four pockets in it.

W1: Will you sing for us?

W2: Asked da teacher. So I sang and she put a penny in each of the four pockets. I liked larning but I didn't like the cane. [W1 *swishes.* MAN *puts his hand out.* W1 *comes down three times.* MAN *continues to stand with his hand out without budging.*] And it was bad enough to be hit yourself, but to see my brother hit. And across the knuckles.

W1: They were fuckers – excuse me – for across the knuckles.

W2: I hated it.

[MAN *walks away slowly.*]

W2: I'd rather she had hit me.

[*Pause.*]

MAN: I went on the run and hid out in the bog.

W2: He has the masles, Sister.

W1: Has he indeed.

W2: Covered in them.

MAN: I spent the day be Cannings' bank without a spot of bread for three days running. I kept on the lookout. No-one. Nothing. There I was considering my lot when Sergeant Leary swung out from behind a head of gorse and what did he do – he handcuffed me to him, and said nottin, and he took me off the bog and marched me past our house, and into the school.

W1: Can I see your spots?

W2: Said the nun.

W1: And he was leathered.

[*Pause.*]

MAN: But I got me larning and it stood by me. So thank you Sergeant Leary, thank you, Sister Raymond, thank you.

[*All sit.*]

W2: I don't know why they were so cruel. I made myself sick to get away from the nun. She said . . .

W1: The only daughter of Mick Foley is an idiot.

[*Pause.*]

W2: At school? Wait till I think. I suppose I was about average.

[*Pause.*]

W1: Oh Miss X. To this day I can't bear to hear her name. Miss X was vicious out. With beads and pigtails and cruel. She made life a sheer misery.

W2: Class!

W1/W2/MAN: Na na na
Du du duairt
No no Nora
Fuck Fuck Fuckle.*

W2: Hazel Foley!

*Irish: "I didn't say a word."

W1: Me?
W2: Yes you, I'm talking to you.
W1: Miss?
W2: Please explain to the class what's so funny.
W1: Nottin.
W2: Nothing what?
W1: Nothing Miss.
W2: I'm sure we'd all like to hear what you found so funny. Stand up!

[W2 *stands.*]

W1: She was mocked, laughed at, kept in at break and lunch time, made to pull briars and nettles with her bare hands for getting something wrong. And one day she had the back of her hand blackened and skinned because of being smacked with a sooty saucepan. Most days saw her in tears.
W2: Then back to the house and drop potatoes into drills that seemed to go on forever and ever.
W1: And we reported nothing.
W2: No.

[W2 *sits. Distant train.* MAN *leans his elbow onto the pram. The women kneel sideways to their chairs.*]

W1: Bless me, father . . .
W2: For I have sinned.
W1: [*Quietly.*] It's a week since my last confession.
MAN: Speak up!
W1: I nearly died of shame.
MAN: Speak up, I say!
W2: [*Loud.*] I stole apples from Benny Maguire's.
MAN: Poor Benny.
W2: [*Quiet.*] I only took the few.
MAN: It's a wonder there's any left to steal. Go on.
W1: Pears from Tom Bell's summer pear tree.
MAN: Are they out, be God.
W2: I didn't pay attention at the Rosary.
W1: I never heard the trimmings.
MAN: Go on.
W2: I was a hypocrite.

MAN: You were what?

W2: I was a hypocrite, Father.

MAN: Well that's a new one.

W2: And he smiled and I could see the gold filling in one of his front teeth as he smiled.

MAN: Go on.

W2: It's Auntie Mary.

MAN: Hah. Is she the one married to Charlie Fay be any chance?

W1: That's right.

MAN: I have her. And pray tell, what about Auntie Mary?

W2: Well, the mother lines us up to say . . .

W1/W2: Glad to see you Auntie Mary . . .

W2: When she comes to visit on her donkey and trap and there's a hug and a kiss and then we all say . . .

W1/W2: Auntie Mary you are welcome.

W1: Well now, she says, with the big false smile . . .

W2: I'm so glad to see you, we say, and she says . . .

W1: [*Over-the-top, patronising.*] Hullo Auby, are you a good girl today?

W2: Or . . .

W1: [*More patronising.*] Haven't you the lovely dress on?

W2: And we have to smile and smile.

W1: [*Patronising.*] What beautiful children, Maeve . . .

W2: She says to my mother. And on she goes, so one day I asked my mother if a person said they were glad to see you and they didn't mean it, who would they be and she said . . .

W1: Oh they'd be a hypocrite.

W2: And that's why I'm a hypocrite, Father.

MAN: I see.

W2: Because behind her back I stuck out my tongue at her as far as it would go.

MAN: No.

W1: Did.

MAN: No.

W1: And spat.

MAN: You what!?

W2: Yes Father, and I'm not that sorry.

MAN: I can see that.

W1: So that's what it is to be a hypocrite. But Father?

MAN: Yes?

W2: I think Auntie Mary is a bigger hypocrite than me.

MAN: That'll do now. [*Wags finger.*] Whist, enough! [*He goes to his knees by his chair and so does* W2. *In low voices they pray.*] Holy Mary, Mother . . .

W2: And while you're at it go down to Hourigan's shop and don't be kept, do you hear, by those pair, gossiping, Hail Holy Queen . . .

[W1 *gets up and enters shop and knocks.*]

W1: Hallo.

W2: Hail Mary, full of grace . . .

MAN: The Lord is with . . .

W1: Hallo Mrs Hourigan?

W2: Blessed art thou . . .

W1: Hallo in there!

MAN: And blessed is . . .

W1: Is the shop open?

W2: Hail Mary, did you hear someone?

W1: The place only opened when a customer came. No matter what day or hour they were always kneeling down and praying in the shop.

MAN: Art thou among women.

W2: And blessed is the fruit. Who is it?

MAN: The young Foley lassie.

W2: Oh! Now and at the hour of our death. Holy Mary, and what does she want?

MAN: [*Rises.*] We have the lot.

W2: [W2 *rises.*] Indeed we have.

W1: Raisins, please.

[MAN *and* W2 *look at each other.*]

MAN: That's a hard one.

W2: [*Clearing throat.*] It is.

MAN: She's testing us.

W2: Well we'll soon put that out of her head, now – you were saying, Miss?

W1: Raisins.

W2: Raisins what?

W1: Raisins please.

MAN: [*Looking round him puzzled.*] I heard that voice before somewhere.

W2: And what do you want with raisins? Sure you don't want raisins, do ya?

W1: I do.

MAN: And why wouldn't you?

W2: Well some people can't be plazed.

W1: I'll have to go. Me Mammy is in a hurry.

MAN: Now wait.

W1: I can't wait. I'm not allowed gossip.

MAN: We have things like tay and sugar.

W1: I want raisins.

MAN: I know, I know you do, indeed you do. We have . . .

W2: [*Black low voice.*] We have traycle.*

MAN: [*Trying to brighten it up.*] Aye indeed, we have various assorted items as they say, we have Boland's bread and we have tobacco, we have Players, John Players in fact, now what have we got now . . .

W2: [*Darker still.*] We have more traycle.

MAN: Aye. [*Going over to the shelves and licking his finger to point.*] We have Tide, we have dried parsley. [*Peering closer.*] We have queen cakes . . .

W1: Raisins, I said.

MAN: Shoe polish, boiled swates and macaroons, cod-liver-oil, wrapping paper – what's that?

W2: [*Leans in to look.*] Cough syrup.

MAN: Ah, cough syrup, lozenges, laxatives . . . [*Lifts and looks.*] Did ya hear they have the cure for da cauld sore in Castleblaney? – syrup of figs, rat-traps . . .

W1: I want raisins!

MAN: Hold it now.

* Treacle.

W2: There's a problem there.

MAN: Would you kindly forget about the raisins.

W1: I can't.

MAN: You'll have ta.

W1: Why?

W2: Because the last of the raisins is gone.

MAN: Now.

W1: Oh I see, I said, pouting my shoulders, well I'm surprised, says I mimicking Bennie Smith – [*Old Voice.*] – that you haven't got raisins in a concern like this.

MAN: [*Imitating Benny Smith.*] Oh do you hear the grown-up voice.

W2: But if you hold on, there'll be candles and raisins when Owen comes home.

MAN: The last of the candles went last night.

W2: The raisins this morning.

MAN: So Owen is gone to Monaghan.

W2: [*Closing in.*] On the bike.

MAN: [*Closing in.*] At cock crow this very morning.

W2: He'll not be long the cratur . . .

MAN: And he'll be back . . .

W2: With the confounded raisins.

[*The two close in on her, and stop.*]

MAN: So now . . .

W2: What?

[W1 *backs away.*]

W1: My mother wants raisins now.

W2: [*Breakdown.*] Oh dear.

MAN: I hear ya, daughter. You've spent a lot of time on the raisins you have. Longer than most I'd say. You've them all bet arseways. You'll get the prize. Well now, listen to me, after all that, while you're waiting, like, will you have a sweeeeeet?

W1: I can't.

MAN: You can.

W1: I can't.

MAN: [*Close.*] Always give in to temptation.

W1: [*Close.*] It's a sin.

MAN: [*Soft and intimate with fierce tempting eyes.*] Well take the sweet anyway.

W1: [*Soft and intimate.*] Thank you. Goodbye now, said I as Benny would, and thank ya ver' ver' much. [W1 *goes.*]

W2: [*Turning to* MAN *seriously.*] Will you have something?

MAN: [*To* W2, *elderly grateful voice.*] After all that I think I'll have cup of Complan, thank you.

[*He goes to his knees.* W2 *goes to her knees.*]

W2: Hail Holy Queen . . .

MAN: Mother of Mercy . . .

W2: Hail our light our sweetness and our hope . . .

[MAN *rises, pulls the pulley. Mother throws open the gates. Light drops, in the far distance the sound of train bells. The train goes by, the light rises, and hummed music begins.*]

W1: And it was . . .

MAN: Men to the right . . .

W2: Women to the left . . .

W1: And off you'd go.

[*Pause. Humming continues from all three as they rise to dance.*]

W2: The minute the music started . . .

W1: They started . . .

W2: Across the floor . . .

W1: In a stampede.

W2: They'd come at you like a tide.

W1: They'd come at you like cattle.

MAN: Would ya care to dance?

W2: [*Imitating* MAN'*s flirting.*] Would ya – like ta – take the floor?

MAN: Hi Missus, will you face me?

W1: I'm not your Missus.

MAN: You might be wan day.

W1: Dream on.

MAN: Can I back you round the floor, Nan?

W2: There were two lots, fellows you knew and fellow you didn't and you'd dance with fellows you did – [W2 *starts humming.*] – and they'd say . . .

MAN: Will ya have a go?

W1: And the ones you didn't know well you took your time there, be ladylike you know, down with the eyes, nothing too forward . . .

W2: Oh no.

W1: A little at a time . . .

W2: Just enough . . .

W1: Cautious . . .

W2: That would be it.

W1: Yes, act cautious, though they were the ones in the long run you wanted to be with, and they'd say . . .

MAN: Will you dance, Miss, please?

W1: And if you took a chance on him . . .

W2: And refused another . . .

W1: And took the stranger out onto the floor . . .

W2: Well the wan ye knew might have a word with the bandleader . . .

W1: Oh God.

[MAN *makes a big long walk, about business, to the bottom of the stage where the bandleader is playing a trumpet. He calls him down, one eye closed, with a few wags of the index finger.*]

MAN: [*Points at* W1.] Hi. What? Yon Wan refused me. [*Bandleader dropping trumpet.*] Which one? Yon Wan. The Wan in Blue? The Very Wan. I see. [*The bandleader waves his hand.*].

[*The humming stops. The movement stops. All look at* W1.]

W1: The shame of it.

W2: Everyone looking.

W1: They'd stop the dance because if you refused him you were not to dance another.

W2: Now!

W1: [*To* W2.] Indeed you could be put out of the hall for refusing a man.

W2: [*To* W1.] Indeed you could.

W1: Or left sitting be yourself for the night.

W2: [*Nodding.*] That's right.

W1: And the crowd'd go by you like you didn't exist.

W2: That's right.

MAN: Have you your knitting with ya tonight?
W1: It was humiliating.
W2: It was.
W1: The two-faced bitches.
W2: And you'd be sitting there with a sore arse on you after coming for miles on the bar of a bike.
W1: That's right.
W2: But did it stop you dancing?
W1: [*Nod.*] It did not.
W2: I'd spite them, I would.
MAN: [*Whispers.*] Can I see you outside?
W2: [*Conspiratorial.*] I'll think about it.
MAN: [*Conspiratorial.*] Very good.
W2: Outside is a big place mister.
MAN: It is surely.
W2: The gom.
MAN: Would you like a lift home on the bar of me bike?
W1: Take care there.
W2: What do you mean?
W1: [*Whispered too low to hear.*] There might be no bar on his bike.
W2: [*Laughing.*] Oh dear.
W1: But did it stop you dancing?
W2: No.
W1: It did not. We'd get a load together in Jackson's bus and off we'd go. Bollax to the lot of them. Distance was no obstacle. To the dress dances.
W2: [*Off together again.*] McCarron's. The Tennis Club.
W1: Up the town archway for a court.
W2: In your wellies across a field of muck.
W1: To the Carnival.
W2: And into this enormous tent.
W1: With your season ticket.
W2: And your high heels in your hand.
W2: I said . . .
W1: What do you take me for?
MAN: Ah Gertie.

W1: Don't Gertie me . . .
W2: I said.
W1: Oh boys. I saw myself dancing . . .
W2: Sunday, The Pavilion in Cavan . . .
W1: Monday, St Joseph's here in Clones . . .
W2: Tuesday, The Farmer's Ballroom . . .
W1: Vargini . . .*
W2: Aye.
W1: Wednesday . . .
W2: Somewhere over the border.
W1: And that was very nice thank you.
MAN: No bother.
W1: And then . . .
W2: Thursday, The Pavilion again . . .
W1: With the same crowd . . .
MAN: Belly bumping.
W2: And . . .
W1: It was from the dancing . . .
W2: That I got the knack of travelling.
W1: Ya did.
W2: The minute I was trained as a midwife I was off to where . . .
W1: Australia.
W2: The two sides of the USA.
W1: And she went to Norway, she did.
W2: Practically all of Europe.
W1: Egypt as well, didn't ya?
W2: And the Bahamas.
W1: Aye, but that was only the once though.
W2: Once only. Yes.
W1: That's what I thought.
[*Nod to each other.*]
W2: Yes. And a banker asked me up of a Friday . . .
MAN: Will you come to Oldcastle tonight?
W1: No I said, though I thought he was cute . . .
W2: I can hardly keep my eyes open.
MAN: It's the Clipper Carlton.

* Virginia, Co. Cavan.

W1: No I can't.

W2: I'm sorry.

W1: I'm whacked.

MAN: Ah, and I got the new shoes.

W2: Oh?

MAN: All for you.

W1: And they're lovely.

W2: I was on my last legs behind the counter. And the bitch I worked for overheard me in the shop and what did she say? She said . . .

W1: Don't tell me, Miss Coyle, you're not going out tonight.

W2: No.

W1: Oh dear, dear, dear. Oh dear, you must not feel well.

W2: I'm fine, thank you.

W1: All those late nights – how romantic.

W2: Jesus!

W1: And what will the men do without you. [*Hoity-toity.*] The Rose of Latt has the vapours. [*Hand to her forehead.*] Oh do excuse me while I ponder my travail.

W2: I coulda kilt her.

W1: Now here's a customer coming in and I do believe he's a bachelor – now's your chance, you never know, put on your best face.

MAN: Do ya have the cure here for the cauld sore?

W2: When I think of it! Her idea of excitement was to try and have her hyacinths in bloom for Christmas before anyone else. I could have . . .

[MAN *steps in, hat in hand.*]

MAN: Hallo there, Miss Burns.

W2: He was a young farmer from Cootehill.

W1: [*To* W2, *chats again.*] A town, I mind, with a wide lonesome street.

W2: [*To* W1.] True. He was one of the load you know. Off the bus . . .

W1: Ah I see . . .

W2: Always sat in the back.

W1: I know the type.

W2: With the collar up directing operations.
W1: [*Signals finger.*] The very one . . .
W2: And sloping about.
W1: A daunderer!*
W2: Right.
W1: Got ya.
MAN: I love a daunder, I do.
W2: Oh, indeed.
MAN: Would you care for . . .
W2: I don't mind.
W1: We became an item after a foxtrot in The Maple in Rockcorry.
W2: First came the lemonade and then came the soup. [*They sit in a circle by the table.*] I dreaded meeting his family. Mr Heaslip.
MAN: Ah, Hazel, isn't it?
W2: Mrs Heaslip.
W1: I believe our fellow has taken a shine to you.
W2: Ah, well, he's very nice.
MAN: He's a hames.
W1: I'd rather you than me, miss.
MAN: Brave soup, Hazel.
W1: I'll tell you this daughter, for nothing.
MAN: You tell her . . .
W1: Put a bit by for yourself. For after the flowery talk. And the bad talk. And you'll hear plenty of that.
MAN: You're not so bad at it yourself.
W1: Shut your trap ya half-wit. [*Taps skull, and calls her in.*] I have a conundrum. [*With widening eyes.*] Did you know that Machine Gun Kelly was an altar boy?
W2: Oh?
W1: [*Nods.*] Mark my words. No one ever escaped from Alcatraz.
MAN: No.
W1: You see one of the rules is . . .
MAN: Ya can't break the rules.
W1: And there ya have it. Now would you care for a tot of

* A person who is easy-going.

Buckfast, daughter?

MAN: The very thing.

W2: And eventually he asked me.

MAN: [*Stands behind his chair, hesitates, smartens himself as she waits expectantly.*] Will you . . . marry me?

W2: [*Turning to him.*] When?

MAN: Well any Thursday that will suit. [*Sits.*]

W2: I could not believe my ears. You see – Thursday was marrying day.

[*Pause.*]

W1: The first man I ever fancied . . .

W2: That's my line!

MAN: Hah?

W1: Never mind, you.

W2: All right then, go on.

W1: If you don't mind. The first man I ever fancied was the best part of twenty.

MAN: Was he now?

W1: Yes.

MAN: Well I never heard about him.

W1: And I was only seven.

MAN: Oh, excuse me.

W1: He used come to my grandpa's shop. Keenan was his name.

MAN: Keenan, ha-ha, that yoke.

W1: Yes. I thought he was lovely. I used decorate the handlebars of his bike with daisies. I'm sure he was mortified. He was a turf cutter come to help on the bog. We had great days on the bog.

W2: The best days.

W1: By far.

MAN: I never liked it. I hated it, every bucken moment of it.

W1: Ya did not.

MAN: I did. The bog is well named.

W2: You're only saying.

MAN: [*Low snarl.*] Get up out of that bed!

W2: [*Rises to feet.*] Cutting, standing, stacking, drinking tay.

MAN: [*Snarl.*] Get into your britches!

W1: Making mud turf with your feet.

MAN: Drinking sour tay.

W1: And the turf cutter never spoke to my uncle. He was not chatty. He'd take the slean and cut and cut. Not a word. Except to say . . .

MAN: That's the best hand crame there is.

W1: And then he'd come home and eat in silence. He never spoke to my uncle, but he spoke to us. He said . . .

MAN: The one that makes me doesn't want me. The one that buys me doesn't use me. The one that uses me doesn't see me, but I can't refuse. Who or what am I?

W1: I don't know.

MAN: There you go.

W2: [*To* MAN.] Well, tell us.

MAN: [*To* W2.] My lips are sealed.

W1: He was there a week, a full seven days, and each night I asked him but he would not tell.

MAN: [*Finger up, quietly.*] No.

W2: [*To* MAN.] Please.

MAN: No.

W2: We were demented wondering.

W1: And at the end of the week when he was being paid off and about to go he said to my uncle . . .

MAN: Tell the young fry it's a coffin.

W1: My uncle didn't know what he was talking about so he came into us and said . . .

MAN: Your man Mister No-speak-to-anyone-no-matter-what-the-fuck-you-say broke his silence and said: It's a coffin. Have you got that? It's a coffin. Whatever the hell that means.

W1: And there you have it.

[*Women rise and exchange seats.*]

W2: The one that makes me doesn't want me.

W1: The one that buys me doesn't use me.

W2: The one that uses me doesn't see me.

MAN: But I can't refuse.

[*Pause. Light down a little. Slowly* MAN *rises and pulls the chain, then stands there alone. Train bells. The train comes thundering and goes by. The two women follow it with their eyes.* MAN *looks straight ahead. Light rises.*]

W2: My brother disappeared.

[MAN *rises and moves towards back.*]

W1: Just like that.

W2: [*She moves towards his seat.*] He was my half-brother. Although I didn't know the meaning of that at the time either.

W1: He always called me . . .

MAN: Baby.

W2: [*Sits in his seat.*] He spent some years in Artane reformatory school for what I don't know. And I don't know whether he was in the band, but when we'd go up to a neighbour's house to hear the All-Ireland on the radio, I used love to listen to the Artane Boys Band at half-time thinking he was in it.

W1: He'd come and go.

W2: It was after he joined the Irish Army that he disappeared.

W1: I used love the smell of Brasso when he cleaned up his uniform buttons.

W2: He'd grease his hair with bone marrow.

W1: He became corporal, then sergeant, but they wouldn't let him mix with boys in his previous rank, they thought they were below him so he lit out and went to England.

W2: A letter arrived.

W1: He said . . .

MAN: Send me on my Birth Cert . . .

W2: And my Baptismal Cert if you can find it . . .

MAN: I'm getting married . . .

W1: Ma, he's met a woman!

MAN: And I'll be back for me honeymoon.

W2: We got our finery ready . . .

W1: But he never came.

W2: The mother got very sad.

W1: I think she was more fond of him than she was of me.

W2: Years later the father died calling out me brother's name.

MAN: [*In the background, in half-profile, the* MAN *mutters.*]

Seán . . .

W1: Then our mother sent letters all over and she died not knowing where he was.

W2: And only a few weeks after she died a letter came from the States. I don't know how to put this. It had been sent ages before, and lain in the priest's house. We had moved and the priest must have put it aside. And forgot about it. Never thought about it no more. The letter had lain there forgotten till someone found it.

W1: And by then it was too late.

W2: Me mother was dead. Me father was dead.

W1: And now I understood.

W2: My brother John had not deserted us. He'd . . . he'd been searching for us. He'd been a prisoner of war in Vietnam. I wrote back telling how we all loved him.

W1: He rang the house.

W2: I answered it.

MAN: Baby . . .

W2: He said . . .

MAN: Is that Baby?

W2: I couldn't speak. [*Pause.* W2 *returns to her own seat. Child cries.* MAN *returns and rocks pram.*] And so we came to Thursday, marrying day.

MAN: Hold on.

W2: What.

MAN: Tell the truth.

W2: Well first I spent a few months in the US of A, okay?

MAN: Go on.

W1: Motoring through the Everglades she was.

MAN: Listen to that – motoring through the blasted Everglades . . .

W2: And next thing I'm standing in the Presbytery with me sister to make the arrangements as they call it and the priest says . . .

MAN: I'm afraid you'll have to get married at eight in the

morning.

W2: Ah Father.

W1: Well I saw red.

W2: You must be joking, Father . . .

W1: I said . . .

W2: It's not a shotgun wedding you know . . .

W1: I said.

MAN: It's not my fault. There's two already booked. I can move it to 8.30 but then we won't have a priest available.

W1: And how in the name of God do you expect us to get married without a priest?

MAN: You'll have to get one of your own.

W2: That's nice. I never heard of that before.

W1: In the event that's what we had to do.

W2: Get married at 8.30.

W1: At cockcrow.

W2: And then the priest said . . .

MAN: Unfortunately there may be another Mass going on in the church.

W1: Is there anything else, Father, you'd like to add?

MAN: No.

W2: Well I said, never mind, Father . . .

W1: Go ahead and book us.

W2: Anything would do.

W1: Anything, so we booked one of the White Fathers to do the job.

MAN: A fiver.

W2: And before you knew it . . .

W1: Me father bawled out . . .

MAN: Get up out of that bed, it's Thursday.

W2: And so the morning of the wedding we entered the sacristy and I mind something odd, my dress brushed against something as we came out onto the altar, but I was so excited I suppose I just went on, and as our service began – [MAN *rises and moves towards* W2.] – another was just ending to the side of the cathedral, well that was alright but their priest was in black and then I saw the coffin that I'd brushed against, and my heart went cold. Some poor soul was dead up there. But my man consoled me.

MAN: Aisy.

W2: I felt faint. Some poor soul was dead up there. [*Pause.*] Then the White Father turned to me as we stood on the altar and I could see he was nervous too, and he said . . .

MAN: This is my first wedding.

W2: This is my first wedding also, Father, I said.

[*Pause.* MAN *returns to chair slowly. Looks into pram, sits.*]

W1: My mother was always poorly.

W2: I was calm.

W1: She would not say boo to a goose.

W2: I was never really strong from . . .

W1: From when I was born.

W2: It was difficult. I had my own life then I hadn't. The others came and I was wore out.

MAN: Mammy, don't cry.

W1: She put the tartan fur rug round her knees, but she was always cold.

W2: Good night, mammy, I said to my mother, I love you. Those days the women died before the men. She grew wretched. You could hear the silence from acres away. And when she died a neighbour said . . .

W1: She was a lady.

W2: But Norman the workman got angry.

W1: I never saw him like that.

W2: He reared up and shouted . . .

MAN: [*Rises.*] Why say it now?

W1: What!

MAN: Why say it now!

W1: He said, and he was angry . . .

W2: And he went on . . .

MAN: Why didn't you tell her when she was alive!

W2: He could not be comforted.

MAN: [*Quietly, sitting.*] She was a mother to me.

W1: Norman was standing below our house one night when we were childer and Mammy shouted to me . . .

W2: You better come in for your supper!

W1: [*To* MAN.] So I said to Norman you had better come too.

MAN: [*To* W1.] Won't she mind?

W1: [*To* MAN.] No.

MAN: [*To* W1.] Are you sure?

W1: [*To* MAN.] I am.

MAN: [*To* W1.] All right then.

W1: [*To* W2.] Now to Mamma, I said, say all to his face that you said behind his back. She couldn't speak a word. She was never done giving off about this fellow Norman. She'd say . . .

W2: Who does he think he is, anyway, hah?

W1: Well he's here now and you ask him yourself.

[MAN *stands, then sits.*]

MAN: Norman Jackson. I'm sixteen years of age this June the 24th coming.

W1: And he started eating. She couldn't say anything. And he was back the next day, Sunday, at dinner time, right on the dot.

MAN: Hallo, Missus.

W1: And just sat down to the table like he was one of us.

MAN: Ojus* warm out there . . .

W2: He said, and he stayed.

MAN: I'll have the gravy, thank you.

W2: He came to dinner and he stayed for the rest of his life.

W1: We never asked him more than he wanted to tell.

W2: First he worked on the farm as a labourer, then when he went off to be a mechanic, I said to the mother . . .

W1: Can Norman stay here till he finds somewhere else?

W2: All right, but he'll get the same treatment as the rest of ye.

W1: And this went on for years.

W2: There you go.

MAN: Aye.

W2: I hear your courting up Newbliss way.

MAN: Now, now, now.

* Fierce or terrible.

W2: Ya dirty divil, ya.

MAN: Ah stop, Ma.

W1: Then he got married from here to a nice wee lassie we knew, Rosie, and they went to live with her mother.

W2: But a year later the child was born and after the child was born, Norman could not stick it any longer.

W1: A knock came to the door late one night.

W2: I got a hop.

MAN: [MAN *rises.*] Ma, can I come back home?

W2: What?

MAN: Can I come back home at night and stay here.

W2: No, back you go.

MAN: Ah, Ma.

W2: I told you when you got a wife that you should find a home, even a bloody room. But no you didn't ya jackass. So go on.

MAN: Ah, Ma.

W2: Back with you Norman to your wife, but you can call with Rosie anytime.

[MAN *starts to return to the chair.*]

W1: [*To* W2.] And he was back the next day.

W2: [*To* W1.] And the day after.

W1: [*To* W2.] [*Nodding.*] And when Mammy died he cried.

W2: [*Nodding.*] He cried like a child.

MAN: I missed her something dreadful, your mother.

[*Pause.*]

W1: Poor Norman, he always said . . .

MAN: You can't take back the spoken word.

[*Pause.*]

W1: And . . .

MAN: See all of that out there – that's on loan. [*Pause.*] That's on loan.

[*Pause.*]

W1: And some people like to sit down and have a chat and that's what they do and some are all always on the go like Norman.

W2: Six months after Mammy died, he died. He was mending a lorry. The jack slipped and down it came onto him. He'd been reared by his granny. Never knew his father and mother.

We never asked him anything more than he wanted to tell. I loved him dearly. I could have married him but one thing I could not stand was his laugh. [MAN *laughs.*] More's the pity. [*Pause.*] There was this old man, Sam Hall, I used meet when I was young. And if you broke a finger he'd say, that's nottin, that's nottin at all, there's worse, I'll tell you this – there's nothing worse than a broken marriage. Whatever happened you . . .

MAN: [W1 *moves lips aping his speech.*] There's nothing worse than a broken marriage . . .

W2: He'd say. And I forgot all about him when I grew up. Never thought of him once till I got married myself.

W1: And not even then.

W2: You're right. That was later. Sam Hall was a thing of the past. The marriage lasted three months because the man I married started to clock me. Then he went too far so I came home.

MAN: Go back to your husband!

W2: But I would not go back. No.

W1: You made your bed, you can lie on it.

W2: So I moved into my Granny's and she was kind to me. And then one day, one of those long days, I heard this something in the back of my head, I thought, what was it, what was that, what was that being said, and then I heard him, I thought back on what Sam Hall used to say . . .

MAN: [*Quietly.*] There's nothing worse than a broken marriage.

W1: And I got the meaning of it at last.

[*Pause. Child cries. Father rocks the pram.*]

W2: The vinegar plant . . .

W1: The ale plant, and . . .

MAN: The buttermilk plant.

W2: The smell of flax and the dandelion wine.

MAN: The bath in the tub on Saturday morning.

W1: The bellows and the gramophone.

MAN: The cursed Senna dished out on Saturday night.

W2: The crook.

MAN: The traycle.

W1: And the black black lead.

[*Pause. Distant sound of train.*]

MAN: [*Rises.*] I was above shaving and listening to Chamberlain the day war was declared.

W2: And along came the rationing.

W1: In came identification cards.

W2: Work permits.

W1: The lot.

MAN: But things were going well enough when . . .

W2: Along came Winston Churchill . . .

MAN: The blaggart!

W2: Asking us to hand over our ports to the British navy.

MAN: Who does he think he is?

W1: The grownups were afraid.

MAN: [*Turns sideways on chair to read newspaper.*] We'll be killed in our bloody beds, mark my words. Stalin will not be able to save us. I tell you, Hitler will be above in Cavan town before the Christmas. There won't be a house left standing. Jesus.

W2: Eamon de Valera had to make the big decision as to what to do.

MAN: Don't do it, Dev, don't!

W1: His reply was scheduled to come on the radio.

MAN: Don't!

W2: The whole country held its breath.

W1: We gathered in a neighbour's up the road to hear the broadcast.

W2: Even though I was a child I sensed the strain in the air.

MAN: Quiet, now, you. [*Silence. Loud whisper.*] Put out the damn dog. [*Silence. Whisper.*] Will you tune it right. [*Silence.*]

W2: Then Dev's voice came over the air – in slow and solemn tones . . .

MAN: Ireland will not hand over the ports to anyone, neither England nor Germany.

W1: My hero did the right thing.

MAN: Good man Dev.

[*Pause.*]

W2: Dev was kind to Henry Blake who was blind. We used visit his area down South during the summer. Henry used say . . .

MAN: The wind is a blind man's fog.

W1: With the sound of the wind he could not hear his stick tapping.

W2: He could not hear traffic.

MAN: It's no use saying "If only" . . .

W2: He would say.

W1: He always knew my voice . . .

MAN: Is them the swallows?

W2: He called us swallows because we only came in the summer and went away in the winter.

W1: But then when he got old he used go away for the winter to the hospital and we called him . . .

W2: King Swallow.

W1: And once King Swallow danced with Joan Denise Moriarty, the ballet queen . . .

W2: And he said . . .

MAN: Yon woman is a great dancer. She doesn't sweat at all.

W1: And Henry Blake and De Valera met . . .

W2: And compared notes on their blindness . . .

MAN: In a schoolhouse in Clare. [*Pause.*] Yes.

[*Pause.*]

W2: For smuggling on the train, what did you need? Let me see. First of all you needed . . .

W1: A pair of interlock knickers with good elastic in the legs!

MAN: [*Nodding vehemently.*] Damn right you did!

W1: A drindle skirt . . .*

W2: And a wide one at that.

W1: And you had to make sure that whatever it was you were smuggling did not fall down the arse at the back as it would be uncomfortable sitting down.

W2: You could not sit with your bum for half an hour on a few pound of butter.

MAN: You could not.

W1: And the newspaper.

* A dirndl skirt is a light circular dress, gathered at the waist, which falls just below the knee.

MAN: [*Tapping it in the pocket.*] You forgot the newspaper.

W2: I forgot the newspaper. You needed the newspaper to pretend to read and cover yourself as best you could. Because you didn't smuggle one item, oh no, you smuggled a dozen.

MAN: And maybe more.

W1: And watches, how did you smuggle watches? Well, you smuggled them in a taypot.

W2: Is right woman.

W1: You ordered your tay, filled a cup, and fecked the rest out the window. And dropped the watches into the taypot. And off you went. Once the train passed south of the Northern customs you were away.

MAN: You were. That'd be her. Everything came across that damn border.

W1: Even my First Communion shoes.

MAN: Very true. I mind there was no white leather in Clones.

W2: The women were over and back across the border . . .

W1: Pushing prams with false bottoms.

W2: I used walk across the border with you in it.

MAN: [MAN *rises.*] I saw her goin' over and back. I'll catch her, I said. Have you anything to declare? Well she stopped up and looked at me like I was an idiot.

W2: No . . .

MAN: She said, but I knew there was something bloody wrong with that damn pram.

W2: I might have a few pound of flour under you and the thing was to keep a straight face as you passed your man.

MAN: [*Looking into the pram.*] What you got there Missus?

W2: I have my bairn.

MAN: Hah.

W1: And the B-Special said . . .

MAN: Stop. I want to look in yon pram.

W1: [*Sniff.*]

W2: And disturb my child? You will not. [*Aside.*] Good girl yourself. A very timely cry. And I kept moving.

MAN: If I get the gun you'll stop. [*The two of them look at each other. He looks into the pram.*] Go on, then.

W2: I nearly peed myself!

MAN: [MAN *sits.*] I'll get ya, you know, one of these fine days, I'll get ya, of that you can be certain . . .

W1: He said, and the next day I was back.

MAN: Is it you again?

W2: It is.

MAN: And of course you've nottin to declare.

W2: No.

MAN: No. I thought so. You have some nerve, Missus, I'll grant you that. [*Pause.* MAN *gets up and moves to back of the stage.*] Get up now, daughter.

W2: [W2 *gets up and sits in his chair.*] I used to go through the fields in my wellies, half-asleep, mushroom picking with my father.

W1: The only blot on the landscape was the gander guldering madly.

W2: Da and I would race the moon.

W1: The moon always won.

W2: I loved the smell of his rashers.

W1: He'd sing as he cooked.

[MAN *hums.*]

W2: Then he took to sitting outside under a pruned tree on the crocus slope in the garden. He had a shock of white hair. [MAN *stops humming.*] For hours he'd sit there looking into the orchard. [W2 *rises.*] He never spoke about what was going through his head.

W1: The mother might go down and touch his shoulder and he'd nod and look on. [MAN *and* W2 *look a moment at each other. He nods.*] Then one day he rose and shouted . . .

MAN: Look!

W2: [*Standing behind* W1.] It was the first plane I ever saw. I was standing on the roof of a shed in Green's mill. It was flying very low and trying to land.

MAN: And by Christ it crashed out on Lord Farnham's.

W2: [W2 *sits.*] The remains of it came down College Street next day on the back of a lorry.

W1: Imagine that.

[*Pause. Child cries.* MAN *sits again, and rocks pram.*]

MAN: I'm getting on, bedad.

W2: What?

MAN: I'm getting on, I said.

W2: Ah, not at all.

MAN: I am. I'm too old for doing my lessons.

W2: That's true.

MAN: I've had enough of lessons. [*Points over at* W1.] You see that woman over there. That one. [W1 *turns.*] That woman over there is my minder.

W1: [*Turns back.*] I am.

MAN: [*Winking.*] You see what I'm saying – I never had it so good. Never. Got the new house. Everything comes on at a touch. Settling in. Regretting nottin, not a thing. No bother to me. I might even cross the hundred. Despite go-boys. Spivs. Profligates and Procrastinators. That lot. You might as well be rubbing butter on a fat arse.

W1: Daddy!

MAN: I saw them in my day about the place. The go-boys. Irondafts.* Still waters run deep. A hard gathering gets a wide scattering. Fortune flavours the bone. It was all go-go-go. Up ya boy-ya.

W1: [*To* W2.] A girl beside us got married and she got married because she was pregnant and my mother said, ah well . . .

W2: [*To* W1.] The drip follows the scollup.**

W1: [*To* MAN *louder.*] She says the drip follows the scollup.

MAN: It does. Certainly. You're right there, Mrs. The drip follows the scollup every time. Too true. Breeding is beyond teaching! What's bred in the bone comes out in the marrow. And so on. It's bullocking. By God there was nothing better than the smell from da ayting houses on a Fair Day. It was ojus.

[*Pause. He falls silent and looks out over the audience.*]

* Stubborn.

** Literally, a raindrop going down a sprig of hay on the edge of a thatched roof.

W1: Daddy?

MAN: Yes.

W1: What are you thinking of?

MAN: I was thinking that you never meet an Offaly man outside of Offaly. They must be fierce close. And the things they say about us. I met one once on Ealing Common after a day at the dogs and the tinker said: Did you hear about the Cavan man? No, I said. He used bring his childer to visit Santa's grave on Christmas Day. Ha-ha. I never did that, did I, daughter?

W1: No Daddy. I suppose ya didn't know where it was.

MAN: No. [*Pause.*] And I was thinking of that tinker Scully. He came up here yesterday cheiling, mar ya,* and he says Hallo Mr Foley, I see your hump has got worse. Well don't worry, I said, your good looks have improved.

[*Pause.*]

W1: [*To* MAN.] What will you have?

MAN: [*To* W1.] I'll have a cup of Complan thank you.

W2: He began to ail.

MAN: Is that you Hazel?

W2: It is.

MAN: Good. Stay there now.

W2: I will.

MAN: Good.

[*Pause.*]

W1: I was away boarding with a landlady above a draper's and going to secondary school and when I came home there was a lot of people in the house. I overhead them saying . . .

W2: He would never come back, no-one ever comes back from that place.

W1: It was only later I heard it was the fever hospital. They'd be taking him away on the morrow.

MAN: Hazel?

W1: [*Turning to him.*] Yes.

MAN: You're still there?

* Cheiling: a friendly visit; mar ya: pretending to be.

W1: I am.

MAN: Good. Now don't cry any more.

W1: [*Turning back.*] Then I was sent back to school and a few days later he died alone. It was a trauma. I'll never forget going through the trauma of my father's death and at the same time coping with doing the Leaving Cert. Then to be told by the headmaster when the results came out . . .

MAN: They could have been better.

W1: They could have been better.

MAN: The shite.

W1: In that short week I did all my growing up.

W2: And the animals driven off by a stranger.

[*Despondently the three look away from each other. Pause. Sound of a distant train.*]

W1: I hear Owen is getting married again.

W2: I hope she is not as mean as the last one, she'd not open the door wide in case she'd wear away the hinge.

[*Pause.*]

W2: The first film to Cavan was *The Gay Divorcee* with Fred Astaire and Ginger Rogers.

W1: The first to Clones was *The Third Man* with Orson Welles.

W2: Now!

W1: Now!

W2: And like in the church it was women to the left . . .

MAN: And men to the right.

W1: Till Norman refused.

MAN: I did.

W2: He did.

MAN: I always sit with the girls.

W1: He said . . .

MAN: And I'll not be parted from them now.

W2: And he sat down beside us.

W1: And your man came up and said . . .

MAN: Hi you, you can't sit there.

W1: And Norman said . . .

MAN: I'm not budging.

W2: I'll call the guards.

MAN: Call who you like.

W2: And that was that, he stopped where he was.

[*Pause.*]

W1: We used dress up as film stars in the loft.

W2: And pretend to serve Mass.

W1: And Norman the Prod played the priest.

MAN: Don't tell anyone.

W1/2: We won't.

MAN: Bless youse . . .

W1: He'd say.

W2: And John McGinty, the publican in Cavan, opened up a travel agency. And one night he declared that he'd arrange for all the customers in the pub to take a flight over the town.

MAN: I mean it.

W2: Ah japers, said Andy Brennan . . .

W1: I haven't a head for heights.

MAN: Be this time next week the lot of you will be in the air.

W2: Well he was true to his word. He booked a plane and in time a busload took off for the airport in Dublin. Oh they were midlin scared all right. I mind it was a lovely sunny Sunday. At half-past three the whole town of Cavan was out on the street to see the plane.

MAN: I had me foot driven into the seat in front of me looking for the brake.

W2: And she appeared. Well we clapped. A cheer went up to the plane.

W1: And they clapped up in the clouds.

MAN: We did, looking down on the town.

[*Pause.*]

W2: Yes, indeed. God rest them.

[*Pause. The alarm goes off.*]

MAN: Hup! Get up out of that bed. Come and get the breakfast into you. [*All three throw the chairs aside and clear space.*] You have a long day ahead of you daughter. Now I'll do the cutting.

W2: Right.

MAN: And see that girl?
W2: Yes.
MAN: She can do the catching.
W1: Right.
MAN: And you'll take the windrows.*
W2: Right.
MAN: And the two cubs can do the wheeling. [*Straightening up with the hand to the back.*] Tell me this Norman, are you right-footed or left-footed? [MAN *ponders the question. The women take positions on the bog.*] I see. [*As if he had been answered.*] Well never mind. [*Lifts, throws to* W1, W1 *throws to* W2, W2 *stacks.*] Where's that fecker? We'd get more work done if that fecker didn't go mooching away. Where did he go?
W2: He's gone to loose a button.**
W1: He has not. James's daughter is after arriving at the far bank.
W2: The brazen hussy.
W1: Do you hear the stupid laugh of him?
MAN: [*The laugh.*] Come back here Norman!
W1: The fecker.
MAN: Norman!
W1: The fecker.
W2: What was that song?
[*Stop a moment, leans on the slean.*]
MAN: Well?
W2: I'm trying.
MAN: Well give us a note.
W2: [*Sings.*] Trumpeter.
W1/MAN: [*Sings.*] Trumpeter.
MAN: Yis?
W2: Trumpeter, what are you sounding now?
[*They look at her, waiting.*]
MAN: Indeed, I'm afraid I don't know that air.
[*About to go back to work.*]
W2: I've got another one.
[*Back into waiting position.*]

* Rows of cut hay.

** Gone to the toilet.

W2: [*Sings.*] And she sat in the low-backed car.

MAN: Ah, you poor thing.

[*Start throwing again.*]

W1: And the highlight of the day was to see Mam come over the hill with bottles of hot tea dangling from her hands in thick woollen socks.

MAN: And there we were.

W1: Warding off the bees.

W2: Warding off the clegs.

W1: And it was scorching.

W2: It was.

MAN: Jazus me back.

W1: The thirst was something shocking.

MAN: Who made this tay? . . .

W2: Is what he'd always say.

W1: Always.

W2: Give it a stir can't you . . .

W1: She'd say.

MAN: I'll have a cut of white bread.

W1: I'll have a duck egg.

MAN: There's nothing better than an egg boiled on the bog. [*They stop.*] Holy God, where is me wheeling man gone?

W1: Look, he's talking to her.

MAN: Norman!

W2: The divil.

MAN: He didn't take a blind bit of notice of me.

W2: Ohhhhh, that Norman,

W1: See him now what he's at.

MAN: The dirty hure. Of course the one thing he doesn't know is that when the love wears off the language gets tough. [*No reply as he looks round.*] On!

[*They commence throwing and stacking again.*]

W1: The egg is burning my hand.

MAN: That's more like tay now.

W2: I told you.

MAN: Very good now.

W2: [*Sings.*] And she sat in the low-backed car . . .

MAN: Ah Jesus me blasted back.
W2: Take it slower.
MAN: If I take it slower we'll be here for the night.
W1: Daddy, you're not as young as you used to be.
MAN: You're right. Hold it. Why has the Paddy a bad back? I'll tell you . . .
W1: Ya told us that one before.
MAN: Oh. [*They work away*] And there you are. Good man Norman.
W2: You came back to us.
W1: Do you remember Hourigan's?
W2: Will I ever forget it.
W1: The bould Rinso.
W2: And the Lifebuoy.
W1: The Blue Bags.
MAN: And the feckin Starch.
W2: And he said . . .
MAN: Never again.
W2: And I said . . .
W1: I will.
MAN: [*Quietly flirting.*] Up Crossdoney! . . .
W2: The idiot roared.
MAN: I did. Well, as I said before, but no one took a blind bit of heed – after the first loving the language gets fierce rough.
W1: It does.
MAN: Then comes the second loving.
W2: I hope it comes soon.
MAN: True for ya.
W2: Will we be finished be tonight?
MAN: The weather, woman, it all depends on the weather.

[*Stop, hold, start.*]

W2: Look at the cut of that sky.
MAN: It looks black.
W1: It's got ojus dark.
MAN: It's closing in.
W2: It is.
MAN: We'll stay.

W2: We'll go.
W1: There's the first flash.
MAN: The bog is fierce dangerous in thunder.
W2: It is.
MAN: You see bog damp draws the lightning.
W2: It does. [W2 *stops stacking and looks at the others.*]
MAN: Get a move on.
W1: They were the best days.
MAN: Shift yourselves.
W1: Out on the bog.
MAN: [*Snarl.*] Get a move on, can't you.
W1: Daddy!
MAN: Aw. [*The other two now stop throwing and stand a moment.*] Have you everything Hazel?
W1: Yes.
MAN: [*To* W2.] Is everything packed?
W1: Yes.
MAN: [*To* W2.] The tay things?
W1: Yes.
MAN: Are the porringers* in?
W1: Yes. The whole shebang.
MAN: Well let's cut our hook and hit the road. I think we've had enough for wan day. Did you see that, Christ Almighty! We'll be like drowned rats. I'll be glad to see the house tonight. [*He looks at* W2.] C'mon ladies, let's step under this tree.
W1: We're coming.
W2: We're coming.
MAN: We've a little bit to go yit. [*Train in distance.*] Afore we're there. [*He stands in centre. Women stand each side of him. He reaches up and pulls the rope. Spotlight on three of them. The train comes. Thunders by.*]
[*Spot off.*]

END

* Small bowls.

Metagama

First performed by Theatre Hebrides, Stornoway, Isle of Lewis, Scotland, on 18 August 2004 at Studio Alba, Stornoway. Directed by Muriel Ann Macleod. The extant script is the final rehearsal version, dated "26 July 2004."

CAST

MacKENZIE
MISS MacDONALD
MURDO
MISS TULLO
AENGUS
THE MOUSE MacTAVISH
JOHN CAMPBELL
BBC RADIO VOICE
SERVANT
SIR
FIGURE IN ROBES
OFFICIAL
LAWYER
POLITICIAN
MRS YOUNG
MR YOUNG
LORD LEVERHULME
MR HARDY — Leverhulme's agent
SECRETARY
A MOTHER
A FATHER
A SON
AGENT — a Scots-Canadian

Note: Each of the seven core actors plays several parts, e.g. the actor playing AENGUS can play MR HARDY; MISS TULLO can double as the SECRETARY; MacTAVISH can play the AGENT, etc.

Set: Open space. A mound of kelp, a black boat, a mound of peat, and piles of timber.
Music: Various traditional songs – where necessary, new versions of psalms.
Sound: Throughout the scenes set on Lewis there will be the intermittent sound of the sea when appropriate.
Visuals: Stills and film footage of Canada and of the migrant crowds on the quay waiting for the departure of the Metagama.

Editors' Note: The islanders speak a mixture of English and Gaelic. For the most part, their speech in the text is presented in English. Depending on the linguistic ability of the actors, they can introduce some Gaelic phrases at appropriate points. Any line of Gaelic spoken should be immediately followed by its translation into English. In some key scenes, Gaelic is spoken for dramatic and thematic effect.

ACT I
SCENE 1

A cold wind blowing. Sound of sea in the distance. The villagers are on a rocky inlet collecting kelp. One spotlight overhead lights up the six villagers – four men, two women – forking a pile of seaweed and kelp to the front of the stage to form a ridge. They do not stop moving over and back. Song: In Gaelic and English.

ALL: Togail an fheamainn, tionndadh an fheamainn. (Lifting the kelp, turning the kelp.)
My hair is made of kelp
My legs are kelp
My head is kelp.
ALL: Togail an fheamainn, tionndadh an fheamainn. (Lifting the kelp, turning the kelp.)
My arms are kelp
My blood is kelp

My heart is kelp.
ALL: Lifting the kelp, turning the kelp.
MacKENZIE: Togail an fheamainn. (Lifting the kelp.)
MISS MacDONALD: The slave in Africa is working in paradise.
MURDO: Never was there a dirtier job.
MISS MacDONALD: Never.
MURDO: And what does the kelp make I ask you?
MISS TULLO: Something we never see.
MISS MacDONALD: And that is?
MURDO: Soap, dear God.
MISS TULLO: Ah soap!

[*In the distance a ship's horn. They stop to listen, then carry on.*]

MISS MacDONALD: In London the ladies are cleaning their faces with the weed that we collect.
MISS TULLO: Indeed they are, Miss MacDonald.
AENGUS: So that the rest of the country can wash themselves and preen themselves we must be covered in dirt.
MISS TULLO: Quite so.
MacKENZIE: [*Dressed in beard and round hat.*] The slave is a quiet man, a thing that you are not.
AENGUS: You poor, poor soul.
MacKENZIE: Will you stop your gurning – your eternal gurning – it's driving me mad. How does complaining help – it only makes the work worse. Let it be, I ask ye.
MISS MacDONALD: And the thing is, I never once saw the soap that comes from the kelp.
MISS TULLO: Nor did I.
MacKENZIE: Well please the Lord you will, one day, far beyond these parts – and then it might put a stop to the complaining, the incessant complaining,
MISS MacDONALD: You think I will see that soap someday?
MacKENZIE: I do – if you were meant to see the soap then you can take the boat.
MacTAVISH: To Canada.
MISS MacDONALD: And I can give myself a good rinse there.
MISS TULLO: A good rinse.
MacKENZIE: You can if you want, with the rest of them, who

left – the incessant complainers.

MISS MacDONALD: [*Putting on accent.*] He's ever so kind, isn't he Gertrude?

MISS TULLO: [*Putting on accent.*] Oh he is, my dear.

MacKENZIE: Go where you will and have your wash, but no more singing, no more singing, if you'd be so kind. As for soap, I've heard enough about soap for one day. And as for whingeing, I've had enough of whingeing for one day.

ALL:

My hair is kelp
My foot is kelp.

MacKENZIE: No, no, no.

MISS MacDONALD: Do you not think it's strange that soap rhymes with kelp?

AENGUS: You're wrong there Blondie, kelp rhymes with help.

MISS TULLO: And soap rhymes with boat.

AENGUS: And that's the story.

[*Black-armed, they slap the seaweed to dry. One person cuts with a sickle, and there should be a basin of water for washing. One person moves a long iron poker known as a "clatts." This is tight, concentrated work. It is done neatly, like making a grave. No other sound but at odd times they stop when a sheep bleats; they wait, then go on. As they make the ridge, bags are being filled with kelp and handed off into the dark.*]

BBC RADIO VOICE: [*Bad reception.*] Predestination weighs very heavily on these people . . . They are a people, I'm afraid, condemned to predestination . . . Where the people cut . . . Yes, cutting . . . Then gather . . . Highland army . . . Crofts as a curse . . . And drying . . . To incinerate on the tidal sounds or rocky inlet . . . peat fired . . . blue ash . . . Yes, very brittle to the mouth . . . On a diet of oatmeal and water, limpets and crabs . . . And for cutting, the tools are sickles to cut, yes . . .

[*As the ridge is near finished, the bleating gets louder. Soon the sound of the sheep dominates.*]

SCENE 2

The work stops, they all stand still, then move into two lots right and left of stage.

SERVANT: Sir, one of your tenants has removed some kelp for his own use.
SIR: Step forward. [*The man* – MURDO – *steps forward with a bag of kelp.*] Murdo?
MURDO: Yes.
SIR: What have you in that bag?
MURDO: History.
SIR: I see. Seaweed.
MURDO: Yes.
SIR: You are aware that the use of kelp as a fertiliser is forbidden?
MURDO: I am.
SIR: So what are you doing with yon bag?
MURDO: I am bringing it home.
SIR: For what reason?
MURDO: Bia dhan bhuntat. (To feed the potato.)
SIR: You will not take that bag of kelp from this place.
MURDO: It is dulse, sir, mostly dulse, to feed the children.
SIR: It is kelp. And it is forbidden.
MURDO: Duilisg a th'ann. (It is dulse.)
SIR: [*Angry.*] It is kelp. Kelp! Take it off him.
MURDO: What will I do? Will I boil boots?
SIR: Do what you will. The kelp is for incineration. It shall not manure the land. Every scrap of seaweed shall find its way to the kiln. You hear me?
MURDO: How am I to maintain the earth?
SIR: The earth is not my concern.
MURDO: But it is mine.
SIR: [*With emphasis.*] The kelp is your concern.
MURDO: That along with the machair has gone to manure the earth for centuries. You are trying to kill off the earth and kill off my family. The island will turn to moor.
SIR: Take that bag off that man.

[SERVANT *steps forwards. Takes the bag off the crofter who hands it over to him very slowly. The* SERVANT *empties it onto the ridge.*]

MISS MacDONALD: It's the sheep will drive us out of here.

MISS TULLO: Instead of turning kelp we'll be spinning thread.

[*The women now begin to banter – as they do occasionally throughout the play. The tone is playful but edgy and watchful at the same time in case one of them might overdo it.*]

MISS MacDONALD: Did you know St Columba was born on a Thursday?

MISS TULLO: Was he indeed?

MISS MacDONALD: He was.

MISS TULLO: So He could go to Heaven every Thursday if he liked.

MISS MacDONALD: That's right.

MISS TULLO: Every Thursday.

MISS MacDONALD: Yes.

MISS TULLO: Thursday brings luck.

MISS MacDONALD: Ah Thursdays.

[*They all return to work the kelp. Lights slowly down on them.*]

SCENE 3

Spotlight on centre: A FIGURE IN ROBES *appears, spreads his sheet before him, and addresses the audience.*

FIGURE IN ROBES: Good afternoon gentlemen. [*Large smile.*] I well understand that the lairds do not like emigration. [*Distant sound of sophisticated laughter.*] They want to retain the kelp labourers for their farms. But the kelp industry has collapsed, and the kelp worker is a burden on the state. To date, tenants have paid their rent in cash and produce, but from this out I suggest that all rent be paid in hard cash. [*Pause.*] This will spur on emigration. [*Roars of complaint off-stage.*] For your information – I repeat, for your information, in this year 1850 there are 12,829 individuals on Lewis in receipt of charity. I repeat: 12,829. In receipt of charity! [*Loud diverse sounds.*] This is the most extreme case of charity in the entire country and it must stop. [*Ayes.*] I do not agree that improved housing should be built. [*Ayes.*] Improvement should be strenuously resisted as it will only make the people stay at home. These black houses reared healthy men. Talk of illness is mere lies. There is nothing wrong with the houses if you lead a healthy life in them. I believe the powers-that-be are spoiling the Hebrideans. [*Ayes.*] The Hebrideans are lying on their backs waiting for you to feed them. I think the people should be left to work out their own salvation. [*Roars.*] There is no such thing as poverty on Lewis. [*Roars of hatred.*] The good men on the island are being undermined by the bad. Separate the two, and put the offenders on an outbound steamer. [*Roars.*] And let the vacated land become sheep walks. What the crofter has done has exhausted the soil. [*Roars.*] I have made a round of the parishes to ascertain the numbers willing to emigrate from Lewis. And despite the slavish outcry of certain parties – yes, certain parties [*Uproar.*] – I can guarantee that quite a number, for instance in the parish of Uig, are rather disposed to emigration. [*Shouts of "Lies! Lies!"*] The population of this island has over the last fifty years increased by 127%, that is, by some thousands of souls. [*Low murmurs.*] I suggest that a third of the population should be moved abroad. [*Sustained roars of disagreement.*] Immediately. [*More cheers of agreement.*] To the new lands of Canada. [*Spotlight off.*]

[*Darkness. The sound of sheep turns into a nightmarish sound. Then comes a very faraway sound of a ship's horn. In darkness, the sound of the sheep and the ship's horn give way to an almighty sound of wind and sound of rain. Then a man sings mouth-music. Light up slowly, and slowly pans across the stage. No human on stage. Silence, then the wind again as the scene is established. At the front of the stage a small bank of kelp. To left, a stack of potatoes. A black boat, upside down at the back of the stage, with small window in the stern. On one side a quern [hand-mill] placed on a sheep skin. To the other side, a line of washing, blowing. Beside it a tall black pot. Light comes fully up on the washing. The washing includes a complete soldier's army outfit with rifle; a fisherman's outfit from the eighteenth century; a kelp worker's clothes; a large wet cloth of tweed ready for walking; a landlord's silks;* MISS MacDONALDS*'s dark church-going clothes; a child's nineteenth-century long trousers outfit complete with cap; a Viking outfit with the headgear; a Red Indian's headdress; and, lastly, a vicar's outfit with collar. The wind eases, the clothes go still, the wind turns into a version of mouth-music. Then suddenly, a ship's horn screeches. Darkness.*]

SCENE 4

Playwright's Note: *This scene can be cut if deemed unnecessary.*

MISS TULLO *enters stage left and stands and speaks as* MISS MacDONALD *and* AENGUS *come in through the door and begin taking down the clothes and putting them away. Slowly they clear the space.*

MISS TULLO: [*Watching* MISS MacDONALD *and* AENGUS.] When the bad times came, and the potatoes failed again, they sold off their last stock, but did not pay the rent that was due. Instead they said "That's it, we're going. We're going to Canada. Out to a colony on the Red River to another life." They signed on for the passage and they came back to the house along the windswept coast, and without a word came in through the door one last time, and sat a moment, and he got up and started, and then she got up and started, and they took everything. [*They start carrying bags out the back door.*] Every last thing. Except for the soot, the piles of soot and the peat. They took the wheels, the looms, the boiler, and the frame for the hanks of wool. And the peat irons and the spades. And the big chest, the girnel. They took every stitch of clothes. Soon all that was inside was outside. [MISS

MacDONALD *faces the audience.*] She went to look out the window one last time, and then she stepped through the door and he banged it behind him. [*He bangs the door.*] All day they were hauling their gear down to the quay. But when it came to putting it on board, the Captain said no. There was a further charge for this, and then another charge for that, and then another. They last they saw of Lewis was all their possessions sitting on the pier. And they themselves were never seen again. But it's said that they did not get much satisfaction or comfort in the new land. That their heads turned white as seagulls while they were still young. [*Lights out.*]

SCENE 5

Two women sit on sods of peat, a man is taking one potato after the other from the earth. Then MISS MacDONALD *washes the potatoes and puts them into two buckets. All are in black.* MURDO *stands backstage, walks down towards the front, then moves back planting potatoes. When he reaches backstage right,* MURDO *rests a moment on a stack of peat, then heads off again like a man possessed. His white face has streaks of black across it. They keep moving throughout the scene.*

AENGUS: I have a mystery.
JOHN CAMPBELL: Tell us.
AENGUS: We have songs for planting.
JOHN CAMPBELL: True.
AENGUS: And we have songs for harvesting.
JOHN CAMPBELL: Aye.
AENGUS: But we have no songs for weeding. Not a one. And we do more weeding then we do planting or harvesting.
MISS MacDONALD: True.
MacTAVISH: I'm a nobody.
MISS TULLO: You are.
MacTAVISH: Neither fisherman nor farmer. They will not allow us be either. I have listened to so much gurning. I have

become a gurner.

[*They work on in silence.*]

MacKENZIE: There is nothing worse than the smell of rotten potatoes – it poisons the air.

MISS TULLO: It does.

MISS MacDONALD: I hope those that come to these places years after us can smell it. I would not like them that come after us to get away with it. They should know the smell of decay. The sickness in the air.

MacKENZIE: I curse the blight, I do.

MISS MacDONALD: That they may feel the blight.

MURDO: They say there's near twenty thousand people from these parts gone.

MacKENZIE: Two thousand in ten years from Lewis itself.

MURDO: First they wanted us to go.

MISS MacDONALD: To make room for the sheep.

MacKENZIE: And the deer.

MISS TULLO: Then they didn't want us to go.

AENGUS: So that we could harvest the kelp.

MacKENZIE: Huh! The kelp.

AENGUS: But never should we be allowed to fertilize the land.

MISS TULLO: Only for the roof.

AENGUS: Only for the roof Miss Tullo – only for the thatch that we throw on the fields. I wonder do they have to throw their roof onto the field each year over there?

JOHN CAMPBELL: I doubt it.

MacKENZIE: Now they say if we leave that we are turning against our own country.

AENGUS: It was them that started the emigration.

MURDO: It was.

MISS TULLO: And them that stopped it.

JOHN CAMPBELL: And them that will start it again.

[*In the distance the ship's horn. They pause and listen, then go on.*]

MacKENZIE: The land is left to the snipe. They put us where we cannot earn a living, from the fishing or the farm. "Improvements" they say. They speak of improvements. Each improvement starts another famine.

MISS MacDONALD: I hate the sheep.

MacKENZIE: I hate the deer.

MISS MacDONALD: I hate the sheep even more. Where one sheep feeds there once lived an entire human family.

MacKENZIE: His wool is worth more than the skin on my back.

JOHN CAMPBELL: Or the inside of my head.

MURDO: You know why they want us to stay here on the island?

MacKENZIE: I thought they wanted us to go. Did they not hunt down the people of Barra and South Uist with dogs, bind them and transport them onto the ships in '44?

MURDO: Yes, they did, but that is the past – now they want us to stay.

MacKENZIE: Is that it? Well I'm light in the head. If that is the past there is also the future, so where are we now?

MISS MacDONALD: Back.

MacKENZIE: Back: good, good, I have you – the past is back there, the past is yesterday, when they wanted us to stay. Tomorrow they'll want us to go.

MURDO: Tomorrow yes.

JOHN CAMPBELL: But not today.

MURDO: No, tomorrow.

JOHN CAMPBELL: But not today,

MacKENZIE: Oh dear,

AENGUS: No. Not today. If we left yesterday we'd be gone. But now we are here. It's the way it is. Today we stay. Aye. They don't want to see the place de-populated. Why?

MacKENZIE: Once they needed us for the kelp.

MURDO: Fuck the blasted kelp!

MacKENZIE: But Napoleon put paid to that. He was the big boy. It's not only for the kelp now. Not now. Though once it was.

[*Sound of ship's horn.*]

MURDO: No.

MacTAVISH: Nor the fishing.
MacKENZIE: Nor the meagre food that we draw from the earth.
MURDO: No. It's something else entirely.
MacKENZIE: It is.
MURDO: But can I say it?
AENGUS: Do.
[*Sound of the sea.*]
MURDO: Can I?
AENGUS: Can you?
MURDO: Can I say what's inside my head. If they want the land for sheep why keep us here? Why try and stop us going? They are out to prevent emigration. They've risen the price of passage from £3 to £10 and then to £12, and on, so no man can go. Tell me why?
MacKENZIE: Can you say it?
MURDO: The price has gone beyond our reach. And now the words have gone beyond my reach. They want to keep us here.
MacKENZIE: They do.
MURDO: Why?
MacKENZIE: Say it.
[*Bending and picking.*]
AENGUS: Do.
[MURDO *stands up and stays still.*]
MURDO: They want to raise an army to protect England.
[JOHN CAMPBELL *stops.*]
JOHN CAMPBELL: To make the opium landlords richer.
[*All bend again.*]
MacKENZIE: Ah, ah, aye right again John C.
AENGUS: That's it.
MacKENZIE: Think of the money the landlords would lose if they could not recruit a Highland regiment. To them we are naught but soldiers. That's what we are – soldiers in waiting.
[*Bending and picking.*]
MURDO: If we leave for Canada they lose their soldiers.
MacKENZIE: If we stay we starve.

MURDO: So meanwhile they'll find a way to feed us so that we can fight.

MacKENZIE: But who will want us for an army if we are too hungry to fight?

MURDO: They will feed us sufficient to keep us here. And this will increase our debt to them that we have no hope of ever paying off. Nor can we ever be paid for the work we do since our labour is set against the rent that's owed. [*Pause.*] Who was it that worked out this terrible riddle?

MacKENZIE: I would kill that man.

[MURDO *stands. They all speak down as if saying a rhyme.*]

MURDO: They are keeping us here for the next war . . .

[AENGUS *stands.*]

AENGUS: And the one after that.

[JOHN CAMPBELL *stands.*]

JOHN CAMPBELL: And the one after that.

MacKENZIE: And what does a war give us?

[*All bend again.*]

MURDO: A pension.

MacKENZIE: A wage.

AENGUS: And a free coffin.

MacKENZIE: Aye.

MURDO: And the stab in the back. [*He stands.*] After we won the last war the price of kelp dropped to nothing. Our own neighbours down South knifed us in the back and imported the kelp from abroad. For a cheaper wash they hurled us into poverty. Watch the next war.

AENGUS: That's what Lewis is – an army in waiting. You hear me? And you'll see – they'll knife us in the back again. We are naught but cannon fodder. If I had my way I'd be gone in the morning to join the others that left.

MacKENZIE: Aye.

MURDO: Abroad in Canada.

MacKENZIE: Lie low a while and come back.

MURDO: Come back, yes. Maybe. But in the morning I'd go. I would.

[*They pick on for a while in silence. Slowly lights out; sea sound, wind sound.*]

SCENE 6

OFFICIAL *at table.* MacKENZIE *standing to the left, his hands in his pockets.*

OFFICIAL: You are aware that you are in my office, Mr MacKenzie, so that we may speak of the raiders?

MacKENZIE: Yes.

OFFICIAL: And I take it you understand the meaning of the word "manners"?

MacKENZIE: [*Bitter.*] I do. I understand it well. There will be your story and my story.

OFFICIAL: Indeed. It takes two to make history Mister MacKenzie. And perhaps my story will outlast yours.

MacKENZIE: You think so? There is a saying sir. "'Na biasta mor ag itheadh nam biasta beag; na biasta beag a deanamh mar dh'fhaodas iad." ("The big beasts eating the little beasts; the little beasts doing as best they may.")

OFFICIAL: I will allow you your gift for words, but like your farming methods they are promiscuous. On our side we try our best to improve your lot, but now sir, we shall leave those arguments aside. So?

MacKENZIE: So what?

OFFICIAL: Mr MacKenzie, let's establish this – do you know where you are?

MacKENZIE: I do.

OFFICIAL: Well?

MacKENZIE: Well what?

OFFICIAL: Your hands.

MacKENZIE: My hands?

OFFICIAL: Yes.

MacKENZIE: What is wrong with my hands? Do they offend you?

OFFICIAL: They are in your pockets.

MacKENZIE: Indeed they are. It was me that put them there.

OFFICIAL: You know what you have to do.

MacKENZIE: I do – stand here and listen to your latest edict. To hear what you decree.

OFFICIAL: If you wish me to begin, you will please take your hands out of your pockets.

MacKENZIE: I did not come here to attend finishing school.

OFFICIAL: Take them out. [MacKENZIE *does not move.*] Take them out or you will face a fine MacKenzie. You hear me?

MacKENZIE: I hear you well Mister. You can fine me what you will. Since I have nothing, there is nothing you can take away from me.

[OFFICIAL *turns to him, and his voice rises.*]

OFFICIAL: You're wrong there.

MacKENZIE: What are you saying?

OFFICIAL: There is much that I can take away from you Mister MacKenzie. Be sure of that.

MacKENZIE: I am not ready to turn my house into a boat.

OFFICIAL: Take your hands out of your pockets!

MacKENZIE: If houses lie out there with no one in them on the sheep farms, we have a right to enter them.

OFFICIAL: Take your hands out of your pockets! [*Slowly* MacKENZIE *takes his hands out of his pockets. They face each other.*] Thank you Mister MacKenzie. Now let us begin. [*Lights go slowly down as* OFFICIAL *talks away into the distance.*] You will inform those . . . raiders in these parishes . . . that they must remove their cattle herewith. And leave the farms. Summons will be served on all crofters, cotters and squatters who do not clear the lands. They only aggravate the indigence, squalor and lethargy which too much abound already. You will, etc., etc.

[*Darkness.*]

SCENE 7

In the distance the sound of a ship's horn. MISS MacDONALD *and* MISS TULLO *are gutting fish. There are two small barrels into which they bend.*

MISS MacDONALD: The croft is a terrible weight.

MISS TULLO: It's worse than a drunk man.

MISS MacDONALD: True.

MISS TULLO: Till ye get so used to it. One day you don't know it's there.

MISS MacDONALD: But the others see it on you.

MISS TULLO: They do Miss MacDonald. They do with their black eyes.

MISS MacDONALD: "Why don't we just go?" I said to him. "Why don't we just leave?"

MISS TULLO: And he said?

MAN'S VOICE: [*Off-stage.*] Nah.

MISS TULLO: Aye, I knew it. [*Smacks her hands.*] Same as mine. The men of Lewis are spoiled. All the bloody same. Not a hand's turn will they do. I have not lived in my own house for fifteen years and never will.

MISS MacDONALD: The coast is a poor lonesome place.

MISS TULLO: It is, Miss MacDonald. There will be naught to do except grow more lonesome.

MISS MacDONALD: And gut.

MISS TULLO: And gut is right.

MISS MacDONALD: Till the insides of a fish . . .

MISS TULLO: . . . would sicken ya.

MISS MacDONALD: And bait lines.

MISS TULLO: And head to town barefoot with butter and crowdie.

MISS MacDONALD: And a string of fish to sell round the closed doors, knitting a stitch for the bairn as we go.

MISS TULLO: Sixpence for a gat!

MISS MacDONALD: Sixpence for a gat, ya tramp!

MISS TULLO: I had a dream, Miss MacDonald, that I had not a stitch on me and where was I? I'll tell you. I was in the middle of Stornoway with a basket of fishing shouting . . .

MISS MacDONALD: "Sixpence for a gat!"

MISS TULLO: Not a stitch on in front of the world shouting . . .

MISS MacDONALD: "Sixpence for a gat!"

MISS TULLO: And I saw the men in black looking at me. I

could have died. But worse was to come. They began to drive me from the town with sticks. The sticks rained down on me. I ran home to find the house was in the sea. And The Mouse MacTavish said to me: "Now see what you've earned."

MISS MacDONALD: We came here to the sea through force, Miss Tullo, not good will.

MISS TULLO: We did.

MISS MacDONALD: And now there's more women off the island at the fishing than there is men.

MISS TULLO: Five hundred more.

[MISS MacDONALD *stops. Sound of sea and sound of wind.*]

MISS MacDONALD: My father could've gone across the water in '81 but oh no, he'd wait he'd wait, he'd wait till '86 and the place would be his again with security of tenure. I was not born then but I often heard them argue about it. The house became his, but it made no difference. The croft still belonged to the landlord. Not to my father. He didn't go and since then he's just been wasting his life away. He could have gone in 1902, but . . .

MALE VOICE: [*Off-stage.*] No.

MISS MacDONALD: And then I was born. In 1906 we had another chance of assisted passage. She said to him, "Let's go," and he said . . .

MALE VOICE: [*Off-stage.*] No.

MISS MacDONALD: "Can you not see what's happening to us, can you not see what's happening before your very eyes," she screamed.

MALE VOICE: [*Off-stage.*] In Canada they speak a different language.

MISS MacDONALD: "And is our language to keep us poor?" she screamed. [*Loud.*] "I can be a Christian in any language!" [*Quieter.*] He didn't answer her. She had him beat. [*She goes back to* work.] And now he just sits there by the window looking out to sea, with longing. With great longing. And then the shouting would start. The swearing like he was back again out on a boat and swearing at the crew. The whole night through roaring orders.

[*Curses in Gaelic.*]

MALE VOICE: To port, you fucking idiot. Heave, you fucker.

MALE VOICE: Damn ya to hell. Heave, you fucker. That you may die fucking roaring.

MISS MacDONALD: If only he'd turn to God. But no. He turned to despair. There is nothing worse. You can hardly pity him.

MISS TULLO: I see it.

MISS MacDONALD: You see me – since I was a child I wanted to be free. They'd say to me, "Do you want to be a nurse?" No, I'd say, I want to be a gypsy. And I tried, honest I did, I left here twice for the mainland, I did. So close and so far. [*Pause.*] If we went we might see Iceland.

[MISS TULLO *stops.*]

MISS TULLO: Iceland. [*Bends again.*] That might be nice!

MISS MacDONALD: Then there's Greenland.

MISS TULLO: But I heard that Greenland is a lie. It's whiter than Iceland.

MISS MacDONALD: No!

MISS TULLO: Oh yes. I have that on good authority.

MISS MacDONALD: Well let's forget about Greenland and go to Canada. I might meet my relations over there and they'll look after me. If I get there I'll get hens and sell eggs. It'll be a business. I'll have no end of vegetables. No end. And I'll have my own milk. And you?

MISS TULLO: I'll be a dressmaker.

MISS MacDONALD: Good for you, Miss Tullo, I can see you in a fine dress.

MISS TULLO: I don't care if I never see this place again. What's the difference between a shieling in Lewis and a wigwam in Canada?

MISS MacDONALD: None but a few thousand miles. [*Pause. They both stop working.*] You see yon mainland?

MISS TULLO: Aye.

[*They stop, and look towards audience.*]

MISS MacDONALD: Well there's a boat leaves Glasgow with nothing on board but women bound for Canada. And they call it the bride ship.

MISS TULLO: That's a nice name.

MISS MacDONALD: We'll go and join the bride ship.

[MISS TULLO *starts work again.*]

MISS TULLO: [*Slowly, enunciating each word.*] We will, aye, but . . . there again Miss MacDonald . . . Cape Wrath . . . is well named as far as women go.

[MISS MacDONALD *stands still.*]

MISS MacDONALD: Can you hear them?

MISS TULLO: Hear what?

MISS MacDONALD: The bells.

MISS TULLO: [*Warily.*] What bells?

MISS MacDONALD: Wedding bells in Canada.

MISS TULLO: [*Looks, listens, shakes her head, works.*] Miss MacDonald, I'm sorry.

MISS MacDONALD: [*Urgently, forcefully.*] Listen.

MISS TULLO: [*Angrily, almost sharp.*] I'm listening.

[*Sound of sea and sound of wind.*]

MISS MacDONALD: You must hear them?

MISS TULLO: [*Forcefully.*] I hear nothing. Nothing.

MISS MacDONALD: Well, if you don't hear them neither do I.

[*Returns to work, happily, as if it was all a joke.*]

MISS TULLO: All right then, things are back to normal.

MISS MacDONALD: So there's nothing to do.

MISS TULLO: But gut.

MISS MacDONALD: [*Wearily, and angrily.*] But gut the gat.

MISS TULLO: And gut the gat.

MISS MacDONALD: And bend.

MISS TULLO: And bend.

MISS MacDONALD: I'm tired bending.

MISS TULLO: To gut the gat.

MISS MacDONALD: A thousand herring to a barrel.

MISS TULLO: Nine shillings a week. There is nothing wrong with that.

MISS MacDONALD: No.

MISS TULLO: So no gurning.
MISS MacDONALD: No.
MISS TULLO: We'll go from here one day.
MISS MacDONALD: We will.
MISS TULLO: [*Happily.*] Till then . . .
MISS MacDONALD: [*Happily.*] It's bend . . .
MISS TULLO: . . . and gut . . .
MISS MacDONALD: . . . and bend . . .
MISS TULLO: . . . and gut.
MISS MacDONALD: And gut the gat.
MISS TULLO: Sixpence for a gat!
MISS MacDONALD: Sixpence a gat!
TOGETHER: Gut the gat!

[*Turning it into a song.*]
Gut the gat!
Sixpence a gat!
Sixpence a gat!

[*The wind rises, the sound of the sea rises. The other villagers begin to gather, with their bibles. The five men join the two women singing. The voices turn to Gaelic psalms.*]

SCENE 8

The group kneel towards a central figure, who gives the first few phrases. The singing starts in earnest. A psalm in Gaelic starts. The five men and two women are seated in a half-circle in a low light, each with a bible, around one man, AENGUS. *When it has ended* AENGUS *rises.*

AENGUS: I would like to remind you of the sermon given by a man who had not the safety of a church but a gravel-pit in Mull. As you enter the new days remember his words, as a reminder to yourself, that we need nothing. These are the words he said: "We have a religion and a language to translate that religion. We do not need church walls. Let those that need those walls go sup with the lairds. We don't need them. This place will do us. This gravel-pit below the high-water mark. I like it here. The Lord does not deny us the smile of his countenance. [*He waves to the sky.*] That we, gathered here in the open air this Sabbath, are obliged to worship in a gravel-pit is a sign of our faith. The water that fills this pit at high tide is another sign – not something to be feared or humiliated by. These waters come through the generosity of God. And the wind that drives them is His breath. And when the waters empty the world is a fierce lonesome place. Aye. But when the waters empty we pray. In the emptiness we pray to escape Hell. [*Very loudly.*] If you do not believe in Christ the waters of the sea will testify against you in the day of judgement; if you do not believe in Christ the wind will testify against you in the day of judgement; if you do not believe in Christ these rocks will testify against you in the day of judgement."

[*The sermon stops suddenly. Commotion backstage.*]

SCENE 9

Darkness. Loud commotion backstage. The door backstage begins to swing on its hinges as the raiders begin hacking. Loud hacking and crashing sounds continue. The door opens and men appear with lights. They run to and fro.

AENGUS: [*Quietly, in a whisper.*] Anyone?
MacKENZIE: [*Quietly.*] No.
MURDO: It is empty.
MacKENZIE: There is no-one Aengus.
AENGUS: Are you sure?
MacKENZIE: Yes, there is not a soul.
AENGUS: [*Whispers.*] John Campbell – where are you?
JOHN CAMPBELL: [*Stepping in.*] I'm here.

[JOHN CAMPBELL *steps in with a torch to his face. Then* MISS MacDONALD appears with a torch.]

AENGUS: Are you sure you want to do this Miss MacDonald?
MISS MacDONALD: I don't know.

AENGUS: There is still time for you to go home.

MISS MacDONALD: I want to stay on account of the women.

AENGUS: It's your choice. We will remain outside till dawn to guard you. Do not show yourself at the door John Campbell. Light no fire. Pray. Listen to every sound. Be on your guard. [*They go. The place goes quiet.*]

MISS MacDONALD: [*Fearful.*] John?

JOHN CAMPBELL: Aye Miss MacDonald?

MISS MacDONALD: You're there. I'm so glad you're there. I could not see a thing getting here. I got out the window and into the cart. They kept us in the back of the cart under a cloth so that we could not see. We came a long way in the dark. I could not tell what direction we took. Who were those men?

JOHN CAMPBELL: [*Nonchalantly.*] All pious men from Ness.

MISS MacDONALD: This house is huge. There must be five rooms. Who owns it John?

JOHN CAMPBELL: We do. [*Pause.*] Now.

MISS MacDONALD: And for how long?

JOHN CAMPBELL: For a while, I suppose.

MISS MacDONALD: What will people think of me? Bad enough to be a raider, but to be unmarried as well is a worse crime.

JOHN CAMPBELL: You will sleep there, and I will sleep here.

MISS MacDONALD: And who will believe us? Either way I will be known as a scandalous woman. [*She moves towards him.*] Is it not arrogance John?

JOHN CAMPBELL: No – it is justice. These houses are lying idle.

[MISS MacDONALD *wanders the space.*]

MISS MacDONALD: Where are we?

JOHN CAMPBELL: As the famous minister once said . . .

MISS MacDONALD: [*Sharply.*] Yes?

JOHN CAMPBELL: "We are somewhere between Genesis and Revelation" – [*Pause.*] – "in the parish of Back."

MISS MacDONALD: How can you joke John Campbell? This

is no time for joking. I wish you would not joke. We can expect the soldiers to come through that door in the morning.
JOHN CAMPBELL: Well till that time let us be content.
MISS MacDONALD: John?
JOHN CAMPBELL: Yes?
MISS MacDONALD: What will my parents think?
JOHN CAMPBELL: I don't know.
MISS MacDONALD: I'm frightened.
JOHN CAMPBELL: You're not the first, and not the last.
MISS MacDONALD: [*Angrily.*] I said I'm frightened!
JOHN CAMPBELL: [*Loud whisper.*] Stop your screaming woman.
MISS MacDONALD: [*Loud whisper.*] Stop your roaring.
JOHN CAMPBELL: Don't let them hear you scream. [*Pause.*] If you must go home, do. We can't go on like this.
[*They stand lightly lit to the right of the empty stage.*]
MISS MacDONALD: Think of the shame I'll bring on the others at home. I have to think of the others at home.
JOHN CAMPBELL: Then go Miss MacDonald. I will not keep you here.
[*Long pause.*]
MISS MacDONALD: John?
JOHN CAMPBELL: Yes?
MISS MacDONALD: [*Calm.*] Three things John.
JOHN CAMPBELL: Aye.
MISS MacDONALD: Three things only.
JOHN CAMPBELL: Yes.
MISS MacDONALD: You have them?
JOHN CAMPBELL: I have them by me.
MISS MacDONALD: Count them.
JOHN CAMPBELL: I will.
MISS MacDONALD: Now.
JOHN CAMPBELL: Now?
MISS MacDONALD: Aye, for me.
JOHN CAMPBELL: [*Emphasising each on a finger.*] Three things that come without asking: fear, love and jealousy. I

have them.

MISS MacDONALD: Good. Keep them by you. For again. You know where you are going.

JOHN CAMPBELL: I do.

[*She goes to the door, opens it, closes it and remains inside. They stand with their torches to their faces, well away from each other. One by one the torches die.*]

SCENE 10

Lights full up. JOHN CAMPBELL *and* AENGUS *seated in two chairs. A* LAWYER *addresses the audience as jury.*

LAWYER: You see here before you the two accused – John Campbell and Aengus McKay – who were summoned to appear in court for being part of a raiding party that broke into a certain premises in Back. You have heard much high talk today and yesterday and other days. How these men are criminals. Are cowards. But let me remind you if you find these men guilty, and these summons are implemented, the effect will be the turning out of house and home of several hundreds of beings. You heard what John Campbell said when asked "What is a croft?" "A croft, sir," he said, is "a half-acre of land surrounded by legislation." A half-acre of land surrounded by legislation. I would ask you to dwell on those words. These men were turned out of their homes and sought sanctuary in houses that lay empty on sheep lands. The crime was not seeking shelter but the real crime was the eviction itself. From the way in which these poor people have been treated, one would naturally be led to suppose they were undesirables. But though repeatedly asked by me the prosecution could not give any instance of either accused committing any crime. And there was a further injustice to these two men. None of the witnesses on behalf of the defendants were allowed give their evidence in Gaelic. In fact, if it was discovered that they could speak English their resort to Gaelic in the witness box was seen as a further crime. So Gaelic now is the unworthy language of subterfuge and betrayal. The right honourable gentleman has drawn attention to the fact that the empire might in the near future face war, and I have heard it suggested by certain parties and in certain newspapers that these accused, these so-called raiders, in a time of great instability, are trying, not only to avoid conscription, but were acting unpatriotically by illegally breaking into unoccupied houses. In Parliament it has been rumoured that Scotland and its newspapers have remained anti-war. That Scotland, like Ireland, is seeking independence and are turning against England in her time of need. It is said that Irish rebels have been in these parts talking rebellion and selling guns. All this when Britain is facing its enemies. That we – especially those two men sitting there – are in fact cowards. That theirs was an act of betrayal in a time of danger for the empire. But I would suggest that it is the person who evicted them who is guilty of an act of betrayal. The people who let houses lie idle when their fellows were homeless are the ones who were unpatriotic. Lewis Island has and always will provide some of the finest soldiers in this country. To date fifteen hundred men have joined the ranks of the forces, and this without one instance of conscription. And as I have indicated both these men are ready to join the forces. I leave the matter – [*He bows to the audience.*] – in your generous hands.

BBC VOICE: On the 28th of June 1914 a Serb nationalist assassinated the Archduke Ferdinand, heir apparent to the Austro-Hungarian throne. Austria-Hungary declared war on Serbia. The First World War began. On one side the Allies: Great Britain and her Empire, France, Russia, and the USA. On the other side the Central Powers: Germany, Austria-Hungary, and Turkey.

[*War posters and headlines from Scottish newspapers on screen. Film footage.*]

SCENE 11

JOHN CAMPBELL, *now a soldier, is dressing himself. He dons his jacket.* MISS MacDONALD *holds it for him. He throws water on his face, and towels himself.*

JOHN CAMPBELL: One last war and it's over. If you read the *Gazette* that's what it says. And if they are not talking about conscription they're talking of constipation. Conscription on one hand and constipation on the other. [*He takes his boots and puts them on, stands, puts on his cap.*] I hear there is great traffic on the island for widows' weeds. Do not buy widows' weeds.

MISS MacDONALD: Since I am not married to you, I can't.

JOHN CAMPBELL: But even if you were.

MISS MacDONALD: I wouldn't.

JOHN CAMPBELL: No tears.

MISS MacDONALD: No.

JOHN CAMPBELL: We will be married when I return.

MISS MacDONALD: It's a strange time you thought of asking me that.

JOHN CAMPBELL: Well, have you an answer?

MISS MacDONALD: I'll tell you when you come home.

JOHN CAMPBELL: That could be a long time.

MISS MacDONALD. It might.

[*He does a sudden skip on the floor, then stops.*]

SCENE 12

A POLITICIAN *stands.*

POLITICIAN: The Board of Agriculture is preparing schemes in accordance with the provisions of the Small Landholders Act 1911 for dividing into crofts those farms with a rental in excess of £80, or fifteen acres. Eight hundred Lewis families have applied but unfortunately the war has intervened. But when this war is over each man is guaranteed a plot of land – in Gress, in Galson, in Carnish, and Orinsay. Each man that signs on as soldier to protect this empire will be guaranteed a plot of land and a croft upon his return from Europe. This has been guaranteed by Parliament, and will soon become law. Lloyd George recognizes the nation's debt to the people of the Hebrides and especially the people of Lewis. As soon as the war is won the land question in the Highlands will be settled once and for all. Everyone is agreed upon this. Everyone is agreed that the people of the Highlands must be placed in possession of the soil. You go forth onto the front in France not as peasants but as landholders. This promise is . . .

[*Gunfire.*]

SCENE 13

Lights up on front of stage. Behind the bank of kelp, six rifles point towards the audience. The six men lie behind the bank. To the back on each side, the women sleep on the floor under blankets. We cannot see the faces of the soldiers, only their caps, or maybe not even that. The sound of explosions in background.

AENGUS: Aaa-ah-ooh.
JOHN CAMPBELL: Aaa-ah-ooh.
MacKENZIE: Well, Mouse?
MacTAVISH: It's dear bought.
CAPTAIN MURDO: Stop bugling.
AENGUS: Where are we Captain Murdo?
CAPTAIN MURDO: Where do you think?
MacTAVISH: It's not Dark Island.
JOHN CAMPBELL: It's not the Narrows.
MacTAVISH: It's not Aird.

[*Gunfire.*]

CAPTAIN MURDO: I did not come here to fight for land at home. [*Laughing.*] Take a look Mouse.
MacTAVISH: You think I'm bloody mad Captain Murdo. You're mad. I'm not mad. No.

AENGUS: That there man is skew-eyed.

MacTAVISH: Oh that I was.

MacKENZIE: It's going to be a bad day today with the blasted midges.

CAPTAIN MURDO: Oh dear. I didn't know there were midges in France.

AENGUS: That's because you brought them with you.

MacKENZIE: But they're here.

MURDO: Stop it MacKenzie – if you hadn't mentioned them I wouldn't know they were there.

[*Shots, then silence. Behind,* MISS TULLO *rises and walks behind the men towards the door. She opens it, looks out.*]

MacTAVISH: I'd murder a herring.

AENGUS: I'd give my life for a herring.

MacTAVISH: Right now.

JOHN CAMPBELL: For a kipper.

MacKENZIE: For a prawn.

[MISS TULLO *closes the door and stands at the back facing the audience.*]

CAPTAIN MURDO: For a kipper o' Stornoway.

MacTAVISH: Never mind a dame.

CAPTAIN MURDO: It's good that they put something in the soup to drown your want MacTavish. Stop that degrading business. Get down I say. Stay! Stay! I say.

AENGUS: Stop man! Stop the business.

[*A barrage takes place. Each take a shot.*]

JOHN CAMPBELL: For Loch Roag!

AENGUS: And one for Stornoway!

MacTAVISH: For Alice Macleod!

[*Shooting stops. Voices casual.* MISS TULLO *leaves the door and goes back and lies down.*]

AENGUS: You know why the herring left the lochs Captain Murdo?

CAPTAIN MURDO: Pray tell.

AENGUS: It was my father told me. He said the herring did not like the splashing of oars.

CAPTAIN MURDO: No?

AENGUS: No, Captain Murdo, they did not.
JOHN CAMPBELL: The herring would not like it here then.
MacKENZIE: No.
CAPTAIN MURDO: Only the smoked variety. They might prosper.
AENGUS: Aye, Captain Murdo. Good on ya.
MacKENZIE: The poor herring. He has a lot to answer for. He must've sinned in another existence.
AENGUS: Like Jonah.
MacTAVISH: Like us.
AENGUS: Like the Mouse. The Mouse MacTavish.
JOHN CAMPBELL: The poor mouse.
MacKENZIE: Aye. Afflicted with a mighty burden of lust.
MacTAVISH: I'd like to remind ye, it's myself you're speaking of.
AENGUS: Yourself indeed, poor soul, a gimlet soul tipping down Cromwell Street with a face on you.
MacKENZIE: After the ladies.
MacTAVISH: Ah dear. I can't. I can't see it.
MacKENZIE: Well, you will son.
AENGUS: Soon you'll be stepping onto a boat.
MacTAVISH: I can't see it. I can't see it.
CAPTAIN MURDO: You can't lad. It's not in your nature.
AENGUS: Don't worry Mouse. Soon we'll be going home to the island. And if you get left behind, well we'll come back for you.
MacTAVISH: Thank you kindly, you're a most esteemed man Aengus. [*A blast of light as if lightning strikes.*] And did you see the Scottish papers? They were against it. Every day. There would be no war. No, they would not hear of a war. First there would be no war. Then there was. Then there wasn't. Then there was, then there wasn't; no, we would not go to war. Then we did. You see them change their tune? Did you see that Captain?
CAPTAIN MURDO: I did Mouse, I did.
MacKENZIE: I'm being eaten alive.
CAPTAIN MURDO: Shut your gob MacKenzie.

[*A terrible barrage. The two women look up from their bed to listen. The guns disappear behind the bank of kelp. A single shot. A flash of light. In the flash the women rise.*]

[*On Screen: 11 November 1918.*]

BBC VOICE: Peace was declared . . .

[*A number of ships' sirens sound throughout the theatre. Silence.*]

SCENE 14

A huge roar of ocean occurs. In the darkness a spinning light and a ship's horn. The ocean and the wind pound. Jets of light cascade: red, white and green. Figures move to and fro across the stage creating enormous shadows. The siren blow. Voices screaming but mainly the staccato voice of JOHN CAMPBELL.

VOICES: The Arnish Lights one point to port – we're headed for the Beast of Holm – I never saw a ship running this close – he's altering the course – what's he at? – he's running ashore – what's he at? – I never saw a ship run so close to the land – here's Arnish – the Arnish Lights – she's struck – there's Arnish – she's struck – Captain – Captain – Captain, she's broadside on – do not cast the boats adrift! – stand back, man – the Bridge – is there anyone on the bridge? – where is the land? – get the rope – we're gone – help – help – help – help – help – help – help – help – God, starboard – smash the window – watch the rocks – watch the rocks – smash the bloody door – see the rockets – there – what's happening? – throw the line – take it man – take it man – drop the boat – drop her – drop her – where's the lifebelts? – there are no lifebelts – she's going – she's going – help – make her fast to the starboard quarter – he's gone ahead with a heaving line – go on man – on the hawser man – get you on the hawser – go – go – go. [*Silence. One last sluice of coloured light. Silence.*]

SCENE 15

A quiet knock on the door. Then a louder knock. MRS YOUNG *appears in her nightdress.* MR YOUNG *answers the door. When he opens it, the storm rages beyond. A man in uniform enters, drenched, and out of breath.*

JOHN CAMPBELL: Am I in Lewis?
MR YOUNG: You are.
MRS YOUNG: Come in, come in from there.
JOHN CAMPBELL: So I'm home. [*They bring him across to a chair.*] But they are not, the ones out there. [*He points, then pulls his hand down.*]
MR YOUNG: What, what happened son?
JOHN CAMPBELL: The Iolaire is down . . .
MR YOUNG: Dear God!
JOHN CAMPBELL: . . . with more than two hundred souls . . . coming home from the war. Out . . . there . . . on the rocks.
MRS YOUNG: Two hundred!
[*He points again.*]
JOHN CAMPBELL: Just out there.
MR YOUNG: This is terrible. Is there something we can do?
JOHN CAMPBELL: The worst is over. There is nothing you can do. I'm sorry – I saw your light. All the years in France I never saw anything worse than this. I saw a boy out there and could not get to him. We were alright, we were nearly home – we could see the lights from Stornoway. We were nearly home. Only a little to go. I got my gear ready. They were singing in the saloon when she struck. [*Stands open-mouthed and delirious.*] Some of the men broke a window. I climbed up on the port side. And scrambled down before the bridge. She gave a great crash. I made it up to the bow. She was listing badly. [*Sits.*] It was pitch dark but when the distress lights went up I could see the land only yards away. Why did we turn that way? Why? [*He looks at them.*] The sea washed over the ship. I saw maybe fifty men jump overboard and I saw them broken up on the rocks. Aye. [*Pauses, looks round him.*] Is it still New Year's Eve?
MRS YOUNG: It was, my unfortunate man, till three hours ago.
JOHN CAMPBELL: So it's New Year's Day. And here I am. On New Year's Day. Aye.

MR YOUNG: Take this.

[JOHN CAMPBELL *sups.*]

JOHN CAMPBELL: Thank you. To come all this way back from death to die a few yards from home. In the sea, the blasted sea. I thought we had conquered death. I did. I was wrong. [*He remains fixed.*]

MRS YOUNG: Easy son, easy.

JOHN CAMPBELL: It would have been better to die in France than to die out there in the bay. [*He points and holds his hand out rigid.* MRS YOUNG *throws a blanket over him.*] Thank you. [*Drops his arm.*] This is my first time home since I was mobilized on the thirteenth of August 1914.

[*There is another knock on the door.* MRS YOUNG *opens the door. A drenched sailor enters. Then a soldier. Then a sailor. Each person on stage freezes to their spot. Lights slowly down. The mouth-music begins.*]

BBC VOICE: Eight hundred soldiers from Lewis died in the First World War. Two hundred or more drowned on the Iolaire yacht after she struck rocks as she entered Stornoway Bay on New Year's Eve 1919. Appalling catastrophe. "Home at last!" they cried. First the caps floated in, then came the tunics. The whole island plunged into sorrow. In 1918 Lord Leverhulme purchased the Island of Lewis from Lieutenant Colonel Duncan Matheson for a sum of £148,000 on Whit Sunday, May 1918. Lord Leverhulme had made his fortune by manufacturing and selling soap on a scale unequalled by any man before him.

SCENE 16

JOHN CAMPBELL *walks into a room. Opposite him stands* MISS MacDONALD. *Long pause as they look at each other.*

MISS MacDONALD: Yes.

[*They do not move. Lights go slowly down.*]

SCENE 17

Lights up on a sort of small market. MISS MacDONALD *is selling fish.* MacKENZIE *is selling prawns.* JOHN CAMPBELL *is selling hens.* AENGUS *is selling boots.* MISS TULLO *is in her chair knitting.* MURDO *is mending a net, and dozing.* MacTAVISH *is getting dressed in a fine suit.*

MISS MacDONALD: Sgadan Ur! Sgadan Ur! (Herring! Herring!)
AENGUS: [*Singing.*] Boots, boots!
JOHN CAMPBELL: [*Gritty.*] Hens!
AENGUS: [*Trying harder.*] Worthy boots!
JOHN CAMPBELL: Hens!
MacKENZIE: Prawns fresh from the sea!
[*Astonished to find himself saying it.*]
Prawns, prawns, prawns!
AENGUS: Boots to last a lifetime!
MISS MacDONALD: [*Energetically.*] Sgadan Ur! Sgadan Ur!
JOHN CAMPBELL: Chuck-chuck-chuck!
AENGUS: You could walk to London – [*Lifts a pair of boots.*] – in a pair of these.
JOHN CAMPBELL: Chuck-chuck-chuck!
AENGUS: Will you save a herring for me, Blondie?
MISS MacDONALD: I will.
[MacTAVISH *is now fitted into his suit. He lifts an umbrella and adopts a proud bearing – the opposite to* MacTAVISH's *usual stance.* MISS TULLO *in the chair sings a small ditty.*]
MISS TULLO: Is that the old soapman coming?
AENGUS: Hark – it is Mr Sunshine soap himself.
[LORD LEVERHULME *nods. They in turn nod back to him.* LORD LEVERHULME *is accompanied by his agent,* MR HARDY.]
LORD LEVERHULME: Good morning Hardy.
MR HARDY: Good morning Sir.
[MISS MacDONALD *inclines her head.*]
LORD LEVERHULME: Good morning.

[MISS TULLO *bows.*]

MISS TULLO: Your Lordship.

LORD LEVERHULME: Good morning gentlemen. [*He bows.*] And Ladies. Have you noticed that the sun is shining? And this is the first time – I am told – that it has shone in Lewis for ten years. [*They give a slight nod of the head and take off their caps.* LORD LEVERHULME *takes a commanding position.*] Now. Yes. We welcome back all our eminent islanders from the war. They – all gallant men – are welcome back. Those on leave over the years will have found a Ford car at the pier to take them home. So thank you to the YMCA and the Red Triangle Club. Thank you. Thank you for the billiards. And for the cards. [*He gives a polite clap.*] Gentlemen. We do not bring you back to poverty. The war will not have been in vain. There will be a great fishing harbour on this island. A great capital town will be built. Barren land will be turned into gardens. Roads and railways laid to spread prosperity. I promise you this – Stornoway will be a metropolis. The black house will be no more.

MR HARDY: [*Very obediently.*] No more.

MISS MacDONALD: Sgadan Ur! Sgadan Ur!

LORD LEVERHULME: The new house will be one storey high, and will contain a living-room, three bedrooms, scullery, pantry and bathroom. The scullery and larder will have . . .

MR HARDY: . . . concrete floors.

MISS MacDONALD: Sgadan Ur! Sgadan Ur!

LORD LEVERHULME: And the bedroom and living room will have . . .

MR HARDY: . . . boarded floors.

MISS MacDONALD: Sgadan Ur! Sgadan Ur!

LORD LEVERHULME: There will be a nice porch to keep away the wind and the iron sheeting will be painted a nice warm red.

MR HARDY: Yes indeed.

MISS TULLO: Beautiful. How beautiful it sounds.

MISS MacDONALD: I have me a nice fresh low-back here.

LORD LEVERHULME: And ah . . . [*Looks puzzled because of*

interruptions.] Now, what was I about to say Mr Hardy?

MISS MacDONALD: I have me a fluke.

MR HARDY: Be quiet woman. You were about to say, my lord, that every house must have a garden.

LORD LEVERHULME: Indeed, that's right, Mr Hardy, I forgot the garden.

JOHN CAMPBELL: And what land will we have?

LORD LEVERHULME: We will leave that question for again.

MacKENZIE: Sir, could we have a few acres to go with the ones we don't have on the croft?

LORD LEVERHULME: I will not split up farms. They will provide milk for the island. And again, I repeat, this house is a villa. I do not want to hear that other word.

JOHN CAMPBELL: What word sir?

LORD LEVERHULME: You know what I mean. That word.

MR HARDY: [*Quietly.*] No more saying of "croft" now.

MacKENZIE: Ah I see what you mean. I see now. I know the word that offends you sir. Yes, I see. I see. You mean "croft." The word that you do not want to hear is home to me, or was, until it was taken away, and now I'm reduced to being a squatter. What is misery for you, is consolation for me.

LORD LEVERHULME: I am offering you gainful employment.

MacKENZIE: But why would the word – croft – offend thee?

JOHN CAMPBELL: Sir?

LORD LEVERHULME: Yes my good man?

JOHN CAMPBELL: I know you are an enlightened man sir.

MISS MacDONALD: Sgadan Ur! Sgadan Ur!

MR HARDY: Silence woman!

JOHN CAMPBELL: And we welcome you to the island. But there are troubles afoot. There were promises entered into by the government before your time. I would like to ask your good self: what of the promises made to us that every man upon his return from war would be given a new croft with a number of acres?

LORD LEVERHULME: I am promising you something greater than that. Forget the cursed croft. It is an obsession that will keep you impoverished. I will give you a great fishing industry, bridges will be built between isolated areas, there will be canneries, afforestation, handloom weaving, basket making— [*He is interrupted.*]

JOHN CAMPBELL: —I do not doubt you sir. But when will we be given the croft and the land that we were promised?

LORD LEVERHULME: [*To himself.*] Dear God. This constant refrain would drive one senseless.

JOHN CAMPBELL: The last time I saw meat was out of a tin during the war in France.

MISS MacDONALD: Fresh Herrings!

MISS TULLO: Raw suet!

MISS MacDONALD: Sgadan Ur! Sgadan Ur!

MISS TULLO: Raw suet!

[LORD LEVERHULME *starts walking away, accompanied by* MR HARDY.]

LORD LEVERHULME: Hell and damnation, Hardy. Will they never understand?

MR HARDY: I'm afraid not sir.

MISS MacDONALD: Miss Tullo, the soapman is not great with that word.

MISS TULLO: He is not, Miss MacDonald – he's very touchy.

MISS MacDONALD: Yes. Very touchy.

MISS TULLO: Like ourselves.

[LORD LEVEHULME *returns and faces* JOHN CAMPBELL.]

LORD LEVERHULME: Listen here. Listen here, I have gone to the sixteen farms that have been raided – I have offered them land, legally, but not on the crofter's terms, not on fixity of tenure. I do not want to turn to the law, but I will turn to the law if I must. I have high admiration for the crofters. What you are faced with is crofting or emigration. I am offering you a third alternative – a great fishing industry. Out there in that sea – [*He points to the audience.*] – is a great harvest. I want people to move here onto Stornoway.

JOHN CAMPBELL: It is not home.

LORD LEVERHULME: If a man has two jobs, what happens Mr Hardy?

MR HARDY: One job suffers.

LORD LEVERHULME: Correct. Thank you. For you see, the people are divided in their responsibilities. The crofter must leave his trawler in the springtime to attend to his croft. You are fishermen, not farmers. The problem is to separate the fisherman and the crofter.

MISS TULLO: Forgive me your honour, but they have been trying that for centuries.

MR HARDY: What the gentleman is implying, my good lady, is that the land does not pay because of double trade.

MISS TULLO: Surely the land and the sea are not enemies.

LORD LEVERHULME: If managed well they are not enemies Madam. If they are worked along business lines. But the business has to be properly established. And not until certain things change. Speaking of enemies – who are the real enemies sir?

MR HARDY: Why, tradition and inertia.

LORD LEVERHULME: You hear that? Quite right Hardy. Tradition and inertia. Well put. Very good.

MISS MacDONALD: Would you care for a slap of doosh?

MISS TULLO: And there you have it – a pail of sheep's blood.

MR HARDY: The inertia follows from contemplating that repulsive stretch of barren moor – [*Points into audience.*] – and the misery hemmed in between the muck and the sea. [*A long silence.*]

MacKENZIE: Seo, seo, fhiribh. Cha dean so an ghnothach. Bheireadh am bodach milbheulach sin a chreidsinn oirnn gu'm bheil dubh geal is geal dubh! Ciod e dhuinn na bruadairean breagha aige, a thig no nach tig? Se am fearann tha sinn ag iarraidh. Agus se tha mise a faighneachd. [*Points at* LORD LEVERHULME.] An toir thu dhuinn a fearann?

LORD LEVERHULME: I am sorry! It is my great misfortune that I do not understand the Gaelic language. But perhaps you might translate what has just been said.

JOHN CAMPBELL: I will do my best. "Come now men! This will not do the job! This honey-mouthed man would have us believe that black is white and white is black. We are not concerned with his fancy dreams that may or may not come true! What we want is the land – and the question I put to him now is this: will you give us the land?"

LORD LEVERHULME: [*To* MR HARDY.] Let us go from here. These people are impossible.

MISS MacDONALD: Sgadan Ur! Sgadan Ur!

LORD LEVERHULME: I bid you good day. [LORD LEVERHULME *and* MR HARDY *stride off.*]

[MISS MacDONALD *goes over and touches* MURDO*'s shoulder. He awakens from a nightmare.* MURDO *looks around him. Then at her.*]

MURDO: Ah Blondie, it's you.

MISS MacDONALD: You missed all the excitement Murdo. The soapman has been and gone.

MURDO: He was here?

MISS MacDONALD: He spoke to us. Isn't that right Miss Tullo?

MISS TULLO: Oh yes. He spoke to us surely.

MISS MacDONALD: A very charming man.

MISS TULLO: He promised us gardens. Oh yes.

MISS MacDONALD: And basket weaving.

MISS TULLO: And harvests from the sea.

MURDO: Will I tell you of the soapman, Lord Leverhulme?

MISS TULLO: And what is wrong with him?

MURDO: You ask me what is wrong with Lord Leverhulme. There is nothing wrong with him besides the fact that he does not know we are real people. He wants to do good, but we are bad in his eyes because we do not see the good in him, and in his projects; yet we say they are good, have told him so, that his projects are good but not good for us, they may be good for someone else, not for us, at this time; for we have been given promises long ere he came, and these are what we expect to be kept; not his promises but theirs; and because of this he thinks us bad and we think him bad though we know he is good, but he does not know we are good, and there's the problem. [MURDO *closes his eyes again.*]

[*Lights down quickly.*]

SCENE 18

Four men are seated with drinking glasses: AENGUS, JOHN CAMPBELL, MURDO *and* MacTAVISH. MacKENZIE *has the drinks on a table in front of him.* AENGUS *is well inebriated, and they are aware too of his cough and possible sickness, so they give him some leeway.*

AENGUS: To Captain Murdo!
ALL: Aye.
MURDO: To all the gallant men of the Seaforth Regiment!
ALL: Hear, hear!
[*They drink.*]
AENGUS: And is the German not a bonnie fighter?
MURDO: He is.
AENGUS: It's the French were treacherous.
MacKENZIE: Easy, Aengus.
AENGUS: But the people that we returned to are even more treacherous than them. Cowardice has come to the islands. Am I not right Captain?
MURDO: I do not want to speak of it.
AENGUS: And you, what do you say, John Campbell?
JOHN CAMPBELL: It's best not to speak of it.
AENGUS: You are too compromised John Campbell. Too cushy. You are soon to have a wife I hear. I have no wife. I have only you men here. And the Board of Agriculture is with us. We raiders will go where we like. They can bring soldiers in and who will they be facing John Campbell?
JOHN CAMPBELL: They will be facing soldiers.
AENGUS: Right. This is it. They will turn soldiers on soldiers will they?
MacKENZIE: That would be a bad thing.
[*They drink.*]
AENGUS: Was it for this we walked through Hell? [*Pauses, then he suddenly stands up with glass in hand.*] I say to the landlord: what would have become of your estates if the Germans had

come over here? We that defended this land from the Huns have – by the same law – a right to share in its riches. [*He sits.*] Right John Campbell? Am I right?

JOHN CAMPBELL: You're right.

[*They drink.*]

AENGUS: It's Lord Leverhulme on one side and the Church on the other. After what I've seen I cannot follow the Church.

MacKENZIE: You're speaking wild Aengus.

AENGUS: You're very quiet Mouse.

MacTAVISH: I am.

AENGUS: Well, they will not stop me walking into their wind on the Sabbath. I'll go where I like any Sunday I like. You hear me Mouse?

MacTAVISH: I do.

AENGUS: But don't ask me to step on a boat.

JOHN CAMPBELL: Nor me. Never again.

[AENGUS *breaks into a fit of coughing.*]

AENGUS: And the thing is, it wasn't even the Iolaire. It was another boat entirely. If we'd been on the Iolaire we'd have made it. And they never told us when we stepped on board that we were stepping on the wrong ship. Never again. I'd rather go back to war then step on a boat. They did this to us deliberately. [*Angrily and nearly crazily.*] Put us in the wrong boat, then they deliberately turned that boat into the rocks.

MacKENZIE: No Aengus, you're talking madness.

AENGUS: [*Quietly.*] Am I Mouse?

MacTAVISH: It's the drink Aengus.

AENGUS: I'll have my drink, and no-one will stop me.

MURDO: It was the same drink made that boat go astray.

AENGUS: Was it?

MURDO: So I believe.

AENGUS: But I don't. The people who claim that are against the drink. But I do not want to argue with you Captain. We did not come all this way to argue. Is this what we fought for, Captain?

MURDO: No.

AENGUS: Do you hear what the Captain said men? Do you

know what he is saying? He is saying we fought for this land in France and we will die for it in Lewis. [*Pause.* AENGUS *looks around them all, forcing them to speak. A pause, as if he has gone too far this time.*]

JOHN CAMPBELL: A drink to John Macleod who swam ashore from the Iolaire with a life line and saved forty lives.

ALL: To John Macleod.

[*They stand and drink. Then sit.*]

AENGUS: We came back – that's what wrong with us. We should be "Presumed Dead." Or "Missing." Or "Lost in Action." Not in the Great War. But in the Great Lie. On all of the other islands the soldiers are getting the land they were promised. But here we are getting nothing – not a fucking thing. They promised us and what did we get? [*He points at* MacTAVISH.]

MacTAVISH: Nothing.

[*He points at* JOHN CAMPBELL.]

JOHN CAMPBELL: Sweet fuck all.

[*He points at* MacKENZIE.]

MacKENZIE: Nothing.

AENGUS: And what is happening Captain.

MURDO: They're talking of emigration.

AENGUS: Yes, they are talking of emigration. I will not step on a boat again, Captain Murdo. Not even if the soapman himself was to carry me on board. Never. I will never leave this island. Never again, you hear me, I swear, never.

[*He drinks. He breaks into a fit of coughing. The others drink watching him. He points at* MacKENZIE.]

AENGUS: Are you afraid of my cough MacKenzie?

MacKENZIE: No Aengus.

AENGUS: We are ghosts now. Ghosts only. We are not clan. Nor family. [*He stands.*] Home at last our sorrows now are fled. [*He sits.*] We may be back in the Hebrides, but we are not at home. [*He breaks into another fit of coughing.* MacKENZIE *clears away all glasses. All leave, except* MacTAVISH.]

SCENE 19

The SECRETARY to LORD LEVERHULME *enters and sits at a small table, glasses on, pen ready, manuscript before her. As* LORD LEVERHULME *speaks she writes. With each letter he adopts a different tone.*

LORD LEVERHULME: [*Striding about, as he dresses.*]
[*Sharply.*] Dear Sir.
I would like to bring up the subject of the extermination of rats. I think it's high time this matter was given your full attention.
Yours.

[*Caring.*] Dear Sir,
I would speak of Tuberculosis. We are now the worst in the land. And it is to our shame. Please let me know your plans
Yours, etc.

[*Indignant.*] Dear Sir,
At the present time you see children watching cattle all the live long day on the wind-swept grazings; you see women . . .

SECRETARY: . . . carrying creels of peat on their backs, a weight of eighty pounds . . .

LORD LEVERHULME: . . . while in the Congo, no Negro woman is allowed to carry more . . .

SECRETARY: . . . than forty-four pounds.

LORD LEVERHULME:
These people are not adding to their happiness. They are merely existing.
Yours, etc.

[*Can't you understand?*] Dear Sir,
With regard to your letter of the 5th. I would remind you that if you take Stornoway as the centre there are many

square miles of sea in a radius of five hundred miles. Think of the fishing industry that could be established.
Yours.

[*Trying his luck.*] Dear Sir,
With respect to tourism it seems to me that the best manner of arriving to Stornoway . . .
SECRETARY: . . . would be by flying machine . . .
LORD LEVERHULME: . . . and then to continue that journey by way of an electric railway system, there will be . . . There will be . . .
SECRETARY: . . . an all-island laundry service.
LORD LEVERHULME: Yes, Yours, etc.
[*The businessman.*] Dear Sir,
I recommend that carrots, turnips, parsnips . . .
SECRETARY: . . . cabbages . . .
LORD LEVERHULME: . . . leeks and onions be set in these gardens. Also the growth of cranberries, currants, raspberries . . .
SECRETARY: . . . strawberries, gooseberries, and apples . . .
LORD LEVERHULME: . . . should be encouraged.
In five years' time we will have a jam factory. And there is no industry that will possibly thrive better here, than in any other part of the world, namely the growing of . . .
SECRETARY: . . . the willow.
LORD LEVERHULME: Yours.
[*Under pressure.*] Sir,
The difficulties with Lewis ex-servicemen continue. Their attitude to the land, and the support given to them, despite my protests, by the Scottish Secretary, Robert Murdo, is undermining all my plans for the island.
Yours.
How many is that?
SECRETARY: Eight.
LORD LEVERHULME: [*Trying to keep calm.*] Dear Sir,
I hope this finds you well.
These soldiers will have to be integrated back into the

population. It has gone too far. These men are wild. With the invasions of the farm of Tong, the seizure of land at Gress, the raid on Coll Farm, lawlessness is spreading to every part of the island through the actions of a handful of men. I can no longer stand by and watch my every plan being destroyed.

[*Turns to* SECRETARY.]

There must be a better word than "destroyed"?

SECRETARY: Being trampled on?

LORD LEVERHULME: Being trampled on.

I await your reply,

Yours, etc.

[*Steady and guarded.*] Dear Sir,

I would inform you that what you raiders have done is an illegal act for which there can be no justification – and which leaves me with only one of two courses: either I must appeal to your practical common sense, or I must appeal to the strong arm of the law.

[*The* SECRETARY *leaves her desk and goes off. He goes to and fro without looking behind him dictating.*]

I am convinced that on consideration you will withdraw as raiders from these farms.

Yours.

Sir,

In your newspaper you refer to me as a successful soap-boiler who happened to buy up the island. I take exception, not to being called a soap-boiler, but to the implication that I am against the crofters. It is the raiders I am against.

Yours.

[*Enjoying himself.*] Sir,

The House is losing its reason. Today a question in Parliament was posed: "That folksong is outside the domain of conscious art." My, my.

Yours.

[*Enjoying himself even more.*] Sir,

We cannot always agree. It reminds me of the story of the ladies at a tea party who disagreed about something and one of them said, "Well it would not do for all of us to be of the same opinion, for if we were, you would all have wanted my husband." "Oh no," replied another, "if all of us had been of my opinion, none of us would have wanted him."
[*Off-stage, the* SECRETARY *laughs loudly.*]
Yours.

[*Slightly irritated.*] Sir,
Thank you for your concern. I refused to take legal action to evict the raiders because I am unwilling to treat ex-servicemen as criminals. Also I feel that any action taken now may in fact work to the benefit of the raiders.
Yours.
[*The* SECRETARY *returns.* LORD LEVERHULME *getting fierce angry.*]
Sir,
If the raiding does not cease all development work in Lewis will stop. And I mean it.
Yours.

[*Vehement.*] Sir,
I am closing down work on the canning factory. You will inform all interested parties. My purse is not bottomless. I will resume my schemes only when the raiders leave the farms, and when I am left in peaceful possession of them, and not till then.
Yours.
[*Pause.*]
How many is that?
SECRETARY: Sixteen.
LORD LEVERHULME: I suppose that will do for today. Hold it. Just one more.
Sir,
For your information, in every part of Lewis all but one of my schemes were put to a popular vote and received the

unanimous approval of the people.
Yours.
[*He leans down and begins to sign each sheet.*]

SCENE 20

MURDO *is seated by himself.*

VOICES FROM OUTSIDE: You are scum, Murdo. Nothing but scum!
[*Many curses in Gaelic. Improvise.*]

SCENE 21

MISS MacDONALD *is reading the Gazette to* MISS TULLO. *The exchange is lighthearted, sardonic, and naughty.*

MISS MacDONALD: The best man for dry hair is the rubbing in of toilet paraffin or, mark you, brilliantine.
MISS TULLO: You could go up in smoke.
MISS MacDONALD: Oh, and by the way, never ever leave the dead hairs in the scalp.
MISS TULLO: Is that bad?
MISS MacDONALD: Bad out. You have to get out the brush and comb.
MISS TULLO: Oh I will.
MISS MacDONALD: Now here's something for you.
MISS TULLO: Read on.
MISS MacDONALD: It's a recipe for a hair-tonic: one-half ounce of strong liquid ammonia; one-half ounce of chloroform; one-half ounce of sesame oil; one-half ounce of oil of lemon; oh, and I nearly forgot, add some spirit of rosemary.
MISS TULLO: Oh do, if you are going to stink to high heaven, don't forget the rosemary.
MISS MacDONALD: Now Miss Tullo, you do not want to dance away your pin money.

MISS TULLO: I do not.

MISS MacDONALD: Well, wash your stockings.

MISS TULLO: [*Wearing none.*] I will certainly.

MISS MacDONALD: You see silk or imitation stocking should be washed before they're worn, and then daily after that. You see if a pair of stocking is worn several times, perspiration stiffens the feet and they soon fill with holes. And, most important – [*Waving finger like a teacher reprimanding.*] – you must not wring the stockings but gently squeeze them. Have you got that?

MISS TULLO: I will remember that Miss MacDonald. I'll write that down and put it by my bed.

MISS MacDONALD: And lastly here is a question posed by a reader: "Is flirting wrong?"

MISS TULLO: Hah! Pray tell.

MISS MacDONALD: Well, if the woman sets out to collect scalps she rarely makes a good wife and she's left on the shelf in the long run.

MISS TULLO: And what of him – the man fellow?

MISS MacDONALD: Oh, the male flirt may marry but he'll never settle.

MISS TULLO: Oh the poor, poor man.

[MISS MacDONALD *turns a page. Her demeanour changes.*]

MISS MacDONALD: And then there's the advertisements for Canada.

MISS TULLO: [*Coldly.*] Yes.

MISS MacDONALD: They're everywhere. "Wanted for Ontario, domestic servants for first-class farmhouses." [*Reading.*] "To sail in April. Situations guaranteed. Assisted passage."

MISS TULLO: Yes.

MISS MacDONALD: [*Reading.*] In placing the girls in situations, every effort will be made to place them as near each other as possible.

MISS TULLO: [*Cynically.*] That's kind of them, isn't it?

MISS MacDONALD: Immediate application should be made

to Major Goodlife, Ontario Government Representative, 46 Point Street, Stornoway. [MISS MacDONALD *folds the newspaper and puts it away.*]

[*They both look into the middle distance, thinking.*]

[*Advertisements for domestic servants come up on the screen, then a slide show of Canada.*]

BBC VOICE: In 1921 and 1922 the potato crop failed. An official report recorded that forty-two out of ninety-two children in North Tolsta were seriously underweight, some of them looking like famine orphans.

SCENE 22

The five men are standing in a group, shivering. It's a cold winter night. Their hands are deep in their pockets, and their hats are pulled down low.

MURDO: Can things get any worse?

AENGUS: No by God.

JOHN CAMPBELL: They're now importing fresh fish from the mainland.

MacKENZIE: And posters everywhere for Canada.

MURDO: And I believe they've been going round the schools again.

AENGUS: They've been doing that since I was a child. The slide show.

MacKENZIE: Oh the slide show.

AENGUS: In he'd come to the class painting a pretty scene out there in the homesteads. The lush fields. Apples and oranges. Apples and oranges.

MacKENZIE: Your mouth would water at the thought of Canada.

AENGUS: We learned more of that country than we learnt of our own history.

MacTAVISH: I used dream of it, then wake up in the black house.

AENGUS: This man, Major Goodlife – he'll clear the island with his "Domestic Servants for Ontario," and "Farm workers for Ontario." They're manipulating us.

MURDO: It's started again.

MacTAVISH: Aye.

MURDO: You can feel it – the fear.

JOHN CAMPBELL: The inspector of the poor is also the shipping agent.

AENGUS: What do you expect? The poor are always been shepherded abroad.

MacTAVISH: And you get ten shillings a week less over there than you'd get under Leverhulme.

AENGUS: I never thought that I would have had affection for Leverhulme.

MURDO: The other night a crowd gathered outside my door and began to scream abuse. They said it was the raiders had brought us to this. They are turning on us.

JOHN CAMPBELL: I saw it.

AENGUS: It's a conspiracy. Someone put them up to it. The whole thing is a conspiracy. There is no house, there's only ourselves.

[*One by one they go different ways.*]

SCENE 23

A fierce sound of a cock crowing. MISS MacDONALD *appears.* JOHN CAMPBELL *is seated a distance from her.* MacKENZIE *enters.*

MacKENZIE: John C, John C, I have come to talk to you.

[JOHN CAMPBELL *lowers his stick rather dubiously.*]

JOHN CAMPBELL: Sit you down and tell me what you have to say.

MacKENZIE: [*Trying to be secretive.*] What I have to say will not go beyond this room?

JOHN CAMPBELL: [*Alert.*] You have my word.

MacKENZIE: I came to tell you. In recent days I have . . . I have been approached by . . . certain people.

JOHN CAMPBELL: Aye. Who?

MacKENZIE: Certain people in authority. They say we may face jail if we do not accept their terms.

JOHN CAMPBELL: They've said that for years.

MacKENZIE: This is different. The raider is seen as the man who drove Leverhulme and prosperity from the island. The government too know they themselves are at fault. They are trying to put it to right.

JOHN CAMPBELL: Are they now. They created this hell. And what are their terms?

MacKENZIE: The government are offering any ex-soldiers who wish to go a free passage to Canada, with work at the other end. You repay down the line.

JOHN CAMPBELL: They are trying to get rid of the raiders.

MacKENZIE: Better to have a free passage to work abroad than to face jail at home. A list of names were drawn up.

JOHN CAMPBELL: We're the surplus population again.

MacKENZIE: Yes, but you see John, after thinking about it, the others have agreed to sign.

MISS MacDONALD: Sign John, sign.

MacKENZIE: [*Warily.*] I myself am going.

JOHN CAMPBELL: You?

MacKENZIE: There is nothing here for us. It's hopeless. I am going. I'll get to see my Uncle who went out in '89. He'll look after me. In Ontario they are offering each one of us one hundred and sixty acres of virgin ground and a hut for shelter.

MISS MacDONALD: Are you listening John?

JOHN CAMPBELL: [*Angrily.*] I am listening.

MacKENZIE: And do you know who put his pen to paper this very morning? Aengus.

JOHN CAMPBELL: [*Astonished.*] He signed?

MacKENZIE: He did.

JOHN CAMPBELL: Are you telling me the truth?

MacKENZIE: I am.

JOHN CAMPBELL: Above all men, Aengus.

MacKENZIE: As did Captain Murdo. We signed to cross on a

boat called the Metagama.

JOHN CAMPBELL: How easy it was to get rid of us in the end!

MISS MacDONALD: John.

JOHN CAMPBELL: [*Voice goes up into a mad whine.*] Right I'll go. Right I'll go.

MacKENZIE: John. There is one unfortunate thing. This is what I came to tell you. They are only taking single people. I'm sorry John. Ye will have to call off the wedding till you get there. [*Over* JOHN CAMPBELL *whining he backs off. He steps out door and pulls it behind him.*]

MISS MacDONALD: This wedding is taking a long time.

JOHN CAMPBELL: Right, I'll go, and we'll get married over there.

SCENE 24

AENGUS *is sitting without his shirt on.* MURDO *bends and listens to his heart through a stethoscope. He inspects* AENGUS*'s ear with a torch, then opens his mouth and looks in.*

MURDO: Say Ahh!

AENGUS: Ahh!

[*The sound rises into a great long echo of pain that is amplified throughout the theatre.*]

SCENE 25

BBC VOICE: The Metagama was launched at Scotstoun, Glasgow, on the 19th of November 1914 with cabin class for five hundred and sixteen passengers and third class for eleven hundred and thirty. The Metagama acquired the reputation of being a "bride ship" after the First World War, through its transporting of young brides-to-be from Scotland to North America.

VOICE 1: [*Off-stage.*] It's twenty-six pounds one way.

VOICE 2: [*Off-stage.*] Are you going?

VOICE 1: [*Off-stage.*] I am.
VOICE 3: [*Off-stage.*] Suitcases – they are doing a roaring trade in suitcases round the town.

SCENE 26

MURDO *appears in vicar's outfit. Everyone else kneels in a circle facing him.*

MURDO: A Warning against Unbelief. Hebrews 3.
Today if you hear his voice
Do not harden your hearts
As you did in the rebellion,
During the time of testing in the desert,
Where your fathers tested and tried me
And for forty years saw what I did.
That is why I was angry with that generation,
And I said, "Their hearts are always going astray,
And they have not known my ways."
So I declared an oath in my anger,
"They shall never enter my rest."
With whom was he angry? For forty years? Was it now with those who sinned? And to whom did God swear that they would never enter His rest if not to those who disobeyed? So we see they were not able to enter, because of their unbelief. And for those who have fallen away, who have tasted the goodness of God and the powers of the coming age, if they fall away, they will be brought back to repentance.
[*He looks up. Holds gaze.*]
Today is the Sabbath, the day of rest. Rest easy. Wherever you go, wherever you land, God will have been there before you. He is waiting on your arrival. When God made his promise to Abraham, He swore by Himself, saying "I will surely bless you and give you many descendants." And after waiting patiently, Abraham received what was promised.
[*He looks down at his bible.*]

I wish you well. They are talking of a boat by the name of Metagama. There is one good sign – I'm told on good authority that this is an Indian word which means "Where the waters meet." God bless you.

[*A roar of water fills the theatre. Now objects are beginning to be removed from stage. A boy begins filling his case.*].

SCENE 27

A FATHER *and* MOTHER are *lying down. Their* SON *is filling his case. He puts some last things away, then he himself lies down.*

SON: I'm glad to be going. No, I'm happy.
MOTHER: Say hello to everyone. To everyone over there.
SON: I'll write every second Thursday.
MOTHER: At the other end there will be a nice bed.
SON: And don't be helping my father all the time.
MOTHER: No.
SON: Let him get on. I'm going to be coming back soon and you'll see me then, so bye Ma.
MOTHER: I will not see you again so don't say you will.
FATHER: You sleep now. You have riches ahead of you. And don't over-speak to your mother – it will only annoy her. You will walk down on your own. We will not go with you.
SON: Aye.

[*He lies down. The* FATHER *gets up and empties his case again. When the* FATHER *lies down, the* SON *rises and begins filling it again. Slowly, darkness falls.*]

INTERVAL

ACT II
SCENE 28

They line up, one behind the other, all looking one way to stage left. They do not look at each other. Each with a case and a bag. The AGENT *is taking their papers.*

AGENT: Name?

MISS TULLO: Miss Gerty Tullo.

AGENT: Thank you Miss Tullo.

[MISS TULLO *steps on and heads backstage, turns with a smile, waves, no hint of emotion, and goes out the open door at the back.*]

AGENT: Name?

MURDO: Murdo Macaulay.

[*He steps on and heads backstage, and goes out the open door at the back without looking back.*]

AGENT: Name?

MISS MacDONALD: Miss Catherine MacDonald.

[*She steps on and heads backstage, stops a moment with her back to the audience, then turns fully – she is upset but controls it, looks towards the audience, case at her feet, and eventually she goes out the open door at the back.*]

AGENT: Thank you. Name?

MacKENZIE: Donald MacKenzie.

[*He steps on and heads backstage, a quick turn, a nod and a laugh, then out the open door at the back.*]

AGENT: Name?

AENGUS: Aengus MacIver.

[AENGUS *halts. Looks to where he is going with terror.*]

AGENT: Go on man, you're holding up the queue.

AENGUS: Aye.

[*He moves forward slowly, with great reluctance, then stops.*]

AGENT: Mr MacIver, will you kindly board the boat?

AENGUS: Aye.

[*Slowly* AENGUS *heads backstage and stops at the open door at the back. Looks back without turning his body, eyes fearful, then he goes out the door and out of sight.*]

AGENT: Name?

JOHN CAMPBELL: John Campbell. [*Then he continues speaking, giving each name a different inflection as he moves to and fro across the space. The* AGENT *stays in same position accepting each name with a nod. In the background a pipe band starts playing "The Road to the Isles."*] Angus Campbell. John

Kennedy. Rena Logan. Mabel MacAskill. John MacDonald. Allan MacKenzie. John Macleod. Norman Macleod. William Macleod. Roderick Macleod. Alex MacPhail. John MacRae. Angus MacRae. Hector Nicolson. Alex Morrissey. Lionel Morrissey. John Smith. [*The* AGENT *moves towards the door.* JOHN CAMPBELL *steps by him.*] Catherine Montgomery from Keith Street. Malcolm Morrison, 7 Lower Shader, Barvas. John Matheson of Barvas. John Martin, Lower Shader. Donal Morrison of Fivepenny. John Macleod, 27 Laxay, Lochs. [*Projected onto the screen behind is some footage of the Metagama. Photos of the crowd on the quay.*] Alex D. MacPhail, 9 Laxdale. Colin MacPhail, 33 Upper Carloway. [*He turns to place names.*] Lochs. Balallan. Crossbost. Breasclete. Stornoway. Ness. New Shawbost. North Tolsta. Aignish. Battery Park. Achmore. Habost. Coll. Lighthill. Aird of Tong, Aird of Tong, Aird of Tong . . . [JOHN CAMPBELL *at last reaches the door. Looks back and steps through. The* AGENT *pulls the door behind him. The psalm finishes. Then there is a loud, explosion of a ship's horn, repeated five times. There is a crescendo of sound and light, then dark. Lights like a bonfire, then darkness, and finally a single torch that gives three beacon signals – three longs and two dashes, three longs and two dashes, three longs and two dashes – then abruptly dies.*]

SCENE 29

Light slowly up. Foggy. Dark interior of hold. Sound of water hitting the boat. AENGUS *sits alone playing patience and drinking. He coughs. The others sit in a tight group together, talking incessantly in Gaelic and English.*

MISS MacDONALD: Stop moving.
MacKENZIE: I'm sick.
MISS TULLO: Home sickness.
MacKENZIE: Boat sickness.
MISS TULLO: Mother sickness.

[*They start eating raw herrings.*]

JOHN CAMPBELL: My dear father.

MURDO: Aengus has not spoken since we left Stornoway. Aengus! Aengus!

[AENGUS *does not look at him but takes a dram.*]

MISS TULLO: [*She taps her head.*] He has another sickness.

MURDO: He has the cough.

MISS MacDONALD: They'll not take well to that in Canada.

JOHN CAMPBELL: No.

MISS MacDONALD: You know the first thing we must do when we get there?

MISS TULLO: What is that?

MISS MacDONALD: Write home. I remember this boy – he's in America now – he never wrote home once. Not once, the silly beggar – and his fare was raised by a dance my father played at.

[*There is a huge heave above decks.*]

JOHN CAMPBELL: One of us should go up and see what's happening above.

MacKENZIE: Stay where you are.

MISS TULLO: It's bad. The last time I was up there was broken ice out there.

MacKENZIE: You'll not find me going up on deck.

JOHN CAMPBELL: We're beginning to smell.

MISS TULLO: Speak for yourself.

MURDO: That's fear of the boat again.

JOHN CAMPBELL: And are we going to spend the entire journey down here hiding in the Hold?

MURDO: [*Shouts.*] We are. Up above there's naught but men with cameras and men with pens. Special Commissioners, and the like. I do not want to talk to them anymore. They will tell a different story than the one we know. It's in their interest. Isn't that right Aengus? Will you have a herring Aengus? No bother. We're all on a one-way ticket man. Stick together till we get there, then its everyman for himself. Isn't that right Aengus! [AENGUS *does not reply, gets up and walks off.*] Aengus! [*No reply.*] Ah!

[*There is another almighty heave. They cower. There is a screech of bagpipes.* AENGUS *enters playing them. Does a small step to and fro three times, then stops midway, turns with the pipes and walks to the front of the stage.* AENGUS *looks long and hard at the audiences and plays.* MISS TULLO *comes up and joins him, then one by one the others come and stand by him. Lights go slowly down. Eventually the last sound to fade is the sound of the sea.*]

SCENE 30

Silence. No sound of the sea. The door at the back of the stage opens, and the AGENT *enters with a lamp. The others speak in Gaelic and in English.*

AGENT: [*Canadian accent.*] It's five o'clock you people.
MURDO: [*Wakening.*] Aye.
AGENT: Up folks, this is your new life.
[AENGUS *coughs and smothers it.*]
MacKENZIE: Is this a nightmare?
MISS MacDONALD: I'm starving.
MISS TULLO: I thought we still on that train. How long were we on that train?
MacKENZIE: How long were we on that train is right – it seemed like days.
AGENT: Rise and shine. It's past five.
[*They start rising – all except* AENGUS.]
MISS MacDONALD: I was dreaming of the bonfires on Tiumpan Head as we were going out on the Metagama.
AGENT: They told me that big tall highland men were coming. I was expecting a race of giants. Well I don't see them.
MURDO: They must have got off at another stop.
MISS TULLO: Tell the gimp that the one tall man among us was turned back at Stornoway. He was too tall, and too thin.
MURDO: You have it right.
MISS MacDONALD: Indeed she has.
MISS TULLO: He was too tall for Canada, tell the gimp that.

AGENT: What is that woman saying? Clattering around in Gaelic. Hey there – hey, you. Which of you people speak English? I said which you people speak English?

JOHN CAMPBELL: [*After looking round at the others.*] I do.

AGENT: So what is she saying?

JOHN CAMPBELL: [*Hesitates.*] She's saying . . .

AGENT: Yes?

JOHN CAMPBELL: That . . .

AGENT: Yes I'm listening.

[MISS TULLO *looks on.*]

JOHN CAMPBELL: . . . that . . . she thought she recognised you from someplace.

AGENT: Well she can abolish that idea. She has never seen me before but from this on out she'll be seeing me right often. [*He laughs at* MISS TULLO.] Yes sir.

MISS TULLO: Feach leis an bus ar an fear sin. (Look at the mouth on that fellow.)

AGENT: Thank you. Thank you very much. [*Nods to* MISS TULLO *with exaggerated good manners.*] Right, well, you – [*Indicating with nod at* JOHN CAMPBELL.] – yes, you, thank you very much, you can translate for me. Tell that man there to get up now!

JOHN CAMPBELL: Aengus. [*Quietly.*] Aengus.

AENGUS: Aye?

JOHN CAMPBELL: He wants you up.

AENGUS: Aye. [AENGUS *slowly rises, reaches for the support which* MISS TULLO *gives him, then tries to stay upright.*]

AGENT: Now that we are all on our feet I will begin, and you will translate. Right?

JOHN CAMPBELL: Aye.

[*The* AGENT *turns to the others and enunciates each word.*]

AGENT: In a year's time – I repeat – in a year's time, you will be brought to a farm of fifteen acres, with a house half-built, timbers at the ready, and a well with water, two pigs, two oxen, and some chickens. Till then, the men will work this farm, and the women will act as domestic servants.

MURDO: Cad a duirt se? (What did he say?)

JOHN CAMPBELL: [*Translates.*] He said we'll have to head to the Rocky Mountains on the backs of donkeys through the snow, so put on your best clothes. And there's a fine for anyone with a tear in their stockings but don't worry – there'll be no end of warm toast.

AGENT: Each man will be given a woollen coat and two pairs of boots.

MISS TULLO: Cad a duirt se? (What did he say?)

JOHN CAMPBELL: [*Translates.*] The crossing will take six nights. There is a risk of losing fingers with the cold so keep them between your legs. And marriage is not allowed.

MISS MacDONALD: Ah dearie me.

AGENT: Each man will be given two tillies, one bale of straw, and a barrel of seed.

JOHN CAMPBELL: [*Translates.*] On the seventh day we'll cross the river. We'll go on skates. You'll spend three days learning French. Then we'll be given our pass to the car factories in Detroit and a hundred dollars to see us there. The thing you need to watch out for . . .

MURDO: Cad é sin? (What's that?)

JOHN CAMPBELL: The blooming bears on the other side.

[AENGUS *smothers a cough. The* AGENT *is looking at* AENGUS.]

AGENT: What is wrong with that man? Why does he look so despairing?

JOHN CAMPBELL: He's just sad at his lack of English.

AGENT: Oh. [*He goes over and claps* AENGUS *on the shoulder.*] You'll be fine.

AENGUS: Aye.

[*Alan MacDonald's version of "The Exile" is sung.*]

SCENE 31

Four of the men – MacKENZIE, JOHN CAMPBELL, AENGUS and MURDO *– are weeding again in a position similar to that at the start of the play. They continually move throughout the scene.*

JOHN CAMPBELL: It's very hard on the blooming conscience to burn timber in a fire.

MURDO: It is. And then there's worse – to burn down an entire field of trees. It's a crying shame. It's like burning money.

JOHN CAMPBELL: The first few nights I felt the cold and I gave in, a little at a time.

MacKENZIE: This place is well named – Hardscrabble Farm.

MURDO: When they were showing us the slides, they didn't mention the snow.

JOHN CAMPBELL: They did not Captain, nor the prairie fires.

MacKENZIE: I miss the peat. I miss the shielings. There is no peat in this soil.

MURDO: If there is one thing I do not miss it is the blasted peat.

MacKENZIE: Well if there is one thing I've had enough of is milking, milking, milking – I'm milking in my bucking dreams.

MURDO: And weeding turnips. I wake up weeding turnips.

[AENGUS *stops and sits.*]

MacKENZIE: And stoking wheat. And wherever you look in your sleep there's stumps of trees that have to be got out, and then you wake and step out and you can see the actual wind, and then there's the prairie – it's as wide as the moon and when you find yourself out there you're so small you get a fever of loneliness.

MURDO: You know what's wrong with this country MacKenzie?

MacKENZIE: What's that Captain?

MURDO: There is too much land. Isn't that right Aengus?

[*They all stop to look at* AENGUS. *He answers without looking at them.*]

AENGUS: [*Quietly.*] Aye.

MURDO: [*Chuckles.*] If there was less land the people would be more God-fearing.

[AENGUS *gets up and continues to work.*]

JOHN CAMPBELL: Listen to the raider. So that is why we were the way we were. We've come a long way. So if a man ends up with a hundred acres he'll lose his God?

MURDO: John C?
JOHN CAMPBELL: Aye?
MURDO: Watch it.
JOHN CAMPBELL: We are some cases the lot of us. Do you know the real meaning of that there word croft?
MURDO: I've heard many a meaning over the years.
JOHN CAMPBELL: Well on good authority I'm told it means "hump."
MURDO: No!
JOHN CAMPBELL: Aye.
MacKENZIE. Hump? Aye, ahahh hahaha.
MURDO: Did you hear that Aengus?
AENGUS: [*Quietly.*] I did.
MURDO: I knew I had something on my back for all those years.
JOHN CAMPBELL: And the trick is not to bring it with you. [MURDO *straightens up.*]
MURDO: Is that it?
JOHN CAMPBELL: Aye.
MURDO: You hear what he said Aengus? [*No reply from* AENGUS *who slowly and laborious continues to work.*] You're saying don't take the croft with you?
JOHN CAMPBELL: No, I'm not saying that, Captain.
MURDO: So what are you saying?
JOHN CAMPBELL: What I'm saying is leave the hump where it is, and let's find out the meaning of the word prairie. There's no ceilidh on the prairies.
MURDO: You're too cute.
JOHN CAMPBELL: Stop it Captain.
MURDO: [*Disbelief.*] Woe is me. The squatter has turned into a philosopher.
JOHN CAMPBELL: No Captain, the war is over. [AENGUS *coughs.*]
MURDO: Are you all right Aengus?
AENGUS: Aye.
JOHN CAMPBELL: And the slides never mentioned the

blooming grasshoppers that destroy the crops.

MURDO: Oh indeed, there's a lot of beasties in the thatch, there is.

MacKENZIE: You're right there Captain.

[AENGUS *rises and makes his way off the stage.*]

MURDO: I'll tell you a story now. What did they do when the hen died after laying a clutch of four eggs?

JOHN CAMPBELL: I don't know.

MURDO: I'll tell you the story. [*He starts doing the story in movements.*] Well the hen died and the four eggs were sitting there. My father went up to the cliff and wandered about till he saw a gull warming her eggs some way below. What did he do? Why he let himself down by rope to the nest. When she saw him the gull flew off. He popped the gull's eggs into his pocket. Then he substituted the four eggs of the hen for those of the gull. He climbed up, the gull came back, and sat in as if nothing had happened. My father went home to tell the news. They ate the gull's eggs that night. Each day my mother and him came up to check the nest. And there the gull was sitting content on what was not her own. A few days later they duly hatched, out stepped four dark chicks – no problem, the colour made no difference to yon bird, they were carefully attended by the gulls. Oh yes, great parents, firing off in all directions for food, till one day one of the chicks thought she could fly like a gull and she reared out of the nest and fell into the sea. So my father climbed down and the other three chicks were taken back up the cliff and they were reared into fine mature hens.

[*They smile at each other. The* AGENT *enters.*]

AGENT: Where is this man Aengus?

[JOHN CAMPBELL *looks around him.*]

JOHN CAMPBELL: He was there a moment ago.

AGENT: Well he's not here now? Is he?

MURDO: He's just gone off, he'll be back.

AGENT: He refused his first location, now he has failed to arrive here on the day appointed?

MURDO: I tell you, he was here till a few minutes ago.

AGENT: If he has run to the south the police will have him. He will be sent back to the Hebrides.

MacKENZIE: Could he take us with him?

[*The others laugh.*]

AGENT: Is that a joke MacKenzie? Ha-ha-ha. It's nice to have a sense of humour. But my advice to you people is to just keep working. And in time take a native woman and settle down. That's my advice to you. [*He goes.*]

MURDO: We all get used to the faces we see every day. First we recognize them, then we get used to them – I am trying to get used to his puss. But I can't. I was not to know that the man who would become my first enemy here was a Scottish man who came out from over there before me by a few years. You can take meanness from the face of a man that you know. If you say the right thing. But it's harder to take meanness from the face of a man you don't know. He is a stranger to me. And it comes as a shock to me that he is. I cannot get used to him, because I expect him to be otherwise.

MacKENZIE: And where is Aengus?

[*There is a sudden flash of lightning, and they flatten down.*]

MacKENZIE: Jesus, that was close.

JOHN CAMPBELL: Are you afraid Mac?

MacKENZIE: Yes I am. Jesus Christ.

JOHN CAMPBELL: Are you praying?

MacKENZIE: I am.

JOHN CAMPBELL: Or maybe you were cursing?

MacKENZIE: I'm praying and cursing both. When they showed us the slides they didn't mention the cursed lightning. [*Another terrible flash with thunder and the men start crawling to stage left.*] Oh dear. Oh dear. Oh fucking dearie me. Is it the end of the world?

[AENGUS *appears stage left in a large overcoat. He carries on a chair and sits down on it. He watches them intently, but they do not see him.*]

JOHN CAMPBELL: I don't know, I've never been there.

MURDO: Yes you were John C. It's just that you've forgotten.

JOHN CAMPBELL: No Captain, I want to put it behind me. Whatever you do MacKenzie, don't stand under a tree you dummy.

[*They start crawling towards stage left and off.* AENGUS *looks after them; then, when they are gone, he closes his eyes.*]

SCENE 32

Stage suffused with white light. AENGUS *is sitting and coughing; he is covered in snow.* MISS TULLO *appears.*

MISS TULLO: Aengus.
AENGUS: Miss Tullo, Miss Tullo.
MISS TULLO: You are covered in ice.
AENGUS: I know, don't tell anyone. I've never known such cold.
MISS TULLO: Aengus?
AENGUS: Yes?
MISS TULLO: What are you doing out here?
AENGUS: Taking the air.
MISS TULLO: What are doing to yourself man?
AENGUS: I'm trying to get better.
MISS TULLO: Better from what?
AENGUS: The cough.
MISS TULLO: Out here on the porch?
AENGUS: Aye.
MISS TULLO: I don't understand.
AENGUS: [*Whispers.*] They found . . . spots on my lungs, and they said . . . they said I had to sleep outside on the porch . . . that's what they said . . . that this was the cure. You see Miss Tullo, there was no medicine for what I had, and . . . All I can say is that getting better is worse than nearly dying.

[MISS TULLO *mops his forehead.*]

MISS TULLO: You're covered in ice, Aengus.
AENGUS: Yesterday I heard rumbling. Today I heard military aircraft.
MISS TULLO: There is no war here Aengus.

AENGUS: I know. I know that, but it doesn't stop me hearing them.

MISS TULLO: Take it easy now.

AENGUS: Premonition is a terrible affliction, Miss Tullo, no one wants it.

MISS TULLO: You're sick, Aengus, that's what's wrong – you're sick.

AENGUS: Yes, but I'm getting better, I can see myself getting better.

MISS TULLO: You must get up and come inside. [*She reaches down under his back.*] You're freezing. This is madness. [*She gets him slowly to his feet.*] Come Aengus. [*He reaches out for support.*] Just a little more. [*He goes to his knees.*] Come on Aengus. [*They reach the back door.*]

AENGUS: Miss Tullo?

MISS TULLO: Yes?

AENGUS: I'm all in. Don't tell anyone. They'll send me home.

MISS TULLO: I won't tell anyone Aengus.

AENGUS: You promise?

MISS TULLO: I do.

[*They got through the door and it slams shut. Instant darkness.*]

SCENE 33

Stage in darkness. MISS TULLO *and* MISS MacDONALD *speak in the dark.*

MISS TULLO: Go on, do it.

MISS MacDONALD: I can't.

MISS TULLO: Go on.

MISS MacDONALD: Never, you do it.

MISS TULLO: You said you would.

MISS MacDONALD: Wait a second. Give me your hand.

MISS TULLO: For what?

MISS MacDONALD: Just give me your hand, please.

MISS TULLO: Where are you taking me?

MISS MacDONALD: Are you alright?
MISS TULLO: Don't do it Miss MacDonald.
[MISS MacDONALD *hits the light switch. The light comes on. They both have their hands on the switch.*]
MISS MacDONALD: Open your eyes.
[MISS TULLO *slowly opens her eyes and looks up at the light.*]
MISS MacDONALD: Now what you have to do is pretend that you know all about electricity. Don't let them think that you were never on a bus or in a motor car or in a moving picture house. Just put the switch on, and then put the switch off, like this – [*She hits the switch, and they go into darkness.*] – and then put it on again. [*Stage lights up again.*]. Now you do it. [MISS TULLO *nervously lifts her hand to the switch, she hits it, and the lights go off.*]

SCENE 34

The lights come up. To the side is a five-gallon drum. JOHN CAMPBELL *is seated by the table and* MISS MacDONALD is *seated by the fireplace, her hands on her lap. The lights get brighter. The* AGENT, *wearing a suit, is standing with a file in front of him. His speech is littered with questions, even when they are not questions.*

AGENT: Good day? Sorry for intruding on you good people. I am from the Emigration Board? I have a few questions.
MURDO: Go ahead sir.
AGENT: You there, are, so I take it, Murdo Macaulay?
MURDO: I am.
[*The* AGENT *turns to* MISS TULLO.]
AGENT: And you there, I believe, are Miss Gertrude Tullo? [*She looks at him then looks at* MURDO.] It would be wiser if she answered for herself.
MURDO: She does not speak English.
AGENT: I see. So, you have to speak for her?
MURDO: Aye.

AGENT: Well in this country that might prove a handicap. This is not proper conduct but let us proceed. What funds have you?

[*The* AGENT *writes throughout this scene.*]

MURDO: I have my boarding card and landing card still from the ship. I have my emigration documents. I have the receipt for every part of the loan that I've paid.

AGENT: I mean what funds in cash have you?

MURDO: I have ten dollars sixty cents of the eight pounds I brought out with me. My wages are thirty-five dollars a month. I have six dollars twenty cents saved from my wages. I try to pay back my loan to Toronto. It was ninety dollars. I have it down to sixty dollars and thirty-four cents. I find it very hard – it takes all I have. When are we going to see this hut we were promised?

AGENT: That is not in my department.

MURDO: Is there anybody we can speak to?

AGENT: I'm sorry I don't know. And now, what funds has Miss Tullo?

MURDO: She has nothing in cash. All goes on the loan. She knows what I know. That the promise is not true. She has enough stockings for the winter but no clothes.

[*The* AGENT *writes.*]

AGENT: And what animals, what stock?

MURDO: She had a cow. Now she has no cow. She earned an additional cow working as a domestic, then it was killed by lightning, as was my yoke of oxen. One calf survived. [MURDO *points at* MISS TULLO.] Gerty has twelve chickens. I have two pigs. The lightning came again and we lost twenty-five tons of hay to fire.

AGENT: Twenty-five tons. [*He writes.*] Do you like it here, do you like the conditions?

MURDO: [*Uncertainty, long pause.* MURDO *studies the* AGENT *to see if he can be trusted, then decides to take another avenue.*] We have our bible.

AGENT: And that woman there? Does she like it here?

[*The* AGENT *waits, listening.*]

MURDO: She is homesick, but at least there is not the threat of a great war here. [AGENT *writes, waits, listens, and then starts writing again.*] She is sad she is not able to look after the old people that she left behind. Hers was a godly house. And that she has left it has put darkness on her. The old were her responsibility. Now she is troubled by leaving them defenceless. This place is alright, but the people she left in Lewis have followed her here. They are here in this room. They are at the bottom of the bed when she lies down. They are sad, she says. There is no church here, except the church inside her head, and in that same head is all the people she left behind. When she was in Lewis her thoughts were always abroad, away from the Great War, and now that she's abroad she is home in Lewis. She brought Lewis here, so she is at home.

AGENT: [*Finishing his writing.*] She . . . she . . . is at home here. [JOHN CAMPBELL *looks at him in disbelief.*] Thank you. [*The* AGENT *gets up to leave.*]

MURDO: Can I ask you a question of you sir?

AGENT: Certainly.

MURDO: What is it like to be a Canadian?

AGENT: What is it like to be a Canadian? It's a question I often ask myself, as will you in time. Perhaps what we are is a people who do not make statements, but only ask questions. So by asking me what it's like to be Canadian you're already being one. Thank you Mister Campbell, and Miss MacDonald – [*He bows in her direction.*] – for your time. [*The* AGENT *goes.*]

[MISS TULLO *continues sitting there, hands in, lap. Silence a while.*]

MISS TULLO: Did I say the right things?

MURDO: Aye.

SCENE 35

MISS MacDONALD *is sweeping fast with a broom.* MISS TULLO, *dressed elegantly, is pirouetting about happily.*

MISS TULLO: Good morning.

MISS MacDONALD: Good morning to you.

MISS TULLO: And how is your good self this morning?

MISS MacDONALD: I'm fine.

MISS TULLO: I am so glad to hear it. It's truly wonderful. Well now, let me explain the details – the details of everyday life here in Ontario. You will have every other Sunday off, every other Sunday, and then along with that, each Wednesday afternoon. You will have your own bathroom – think of that! Clothes will be boiled in the basement. The children will be in at two o'clock. I expect you here each morning at eight.

MISS MacDONALD: Yes.

MISS TULLO: Oh do call me Gertrude.

MISS MacDONALD: Yes Gertrude. [*She brushes like mad and* MISS TULLO *admires herself.*]

MISS TULLO: You may bring me a drink.

MISS MacDONALD: So early in the day?

MISS TULLO: Yes indeed.

MISS MacDONALD: Your usual, Madam?

MISS TULLO: Yes, thank you.

[MISS MacDONALD *pours a sherry.* MISS TULLO *swallows it down immediately, proffers her glass, then gets another and swallows it down.*]

MISS MacDONALD: Oh by the way, Miss Gertrude. You see the colour of yon outfit?

MISS TULLO: Why yes – do you like it?

MISS MacDONALD: Oh yes.

MISS TULLO: How sweet of you.

MISS MacDONALD: It's a very expensive item, I'm sure.

MISS TULLO: Why I bought it in Masons of Toronto for a mere two dollars.

MISS MacDONALD: No!

MISS TULLO: [*Swooping around.*] Yes! I can show you the receipt if you like.

MISS MacDONALD: No you keep the receipt, Ma'am.

MISS TULLO: I might bring you with me one day to the shops.

MISS MacDONALD: How kind of you.

MISS TULLO: It is nothing. But that you like the frock gives me great pleasure – yes indeed.

MISS MacDONALD: You would not like anything to happen to it, I'm sure.

MISS TULLO: Oh no, no.

MISS MacDONALD: So, I have just one reservation Madam.

MISS TULLO: Gertrude, you silly.

MISS MacDONALD: Forgive me, Miss . . . Gertrude, but it's nearly five and if you don't have that item of clothing off your back within five minutes she'll be through that door to give you your marching orders.

MISS TULLO: Oh. [*She empties her glass and starts stripping off as she heads off stage.*]

MISS MacDONALD: Don't tear it Miss Tullo – and don't fall for goodness sakes. And wash out your mouth!

SCENE 36

MISS MacDONALD *is knitting, and* MacKENZIE *arrives. A sheepskin is thrown across a chair. There is a pile of logs where there used to be timber.*

MacKENZIE: [*He sits and studies her.*] Well, did you write home Miss MacDonald?

MISS MacDONALD: I tried.

MacKENZIE: And?

MISS MacDONALD: Oh I wrote many.

MacKENZIE: And did you send them?

MISS MacDONALD: No.

MacKENZIE: I see.

MISS MacDONALD: I tried, but could not.

MacKENZIE: And why is that?

MISS MacDONALD: It's difficult.

MacKENZIE: It is.

MISS MacDONALD: Maybe there is no need.

MacKENZIE: Did you not say that the minute we arrived we should write home?

MISS MacDONALD: I said that, yes. [*She ponders the question.*] Now I think I said it in the hope that if I wrote they might write back. But neither of us can write. It's like this. They don't want good news and I don't want to send them bad news. So I send the dollars on and say nothing. Just hello. They want to know things are bad so they can feel like it's lucky they never came on out after us. One day they might want to up and follow us – and do I want to put them off? I can't. It's hard work being a herring girl there, and it's tough work stoking wheat here. I could write. But then neither can I tell a lie. If I was to write I would tell a lie. So I say nothing. Only hello. They asked when I left to let them know if my portion of the world was better than theirs. What can I say to that? – it's too early to say. Each evening I write a letter that I tear up the following morning. [*Pause.*] My head is full of letters that I never write.

MacKENZIE: As is mine.

MISS MacDONALD: And I speak more Gaelic here than I ever did at home.

MacKENZIE: Well, this is the thing with you Stornowegians. You're stuck up. If I spoke to you at home in Gaelic, you would answer me in English. Now when I speak to you in English you answer me in Gaelic. Why?

MISS MacDONALD: Maybe I found the language again over here.

MacKENZIE: And now I'm a churchgoer, which I swore I'd never be.

MISS MacDONALD: We travel with ghosts.

MacKENZIE: We do. And sometimes we meet them.

MISS MacDONALD: [*Looks at him sharply.*] What do you mean?

MacKENZIE: I'll tell you a story.

MISS MacDONALD: Oh do.

MacKENZIE: I thought I had no near neighbours where I am.

But I was out cutting – [*He mimes cutting wood.*] – the other day in the woods, trying to clear the bush and the swamp. I had just started when I heard some woodcutting – [*He stops to listen.*] – going on in another place. I thought I was hearing things. I listened, it was sort of to the North and East of me. It was the type of morning when all sounds carry clearly, clear as any sound can carry. There was someone out there surely, so I started chopping towards the sound of the axe. [*He chops, chops, chops.*] He'd stop to listen to me – [*He stops to listen.*] – and I'd stop to listen to him, who-ever-he was, and he'd hit with the axe just to make a sound. It must have taken us all morning. And as we got closer I began to chop like mad. [*Chops like mad.*] And we both kept coming towards one another, until at last we met. And who was it?

MISS MacDONALD: Who?

MacKENZIE: None other but Ian Morrison from Aird Tong.

MISS MacDONALD: I know of him – but they did not take him out on the Metagama.

MacKENZIE: No. He'd come out on the Marloch. We were happy to meet. [*Pause.*] Now since I can't ask you to marry me, may I ask if you'd bake me some butter – [*Aping Canadian accent.*] – cookies? I have an awful longing on me. [*She looks at him. He looks at her.*]

MISS MacDONALD: You're getting very sweet-tongued.

MacKENZIE: I am, thank you. It's a thing I learned since I came out here, you understand?

SCENE 37

MISS TULLO *sings "Loch Roag" – a song of exile. When the song is over, the stage falls into semi-darkness.*

JOHN CAMPBELL: Catherine! Catherine! [*Screams. Pause.*]

MISS MacDONALD: Are you there John?

JOHN CAMPBELL: I am.

MISS MacDONALD: For some reason I thought you were gone.

JOHN CAMPBELL: No, I'm here. I dreamed I was hanging onto the stern of the Iolaire. My hands were numb and I saw to my left Donald MacDonald go, and to my right Aengus Macleod go, right down, crashing onto the deck and into the sea. I was yelling with all my might but my back was buckling. Then no words came out. She was quickly going to port when I saw the lifeboat coming across a sea of oil. They began to shout at me but I could not let go. Then I summoned up all my strength to free myself, I let go the rope, and woke up here.

MISS MacDONALD: [*She touches his shoulder.*] John.

JOHN CAMPBELL: Yes?

MISS MacDONALD: Three things.

JOHN CAMPBELL: Yes.

MISS MacDONALD: You have them?

JOHN CAMPBELL: I have.

MISS MacDONALD: Three things that come without asking . . .

JOHN CAMPBELL: . . . fear, love and jealousy.

SCENE 38

All are weeding except MacTAVISH *and* AENGUS. *There is silence.* AENGUS *appears, takes his place among them.*

MURDO: You came back to us Aengus.

AENGUS: I did Captain, I'm better you see.

MISS TULLO: I'm glad.

AENGUS: I ended up in this hospital. And listen to this: the whole ward spoke Gaelic.

JOHN CAMPBELL: Indeed?

AENGUS: I don't want to ever see the insides of a hospital again. But in there I heard a lot of things. You can learn a lot of things in a hospital that you won't hear here. There's people there from all over. The man next to me was a metalworker from Stornoway who turned to boxing. He said the wind from the Rockies was like a tune from home. The man next to him was a furnace-man from Ness. They told me things. Things we don't hear here. How there's work to be got in Detroit, no problem, in the car factories. And then there's construction work at Niagara Falls. And there's work on the ships of the Great Lakes. At double the wage we're getting here.

MURDO: Did you say double?

AENGUS: I did Captain. We were enticed out here, it was all a fraud. There is no hut, no one hundred and fifty acres – there was none and there never will be. Now let's enter the country by ourselves, without those vultures driving us. Let's go on from here – here you see the top soil turn to dust. The place is lifeless as ashes. I can hear the frames of the animals rattle same as I heard my own bones rattle when my lungs filled with drought.

MacKENZIE: I would like to be near the lakes.

MURDO: Aye – at double the wages.

AENGUS: Hold it there Captain. There's something else I heard. Opposite me was a man and he told me something ye might like to know.

MISS TULLO: Go on then.

AENGUS: First listen.

MacKENZIE: I'm listening.

[*They wait for* AENGUS *to speak.*]

MISS MacDONALD: We're listening Aengus.

AENGUS: But can you hear it, Blondie?

MISS TULLO: Hear what?

AENGUS: It's all around you.

MURDO: What is all around us?

AENGUS: Just listen.

[*They all stand looking around them in silence.*]

MISS TULLO: I'm listening Aengus, but I can't hear anything.

AENGUS: That's just it. What is you can't hear?

MISS TULLO: What is he talking about?

MURDO: I don't know.

AENGUS: I'm asking you – what is that we can't hear?

MURDO: I'm telling you man, I don't know!

AENGUS: I'll tell you Captain. It's the sea. That is what we can't hear. The sea. And we lived with it all our lives.

[*Again they stop to listen.*]

JOHN CAMPBELL: You're right Aengus.

AENGUS: Now I'll tell you what I heard from that man in the bed opposite. I heard that there are farms going on some islands off that city called Vancouver.

MISS MacDONALD: Islands?

AENGUS: Yes, Miss MacDonald, islands – and better still . . .

MISS TULLO: Yes?

AENGUS: There are Lewis islanders living there.

MISS TULLO: Now that he's better he wants to leave.

AENGUS: I'll pay what's due then go.

MacKENZIE: Vancouver is a distance from here.

AENGUS: Nothing compared to the distance we've come.

JOHN CAMPBELL: Well I heard it's about the same and even longer.

AENGUS: A couple of days and we'll be back on an island, same as the one we left. And there you're lifting the potatoes after only eight weeks in the ground. And grass three to five foot high for cutting. No more cursed agents. You hear me?

MURDO: I hear you.

AENGUS: First chance I get I'm out of here – do you hear me?

JOHN CAMPBELL: I hear you.

AENGUS: We have only a few months more, our fare over is nearly paid, if we stop here, we'll be . . .

[*The* AGENT *enters.*]

AGENT: You ladies there, what are you doing here?

MISS MacDONALD: We are working.

AGENT: You will not work in the fields with the men.

MISS TULLO: But we always worked with the men.

AGENT: Not here you don't.

MISS TULLO: But it's Wednesday afternoon, our half day.

AGENT: No matter what day of the week it is you will not work with the men carrying loads like you did in the Hebrides. It is not proper. You will leave the fields now, please. [*The women leave, accompanied by the* AGENT.]

AENGUS: We should go Murdo.
MURDO: I think you're right Aengus.
MacKENZIE: I like the sound of these islands, do you John C?
JOHN CAMPBELL: I do.
MacKENZIE: But somehow I like the sounds of the lakes better.
[*They continue working.*]

SCENE 39

They pull out chairs and sit. All are collected for the reading of the Gazette. JOHN CAMPBELL *spreads out the paper.*

JOHN CAMPBELL: [*Lifting the newspaper high.*] Listen to this pray: the soapman has gone and left the island in trust.
MURDO: What next?
MacKENZIE: Good man.
AENGUS: Meaning?
JOHN CAMPBELL: The island will be given to the people of Lewis and governed by Trustees.
AENGUS: We'll see.
[*He hands it to* MacTAVISH.]
MacTAVISH: I have tried everything.
MISS TULLO: Indeed you have.
MacTAVISH: [*Reads.*] "The crofters have refused to move to new territories and open the farms to dairy herds."
AENGUS: They are still at it.
MURDO: They are.
JOHN CAMPBELL: Go on Mouse.
MacTAVISH: [*Reads.*] "I'm sure history, who judges things impartially, will see I tried my best for Lewis."
MISS TULLO: You did poor man.
MISS MacDONALD: Read on.
MacTAVISH: [*Reads.*] "Look years hence to what has taken place in Harris where I intend to move with the encouragement of the islanders there."
MacKENZIE: So Lord Leverhulme is off to Harris?
JOHN CAMPBELL: He is.

MacTAVISH: [*Reads.*] "Not only the land of Lewis, but the sea is going to waste."

MISS MacDONALD: He must have thought Harris was better looking.

MISS TULLO: You crowd can never be pleased, you were given a guardian angel and what did you do – you sent him to Harris.

AENGUS: Well, we thought he'd get on better there.

JOHN CAMPBELL: We don't begrudge him.

MacTAVISH: [*Reads.*] "My business is my business. I can see finality for myself, an absolute end, but none for my business." [MacTAVISH *hands the paper back to* JOHN CAMPBELL.]

MISS TULLO: Is there anything about us in the paper John?

JOHN CAMPBELL: Not that I can find, except a bit about a farmer in Ontario who was promised Island men and no-one turned up.

MURDO: Read that again.

JOHN CAMPBELL: There was a farmer in Ontario who was promised Island men but none turned up.

MISS TULLO: But we did.

JOHN CAMPBELL: True.

MISS TULLO: And there's no mention of us.

JOHN CAMPBELL: I'll tell you why. We are a better class of citizen or else bigger fools. A quote from the *Toronto Star*: "The men of the Hebrides are a credit to the country of Canada; they are ambitious, hard-working, and religiously inclined." You read the next line Miss Tullo. [*Hands paper to her.*]

JOHN CAMPBELL: [*Points.*] Just there.

MISS TULLO: Why do you always ask me? [*Reads.*] "They are proud but touchy."

MISS MacDONALD: And there you have it.

MISS TULLO: Here you are Miss MacDonald – that's enough out of me for one night. You're the best of us at the reading. [MISS TULLO *hands the paper to* MISS MacDONALD *who flicks through the pages.*]

MISS MacDONALD: Well at home they still have Beecham's pills: "Take the edge off your appetite and restore it with Beecham's pills!" There's rumours of Bolshevism in Stornoway; there's special value in oilskins this week; you can still cure yourself with Wild Cherry Pectoral Cough Mixture; there's theories of atonement and Bermaline bread; there's a man discussing the origins of the kilt.

MURDO: There always is.

JOHN CAMPBELL: True Captain.

[MISS MacDONALD *hands the paper to* MacKENZIE.]

MacKENZIE: Thank you Miss MacDonald. [*He scans it.*] You always give me the good bits to read. Now listen closely to this. There is a hen that lived nineteen years; for the first six years the bird was jet black, from six on it turned grey, and from grey it turned spotless white. So for ten years she was white till at seventeen dark feathers appeared on its neck and by the time it died it was a beautiful black colour. Only for the cruel frost it would still be alive. And on a clear moonlight night a passer-by saw the blue men playing a lively game of shinty out from Aird . . .

MURDO: I'm glad to see they still have whiskey on the island.

MISS MacDONALD: And fools to drink it.

JOHN CAMPBELL: There's an ad here for Sunshine soap – he left us his soap.

AENGUS: And remember he left us the road to nowhere.

MacKENZIE: Ah the bridge at North Tolsta.

AENGUS: One of the most expensive bridges in all of the isles and who uses it? – the sheep.

MacKENZIE: Correct. I'm glad it's only sheep.

MURDO: And why is that MacKenzie?

MacKENZIE: If the people of Ness and Tolsta were joined by road it would be a terrible disaster. [*Laughter.*] It would be better to keep them apart.

MISS TULLO: On good authority they call them a folly.

MISS MacDONALD: A folly it is.

MacTAVISH: I have to go to the toilet – whenever I hear that word I get taken short.

[*Laughter.*]

MURDO: Go ahead Mouse.

[JOHN CAMPBELL *folds the paper and puts it away.*]

MISS MacDONALD: I don't know. We read the paper and I feel worse. As if we were pretending. I have never stood in a graveyard but I seem to be in one now.

AENGUS: Ah beauty.

MISS TULLO: Oh Miss MacDonald.

[*There is a long silence; then, in the far distance, the sound of a locomotive whistle.*]

JOHN CAMPBELL: So now that we know what was going on in Lewis a few months ago, can anyone tell me what is going on here in this country today?

MURDO: A good question.

AENGUS: I say we go and find out,

MISS MacDONALD: Well all I can say is that over here, John C, we no longer have to keep the evening vigil.

MISS TULLO: True, the courting couple may no longer meet in secret. Isn't that right Aengus?

AENGUS: Right Miss Tullo.

MISS TULLO: [*Flirting.*] Gertrude.

AENGUS: Aye. Gertrude.

MacKENZIE: One day the potato, the next day London. Yesterday the peat, today the wheat.

AENGUS: Our days are up here.

MURDO: We have carried out our commitments.

AENGUS: Yes Captain, we're done.

MURDO: What about the rest of you?

MacKENZIE: I'm for the Great Lakes, and then, who knows?

MURDO: Well I'm for Detroit.

AENGUS: And you?

JOHN CAMPBELL: The islands.

MISS MacDONALD: The islands.

MISS TULLO: Like yourselves there, the islands.

[AENGUS *goes to the back door and opens it.*]

AENGUS: [*Shouts.*] Where are you for MacTavish?

MacTAVISH: [*Shouts off.*] I'm for Toronto! Right now!

AENGUS: Good man Mouse. [*He closes the door.*] Well, now we have all some place to go.

SCENE 40

MacTAVISH *appears alone at back on stage in vicar's outfit. The rest appear one after another and surround him. A psalm is sung.*

ALL:

Wait for the Lord
And keep His way
He will exalt you to inherit the land:
When the wicked are cut off, you will see it.

I have seen a wicked and ruthless man
Flourishing like a green tree in its native soil
But he soon passed away and was no more;
Though I looked for him, he could not be found.

Consider the blameless, observe the upright:
There is a future for the man of peace.
But all sinners will be destroyed:
The future of the wicked will be cut off.

The salvation of the righteous comes from the Lord
He is their stronghold in time of trouble.
The Lord helps them and delivers them:
He delivers them from the wicked and saves,
Because they take refuge in Him.

SCENE 41

The women work stage left, the men work stage right. The women mime domestic chores, the men mime working with wheat. Sometimes the women or the men speak loudly so that their voices can carry to each other.

MISS TULLO: I'm frightened.

MISS MacDONALD: So am I.

MISS TULLO: I've heard of people like us being killed out there.

AENGUS: There was a famous Highlander, Miss Tullo, and what he'd say is: "When you are among wolves, howl" – that's what he'd say, Miss Tullo.

MISS TULLO: Well you better roar for the rest of us.

AENGUS: I will, I will.

MURDO: He will surely.

[*In the far distance the sound of a locomotive whistle.*]

MISS MacDONALD: And are there churches there?

AENGUS: There are, with our own churchmen from Lewis, and Gaelic choirs.

MacKENZIE: I think I'll leave the Great Lakes till again. I was thinking of entering the world of insurance, maybe banking.

MURDO: Good man MacKenzie. You'll probably increase the interest on the loans.

MISS TULLO: And you Aengus, what will you do?

AENGUS: It's politics for me.

MURDO: I knew it.

MISS TULLO: And you?

MURDO: I'll enter the world of newspapers. And you Miss Tullo?

MISS MacDONALD: She'll go into dressmaking.

[*Pause.*]

MISS TULLO: I love the psalm.

[*Pause.*]

MISS MacDONALD: Right then, we'll go as good people.

MISS TULLO: Aye, and then I'll settle down.

[*Pause.*]

MISS MacDONALD: Since we've come this far, we might as well go the rest of the way.

[*Pause.*]

MISS MacDONALD: We're going together but I feel as If I were going alone.

JOHN CAMPBELL: That's the way it is.

MacKENZIE: Indeed it is. When you have to do the thing by yourself, there is few to accompany you until you find them. [*Pause.*]

MISS MacDONALD: What I fear will accompany me all my life.

JOHN CAMPBELL: What is that?

MISS MacDONALD: That when I wake up it's still there. I do not want to wake up, once again, with bitterness in my head.

AENGUS: You won't.

MacKENZIE: Aye. You will be able to write home when you get wherever you are going Miss MacDonald.

MISS MacDONALD: I will.

MacKENZIE: And you will be able to marry Catherine when you get there John.

MISS TULLO: Indeed he will.

MISS MacDONALD: I would not count on it.

MacKENZIE: It's been a long courtship.

MISS TULLO: The longest on the island.

MISS MacDONALD: You know how long it is since he asked me Miss Tullo?

MISS TULLO: Indeed I don't Miss MacDonald, you poor unfortunate woman, but it must have been in the dark ages.

MISS MacDONALD: Indeed, it's nigh on ten year.

MISS TULLO: Ten years!

MISS MacDONALD: Ten. And this time we stay where we are, wherever it is we reach, we stay there.

AENGUS: Yes Blondie.

MISS MacDONALD: Not you. I was talking to that fellow Mr Campbell.

JOHN CAMPBELL: Indeed I know you were Miss MacDonald, but Aengus always answers for me.

AENGUS: I can't help it Blondie.

[*Pause.*]

MISS TULLO: I hope I see you all again.

[*They now work in a very orchestrated manner, passing things down the line so that their formation looks very much like it did at the beginning of the play when they were collecting kelp.*]

ALL: Se feamainn tha 'nam chasan. (My feet are made of kelp.) Togail an fheamainn, tionndadh an fheamainn. (Lifting the kelp, turning the kelp.)

[*The work gains momentum, as they sing. Then suddenly they all stop. They take leave of each other, shaking hands. Then one by one they leave the stage.* JOHN CAMPBELL *and* MISS MacDONALD *are the last to go. Enter* MacTAVISH. *He walks around the space. Looks out at the audience with his lamp. Returns to the door. Hits the switch. Darkness. The sound of the sea starts in the dark, and a far distant sound of bells. Then everything stops.*]

END

Serious

First performed by Prisoners from Castlerea Prison, Co. Roscommon, in December 2005. Directed by Dermot Healy.

CAST

MATTIE	
JAMES	the songbird
OLLIE	
DANNY	
JER	
DAVE	
TWO PRISON OFFICERS	
FIVE VOICES FROM THE AUDIENCE	
SERGOSA	Mr Lithuania

Set: Four black curtains on the back walls marking out four cells. In the centre of each black curtain is one white square sewn onto the black curtain. Between each curtain is one upright plank, painted various colours. A pipe runs along the back wall through the various cells. Each cell can contain flags or photos. The cells, going right to left on stage from the audience's POV, are occupied as follows:

Cell 1: MATTIE – *Radio plus earphones, one chair*
Cell 2: JER *and* DAVE – *Two chairs, TV*
Cell 3: OLLIE *and* DANNY – *Two chairs, TV*
Cell 4: JAMES *(The Songbird) – A chair*

Lighting: Lights, overhead, sends out bars of light so that the actors step through the bars throughout. A single bulb in each cell.

SCENE 1

The sound of crows fighting. The fight grows louder and louder, with violent squawking, then sudden silence. In the dark MATTIE *in Cell 1 is screaming.*

MATTIE: What the fuck! Hey! Shit! Take that. What do you think you're at? What! Where are we going? Stay away from me. No one's going to hurt me – where are we going? I ain't saying nothing. To no one.

[*To left in Cell 4 the light comes on.* JAMES *the songbird is alone, already up and dressed, seated in his chair, facing to the side. Pause. The light comes on in* MATTIE*'s cell to the right.* MATTIE *sits down on the chair looking around him, head down. Violent sound of the master lock being unlocked.* MATTIE *heads straight out, and stands on duty. An* OFFICER *appears from the left, walks in front of the cells, left to right.*]

OFFICER: Officer on the ones. Fifty-seven all clear.

[*Light up on Cell 3 with* OLLIE *and* DANNY. *They are getting dressed.*]

OLLIE: So what's the story?
DANNY: The same.
[*Roar of TV Channels.*]
AUDIENCE VOICES: Get up ya lazy fucker ya.
Rise and shine.
Leave us alone.
Turn down the fucking TV.
[OFFICER *returns, walks right to left.*]
OFFICER: Officer on the twos. Forty-five all clear.
AUDIENCE VOICES: What war is that?
You said what?
Slow up will ya.
He got done.
Get the skins, get the skins.
[OFFICER *returns, walks left to right, checks, then walks right to left.*]
OFFICER: Officer on the threes. Forty-five all clear.
AUDIENCE VOICES: What are ya fucking saying?
Why?
Who?
You're talking shite.
[*Sound of doors banging off-stage right and left.* OFFICER *leans into* JAMES*'s door.*]
OFFICER: Breakfast! You going down the yard today James?
JAMES: No.
OFFICER: You staying here?
JAMES: I'm going scrubbing the landing.
[OFFICER *stops at* DANNY *and* OLLIE's *Cell 3.*]
OFFICER: Breakfast!
[*Another door bangs off-stage.* JAMES *heads out and returns with a bucket and mop.* OFFICER *heads into* JER *and* DAVE*'s Cell 2, still dark.*]
OFFICER: Breakfast!
[*Then he looks round him, and goes back left.* MATTIE *returns into cell, sits, lifts headphone.* DANNY *in cell 3 is first up, standing on his chair, looking right through the back window.*]
DANNY: There's not a soul.

DAVE: 8.15. Don't get up. [*To himself.*] They're going too fast out there.

[*Bang of another door.*]

JER: No boss.

DAVE: 8.20. Don't get up. We'll wait till it quietens down.

OFFICER: [*Shouts going away.*] Breakfast!

[*Bang. No stir.* MATTIE *steps out of his cell and goes to Cell 2.*]

MATTIE: Hup! [*He then goes into cell 3.*] Hup! [*Back into his own cell.*]

[OLLIE *sits in his chair.* DANNY *turns away from the window and stands beside him, and sits looking at the ground. The sound of crows.* MATTIE *gives an imaginary guitar a rattle.* OLLIE *changes channels on the TV.*]

OLLIE: It's the fucking crows tell you when to change the channel.

DANNY: Is there an engine under Mattie's arse?

[JER *claps his hands and gets up and puts on the light in Cell 2 and puts on his shirt and trousers, then steps out.* JAMES *stirs the mop in the bucket over and over.* MATTIE, *in his vest, is listening to earphones.* JER *steps out and faces the audience; audience shouts at him.*]

AUDIENCE VOICES: You're only a rat. Wait till the yard!

Listen bollix.

Bang, bang, you're fucking dead.

Hi boy!

Get out of that bed.

Breakfast.

I want to stay in the bucking bed.

Stay in the bucking bed.

Hallo sweetie.

JAMES: [*Sings.*] The pipes, the pipes are calling . . .

AUDIENCE VOICES: Do you think you are a fucking doorman?

Breakfast.

I'm getting out today.

Up Leeds!

Eejits.

Good luck.
Fuck you and Sligo.
And fuck Limerick too.
[JER *steps in, shakes his head.*]

JER: Fucking bastards.

DAVE: Have you got the remote control?

OFFICER: All right on the ones!

JER: It won't get rid of them.

DAVE: I was somewhere else till that din started.

JER: Where were you?

DAVE: I was on my way to the nightclub.

JER: The Asylum?

DAVE: No, the Oz. I had everything. Yeh, having a fine time. [DANNY *puts on the kettle.* JER *puts on the kettle.* MATTIE *writes down something into notebook, then stands.* JAMES *hits the bucket a kick.*] Yes Ollie. [DAVE *turns to the left, and shouts at the wall as on the other side* OLLIE *dresses.*] Are you up yet Mister Ollie? I'll bet you he has his shirt on. Now the trousers. You're losing weight ya fucker ya. [*Turns to the right, shouts at the wall.*] Look in the mirror Mattie – are you still there? Who's not a happy fellow? You missed under your ear. Who do you see? Don't do it Mattie. Ah don't. Ah Jazus Mattie. Just push it out Mattie, easy this once, please, not all the way, and we'll wait till it quietens down a little. MATTIE *imitates banging of door, and goes out onto the landing.* JAMES *hits the bucket.*] Jesus. Bang it out straight. Right! [MATTIE *re-enters like a soldier on parade.* JAMES *hits the bucket.*] And then will you bang it out for the dinner. [OLLIE *goes out, bangs the imaginary door and re-enters.*] Thank you Ollie. After tea, bang it out. [OLLIE *leaves and re-enters.* JAMES *hits the bucket.*] Bang it out for the night. Good man Mattie. I hear you.

[DANNY *looks at* OLLIE, *then at the floor, joins his hands, a bit down in himself. He lifts out a pretend mobile, looks at it, reads it.*]

OFFICER: All right on two! Breakfast.

[MATTIE *rises and gets up again, pulls the imaginary door*

after him with a bang, then sits down and puts on his earphones.]

DAVE: Good man Mattie. Bang it out good and loud. Up for breakfast, bang it. Fall out, bang it.

JER: Clean out cell . . .

DAVE: Bang it. Off to school.

JER: Or out for a few laps, yes, out to D yard for a few laps.

DAVE: Head back to the landing, and . . .

JER: Bang it.

DAVE: Back out for dinner. Then up maybe for a bit of woodwork.

JER: Nice one.

DAVE: Now come back in after tea, and . . .

JER: What about the gym?

DAVE: Right, into the gym for a few exercises, will that do ya, but not today, and don't forget, and . . .

JER: Bang it.

MATTIE: [*Ear phones on.*] All stations . . .

DAVE: Right. Fall into the rec for a game of pool.

MATTIE: Calling all stations . . .

JER: And the buzz.

DAVE: Then fall in, fall in, and . . .

JER: And bang it out.

DAVE: For the night.

MATTIE: Calling all stations, this is three nines. Over.

JER: Done boss.

DANNY: Then the car hit the milk truck.

OLLIE: Hah?

OFFICER: All right on the three's.

[JAMES *the songbird is mopping his cell.* OLLIE *is eating a bowl of cornflakes.* DANNY *is rolling fags. On both sides the kettles boils.* MATTIE *writes as he speaks.*]

MATTIE: Groundhog, Over.
Pull back there! Over.
What's going on? Over.
Receiving you, do I read you?
You have no way out. Over.

SCENE 2

DAVE *gets up and shakes his shoulders and stands as if playing on a golf tee.* JER *pours tea.* DANNY *pours tea. Pause.* OLLIE *eats without looking at* DANNY. MATTIE *puts down his earphones, sits a moment, then rises to shave.* DAVE *plays a golf stroke, and he and* JER *watch an imaginary ball cross the green and then maybe drop.* DAVE *nods to the imaginary crowd, tips his cap, leans down and takes the imaginary ball out, blows on it, gives it a rub under his oxter, and turns to go.*

JER: You missed it again.

DAVE: I know. But I'm getting better

JER: If you got up earlier, you'd improve.

DAVE: It's the screws are putting me off. I'm trying not to hear them.

JER: Well I've tuned me head in not to hear them. [DAVE *steadies himself to take another golf shot. In the distance a further bang.* MATTIE *begins to shave.*] They play golf where you came from?

DANNY: Ollie I'm fucked.

OLLIE: Easy man.

DAVE: No. I only took it up since I came inside. Golf is good for the head. You get a lotta fresh air, like. [JER *lies back.*] Even if it's only in your head. And you don't need to talk if you don't want to. Life is not all one rap. [*Taps his head.*] Like in here. [*Taps temple, forelock. Stands at imaginary wall between Cell 1 and Cell 2.* MATTIE *is facing him, shaving.*]

DAVE: You in there Mister Heavy, Mister fucking serious? You hear me Sergeant? Below the left ear I told you. I can see what you're thinking. NO, LIFE IS NOT ALL ONE RAP. Unless it's heavy. If it's heavy I'll chat. If you don't chat when it's heavy you'd go light in the head. [*He turns and goes to the wall of Cell 3.*] Right Ollie, okay? You hear me Ollie? [*He turns, leans down and shouts to his left, along the pipe in* OLLIE*'s direction.*] Hi Ollie. [OLLIE *makes no reply, nor does he move.*] Tell me this OLLIE . . .

DANNY: [*Into pretend mobile.*] Hallo.
OLLIE: You hear something?
DANNY: No.
[JAMES *leans down to the pipe.*]
JAMES: Wrong number.
OLLIE: Neither did I.
DAVE: Are you there Oliver?
DANNY: Hallo?
OLLIE: There it goes again.
DANNY: It must be your imagination.
OLLIE: Yeh. As long as it's not my fucking paranoia.
DANNY: Are they not the same thing?
OLLIE: Fuck sake man.
DAVE: [*Through wall.*] You gay Ollie?
OLLIE: I think you're fucking right. You ever get bad vibes about this place?
DANNY: If you're going to stand there looking at the wall man, what do you think you get – fucking good vibrations?
JER: One of these days the boys will hear ya.
DAVE: They're too thick.
JER: Who, the walls or the blokes?
OLLIE: Yeh right, you'll like this one. Do you know what the light at the end of the tunnel is?
DANNY: No.
OLLIE: A boy in the Grove told me. The light at the end of the tunnel is the light of the approaching train.
DANNY: I like it. Yeh man, got ya, step out of the way real fast like.
[OLLIE *steps back from walls, and he and* DAVE *move till they are actually facing each other.*]
DAVE: You fucked up Ollie.
OLLIE: I wonder what he's saying right now.
DAVE: I'm saying Bang. Bang. Bang. So what's the story, so what's the fucking story? Jesus H. Christ, yes, another day. Right.
[*He turns away as does* OLLIE *after him.*]
DANNY: [*Into pretend mobile, no answer.*] Hallo, hallo.

[MATTIE *leaves down his shaving gear, and puts on his earphones.* OLLIE *starts mopping.* JAMES *mops.* DAVE *plays imaginary golf.*]

MATTIE: 6-10, this is thirty-four alpha. It's raining in the desert. The sand sticks like glue.

DAVE: I'm down to a handicap of nine. Nine to go. I opened at a handicap of 18 months. Not bad, huh?

JER: Not bad. [*Shouting outside.*] Listen to that, the shirts and ties, shouting about absolutely nothing.

OFFICER: [*Shouting.*] Teddy Moran, where's Teddy Moran?

[DAVE *plays a low putt.*]

JER: Nice one, nice one.

[*Next door* JAMES *mops.*]

DAVE: Me stroke is getting better but I'm running out of dirty thoughts.

JER: Put your name down for a phone call.

DAVE: She won't talk to me.

[*Tries a golf putt.*]

JER: I'm not surprised.

OFFICER: Teddy Moran!

JAMES: [*Singing.*] Help, I need somebody . . .

DANNY: Someone should tell him that Teddy Moran is still snoring. I was going to see my father but I didn't. I should have.

OLLIE: It's better to leave the stuffing in.

DANNY: Life is just a break from being dead.

OLLIE: Yes, Danny.

JER: She won't talk to you.

DAVE: No. But she will. In time.

JER: Send her a letter.

DAVE: Maybe later. Send her a letter? Right, I will then. Tonight?

JER: Whenever you want.

DAVE: You're one sound man. Aye.

MATTIE: All stations this is zero. Where are you, where are you? Over.

[DAVE *goes to lift a pretend ball.*]

OFFICER: Fall out!

[MATTIE *puts down earphones. All six of them stand outside their cells in various postures:* DAVE *smiling,* JER *watchful,* DANNY *looking about him,* MATTIE *looking straight ahead,* OLLIE *at the floor,* JAMES *standing solid. They all take a look towards* JAMES, *then face forward as the* OFFICER *approaches.*]

OLLIE: What was her first name?

DANNY: [*Fast.*] Rita.

DAVE: [*Fast.*] Alice.

JER: [*Fast.*] Catherine.

OLLIE: Hey – [*Looks at* JER, *then looks back to the front.*] – that's my bird.

OFFICER: Warder Wilson, one hundred and 24, B Wing, nine o'clock.

JER: It's been downhill since James Bond became an Irishman – that's what my Da used ta say. I didn't know he was Irish, did you?

DANNY: Who, your father?

JER: Fuck sake.

[OFFICER *walks by each prisoner; looks into their faces. The* OFFICER *goes out to the extreme right.*]

OFFICER: All clear on three. Clear the landing.

SCENE 3

They all step back into their cells, moving more quickly, all getting ready to go out – dressing up, doing their hair, etc.

DAVE: Jer, where's me mobile?

JER: The Cherokee took it. Steady. Here. [*Hands him nothing.*] You hid it in my fucking locker. So I'd get the fucking blame. If you were there without your mobile on the top of Everest what would you do?

DAVE: I'd throw myself off.

JER: Good one.

DAVE: [DAVE *starts tapping off numbers on pretend mobile.*]

Bump! Bump! Bum! [*He looks at the palm of his hand.*] Fuck, it's the wrong number. [*He rings again.*] Flip! Bump! Bump! Bum! Bum! Bup! Bup! Bo-bo! [*Listens.*] Hallo? Is that you? What are you saying? Where am I? Where the fuck do you think I am? In Paris or maybe Amsterdam. [*He slaps palm.*] I say, there. [*To* JER *in a posh accent.*] I say there old boy, where are we? [*Phone back to ear.*] He doesn't know where we are either. What? You feckin half-wit. [*Puts away the phone.*] Do you hear that, he asked me where I was ringing from – and then he said he was sorry.

[MATTIE *begins push-ups.*]

DANNY: How did the car hit the milk truck? That boy I'm with in three lost me two bottles of coke. I'll have one of them straights. Is there any water left in the kettle?

OLLIE: Slow down, will ya.

DANNY: I met that fat bollix from that fucking hole, Limerick – you know what he sez? He sez just out there to me . . .

JER: "You're sweet enough without sugar."

DANNY: He sez to me, "You're sweet enough without sugar."

OLLIE: Just nod and listen to his story, okay – just listen and say nothing, okay?

DANNY: Right.

OLLIE: Are you clean like?

DANNY: Yeh.

JER: Well give us a drag of that after ya then, will ya?

[JAMES *begins mopping madly. All of them begin putting their cell equipment out of sight, and move the chairs straight against the back wall.* JAMES *begins with the mop and bucket and heads off stage, mopping to stage right.* MATTIE *lifts headphones and begins writing.*]

DANNY: She loved me like no other one before her and all I gave her was the three H's. The three H's. And that's how I broke her heart. [*Hands fag over.*]

OLLIE: Thanks Danny. [*Stops and Smokes.*]

MATTIE: Take the road to the left.

No, they're dug in there.

Take it out.

Groundhog, all stations, this is three.

All stations, this is three nines. Lebanon. 6-4-2.

This is zero. Over.

[*Looks away.*] I can't talk right now.

[*Back in to headphones.*] Zero. Over.

Pull back there. Over.

What's going on? Over.

Over. [MATTIE *puts down his headphones and reads the notebook and then starts correcting it.*]

DANNY: My nerves hum with fear and I had great feelings of loss. Am I on my own now, or was I thinking too much? [DANNY *sits, takes cigarette, stands, sits, lifts out folder, and writes.*]

[JAMES *appears from stage left and mops across the front of the stage.*]

JAMES: Put that thing back where it was, will ya?

DANNY: I just wrote down my name. I want to practise my signature before I get out.

OLLIE: You wanna get it right the next time.

DANNY: That's right. But I don't know which road to go.

JAMES: Room, please.

OLLIE: [*Takes back fag.*] You're thinking too much.

[DAVE *looks at his pretend mobile. He puts it away after switching off.*]

DANNY: Maybe. Maybe, maybe. When I was young I was put on the honours list.

OLLIE: Fuck sake, you were lucky you weren't on a hit list.

DANNY: Yes. I was granted an OBE.

OLLIE: Oh yeah?

DANNY: Yeh. An OBE.

OLLIE: What da fuck is an OBE?

DANNY: I'll tell you. An outta body experience.

JAMES: Nice day.

DANNY: There was darkness with a bright light. There I am. I see an uncontrollable light. Now wait a second. An uncolourable light, knowing everything is a split second that lasts a lifetime. I was touched as a child by a man dressed as a clown.

OLLIE: Don't start.

DANNY: I was touched by a man dressed as a clown.

OLLIE: Yes Danny, but let's not go back there again.

[DAVE *and* JER *start going outside,* JER *looks round the cell, and switches off the light.*]

DANNY: You don't like it. I was abused as a child.

OLLIE: I hear you Danny.

DANNY: Twenty years of overdosing and not being allowed to die. Watching my own son born through a smacked-up haze, having him taken away, because I'm the biggest waster in this room. You hear me.

OLLIE: Yes Danny. We better get a move on.

[JER *and* DAVE *face the audience.* OFFICER *strolls out front by* AUDIENCE, *then turns and goes the other way.*]

AUDIENCE: Well sham.
Bush sucks, fuck Saddam.
Every day is a war.
Watch the rabbits.
Watch your back.
I like the goats.
Look at that, it's a Sligo tash.
Take it off.

[JAMES *is mouthing a song as he mops very tightly at one spot.*]

JAMES: Oh Danny boy, the pipes the pipes are calling . . .

[DANNY *and* OLLIE *doing the last clean-up of their cell.* OFFICER *comes back on stage.*]

DANNY: I am responsible for my own actions. Okay?

OLLIE: I know you are, let's go.

DANNY: I have a kettle, I have a bed, I have a remote.

DAVE: He asked me where I fucking was. And then he said he was fucking sorry. I should have said I was on the steps of a church going into me wedding.

[MATTIE *switches off his room light, leaves his cell, and stands in front of it.* JAMES *turns to another song.*]

JAMES: Mona Lisa, Mona Lisa . . .

DANNY: I should not have let him touch me. [*Pause.*] The clown. And still I live with this weight of guilt, bearing down on me like a universe of souls. [*Pause.*] Between Heaven and Hell. [*Pause.*] For twenty years I've tried to forget, but now all I want to do is wake up from this dream.

OLLIE: It's not your fault, come on.

DANNY: Filled to boiling point with hate and confusion and only myself to blame. I'm fucked Ollie . . .

OLLIE: I know. [OLLIE *douses cigarette, switches off his cell light, and he and* DANNY *step out.*]

[*They stand facing the audience with* JER *and* DANNY. JAMES *reaches his own cell and enters. His is the only cell still lit.* DANNY *looks into* JAMES*'s cell, as do* JER *and* DAVE.]

DAVE: Morning James.

JAMES: Morning.

JER: James.

JAMES: Not so bad.

OFFICER: You going mopping today James?

JAMES: I am. [*Sings.*] From glen to glen and down the mountainside, the summer's gone, and all the . . . [He hums the rest.] . . . I need you so. [JAMES *continues to hum, leans up, and switches off the light. The stage goes dark.* JAMES*'s hum continues as he moves towards the audience.*]

SCENE 4
The First Lap

A wide light comes on. The prisoners begin moving around in a circle. JAMES, *pushing his mop ahead of him, has descended amongst the audience and pushes his mop up one of the side aisles in the theatre. The routine of getting together to go outside and do the laps begins. First they walk by the* OFFICER *who watches them. Then they wait for one and another, one stepping ahead, one looking back, the others catching up and looking round. Waiting.* MATTIE *starts moving by himself. They watch him. Then* OLLIE *starts his walk and steps off, stage right, alone.*

DANNY: What's up Dave?

DAVE: I was out last night for a while.

[*The lap begins with* MATTIE *ahead.*]

DANNY: Good for you Dave.

DAVE: I surely was, no bother, I got to the Asylum.

DANNY: The Asylum is a good old nightclub.

JER: I never liked it.

DANNY: No-one asked you.

JER: It's a shithole.

[MATTIE *drops back behind them.*]

DAVE: On the way, the wipers were going like hell. Hit a ditch again going at a hundred miles an hour. Didn't get a scratch this time either. It was very spooky. This auld fella said I had nine lives. Went onto a nightclub and got a round.

JAMES: [*Down somewhere in the theatre.*] Excuse me.

[*The lap now starts at a certain pace.* MATTIE*'s walk is continuous, without looking at the others.*]

MATTIE: Could we have less of the fucking fantasy?

DAVE: I was only saying.

MATTIE: I was only saying. I was only fucking saying.

DAVE: I say to myself each morning, I won't talk to him, fuck him, and I don't.

JER: You don't.

DAVE: And then I fucking do.

JER: You do.

DANNY: You can't help it.

DAVE: Were you out last night Mattie?

[MATTIE *stops; they all stop.*]

MATTIE: Yeh, I had gun against a guy's head and I waited maybe a long time then I pulled the trigger, and woke up saying that it was only a dream. Then I looked around and found myself in a cell in D wing, and that was real.

DANNY: That's heavy.

MATTIE: It was only a dream, you want to have been round for the real thing.

JAMES: [*Sings.*] Along the Banks of the Royal Canal . . . Take me home, Take me home . . .

DANNY: It's serious, Sergeant.

MATTIE: Yeh son, its serious shit.

[*They start moving slow.*]

DAVE: I see what you mean. Same for me. Like, if everything is alright, I'll say nothing.

MATTIE: No?

DAVE: No. Unless it's heavy. Like what you're saying like. If it's heavy I'll chat. If you don't chat when it's heavy you'd go light in the head. So you see, I'm only saying. Right Mattie, Okay?

MATTIE: That's your problem. I was only saying. I was only fucking saying. Shit.

[*They start moving faster as* MATTIE *gets faster.*]

DAVE: What's wrong with ya?

MATTIE: You see what you were saying there drives me fucking up the wall, you were only saying something like you wouldn't talk to him, what the fuck are you saying, you fuckin chat non-stop man. [*He turns.*] It's bang this, and bang that, bang-bang you're fucking dead, a man can't enjoy his fucking breakfast, move your fucking legs, is it heavy Mister Dave this morning, is it heavy?

DAVE: No.

MATTIE: No? Well then you should not be talking. Stay quiet. Give her a rest. "Dún do hole and practise self-control."

DAVE: [*Humouring him.*] How do you do that, soldier?

MATTIE: You don't get caught. The ones that get caught can't keep their trap shut.

DAVE: [*Sharply.*] What are you saying?

[*All stop.*]

MATTIE: Nothing – you don't fucking like it?

DAVE: No, I don't fucking like it.

MATTIE: Well I'm sorry auld skin.

DAVE: Man, I don't want to speak outta place but you're always acting like you're above us . . .

MATTIE: No, I'm no better than you, meaning I'm worse, that's why I'm trying to advise you.

DAVE: Right, but you're in here.

MATTIE: Yeh, but I'm not with your fucking gang.

JER: But if you're in here it means you got caught as well, didn't ya?

DAVE: Yes, that's right, you got fucking caught too – [*Nodding triumphantly at the insight and the logic.*] – like the rest of us.

MATTIE: Did I?

JER: Course you did.

DANNY: Yeh, aren't you in here with us, aren't ya?

MATTIE: No, I'm not with you shites. You do what you like – but leave me alone. You're a new boy, you'll learn.

DANNY: I'm in here a fucking year.

MATTIE: Yeh, that's what I mean.

DANNY: Learn what?

MATTIE: It depends how you behave yourself son.

DAVE: What's the fucking difference between you and us?

MATTIE: I'll tell ya.

DAVE: Go ahead then.

MATTIE: I don't intend to get caught the next time, that's the difference.

DANNY: Neither do I.

MATTIE: Good for you.

DANNY: Cause I'm going straight.

DAVE: Fuck sake.

MATTIE: I don't intend to get caught either way. That's why I don't watch telly. So meanwhile no head-banging. [*He puts his finger to his lips.*] See, till then – it's . . . [*Silence.*]

DANNY: Sh!

JER: Bang!

DAVE: Fucking – [*Pause.*] – bang-bang!

MATTIE: [*Finger up.*] The fucking drugs. Yeh, the fucking drugs.

DAVE: I think you take the odd snort yourself, Mattie.

MATTIE: You are fucking druggies.

JER: Would you like us better if we were in the IRA?

MATTIE: If you were political, I'd be fucking well away because you wouldn't be talking to me. And because you're fucking sky high half the time no one can know what the fuck you're talking about anyway.

DAVE: Ah but you do, Sergeant.

MATTIE: [*Quietly, bringing it to an end.*] Yeh, I was young once.
[MATTIE *heads off alone ahead of them.*]
DAVE: He's like a fucking flashback. Sometimes I think I invented him. You know like he's in here. [*Taps head, as before.*] He's a bit like – [*Upper class accent.*] – "Oh dear so, oh dear so," is Mattie – you know the type I mean.
OLLIE: It's all them years in the Leb.
DANNY: The laughing shaft.
JER: The Phoenix Park.
[*They start after him, laughing.*]
MATTIE: Shites.

SCENE 5
The Second Lap

The lap continues. A stronger pace. They go around twice in silence. MATTIE*'s walk is continuous, without looking back at the others. And then he disappears. Then* OLLIE *appears watching them all, and begins moving at a slower rate.*

JER: You see that drink you ordered last night in the Asylum?
DAVE: Yeh?
JER: Well you better put in the order again.
DAVE: What d'ya mean?
JER: Here's your auld mate.
[*All turn.*]
DANNY: Mister So-what is coming.
DAVE: I think I need a vacation from this planet.
JER: He has his eye on ya.
DANNY: He's waving.
JER: Watch him.
DANNY: He looks high.
DAVE: Fuck.
JER: Will you fucking look at him.
[*All turn.*]
DAVE: Don't fucking look at him.

DANNY: He's fucking high.

JER: He is.

DANNY: There's no chemical solution to a spiritual problem.

DAVE: If I hear – [*Imitating* OLLIE's *accent.*] – "What's the story?" again, I'll give him one.

OLLIE: Lads . . .

JER: Ollie.

DANNY: Well sham?

[*All turn.*]

OLLIE: Hallo Sligo, Jer, so what's . . .

JER: [*Interrupts. Long drawn out tone of here-we-go-again.*] Yeh?

DANNY: [*Contemptuous.*] Yeh?

OLLIE: [*Brief, and flirty, agreeably.*]Yeh?

DANNY: Go on.

JER: Get it over with.

OLLIE: Well, I was going to say, so . . .

[*All stop.*]

JAMES: [*Sings, down in the theatre.*]

The Auld Triangle.
Goes Jingle Jangle.
Along the banks of the Royal Canal.

DANNY: Yeh?

JER: Go for it.

[*All turn away from* OLLIE.]

OLLIE: Wha?

JER: Don't say it mate.

OLLIE: Say what?

DANNY: It doesn't go down well . . .

JER: . . .First thing in the morning.

OLLIE: I said nothing.

DAVE: So far.

[*They begin to move.*]

JER: Oh but you will.

DANNY: You fucker ya.

OLLIE: Look, what's . . .

[*The lap starts going faster.*]

DANNY: Go on.

OLLIE: I said nuttin.

JER: It's not what you said, sham, it was what you were going to say.

OLLIE: Say what? I don't know what I was going to say.

DANNY: Well don't say it.

OLLIE: Do you hear me – I haven't a clue what de be Jazus I was going to say.

DANNY: Well I know what you were going to say.

OLLIE: What the fuck was I going to say?

[*They start slowing down.*]

DANNY: You were going to say . . .

OLLIE: I can't think.

DANNY: Don't tell us what you're thinking.

JER: We don't want to know.

DANNY: Keep your mind to yourself.

JER: Ya dirty fucker.

[*They stop.*]

DANNY: So out with it.

JER: That's it . . .

DANNY: Go on son . . .

JER: Come on Ollie. Go on, say it.

DAVE: Out with it.

OLLIE: Out with what Dave?

DAVE: Say it you fucker ya.

OLLIE: I haven't opened me fucking mouth.

DAVE: Ah but when you do, you'll say it.

OLLIE: Say what! Ya fuckin Dublin ginnet!

DANNY: Ya fucking Atlantic savage, say it!

JER: Just say it.

OLLIE: Ah fuck. Alright. [*Pause, poses, touches chest like opera singer.*] So: what's the story, morning glory?

JER: Ohohhh.

OLLIE: Ah.

[*They head off again at a fast rate.*]

JAMES: [*Sings down at the back of the theatre.*]

You go your way,
And I'll go mine,

Done for ever till the end of time,
I'll find somebody new,
And baby we'll say we're through,
So I guess it doesn't matter anymore.

SCENE 6
The Third Lap

OLLIE: You know what happened to Sarah Smith?

JER: No, tell us, but no-one is to laugh.

OLLIE: She smoked banana skins and got pregnant.

[*No-one laughs. Pause.*]

JER: Try again boss.

DAVE: And no . . .

JER: . . .Fucking laughing . . .

DANNY: . . .Okay?

OLLIE: [*Putting on a child's voice.*] You can't have your ball back, I know your parents.

[*No-one laughs. Then* DANNY *bursts out laughing.*]

DAVE: You're like that wall – see that wall? – that wall is thick.

OLLIE: I am the wall right round this prison. I'm the one what keeps you in. Isn't that right, Mister Lithuania? I say, Mister Lithuania?

SERGOSA: [SERGOSA *answers down in the audience.*] Yes Holly.

OLLIE: You hear me, Sergosa?

SERGOSA: Twelve luin didaps mig am twenty-six di ani.

DANNY: [*Disbelievingly.*] Go on.

SERGOSA: Se frau cand mauc aicasa.

DANNY: Wow! Far out!

SERGOSA: Frau casa, frau casa.

DANNY: Got ya.

JER: You understand him?

OLLIE: Yeh, he does, they're auld mates.

JER: What's he saying?

DANNY: He's saying: "Time bandits, with the midgets, are travelling through space."

JER: Is that what he said?

DANNY: Yeh.

JER: Yeh.

DANNY: No problem. You learn a lot of languages as a doorman. It's serious stuff.

[MATTIE *reappears and re-joins the walk, like a soldier on parade.*]

MATTIE: You said serious.

DANNY: Yeh, I did.

MATTIE: So you guys are talking serious.

DAVE: He is, not me, I can't do serious.

MATTIE: Well. What I say is keep it real.

DAVE: I'll try.

MATTIE: Try harder.

DAVE: I'm trying.

MATTIE: Right, because life is too short. You know what we are – we're an army.

OLLIE: Well I'm not going tootin' guns to Baghdad.

MATTIE: We're an army without a war.

DAVE: Yeh, Sergeant. But I can't do serious.

DANNY: Why, what happened ya?

MATTIE: He began laughing at his own jokes.

DAVE: No, Mattie, wrong. On the first count. What happens is – I listen to you and you listen to me. The difference is – when you're speaking it's not my story, ye see, it's yours. And yours is serious.

MATTIE: Cut the crap. Everyone is serious.

DANNY: Tell me this – why would someone like you for fifteen minutes, and then not like you for the second fifteen minutes?

OLLIE: That's easy.

DANNY: Is it?

OLLIE: Yeh, they were only getting to know you.

JER: Then they found out you were a bollix.

DANNY: Ha-ha.

JER: My friends blew me out soon as I went to jail. The fucking shitheads, may they suffer badly, even more.

MATTIE: You want outta here, you gotta be serious.

DAVE: Serious, no. I had a plan. I was going to grow old, have a happy life, be adored, and . . .

MATTIE: Life is a bitch and then you die.

DAVE: No, Mattie, none of that dying shit – I ripped that plan up. I looked at it and I said no. I got it out of my brain.

DANNY: Listen . . .

OLLIE: Go for it Danny.

DANNY: . . .The brain is an alien that gets in your ear at night when you're a baby and sends you looking for trouble.

JER: And looking for women, but you don't mention that.

MATTIE: Alright boys. You could call the brain a pussy, but I don't want anyone fucking with mine. You hear me?

DAVE: You're back being serious. I'm good at thinking serious, but I'm not good at talking serious.

MATTIE: Well be serious. If you want to do time, you have to be serious. You can't tell jokes all your fucking life.

[DAVE *stops. Then the rest stop.*]

DAVE: Mom told me to be still, to stand still, and it wouldn't sting me. I stood still and it stung the fuck out of me.

MATTIE: So what?

DANNY: [*Suddenly, a note of sympathy.*] You see, he forgave her.

DAVE: Yeh, I forgave her. [*Kind of surprised by himself.*] Yes Danny. But . . . I said I don't do serious. [*Slow.*] Serious is bitter. [*Slow.*] And bitter is sour. [*Pause.*] And I'm not sour. Okay?

DANNY: Good one Dave.

MATTIE: Yeh, but bitterness – [*He bites the word.*] – is real.

[DAVE *starts walking. Then the others start walking.*]

DAVE: Do you know what bitterness is?

MATTIE: Yeh, I can hear it in your voice.

DAVE: Wanker.

DANNY: Bitterness is real s-e-r-i-o-u-s.

OLLIE: Fuck sake.

DANNY: What happen is you – [*Points at* OLLIE.] – start talking to the wall.

OLLIE: Hey – watch it.

DAVE: Okay, Ollie, you tell us what bitterness is.

OLLIE: Alright, let me think. [*Pause.*] Bitterness is the disease that stops you breaking life's chain.

JER: And that's when it hurts.

DAVE: Not bad Ollie, but it's worse than that.

OLLIE: Yeh okay, you take it away Danny.

DANNY: Bitterness is the rust on the chain.

DAVE: You got it Danny.

DANNY: [*Getting better at it.*] Bitterness is regret.

DAVE: Yeah man – you hear that, Mattie?

MATTIE: I regret nothing.

DANNY: [*Looking at* MATTIE, *then* DAVE.] Bitterness is futile.

DAVE: Good man Danny, but why are you saying it to me, like? [DAVE *stops walking.*] Why are you looking at me like that? Do you think I come across as bitter?

DANNY: No. [*Studies him.*] But you could always get a haircut.

OLLIE: When you get out.

DANNY: Like get it cut off for charity, or something.

[*They all start walking again.*]

DAVE: Fuck me, thanks lads. Are you two on the same medication?

DANNY: Yeh.

OLLIE: What I have he takes for my headache.

DANNY: And what I've got I can't take because it's gone down his gullet.

DAVE: Could I have some of what you're on?

OLLIE: We'll have to think about it.

DANNY: And it'll cost you.

DAVE: And then I'll end up looking like you.

MATTIE: You think it's a joke, Dave – it's not a joke.

DAVE: If it's not a joke what is it?

DANNY: It's heavy.

DAVE: Exactly.

DANNY: And heavy . . .

DAVE: . . .Is a drag.

MATTIE: [*To* DAVE.] That you can't carry.

JER: Easy Mattie.

DANNY: Hey man, I wouldn't like to be coming down off an E with you at the party.

MATTIE: I wouldn't go to no party with you.

DANNY: Pity. It was nice while it lasted.

MATTIE: See the guy from Nairobi, he kissed the ground when he got out.

DAVE: All right, when I get out, I'll kiss your arse, alright? But funny thing is, you might be still in here, see what I mean? Now see what you're missing. And that's what you get for being serious – you make the journey longer, and you don't get me to kiss your arse, alright?

MATTIE: Wrong boss, I'm biding my time. [MATTIE *stops. The rest move on. He follows on talking.*] And you're doing it. I'm doing my time out there man, and not in here, with you fuckers, see. So keep it real, yeh. I'm gonna hang a sign on the door, right, and what will it say? It'll say "Real." Right? Fucking real, okay?

DAVE: Okay Mattie. Okay. Got ya. But I don't care. I don't do serious.

[*They all stop walking.*]

JER: Did you volunteer Mattie?

MATTIE: I might have volunteered. To the bomb squad. I don't know. I was too drunk at the time to remember.

DANNY: The whole thing is a mystery.

JER: Yeh.

DANNY: And wherever there's mystery there's shit. The two go together – shit and mystery. I've known plenty of shit and that's why I know there must be a mystery.

[*Stop. They stand together.*]

END

A Night at the Disco

Written and directed in 2006 by Dermot Healy in collaboration with the teachers and students of St Mary's Secondary School, Ballina, Co. Mayo. Part of the "Writers in Schools Project" for Amnesty International, Ireland.

CAST

LAURA
MARGO
SHEILA
JANE
MOTHER
MARY
SHARON
JACINTA
WINNIE
DRIVER
TICKET COLLECTOR
LAD
BOY

Playwright's Note

The script of *A Night at the Disco* would not have been written without the girls and their teacher, Sinead Leonard, at St Mary's School in Ballina. Like everyone else involved in the project, I did not know what to expect when I arrived. It was up to them to direct me towards what might be occupying their minds.

We did a couple of hours work, role-playing, improvising movement and language, and before long a pattern began to emerge: this jarring jaunt the girls reluctantly took by bus each weekend to a disco in Crossmolina, because at the time there was no disco or no cinema available for their age group in Ballina town.

Once this theme was established the language flew. As Sinead pointed out in her notes to me, certain problems in Ballina – a sense of tribalism and the taunting of traveller families – was being exported down the road, by bus, to small parish halls unsuited to the numbers of young people arriving there. Plus the weekly trip created resentment among locals. And this was further exasperated by drinking among the few, and the sense the girls felt of being hated, ignored, and perhaps even feared.

And so the insults and the anger and the bullying and the humour started.

The chatter of the mobiles could not hide the girls' panic.

Out came their sense of being ostracised. Their fear of violence. As Sheila puts it, "there's murder in the women's toilets." And they were all too aware of how they were being judged by their elders: "The cursed hormones," as it was put. Or, in another meaningful dimension, on the mobile phone: "You're breaking up, Ma." The girls provided us with their idioms, Sinead Leonard kept the notes, and eventually I saw that for some, a night at the disco might actually mean being left outside the hall for the entire evening until the bus came back to take them home. This was the worst scenario – the shame of being barred.

> MARY: It's not a crime to come from Ballina, you know.
> TICKET COLLECTOR: No, but if you're looking for trouble it is.

It may be local, and appear trivial, but to them at the time it was all important.

I hope the school get to see the play sometime.

They wrote it, and I listened in.

I'd like to thank them.

—Dermot Healy, 2006

SCENE 1

Two girls – LAURA *and* MARGO *– appear stage right. Two girls –* SHEILA *and* JANE *– appear stage left. All of them are done up for the night. They look at each other, turn away, then begin circling the space.*

LAURA: Who do you think you are?
SHEILA: Are you starten?
LAURA: Go way and wash yourself.
SHEILA: [*Smiles.*] Settle Laura.
[*They circle the space again.*]
LAURA: Who do you think you're looking at, you tramp?
SHEILA: [*Laughing.*] Sooney geth – go away and wash yourself.
LAURA: You knacker.
SHEILA: [*Points at* LAURA*'s shoes.*] Will you look at the state of her in yon gullies.
LAURA: Look at your own.
SHEILA: What's wrong with them?
LAURA: They're sad.
[LAURA *and* MARGO *laugh.*]
SHEILA: I never heard a' shoes being sad. Did you Jane?
JANE: No.
SHEILA: So what do you mean they're sad?
LAURA: They look lonely.
SHEILA: What's so funny?
MARGO: You are.
SHEILA: Go home to Greenhills you.
LAURA: And you go back to St Patrick's.
MARGO: Cholla hollas.
JANE: Snotty bitches.
SHEILA: One of these days . . .
LAURA: You'll what? You'll what, you knacker.

JANE: You'll see, you loser.

[*The four face each other. They smile cruelly at each other. Lights down a little.*]

SCENE 2

MOTHER *is standing with her daughter,* SHEILA.

MOTHER: I don't know what's getting into youse. What is so wrong that youse have to go fighting on the bloody street?

SHEILA: They called us names because of what we were.

MOTHER: Well, why walk the streets?

SHEILA: We have nowhere to go.

MOTHER: You could at least mind your manners.

SHEILA: There's no cinema and no disco.

MOTHER: When I grew up we had no disco and it didn't mean we went fighting like cats.

SHEILA: I hate Ballina.

MOTHER: Well in another couple of years you can up and go.

SHEILA: Everybody is looking for a row, and then when we try to get away they turn on us because we're from Ballina. Some of the people hate us.

MOTHER: I get the picture.

SHEILA: They hate us and turn on us. You want to hear the verbals. They call us anything that comes into their heads.

MOTHER: Well then, don't go to Crossmolina.

SHEILA: It's the only place I can go for a dance.

MOTHER: Every Friday it's the same story.

SHEILA: At first it was grand. Maybe fifty, maybe sixty of us, now there's up on four hundred going, from all over the place, and then the lads from Killala start into the lads from Ballina, and then the girls go ape and there's murder in the women's toilets. It's pure shite.

MOTHER: God in heaven, so now youse are bringing the problem with you to another place?

SHEILA: Is my hair alright?

MOTHER: "Is my hair alright?" Do you hear yourself? Jesus. In the middle of this you ask me that. You and your bloody hair. Your hair is fine.
SHEILA: Cool. Well then I'm for the bus.
MOTHER: Be back, hear, at one. You hear me?
SHEILA: I hear you. Bye Ma.
MOTHER: Bye. And no bad language out there.
SHEILA: No Ma.
MOTHER: I've heard youse at it you know.
SHEILA: And I've heard you. Bye Ma.

[SHEILA *goes off. The* MOTHER *stands a moment looking after her. Shakes her head towards the audience. Lights down.*]

SCENE 3

Lights up. Three girls – MARY, SHARON *and* JACINTA – *getting ready for the dance in Crossmolina.*

MARY: Can I have your jumper?
SHARON: Why do you always want my gear?
MARY: Because it's nicer than mine.
JACINTA: Your gear is pure cool Mary.
SHARON: That's too much lipstick.
MARY: You think so?

[SHARON *swings around in her dress.*]

SHARON: Jacinta, are you going to be dancing with yon yoke?
JACINTA: I might.
SHARON: You must be out of your head. Amn't I right Mary?
MARY: I'm saying nuttin.
JACINTA: You're just a sickener Sharon.
SHARON: I couldn't fancy yon. He gave me a kiss last Christmas and I can still smell him off me.
JACINTA: Well I think he's a finer.
SHARON: It's a good job we don't all have the one taste.
MARY: Is right. What you have to say to yourself is: he's for me, or he's not for me, and if he's for me, well then, he's not for

her or her, that one over there – you see what I mean? [MARY *takes out a bottle and has a slug.*]

JACINTA: What is she saying?

SHARON: Too much Home Economics, I think.

MARY: [*She points at* JACINTA.] Or that one. Not her either, no, no, only for me, little me – that's the way to think.

JACINTA: You're a mean flirt, Miss Meehan.

MARY: I am. I'm a red hot chilli pepper. [MARY *has another slug.*]

SHARON: I'm not going to talk to anybody. If anything starts, I'm off. You hear me. I'm back out and onto the bus like a shot.

MARY: Okay Sharon, okay.

SHARON: I can't face any more trouble. I just feel sick when it starts. [*She taps her head and then her heart.*] In here. Here and here.

JACINTA: It's cool Sharon.

MARY: [*Nodding.*] Yeh.

SCENE 4

From all sides the girls gather and form a bus queue.

SHEILA: How are you Sharon?

SHARON: I'm grand.

[LAURA *and* MARGO *arrive.*]

LAURA: Oh Lord, look at the state of you.

SHEILA: Don't you start again.

LAURA: I might.

SHEILA: Go away from me.

LAURA: We're not looking for a fight. It's like this – when we go to Crossmolina we're all on the one side.

MARGO: All the one tribe.

JANE: For tonight anyway.

MARGO: Aye, for tonight.

MARY: But not Monday.

LAURA: No.

MARY: [*A little bit of a snarl.*] No.
SHARON: [*Changing conversation.*] Where's your man?
SHEILA: He's always late.
[*More girls arrive.*]
WINNIE: Same as mine. The fecker. He's gone lushen. The blasted drink. And do you know what he said last week? He said to me, can I see you after – after what I said – and he sort went all red and tried to speak but all these words came out that he didn't mean to say, he just bumped along. I was nearly sorry for the yoke, so I gave him an auld thump and said go on you idiot.
JANE: Oh I know what you mean. [*A few girls arrive silently.*] Well sham.
JACINTA: I'm grand.
[*Pause.*]
MARY: Why do we do this, tell me.
LAURA: I don't know.
MARY: Well I do.
SHARON: Oh don't start.
MARY: It's like this: if I failed the Leaving it would be worse than getting pregnant – yes?
SHEILA: True.
MARY: And who is it makes that happen?
SHEILA: I don't know.
MARY: Well I'll tell you – you lot. Not the teacher – you.
SHARON: Ah Jazus Mary.
MARY: This is it. You lot, yes. We go bucking discoing in another town, thinking the enemy is out there in Crossmolina and that we are the best of friends. But the truth is we bring the enemy with us. Oh tonight we're the best of friends, but when we sit down at our desks on Monday morning it's you are the enemy. It's all competition and then the bullies come along.
LAURA: Who are you saying is a bully?
MARY: Yes, they say how did you get on sham, oh did ya, did she, oh I'm sorry for her, you loser, you know what I mean, and behind your back they call you . . .

JANE: Granny!
MARGO: Bitch!
WINNIE: Bluebottle!
MARY: They call you Granny because you have a hearing aid.
JACINTA: Ah easy Mary.
MARY: I think it's terrible cruel and I could say worse.
SHARON: Don't.
JANE: I hate when this starts.
SHARON: If you keep on, I'm going home.
LAURA: Yes, will you shut your feckin mouth. I can never make out a word you're saying but I know you're trying to get at me, so stop it – you're driving me crazy.
MARY: [*Screams.*] Own up, all you bullies!
SHARON: Oh Jesus.
LAURA: She's asking for it.
WINNIE: Wait a second girls. A bully is one thing, but on the other hand, all you need is a teacher to get a fix on you, and then you're really in trouble.
JANE: I had that in first year.
SHARON: Look it, we are all in this together, Laura.
LAURA: Aye, and some of us come out of it better than others.
SHEILA: Ah quit.
LAURA: I'll quit. But I mean it.
[*Silence.*]
WINNIE: Are you going posing tonight Laura?
LAURA: I will, Winnie, just for you,
[*A mobile rings.* LAURA *and* MARGO *listen ironically as* SHEILA *turns away to speak.*]
SHEILA: Yes Ma. We're just getting on the bus now for Crossmolina. Oh yeh, I know. Yes. We'll all grow old one day and then . . . Yes Ma. I hear ya, I said we are just getting on the bus. Now, yes. Bye. [*Puts away mobile.*] She does that to embarrass me.
[LAURA *laughs. There is a series of mobiles ringing. All the girls but one lift out their mobiles and begin speaking. A female* DRIVER *in uniform and cap comes forward.*]

DRIVER: Come on girls, come on, get on board, we haven't all night. Jesus, will you look at the state of yiz – a feckin talking shop. Will you come on with the bread? The mobile should be banned in Ireland. You'd think you're hearing things. [*The girls hand over their fares, and stand in two behind the* DRIVER. *The* DRIVER *reaches up to adjust rear-mirror; behind her the chat continues. Then the* DRIVER*'s mobile rings.*] Well boss. How's it cutting?

[*Voices continue to speak into the mobiles unabated.*]

ALL TOGETHER:

Where are you?

I did not.

You're where?

Ah I'm just doing a run.

Stop.

Oh cool.

I never said a word.

Where the feck are you, I've been waiting for hours.

I did not.

Ah the usual.

You tell him to go and shove it.

WINNIE: Dad, yeh, hi dad. Well I had potatoes and carrots, no I'm not going vegetarian, but you see we had lamb for the dinner yesterday and the day before and I couldn't face it again this evening, No, I don't know why we have so much lamb, she just puts it out on the plate so I went for potatoes and . . .

ALL TOGETHER:

Oh that's lovely.

Yes Boss.

You're where?

I feel like we can be better than that.

You think so?

I do, I think we can be good, we're not like all them ones that fight.

Right boss.

See ya.
No I'm on the bus to Crossmolina.
Yeh.
Go away and wash yourself.
Oh pure cool.
Ballina? Ballina is a trap.
Yeh, I suppose you're right, boss.
See ya.
Yeh, I'll be there.
Yeh.
Cool.
We're nearly there.
I'll let you know.
Cool.
See ya.
Bye.
Yeh.
[*Mobiles away. Lights down.*]

SCENE 5

A crowd of girls circle the bus. The Ballina girls start to disembark. The gangs face each other. Sound of music in distance.

VARIOUS ANGRY VOICES OUTSIDE:
Go home where you came from.
If I get as far as ya, you'll know about it.
Go back to Ballina.
Ya scum.
Ya bitches.
Knackers.
MARGO: Look at the face on that one.
LAURA: Come here to me ya bitch.
VOICE: Tramps.
VOICE: Cholla hollas.
[TICKET COLLECTOR *at dance hall appears.*]

TICKET COLLECTOR: Tickets. [*Pause.*] Will you stay quiet? Stop the roaring.
SHARON: One ticket please.
TICKET COLLECTOR: Here you are. Next.
[SHARON *enters.*]
VOICE: Youse are sickeners.
MARY: [*Screams.*] Shut your face.
VOICE: And who will make me?
MARY: Piss off.
TICKET COLLECTOR: I said stay quiet. Next.
JANE: One.
TICKET COLLECTOR: On you go. Next.
WINNIE: A single please.
TICKET COLLECTOR: There you are. [MARY *moves up to him.*] Next! Excuse me, where do you think you're going?
MARY: I'm going to the disco mister.
TICKET COLLECTOR: Is that so, well, stand aside for the moment.
MARY: What?
TICKET COLLECTOR: You heard me – stand aside from the queue.
SHEILA: But she's with us.
TICKET COLLECTOR: I don't care who she's with.
LAURA: Hard luck Mary.
SHEILA: But she's with us.
TICKET COLLECTOR: Do you want to join her? Okay, right. Go on in. C'mon, on with the rest of you. [*The girls file past.*] So you're going to the disco?
MARY: Yes. I'm not standing here for nothing.
TICKET COLLECTOR: I suppose you're not. I'll grant you that.
MARY: So can I have one ticket please?
TICKET COLLECTOR: Where are you from?
MARY: Swinford.
TICKET COLLECTOR: No you're not.
MARY: Yes I am.
TICKET COLLECTOR: No you're not.

MARY: How would you know?

TICKET COLLECTOR: That's easy. I saw you get off the Ballina Bus.

MARY: I did not.

TICKET COLLECTOR: Yes, you did, and you lot cause trouble.

MARY: It's not a crime to come from Ballina, you know.

TICKET COLLECTOR: No, but if you're looking for trouble it is.

MARY: And now you brand us by the bus we got off?

TICKET COLLECTOR: Aye.

MARY: We get blamed for everything.

TICKET COLLECTOR: And sometimes rightly so.

MARY: I've done nothing.

TICKET COLLECTOR: I heard you roaring in the queue.

MARY: I was being got at.

TICKET COLLECTOR: And you've been drinking.

MARY: Could I have my ticket please?

TICKET COLLECTOR: No.

MARY: What do you mean, "no"?

TICKET COLLECTOR: I mean no, you are not getting in.

MARY: What!

TICKET COLLECTOR: You heard me.

MARY: But why? I did nothing to you.

TICKET COLLECTOR: You were shouting, you told me lies, and you've been drinking, and that's enough. Next!

[*A pair of girls go through smiling sarcastically at* MARY.]

MARY: Ah Christ, you're not going to leave me out there for the night?

TICKET COLLECTOR: That's not my problem. Next.

[*Another girl goes through.*]

MARY: I'll have no way home.

TICKET COLLECTOR: You should have thought of that when you turned up at this door drunk.

MARY: I'm not drunk.

TICKET COLLECTOR: Next.

[*Two girls go through.*]

MARY: I wasn't lushen. Ah please.

TICKET COLLECTOR: Next!

[MARY *moves back a bit.*]

VOICE: So he caught on to you, did he, you slut?

MARY: Mind your business.

VOICE: Have a nice night.

TICKET COLLECTOR: Next.

[*The girls file up and march off the stage till there is only* MARY *left. She sits down, looks back at the* TICKET COLLECTOR, *takes a bottle from her bag and swigs, and lowers her head. The sound of music goes up into a crescendo then down again.* MARY *rises and stands.*]

MARY: Hey, you in there – I want to be with my friends. I came here with my friends. And I want to be with them. You hear me! Who do you think you are putting me out into the night? I did nothing. It's always the bloody same. You can brand me any way you like but you won't frighten me. Do you hear me? Why do you hate us, hah! [*Pause.*] I did nothing to you. [*Pause.*] Please. [*Pause. Quietly.*] I said I want to be with my friends.

TICKET COLLECTOR: [*Off-stage.*] Your friends have deserted you Madam.

[*Silence. She backs off and sits. Lights down, music up, cheers off-stage.*]

SCENE 6

MARY *is sitting outside eating chips. A* LAD *comes along.*

LAD: Well you poor thing, did they put you out? [MARY *says nothing.*] Do you want to go for a spin? I have a car back the road. Are you not talking? Sure c'mon.

MARY: Will you do me a favour?

LAD: Sure.

MARY: Leave me alone.

LAD: Have it your own way.

[*As he leaves,* SHARON *comes out. Distant sound of music.*]

SHARON: Hallo, Mary, hi, is that you?

MARY: Yeh.

SHARON: I'm only after finding out.

MARY: Is that right.

SHARON: What happened?

MARY: I don't know. Like he just wasn't going to let me in. And if he sees you talking to me he won't let you back in.

SHARON: It's too late now. He said: well if you want to go out to see your friend then on you go, and make sure you have everything with you because you won't be let back in.

MARY: Ah Jazus Sharon, you didn't have to.

SHARON: It's okay. I wasn't that happy anyway.

MARY: What's going on?

SHARON: The usual. The preening and posing is something shocking. Your one Laura is a right pain. Any then my fellow didn't appear.

MARY: Oh, I had an offer here a few minutes ago. A jerk. He thought I was an easy pick-up.

SHARON: If we're not being hated we're being ignored.

MARY: And feared.

SHARON: That too. You know what your man on the door said to me, he said . . .

MARY: What?

SHARON: He said: tell your friend she's barred for next week and the week after – you tell her that, he said.

MARY: Ah Christ.

SHARON: Can I have a taste?

MARY: Barred. Shite.

SHARON: Just a taste.

MARY: Do you know what that means. I'm shagging barred. [*She stands, and she shouts towards hall.*] Fuck you!

TICKET COLLECTOR: [*Off-stage.*] I'll ban you for life.

[MARY *sits back down and hands the bottle to* SHARON.]

MARY: I knew you were after something.

SHARON: Now if I had to choose between a dance with an idiot and a taste of vodka with a friend I think I'd know what I'd go for. [*She drinks.*]

MARY: That's shameful Sharon. "Shameful Sharon" – that's a nice name for you. It suits you. Here comes Shameful Sharon.

SHARON: With her friend . . . Morbid Mary. That's you – to a T.

[MARY *and* SHARON *put on older people's voices and act out over-the-top.*]

MARY: Hallo Shameful!

SHARON: Hallo Morbid!

MARY: Terrible weather.

SHARON: A fright.

MARY: And how is things?

SHARON: Things are mighty, Morbid. Just take a look around ya.

[*Out of the hall come a couple with their arms around each other. They pass without looking at the girls.*]

MARY: Would ya quit.

SHARON: Ah sure the young ones these days.

MARY: God bless us, listen to that blasted music.

SHARON: It's a living terror.

MARY: I would not like to be young again.

SHARON: You'd be deaf.

MARY: You would.

SHARON: And then there's the . . .

MARY: Rampant hormones.

SHARON: Don't mention the cursed hormones.

MARY: They gather like fleas.

SHARON: Worse than the blasted midges.

MARY: They were not around in our day.

SHARON: No.

MARY: They were not.

SHARON: Thanks be to God. And while you're at it . . .

MARY: Yes me dear?

SHARON: Just take a look at the height of the micro-mini. Never mind the blasted depths of the plunging neckline.

MARY: The highs and lows is right.

SHARON: It's a terror to the world.

MARY: God help the puberty-ridden teenagers of this world

– those girls are a temptation to the poor young boys.
SHARON: It's disgusting Shamus.
MARY: It is shameful Martin.
SHARON: It is morbid.
[*Pause. They both have a drink. A burst of music. A girl appears across from them and gets sick.*]
MARY: Ah dear, dear, dear. [*Pause. Normal voice.*] Thanks Sharon for coming out.
SHARON: No bother sham,
MARY: Do you know what I regret? Not that I didn't get in but that I should have gone with your man when he asked me. I was just too thick.
[*Lights down.*]

SCENE 7

The girls line up two-by-two on the bus. Outside there is jeering. The driver comes on and sits.

SHEILA: How is the boy?
BOY: Grand entirely. There's a lotta talk of misery in Georgetown.
LAURA: There is indeed.
SHARON: I'm as high as a pony.
MARY: Never mind.
LAURA: Well Mary, did you enjoy yourself?
MARY: Aye, it was a great disco – the best I've been at.
MARGO: You're something else Mary.
SHARON: Morbid.
MARY: Shameful.
SHARON: Seamus.
MARY: Martin.
[*They laugh.*]
MARGO: What the feck are ye at?
JANE: They're high.
JACINTA: They always go like that.
WINNIE: It's weird.

MARY: I was never off the floor.

SHARON: Indeed you were not.

WINNIE: You must have been going awful fast cause I never saw you.

LAURA: I heard he barred you.

MARY: You're just rippen.

LAURA: About what? About you spending the night standing outside?

MARY: Myself and Sharon were taken for a spin. [*Putting on accent.*] By a lad from Swinford. To Castlebar.

SHARON: And back.

MARY: It was fan-tas-tic, right Sharon?

SHARON: Dead on, and don't forget to give me back me jumper.

LAURA: And what will you do next week?

MARY: We'll go in a different direction.

MARGO: What do you mean?

MARY: I'll just go someplace else

LAURA: There is no place else.

MARY: I'll find one.

LAURA: You're a loser, do you know that.

MARY: Well I'm a cool loser.

WINNIE: Now, wait a minute. Listen to this. I was in the toilet. Minding me own business.

SHEILA: As usual.

WINNIE: Shut up you. And do you know what happened?

JACINTA: No.

WINNIE: Well I'll tell you. Like, this one came over, she was all glitz, and what did she do, she bucking pinched me. Like, she said she wanted to see what muscles I had. "Muscles?" I said – and then before I could stop her, Christ she nipped me. But the pinch left a bruise. Look.

MARY: Ah poor Winnie.

WINNIE: It's not funny. A pinch can stop the flow of blood to your head.

MARGO: Is that right.

WINNIE: It is. And you drop down dead. It's serious you know.
[*Mobile rings.*]

SHEILA: Yes Ma, we're on our way. What did you say? You're breaking up Ma. I said you're breaking up Ma. Come again? "The poppy closes his head at night like ourselves." I'm sure he does Ma. I'm glad to hear it. That's cute Ma. Yes, I'll be there. Okay. Cool. Bye.

[*The girls sway in the bus. The all freeze and the lights slowly down. A chorus of voices from all sides starts as the lights go down.*]

VOICES:
Go back where you came from.
Ya poor idiots.
Bitches.
I'll get ya.
One of these days.
If I get as far as ya.
Ya hear me?
Who do you think youse are?
Ha? I said who do you think youse are?

[DRIVER *turns on the midnight radio. Darkness.*]

END

Where Are You?

First performed by Sligo Drama Circle Young People's Theatre, at The Fridge, Factory Performance Space, Sligo, on 27 April 2010. Directed by Peter Milne.

CAST

ROBERTO
GEORGINA
SHELLEY
DANIEL
JIMMY
NOREEN
TIM
BRIDGET
GOSLING
ZERO

Set: The stage is surrounded by dark curtains. At the back of the stage, slightly to stage right, is a bird hide – a watching area made of timber and straw and a see-through curtain. It has seats inside. The entrance to it is on the right. When people enter it we can see their shapes and shadows. One of the cast, DANIEL, *is seated amongst the audience.*

SCENE 1

Stage in darkness. In the dark a sound of geese is heard in the distance. A mobile rings unanswered and then stops. The lights come up. A hand appears at the back of the stage; it reaches out towards the audience palm-upwards, then slowly withdraws. A young man, ROBERTO, *steps out onto the stage from stage right, looks around him as if lost, looks at the audience, shakes his head, then lifts a pair of binoculars.*

ROBERTO: [*In a loud whisper.*] Please turn off your mobiles. [*He looks straight out to the back of the audience, and swings the binoculars towards where* DANIEL *sits; he then walks in a circle around the stage.* ROBERTO *prepares to head off stage left, but a hand comes up in front of him, flat palm upward, signalling that he cannot enter stage left. He steps back.*] Excuse me – is this starting all over again? [*No reply. He faces the hand and bows his head with resignation.*] Come on now – you're joking. [*Serious, nearly angry. The hand grows firmer.*] I want to get off, you hear me? Why can I not continue on the way I was going? [*Pleading softly. He stands listening. The hand slowly drops,* ROBERTO *prepares himself, and then steps forward facing stage left, but the hand quickly comes up again.*] Ah Christ don't tell me. [*He turns sharply, spins.*] The same old story. [*He now prepares to go back the way he came in, but just then, stage right, another hand appears high in the air with the palm facing him.* ROBERTO *throws his hands up in frustration.*] Have it your own way then. [*He turns, bows dramatically to the audience, and with a nod of acceptance goes over and sits outside the hide. He crosses one leg over the other and poses like a gentleman, then lifts the binoculars and stares into the audience. Then he steps into the hide. We see his shape as he sits. Now two hands appear at waist level from stage right and stage left, and in walk two girls who shake hands:* GEORGINA *from stage right, and* SHELLEY *from stage left.* SHELLEY*'s high heels strike a sharp rhythm. They act completely unaware of* ROBERTO*'s presence.* GEORGINA *and* SHELLEY *talk to each other, looking down and around, and sometimes cupping their hands to their ears.*]

SHELLEY: [*Old lady's voice.*] Oh Georgina.

GEORGINA: [*Old lady's voice.*] Oh Shelley.

SHELLEY: [*Younger voice.*] How's the crack?

GEORGINA: Oh sound.

SHELLEY: [*Slowly, older lady's voice.*] The light is very poor.

GEORGINA: [*Old lady's voice.*] Yes it's dim.

SHELLEY: [*Young girl's voice.*] Did you see him?

GEORGINA: [*Young girl's voice.*] I did.

SHELLEY: And?

GEORGINA: I said . . . no.

SHELLEY: Really?

GEORGINA: Yes, I said "No thank you."

SHELLEY: Wow.

GEORGINA: And you – what did you do?

SHELLEY: I said to him: "No, she can't under any circumstances." And you know the way he looks at you – [ROBERTO *looks round the corner of the hide at her.*] – you know the face he makes.

GEORGINA: Oh my God, I do.

[ROBERTO *does not make a funny face but a pretend ordinary glance, then withdraws into the hide.*]

SHELLEY: Well he started into that business and I said "Look at you, you poor idiot – will you cut the crap and listen to me?"

ROBERTO: [*From within the hide.*] Please.

SHELLEY: He said "Please," and I said "No."

ROBERTO: [*Quietly.*] Why?
SHELLEY: He asked why.
GEORGINA: He would.
ROBERTO: [*Even quieter.*] Why?
SHELLEY: And I said: "Enough! Leave Georgina alone. You're doing her head in, do you hear me? I've had enough, you're to blame for getting us into this bother" – and you know what he said after all that?
GEORGINA: Tell me.
SHELLEY: He said . . .
ROBERTO: [*From within the hide.*] . . . nothing.
SHELLEY: Exactly, not a word.
GEORGINA: He did not.
SHELLEY: He did, the idiot.
GEORGINA: Oh Shelley.
SHELLEY: Yes.
GEORGINA: Oh my god – the nerve of some people. [*Old lady's voice.*] But you see I just want peace of mind.
SHELLEY: [*Young girl's voice.*] Don't I know.
GEORGINA: [*Young girl's voice.*] I don't want a flaming row.
SHELLEY: Okay, but you can't go on going out with someone who thinks they're someone else – [*Old lady's voice.*] – that's not on.

[GEORGINA *and* SHELLEY *look at the audience. A sudden silence for a few seconds.*]

GEORGINA: [*Young girl's voice.*] Oh, so what do we do?
SHELLEY: [*Young girl's voice.*] Keep looking, hey?
GEORGINA: And searching . . .
SHELLEY: . . . the spider's web.
GEORGINA: [*Calmly she turns to stage left and picks her way with her fingers.*] Okay.
SHELLEY: Chat ya later, Georgina.
GEORGINA: Grand, Shelley.
ROBERTO: No bother.
SHELLEY: You text me.
GEORGINA: Spot on.
SHELLEY: Right.

GEORGINA: What time are they flying over?
SHELLEY: Sixteen minutes past five.
GEORGINA: Are you all right about this?
ROBERTO/SHELLEY: [ROBERTO *resigned but slightly loud – imitating an elder.*] Oh absolutely.
GEORGINA: That bird can fly quicker than a human can think.
SHELLEY: Now . . . [*They girls look around them.*]
SHELLEY: . . . did you ever get the feeling that . . .
GEORGINA: . . . that we are being watched?
SHELLEY: And that we . . .
GEORGINA: . . . really don't know what we're at?
SHELLEY: Exactly. You could not have put it better.
GEORGINA: I'm made up.
SHELLEY: You are. You were invented.

[*On stage a mobile rings.* GEORGINA *lifts a pretend mobile to her ear.*]

DANIEL: [*From the audience.*] Where are you?
GEORGINA: [*Into phone.*] Where am I? Where am I? [*She looks around her and then she looks down at the audience.*] I'm in the zoo. I'm just at the ducks. "The ducks," I said, you idiot. And where are you? What did you say? In the back row? Out there. I don't believe you. [*She slowly and tentatively waves at the audience.*] Wow. I was just like. Cool. Bob's your uncle. See ya later Daniel!

[*The two girls begin to walk off stage, but up come two hands from off-stage blocking their exits.* SHELLEY *and* GEORGINA *stand back-to-back.*]

SHELLEY: Ah Christ.
GEORGINA: Hey, what's going on?
SHELLEY: Can a body not go where they like?
GEORGINA: [*Old lady's voice.*] Let me out please!
SHELLEY: [*Old lady's voice.*] I am not going to just stand here and wait – you hear me?
GEORGINA: [*Stern old lady's voice.*] And neither am I.
SHELLEY: I won't take it – you hear!

[*The two hands disappear.* SHELLEY *and* GEORGINA

immediately move forward. Up come the hands again. SHELLEY *and* GEORGINA *freeze and look at the ground.*]

SHELLEY: [*Young girl's voice.*] This is bucking nonsense!

GEORGINA: [*Young girl's voice.*] Why are you doing this to me!

SHELLEY: To us.

GEORGINA: Whoever you are?

SHELLEY: Every blooming . . .

GEORGINA: . . . time.

SHELLEY: Do you hear us?

GEORGINA: I want to return.

SHELLEY: And every time . . .

GEORGINA: . . . this happens . . .

SHELLEY: . . . the worse . . .

GEORGINA: . . . it gets.

SHELLEY: You hear me? [*They back towards each other.*] I want out.

GEORGINA: You hear me?

SHELLEY: [*Old lady voice, angrily.*] Right now! [*The two girls back into each other, then turn look at each other, and give up trying to get away.*] What . . .

GEORGINA: . . . the hell.

SHELLEY: Let's head into the hide.

GEORGINA: I'm with you.

SHELLEY: The hide is nice.

GEORGINA: It is.

SHELLEY: [*Intimately.*] The worst about this is that it has all happened before.

GEORGINA: [*Intimately.*] Yes, but at least you will be with me Shelley. [*They promptly go over to the hide. Sound of* SHELLEY*'s heels. They enter and speak from within the hide.*]

GEORGINA: [*From within the hide.*] Oh dear. Is that you Roberto?

ROBERTO: Yes.

GEORGINA: I didn't know you were here in the hide.

ROBERTO: I know.

[*Pause.*]

GEORGINA: We were just talking about you. [*Pause.*] Are the geese out there?

ROBERTO: They're coming.

GEORGINA: Great. This time don't go and become another. Someone I don't know. Will you stay as you are? [*Pause.*] Will you please stay as you are?

[*Lights in hide go down.* JIMMY *comes in from stage left.* NOREEN *comes in from stage right.* JIMMY *and* NOREEN *shake hands, and then begin a conversation without once looking at each other.*]

NOREEN: Any sign?

JIMMY: No.

NOREEN: It's a holy dread.

JIMMY: You see those two lassies?

[GEORGINA *and* SHELLEY *glance out of hide.*]

NOREEN: I do.

JIMMY: Georgina . . .

NOREEN: . . . and Jilly. [GEORGINA *and* SHELLEY *retreat.*]

JIMMY: No she's . . .

SHELLEY/JIMMY: . . .Shelley.

NOREEN: Oh yeh, Shelley is right.

JIMMY: They were above in Castle Street rehearsing in the old Church and talking their heads off about who-do-you-think.

NOREEN: Oh?

JIMMY: Him, what's his name?

NOREEN: Ahm . . . oh . . .

ROBERTO: [*From hide.*] Roberto.

JIMMY: [*Nodding.*] Is right.

NOREEN: [*Nodding.*] I heard that.

JIMMY: And it was . . .

SHELLEY/GEORGINA: [*From hide.*] . . . Roberto . . .

NOREEN: [*From hide.*] . . . this . . .

JIMMY: . . . and . . .

GEORGINA/SHELLEY: [*From hide.*] . . . Roberto . . .

NOREEN: [*From hide.*] . . . that . . .

JIMMY: . . . till it would do your head in.

NOREEN: Someone should have a word in their ear. You know . . .

JIMMY: . . . what Bridie?

NOREEN: Noreen, you idiot!

JIMMY: Oh sorry, Noreen, of course. You were saying?

NOREEN: I was saying – [*Sings in old lady voice as she looks fearfully around the stage.*] – "I am half sick of shadows" . . .

JIMMY: Please?

NOREEN: [*Sings.*] . . . said the Lady of Shallot . . .

JIMMY: [*Old voice.*] You have me there.

NOREEN: Alfred Lord Tennyson.

JIMMY: I could never get into poetry.

NOREEN: Never?

JIMMY: Never. They're for a class of people who won't let go – ever!

NOREEN: I learnt the lines because I want to remember them. [*Pause.*]

JIMMY: And I learned the lines because I want to forget. [*Pause.*]

GEORGINA: [*Whispers in the dark of the hide.*] Shelley.

SHELLEY: [*Whispers in the dark of the hide.*] Yes?

GEORGINA: [*A little louder.*] What's he on about?

SHELLEY: [*Dismissive playful whisper.*] I haven't a clue.

NOREEN: You know . . .

JIMMY: What?

NOREEN: Jimmy . . .

JIMMY: Yes?

NOREEN: . . . it's mental.

[*In the hide* ROBERTO *breaks into a laugh. There is the sudden sound of geese flying over. The three come out slightly from the door of the hide and look at the sky, pointing upwards.*]

JIMMY: You hear that?

NOREEN: I do.

JIMMY: You hear them before you see them.

NOREEN: You do.

JIMMY: The wild has its own laws.

NOREEN: It has. And our parrot won't talk.

JIMMY: He won't.

NOREEN: Domestication breaks the law. That's what happened us.

JIMMY: You said it.

NOREEN: He stopped talking the other night when we were watching "The X Factor." After the show was over I said . . .

GEORGINA: [*Imitating* NOREEN *but slightly uncertain and looks at her while doing it.*] . . . hallo Jerry.

JIMMY: And I gave him a handful of nuts, and what did he do?

SHELLEY: [*Imitating* NOREEN *and speaking as if asking a question.*] He looked away?

NOREEN: He did.

JIMMY: [*For the first time he looks at* NOREEN.] It was sad. I get the feeling he will never talk again.

NOREEN: [*For first time she looks at* JIMMY.] Don't be so hard on yourself Jimmy. [*Pause. The three re-enter the hide.*]

JIMMY: So now . . .

NOREEN: . . . what?

JIMMY: Aye.

NOREEN: Let's . . .

JIMMY: . . . sit . . .

NOREEN: . . . a while . . .

JIMMY: . . . as the swarm gathers.

[*They sit centre stage on the floor. A mobile phone rings in the hide.*]

GEORGINA: Hallo. [*Pause.*] Hallo – I'm losing you.

[*As* DANIEL *and* GEORGINA *speak,* NOREEN *and* JIMMY *get up and perform a series of poses, and some slight hand movements, suggesting the geese. They mirror each other without looking at the other person, and they act out the conversation on the mobile.*]

GEORGINA: [*From inside the hide.*] So what's happening?

DANIEL: Bugger all; just this crowd going over and back across the floor and up the steps and across the boards – you know what I mean? All these bucking metaphors – [*He gives a loud sneeze.*] excuse me – and shagging adjectives: it would do your head in, Georgina. [*Pause.*] I don't know what's going on.

GEORGINA: [*From hide.*] Really.

DANIEL: Are you saying you do?

GEORGINA: [*From hide.*] I do know, I think.

DANIEL: What do you mean?

GEORGINA: [*From hide.*] Well you see . . .

DANIEL: What?

GEORGINA: [*From hide.*] . . . I'm one of them.

DANIEL: Oh I forgot.

GEORGINA: [*From hide.*] And so are you.

DANIEL: You're wrong.

GEORGINA: [*From hide.*] No Daniel. No. You're out there . . .

DANIEL: Okay.

GEORGINA: . . . and we are up here in the bird hide . . .

SHELLEY: [*From hide.*] . . . watching.

ROBERTO: [*From hide.*] Aye.

[*Pause.* JIMMY *and* NOREEN *watch and listen.*]

SHELLEY: [*From hide.*] Watching.

[*Pause.*]

GEORGINA: [*From hide.*] Listening.

[NOREEN *and* JIMMY *shake their hands a little more.*]

DANIEL: I got ya.

[*Faraway sound of geese.*]

GEORGINA: See ya . . .

SHELLEY: . . . later.

[*The three come out of the hide to look up at the sky.* DANIEL *comes up through the audience to the front of the stage.* JIMMY *and* NOREEN *act as if the others are not there; they keep up a knowledge of each other, but do not see the others.* JIMMY *lifts a pretend mobile and taps out number,* ROBERTO *does the same, as does* SHELLEY; *this is all done to a sort of rhythmic beat. Then suddenly they all move and each person on stage looks away to the left and right, as a conversation between them all starts. As they move this way and that, they accidently mirror the action of each other without realising it. Their movements *operate as a kind of innate defence mechanism. They begin to sound like faraway geese.*]

SHELLEY: Yeh – so what can I do for you?

JIMMY: Hallo.

ROBERTO: I can't hear you.

GEORGINA: What?

JIMMY: Hallo.

SHELLEY: Why do we as a people say "ah"?

NOREEN: "Ah"?

GEORGINA: Good one.

JIMMY: I did not.

ROBERTO: Speak up.

SHELLEY: Please don't turn up the ads.

GEORGINA: Do you know who I am?

ROBERTO: No, I do not know who I am.

NOREEN: Well I went into Fergusons and I said . . .

JIMMY: Leave it.

SHELLEY: Stop, will ya?

NOREEN: You're where?

ROBERTO: Here.

GEORGINA: You . . .

ROBERTO: Yes?

GEORGINA: I'm losing you.

JIMMY: Charlie I love you . . .

NOREEN: What!

JIMMY: I mean it.

NOREEN: Stop!

JIMMY: I did not.

NOREEN: [*Bowing and nodding as if in marriage vow.*] I do.

JIMMY: I had only the one.

NOREEN: Tell me another.

JIMMY: I had only the one I'm telling ya.

NOREEN: Ah!

DANIEL: [*From down in audience.*] It's getting personal folks.

GEORGINA: Never mind.

SHELLEY: Is that them?

GEORGINA: My head is tormented by songs.

JIMMY: No, not yet.
ROBERTO: This way.
SHELLEY: Yes Roberto.
ROBERTO: Then that way.
NOREEN: Now listen to me.
DANIEL: [*Quietly.*] Don't do it. [*And he goes back to his seat.*]
JIMMY: I will.
ROBERTO: If you spell "paranoid" backwards . . .
SHELLEY: Yes?
DANIEL: [*Quietly from his seat.*] Stop it.

[*All look around them as if haunted.*]

ROBERTO: . . . if you spell "paranoid" backwards what do you get?
NOREEN: A slap on the gob.
ROBERTO: I'm serious.
SHELLEY: Go away out of that.
ROBERTO: [*Quietly.*] I'll say it again . . .
JIMMY: Don't.
ROBERTO: I will. [*Quietly.*] If you spell "paranoid" backwards and move the "o" and the "i," what do you get?

[*Silence as all move their lips and look around them afraid.*]

ROBERTO: Well? [*Silence.*] You get "doin' a rap."

[*They all move their lips and a rap starts. They drop the mobile phoning gestures and start talking to each other, except for* NOREEN *who is staring down into the audience at* DANIEL. *The rap imitates geese sounds, translated into human terms.*]

GEORGINA: I did not.
ROBERTO: You did.
SHELLEY: Far . . .
GEORGINA: . . . out.
NOREEN: [*She points towards the front.*] Who is that out there?
JIMMY: Take it away.
GEORGINA: Wow.
ROBERTO: You take me for granted.
JIMMY: That will happen.
ROBERTO: You always have.
NOREEN: Tell me please.

SHELLEY: Far . . .
GEORGINA: . . . out
NOREEN: [*Looking down.*] Who you are?
JIMMY: How would I know?
NOREEN: Just tell me.
JIMMY: Ask the boss.
SHELLEY: Far . . .
GEORGINA: . . . out.
JIMMY: Do ye have to go?
NOREEN: Who cares Tommy?
JIMMY: [*Angry.*] Jimmy!
NOREEN: Cool down, will you.
JIMMY: I was only joking.
GEORGINA: The truth is . . .
SHELLEY: . . . behind the scenes . . .
NOREEN: . . . and the sciences . . .
JIMMY: Yeh?
GEORGINA: . . . we all just hate each other.
NOREEN: Is that so?
GEORGINA: But we don't tell each other.

[*Pause.*]

SHELLEY/ROBERTO: [*Quietly.*] No.
GEORGINA: And that's the real problem.

[NOREEN *goes back to the hide and gets a pair of binoculars.*]

DANIEL: [*Speaks from down in the audience.*] I never said a word again any of ye.
SHELLEY: I'm out of here.
GEORGINA: I'm with you.
SHELLEY: Right.
ROBERTO: Settle.
NOREEN: [*Looking through the binoculars.*] I see you.
GEORGINA: Can I have a peep?

[GEORGINA *takes the binoculars and looks down at the audience. The voices begin to slow down like receding bird sounds.*]

GEORGINA: The moon is filling in.

JIMMY: I wish I had been there when Daddy died. [*Pause. Slowly.*] I want to forget.

[*Pause.*]

ROBERTO: As you are.

SHELLEY: As you have been.

GEORGINA: As you will.

JIMMY: [*Sadly.*] Amen.

NOREEN: Don't be sad. Lonesome is . . .

SHELLEY: . . . as . . .

ROBERTO: . . . lonesome . . .

GEORGINA: . . . does.

JIMMY: And so . . .

GEORGINA: . . . the less . . .

ROBERTO: . . . said . . .

JIMMY: . . . the better.

NOREEN: True.

[*Pause.*]

GEORGINA: Act . . .

SHELLEY: . . . One . . .

NOREEN: . . . Scene . . .

JIMMY: [*Thinking.*] . . . Two.

[*Suddenly all movement stops. The gang return to the hide and* JIMMY *and* NOREEN *sit back down centre stage.* NOREEN *gets to her feet, followed by* JIMMY.]

NOREEN: Let's go.

JIMMY: Okay.

[JIMMY *turns to the right, and* NOREEN *to the left, and they advance. Slowly and uncertainly they walk towards the sides of the stage.*]

ROBERTO: [*From inside the hide.*] Go on – try it.

SHELLEY: [*From inside the hide.*] Oh do.

GEORGINA: Look at the blue tit.

SHELLEY: I see him.

[*Slowly* JIMMY *and* NOREEN *approach the sides, but no hands come up. They back away and stand, back-to-back, facing where they want to go.*]

NOREEN: My way is clear. Is yours?
JIMMY: It is.
NOREEN: I don't like it.
JIMMY: You think there's something wrong?
NOREEN: I do.
JIMMY: Let's do it.
NOREEN: Okay.
JIMMY: Right.
NOREEN: Right.

[*They step away from each other towards the side curtains.*]

ROBERTO: Do you hear that song? That old air?

[NOREEN *immediately stops, listens to something only she can hear. She turns back and looks at* JIMMY.]

NOREEN: Jimmy?
JIMMY: Yes?
NOREEN: Can I ask you a favour?
JIMMY: Go ahead.
NOREEN: Can we not go – in the one direction – together? [*Pause.*] Please?
JIMMY: If you want to.
NOREEN: I do.
JIMMY: Okay.
NOREEN: I'm hearing things.
JIMMY: Alright Noreen.
NOREEN: We are better together.
JIMMY: Fair enough.
NOREEN: You see, they – [*Looking round her fearfully.*] – can't stop us.

[*She wheels around and goes behind him. They move together out to the right. At the last moment a hand slowly rises and waves.*]

ROBERTO: [*From inside the hide.*] Got ya boss!
NOREEN: See what I mean?
JIMMY: I do.
NOREEN: Is it a girl?
JIMMY: I don't know.

NOREEN: It could be that lady from way back.

JIMMY: Does it make any difference whether it's a man or a woman?

NOREEN: Yes. It does. [NOREEN *lifts a hand and waves back. The hand at the curtain goes rigid. Out comes another hand in an aggressive manner.*]

JIMMY: What now Noreen?

NOREEN: I don't know.

[*They move further to the right. Out comes a third hand.*]

NOREEN: You know . . .

JIMMY: What?

NOREEN: . . . we can't go.

JIMMY: No.

NOREEN: So we're away with the birds.

JIMMY: It's a curse.

NOREEN: Don't say that ever again.

JIMMY: I won't.

NOREEN: Say you're sorry.

JIMMY: I'm sorry.

NOREEN: Say it again.

JIMMY: I'm sorry.

NOREEN: [*Nodding.*] Good man.

JIMMY: But for what I don't know.

NOREEN: And that's the problem. [*Pause.*] I said that's the problem Tommy.

JIMMY: Jimmy!

NOREEN: You see . . .

JIMMY: Explain.

NOREEN: You say you want to forget.

JIMMY: Yes, and you say you want to remember. [*They look at each other for a nervous moment. Pause. They advance and go into the hide out of sight.*] When did youse get here?

ROBERTO: [*Inside the hide.*] A while back.

[TIM *and* BRIDGET *step in from the right, and* GOSLING *steps in from the left. All on stage stand a moment, looking skywards, and again there is the faraway chant of birds.*]

GEORGINA: [*From the hide.*] Do you hear them?

[TIM *and* BRIDGET *and* GOSLING *go to walk out to the left, but a hand comes up to stop them.*]

BRIDGET: We're on Gosling. [*They step back.*] That's it, we're on. Fan your wings daughter, and measure the property. [GOSLING *carries out her orders.*] Dance the way we should go, pace out the cavity, and then we will have a committee meeting.

TIM: Ah, the Queen bee.

BRIDGET: A nice buzz around.

TIM: Whatever madam wants.

BRIDGET: You see daughter, it's all to do with communal thinking, and fire ants.

[*She falls into* TIM*'s arms.*]

TIM: Holy mackerel!

[BRIDGET *hugs him.*]

DANIEL: [*From audience.*] Less of that please.

JIMMY: [*From hide.*] Oh dear. Is that starting?

NOREEN: Oh dear, dear, dear.

[BRIDGET *rests her head on* TIM*'s shoulder.*]

DANIEL: [*From audience.*] Enough, thank you. Now all hands make light work. [*Lights come up for a second as the gang step out of the hide and form a little choir with the others.* DANIEL *steps in front of centre stage with his back to the audience, lifts a baton, and prepares to conduct.*] Swarm! Flock! [*The group form a choir.* DANIEL *lifts his arm in the air to conduct. Moves his hand to begin. Lights out. Instantly, on the back wall of the stage, comes an image of the gang walking on a beach and looking out to sea. A flock of geese pass overhead. The camera follows them as they wing their way to Inishmurray Island. An "s"-sound chant – like the sound of the sea – begins on stage. The image disappears. Lights up.* DANIEL *has disappeared. All heads move together in one direction.* JIMMY *steps off by himself to a corner to swing his wings. The girls –* SHELLEY, GEORGINA, BRIDGET *and* NOREEN *– form a V-shape with the lads. At the back* GOSLING *waits, ready to fly.*]

BRIDGET: Come on Gosling.

GEORGINA: Come on!
GOSLING: I'm coming.
BRIDGET: You're a dote.

[GOSLING *steps to the front with the others; they form a bird formation for a moment, arms extended but with the tips of the hands up; they sway in the line for a minute, with* JIMMY *flying by himself in the corner, then they all begin mirroring each other without knowing it. They pace out the stage. Then, as the whole crew revert back into ordinary human formations, the chant ends.*]

JIMMY: So tell me Roberto . . .
ROBERTO: Yes Jimmy?
JIMMY: Nothing.
GEORGINA: You're breaking up.
SHELLEY: You what?
BRIDGET: I don't understand.
NOREEN: No one does.
JIMMY: Till it's too late.

[TIM *walks about looking at each person, hands behind his back, with a long enquiring look.*]

GEORGINA: [*Looking at audience.*] It's beautiful out there.
SHELLEY: Can we go down?
BRIDGET: I'd like that, but it's not on.
SHELLEY: Okay.
TIM: By the way . . .
NOREEN: Don't.
TIM: . . . when do I get to talk?
BRIDGET: Whenever.
TIM: I'd like to start now.
SHELLEY: Not yet.
BRIDGET: Go on Tim.
JIMMY: Did you hear the latest from what's-his-name?
ROBERTO: I did.
BRIDGET: Go on Tim.

[*They start moving in little steps around the field looking down, looking up, and looking sideways.*]

TIM: I was in San Francisco with my parents only last week and

who did I meet but Owen Clarke – the schoolteacher – and he asked me to recite a poem I'd written.
JIMMY: Oh of course he did.
TIM: [*Playing a small boy.*] And I said "wow."
SHELLEY: [*Getting fed up.*] What time is it?
TIM: So I started with the low, going out with the high, like . . .
GEORGINA: Oh like . . .
TIM: . . . you know yourself . . .
JIMMY: It's eight o'clock.
SHELLEY: See ya later.
TIM: We were standing on the great San Francisco bridge with the camera rolling, Jimmy . . .
JIMMY: You were Timmy.
NOREEN: We'll be here all night.
TIM: . . . but the problem was . . .
SHELLEY: Ohhh . . .
TIM: . . . you see . . .
JIMMY: Yeh?
GEORGINA: Oh tell us.
TIM: . . . you see, I could not remember the words. Me brain stepped outside of my body . . .
GEORGINA: And flew off.
[*Silence.*]
SHELLEY: Ah lovely.
TIM: . . . and I lost my lines.
JIMMY: I understand.
NOREEN: Don't Jimmy.
TIM: For you see . . .
BRIDGET: It's a curse.
JIMMY: [*Nodding furiously.*] Going way back.
TIM: . . . down the centuries . . .
SHELLEY: Christ, don't mess with it.
TIM: Okay. So there you go, I thought you'd all like to know.
[*He lets out a howl of pain.*]
NOREEN: What's wrong?
TIM: I had a filling fell out of me mouth on Saturday morning

down in the café. Now that's better, I get to talk. At last. Thank you Queen.

BRIDGET: [*American accent.*] No problem buddy.

[*They form the V-shape again, shaking their wings and making the "s" sound at the front of the stage.* DANIEL *strides up, and raises a hand with the palm firmly up to stop them. They stand at the edge without moving.*]

SHELLEY: What is that smell?

NOREEN: What smell?

[SHELLEY *puts hand to her nose.*]

SHELLEY: [*She points at the audience.*] That smell.

DANIEL: Stop it! [DANIEL *impatiently waves an ending and the lights come instantly down. Onto the screen we see the cast walking along the beach, and ahead of them great rolls of waves are seen. A faraway sound of geese.*]

SCENE 2

As the lights come up the cast are regrouping.

GEORGINA: Come on everybody.

ROBERTO: We're coming.

NOREEN: Take your place gentlemen. I said take your place gentlemen! [JIMMY *has wandered off again on his own, as has* GOSLING. *The others form a V, shake their wings, and face the back stage; the first person exchanges with the next:* GEORGINA *to* NOREEN, NOREEN *to* TIM, TIM *to* BRIDGET. *They all turn and face the front in a V-shape. Up comes the loud hiss of the sea on their lips. The sound of a helicopter passes overhead and all flatten themselves in terror.* GOSLING, *who is both terrified and curious, takes the odd look up to follow the flight overhead.* NOREEN *shouts.*] Down Gosling! Down I said.

[*The helicopter makes a fierce roar overhead and all are flat out on the ground – it is like an air attack. Then, as the sound recedes, they remain flat, except for* GOSLING.]

SHELLEY: Oh my God.
GEORGINA: Oh Shelley.
NOREEN: Are you there Jimmy?
JIMMY: I'm here.
BRIDGET: Tim! Tim! Tim!
TIM: It's alright Bridget.

[*Silence. They slowly get up and sit in a ring and imitate everyday speech patterns.*]

ROBERTO: So . . .
TIM: . . . what . . .
BRIDGET: . . . now?
SHELLEY: So . . .
TIM: . . . now . . .
NOREEN: . . . what?
JIMMY: So . . .
SHELLEY: . . .what . . .
GEORGINA: . . . now?
ROBERTO: Oh absolutely . . .
BRIDGET: . . . fabulous.
GEORGINA: Grand!
TIM: At the end of the day.
ROBERTO: Absolutely.
SHELLEY: Like . . .
NOREEN: Oh fabulous.
BRIDGET: Far out.
JIMMY: Oh aye . . .

[*Silence and resignation.*]

GEORGINA: Say something Gosling.
NOREEN: Just one word.
BRIDGET: Just the one.
GEORGINA: Please.

[GOSLING *shakes her head, and sits with her head between her knees.*]

SHELLEY: [*Softly.*] Gosling.

[GOSLING *does not move.*]

NOREEN: [*Imitating an older person's voice.*] The poor cratur.

[*They move round the stage on their hunkers.* GEORGINA's

mobile rings. All of them return to human status.]

GEORGINA: Yeh? Got ya. You're where? [*She looks down into audience. Gives a slight wave. She looks all around her.*] Okay. Have it your way.

[*They get up and start moving frantically; then freeze, move, and again freeze. They make a line facing stage left, and eventually* GOSLING *steps in at the back but faces the wrong way.*]

ROBERTO: Turn around Gosling.

GEORGINA: Turn.

JIMMY: Turn will you, you scut.

TIM: Please gal.

[GOSLING *at last turns. Then comes the far-distant sound of a plane. They move an inch.*]

JIMMY: Let's get out of here.

NOREEN: Okay.

BRIDGET: I want to go.

JIMMY: I want to put all this behind me.

TIM: I'm with you.

GEORGINA: Oh Shelley.

SHELLEY: It feels bad.

ROBERTO: I can't take any more of this.

[ROBERTO *is in front. They move another step. They begin to shake. Up comes a stern hand.*]

GEORGINA: It's starting again.

SHELLEY: Ah Christ.

JIMMY: We are only asking to get off.

TIM: Please.

NOREEN: If you wouldn't mind.

BRIDGET: Just let us through.

ROBERTO: You hear me!

[*The hand rises higher.* ROBERTO *goes to turn.*]

ROBERTO: We'll go the other way.

JIMMY: No, we'll go this way.

ROBERTO: Why do we have to go the one way?

JIMMY: I want to back down. Gosling. [*No reply.*] Gosling, I would be grateful if you went to the front.

[*All stand aside and* GOSLING *walks to the front; they line up again and* GOSLING *turns away from the hand and faces* ROBERTO.]

ROBERTO: Gosling . . .

JIMMY: . . . turn around.

TIM: Please girl.

BRIDGET: Face into it.

SHELLEY: Gosling . . .

NOREEN: . . . if you would . . .

BRIDGET: . . . be so kind.

[*She slowly turns. All of them remain facing the hand. The others take a step as* GOSLING *lifts her foot high in the air, but hardly moves an inch.*]

ROBERTO: Go for it Gosling.

[*They all move another step. Up comes a hand from the right curtain in a fist; the fist opens and feathers fall. Then the hand moves the fingers in small flight patterns.* GOSLING *lifts her hand and answers back with other small flight patterns. The others do finger flights to and fro. There is a distant, faraway sound of thunder. The hand stops gesturing and grows rigid. They all stop their hand movements. They begin to shake with fear, then freeze.*]

NOREEN: Let's leave it.

TIM: Okay.

NOREEN: Please.

BRIDGET: I'm asking you.

NOREEN: Please.

JIMMY: I hear you.

GEORGINA: Now. [*And she leads the way with relief.]*

[*They all turn away from stage left, and as they do out steps* ZERO *from behind the curtain.* ZERO *joins them without their knowing. He is in a long white dress, with a black collar and hip boots. He can look like a priest, but also functions as a computer and a mirror. He follows them from behind, then stands aside and rings a bell. They all head into the hide, and can be seen moving around inside, as if something is afoot, as if they are losing their identity. Inside they look this way and that way, then slowly emerge. They are somehow changed in their demeanour.* GEORGINA *is the last to come out. She looks afraid.* ZERO *goes into a trance, with his hands out each side of him and his lips moving like mad. The others sit and stand around. They look at each other, as if not recognising each other.*]

GEORGINA: Roberto. [*He does not look in her direction.* GEORGINA *goes across and looks in his face.*] Roberto, isn't that you?

ROBERTO: [*Speaking in a very sophisticated way.*] I'm afraid you are speaking to the wrong person.

GEORGINA: I can't be.

ROBERTO: You are unfortunately.

GEORGINA: It's you.

ROBERTO: It's not, I have not been here for some time.

GEORGINA: It has to be you.

ROBERTO: Wrong.

GEORGINA: Now I don't know who I am.

ROBERTO: That's not my fault.

GEORGINA: Please tell me it's you and everything will be alright. [*He does not reply.*] Roberto please! This is Georgina here. [*He looks straight in front of him.*] This is not funny. Tell me it's you. Yahoo! [*She gives a mad bark of laughter, then immediately stops.* GEORGINA *turns to* SHELLEY. *Softly.*] Shelley. [SHELLEY *does not look at her.*] Shelley. [*Loudly. No response.*] What's happening? What's happening, Noreen?

NOREEN: [*Deliberately copying an old person's voice.*]. My name is not Noreen.

GEORGINA: Oh God stop it.

NOREEN: I am not an old lady.

GEORGINA: You are Noreen.

NOREEN: [*Adopting a mad young person's voice.*] No, I am . . . Cynthia.

GEORGINA: Bridget!

BRIDGET: Harriet Keogh if you don't mind.

GEORGINA: Shelley! [*She screams and bangs the floor with her hands.*] Tim! Jimmy! Bridget. Where have you all gone? [*Everyone looks away.*] Oh Shelley [*Softly.*] You're my mate. Please come back to me. Shelley. Shelley, where are you? [*The gang raise a kind of "Oh dear God" sound, and shuffle around shaking their heads.*] Okay, okay then. You want someone else, do you? [*The shuffling stops as* GEORGINA *takes out a scarf, swings it in the air, hurls it round her head, and stamps out a figure eight on the floor. She takes up a completely difference stance from before, then pushes out her knees and elbows. She gives a long sorrowful moan and, changing her personality, she stares at the audience as a new person enters her body.*] Are you happy now? Hah? Okay? Will that do you all? [*She looks around.*] So now ye can all go to fuck.

DANIEL: [*From audience.*] Excuse me. There is no call for that. [ZERO *bends his head forward and places his forehead on his outstretched arms. He goes into a low meditative chant by himself. Then at the back* GOSLING *joins in. To the front,* DANIEL *stands before the stage and lifts a hand high in the air to conduct. Immediately the stage plunges into darkness. The chant reaches all of those on stage. Onto the screen comes the waves rising and falling. Then in the distance the geese appear. They wing their way forward and their chant takes over. The image disappears. Lights suddenly come back on. The whole gang have returned to normality.* DANIEL *has disappeared.*]

TIM: So I said: "Have it your own way and" . . .

ROBERTO: What did she do?

JIMMY: She went yahoo.

GEORGINA: You see I lost myself.

ROBERTO: Oh yes.

JIMMY: That will happen.

DANIEL: At some stage . . .

TIM: . . . in your career.

NOREEN: Then you wake up . . .

BRIDGET: . . . and there's the same . . .

NOREEN: . . . sour pusses . . .

SHELLEY: . . . looking back . . .

ROBERTO: . . . at you.

[*Pause.*]

TIM: Identity is a trick played by fate.

[ZERO *rings a little bell and kneels. From a distance,* GEORGINA *studies* ZERO – *notes the emptiness.*]

GEORGINA: Who are you?

ZERO: Mister Zero.

SHELLEY: Like Google.

ZERO: That's who I am, Madam. [*Stands up straight.*] An individual followed by a thousand zeros.

[*They all line up to take their part in looking into the mirror of* ZERO *who never changes posture.* ZERO *faces a distant empty chair as if he was longing to sit on it.* GEORGINA *goes over and looks into* ZERO*'s eyes, cups a hand to her ear, and nods into his face. Then* JIMMY *comes and looks into* ZERO*'s eyes, then props a hand under his own chin, and studies himself, nearly forming the same expression as* ZERO. JIMMY *winks and he steps aside for* SHELLEY. SHELLEY *kneels down, looks into* ZERO*'s eyes, and begin to comb her hair as if she was looking into a mirror. Then she looks at* ZERO*'s face as if she were looking at her own, pulls back a little, and makes way for* NOREEN. NOREEN *looks up and down as if flipping through TV channels, taps* ZERO*'s chest, taps her own cheeks, leans forward and says something quiet that no-one can hear, like a prayer, into his ear.* NOREEN *makes way for* ROBERTO. ROBERTO *takes out a chair, places it facing* ZERO, *and sits.* ROBERTO *takes one very quick look, nods wildly at the floor as if he is listening to something talking away, and makes way for* TIM. TIM *sits and peers frantically into* ZERO*'s eyes, shocked at what he sees.* TIM *slowly gets up to make way for* BRIDGET. BRIDGET *is pretend-smiley as she looks into* ZERO*'s eyes. She writes something into her notebook, looks coy and questioning, then makes way for* GOSLING. GOSLING *lifts the chair out of the way, looks into* ZERO*'s eyes, taps* ZERO*'s chest twice, then taps the back of* ZERO*'s hand with an index finger. Then* GOSLING *goes off to stand alone.* ZERO *reaches down and rings the bell, and sits down in the chair.*]

ZERO: We go and we become.

TIM: Good man, can I talk again now for a while?

ZERO: Indeed you may.
TIM: That's very nice of you.
NOREEN: Oh dear.
BRIDGET: Oh my.
SHELLEY: Oh sugar.
TIM: So there I was – you know how it is.
JIMMY: I do.
TIM: And anyway I said to him . . .
BRIDGET: . . . five times five is twenty-five . . .
NOREEN: . . . and I'm sure happy to be alive.
TIM: Six times six is thirty-six . . .
JIMMY: . . . I like to go and sit at the flicks.
SHELLEY: Seven times seven is forty-nine . . .
ROBERTO: . . . you have to walk the dotted line.
GEORGINA: Two twos is twenty-two . . .
SHELLEY: . . . and out the window she flew.
GEORGINA: Oh sorry, two times two is only four . . .
TIM: . . . so I'll say no more.
ZERO: So now.
NOREEN: Let's head . . .
ROBERTO: . . . out . . .
JIMMY: . . . that . . .
BRIDGET: . . . open door.

[TIM *looks down at the audience.*]

TIM: Is he looking?
SHELLEY: [*Warning him.*] Yes.

[*They form a V-shape. At the back,* ROBERTO *slips away behind the curtain to the right.* ZERO *rings a bell. They form a line to exit right. Up comes a hand saying no. Overhead comes the plane. They hit the deck. Lights off. Lights up as the sound recedes.* GOSLING *is standing alone on stage. She looks around searching for the others. All around on stage left, at all kinds of angles, hands appear through the curtains, palms up.* GOSLING *says something unintelligible, as if she is working out something in her head. She nods to herself, cracks her fingers, nods again, and as she speaks, all the hands slowly go back behind the curtain.*]

GOSLING: Bala bala laba undi didcumbum si labado do
Dong isakalalaba memit mute mumbo ish ish
Good girl goodbye domball ish hum hum.
Mammytakatoe Mammytakeatoe ishoh a yeh . . .
[*Considers the clue.*] Two across, three down. Markree Castle in the year 1881. [GOSLING *shakes her head forcibly.*] I am not a baba.

[GOSLING *reaches the end of the self-interrogation, nods, throws her arms in the air, and heads off to the right. A single hand comes up in front of her; it is* ZERO*'s hand.* GOSLING *bows her head and kneels in front of the hand. The hand grows more rigid.* GOSLING *prays to herself, then comes off her knees, and lifts one of her hands up in the air. Her hand slowly inches forward towards* ZERO*'s hand. The two hands meet for a moment. Off-stage, all the others begin a fearful chant that slowly turns into the "s"-sound sea chant. The two hands go high in the air, and slowly come apart until only the fingers are touching. Now it is* GOSLING*'s hand that is keeping the stranger out; her hand grows more rigid. The chant ends as* BRIDGET, SHELLEY, NOREEN, GEORGINA, JIMMY, *and* TIM *appear through the curtain on the left. They watch in silence.* GOSLING *swings around and calls them in with her hands.* ROBERTO *slips in behind her, then in comes* ZERO *behind him.* ZERO *rings his bell. They look into each other's faces and their identities are lost again.* GEORGINA *sets off on a patrol through them all.*]

SHELLEY: Please . . .

GEORGINA: Who are you?

SHELLEY: Tracey.

GEORGINA: Oh. Okay Tracey.

SHELLEY: Yeh.

GEORGINA: And you?

NOREEN: Cynthia, I told you.

GEORGINA: I don't hate you.

NOREEN: I never said you did.

GEORGINA: But you make things up.

TIM: What things?

GEORGINA: Can we not go back to being our real selves?
BRIDGET: Why?
GEORGINA: Because Bridget . . .
BRIDGET: [*Correcting her.*] Harry.
GEORGINA: Harriet.
JIMMY: Good man Harry.
BRIDGET: [*Questioning look.*] Thanks?
JIMMY: Mary?
GEORGINA: I'm lost – do you hear me?
NOREEN: That's because you want to blame someone.
GEORGINA: That's a lie.
JIMMY: Nothing is fixed child.
GEORGINA: So you say.
TIM: It's true.
GEORGINA: [*She steps back a little.*] I'm lonely.
ROBERTO: Don't.
GEORGINA: I'm lost.
NOREEN: So are we all.
GEORGINA: I feel like I'm speaking to the dead. [*She starts backing away.*]
TIM: You are too young . . .
BRIDGET: . . . for that sort . . .
NOREEN: . . . of carry on.
JIMMY: You are speaking . . .
SHELLEY: . . . to the living.
BRIDGET: I'm afraid.

[*Pause.*]

GEORGINA: So am I.

[*She looks down into the audience, lifts an imaginary phone and makes a call. A mobile phone rings at the back of the audience.*]

DANIEL: Yes?
GEORGINA: I just want to ask you something.
DANIEL: Fire ahead.
GEORGINA: If you don't mind.
DANIEL: Okay.
GEORGINA: Are you . . .
DANIEL: Yes?

GEORGINA: . . . still Daniel? [*No reply.*] I'm losing you. [*She stands and looks down into the audience.*] Are you there?

[Pause.]

DANIEL: [*Speaking very slowly.*] Yes Georgina.

GEORGINA: Oh thank you, thank you.

[ZERO *rings the bell.*]

ZERO: Now, let's all have a cup of tea.

BRIDGET: Yes sir, Zero. [ZERO *takes off his white coat, and is now another person entirely. He goes round with a pretend teapot and pours out imaginary tea into imaginary cups. While the rest of them hold the imaginary cups with their fingertips,* JIMMY *holds the cup like a pint.*] Will you look at him? Hey boss, that's not tea you're drinking.

JIMMY: What are you saying, Harry?

BRIDGET: I saw you.

JIMMY: Humph! Saw what?

[*Then* TIM *downs a glass. And then* ZERO *shoots a shot into his mouth.*]

BRIDGET: This is getting out of hand. You call yourself Zero – they should call you gargle. You auld tramp – cheers! Youse are animals, that's what youse are, but who am I to tell you; that's right.

[*And* BRIDGET *has a polite shot herself. All of them empty their cups and head off.* JIMMY, TIM, ZERO *and* ROBERTO *fall into a group while* SHELLEY, GEORGINA, BRIDGET *and* NOREEN *retire to the hide. Alone at the back,* GOSLING *sits on the floor facing the back curtain.*]

ZERO: So now men . . .

TIM: . . . what's the crack?

JIMMY: Dude, what's up?

ROBERTO: What's the weather like down there?

DANIEL: [*In the audience.*] Ah a terror.

TIM: [*Lights up an imaginary cigarette.*] You know what?

JIMMY: What?

TIM: I'd like to make a speech.

JIMMY: Oh dear.

TIM: To get back to the start.

BRIDGET: Oh do.

NOREEN: Go ahead son.

TIM: It will concern evolution and microbiology and a new look at how competition does not keep us alive. You see – remember – "we are born losers" is the opening line of that great opera . . .

[*The ordinary world is returning. It's as if they were taking the set down.* JIMMY *begins hauling;* ROBERTO *and* ZERO *begin lifting imaginary boxes and putting them away on a shelf;* TIM *is digging in the garden;* GEORGINA *and* ZERO *are playing a game of cards and shooting pool;* BRIDGET *and* SHELLEY *turn to reading and tuning guitars;* NOREEN *starts washing up. They are all doing something.* ZERO *irons throughout the forthcoming scene, lifting up imaginary shirts and sheets, and then starts putting on his old clothes.*]

ROBERTO: What opera?

BRIDGET: Yes, what opera?

TIM: What does it matter what opera?

BRIDGET: Dear God.

ROBERTO: Tell us its name.

TIM: I'm not in the mood.

JIMMY: [*Angrily.*] Okay then, don't bother.

NOREEN: Just piss off.

TIM: Why?

BRIDGET: [*Roars.*] Why?

JIMMY: Dear Christ.

[*Pause. Anger setting in.*]

TIM: [*Quietly, accepting.*] Okay.

NOREEN: Okay?

JIMMY: Yeh?

TIM: [*Stopping digging.*] It's called . . .

ROBERTO: [*Louder.*] Yeh?

TIM: Hold it . . . [*All wait.*] It's called "You are Some Tulip."

BRIDGET: [*With anger.*] Ha-ha.

JIMMY: Is that supposed to be a joke? Well it's not fucking funny.

ROBERTO: It's blasted nonsense.

NOREEN: Hey men, stop it.

GEORGINA: Thank you Noreen.

[TIM *approaches the front of the stage.* ZERO *is now back in his old outfit, and goes on to his knees; as the gang move about they take the odd look into his eyes.*]

TIM: Thank you. I will speak of prime time and inverted commas, and I will bring the horse into it, you need not fear. The thrush died in the cold . . .

NOREEN: . . . the weight grows . . .

TIM: . . . all of philosophy is written . . .

GEORGINA: . . . in the key . . .

TIM: . . . in the key of C.

ZERO: Tempus fugit.

TIM: Tempers flare as time flies.

BRIDGET: Take it easy Timmy.

[*All of them are now working very hard at everyday chores, to the point of bursting. Improvise these chores.*]

NOREEN: [*To* GOSLING.] Shut him up will ya.

TIM: Abandonment. Trifling. I will leave it at that for . . .

NOREEN: [*Trying to better him.*] . . . the foreseeable future . . .

TIM: . . . for I feel . . .

NOREEN: . . . the hands of the clock turning.

[*All are now working at odd jobs – winding clocks, setting tables, etc. – and looking into* ZERO*'s eyes.*]

TIM: Yes . . .

[GOSLING *rises and looks into* ZERO*'s eyes.*]

NOREEN: . . .through the hieroglyphic . . .

SHELLEY: . . . and the void . . .

BRIDGET: . . . in that never-ending . . .

SHELLEY: . . . cry . . .

ROBERTO: . . . of . . .

GOSLING: . . . remorse . . .

GEORGINA: . . . coming down . . .

JIMMY: . . . from the chorus . . .

ROBERTO: . . . above . . .

JIMMY: . . . in the loft . . .

TIM: . . . and the old-fashioned . . .

DANIEL: . . . harangue . . .
BRIDGET: . . . banter . . .
DANIEL: . . . and rap.
TIM: The cough . . .
NOREEN: . . . the silence . . .
SHELLEY: . . . the whine . . .
NOREEN: . . . the silence . . .
ROBERTO: . . .that accompanies . . .
GEORGINA: . . .you . . .

[*Faraway sound of geese. Slowly the work is coming to an end. Lights begin coming down.*]

SHELLEY: . . . in your head . . .
TIM: . . . as you turn . . .
BRIDGET: . . . out . . .
TIM: . . . the night . . .
GOSLING: . . . light . . .
SHELLEY: Georgina!
GEORGINA: Shelley, you're there.
SHELLEY: I am. It's sixteen minutes past five.

[GOSLING *reaches down and rings* ZERO*'s bell. Silence as all look towards* GOSLING. *She stands to the front and they all form a V-shape behind her.* JIMMY *steps to the side. The "s" sound starts again.* DANIEL *appears to the front of the stage and raises his hand to conduct. The "s" sound sways up a key, then stops. The place immediately goes into darkness. A sudden loud sound of geese going overhead, which then stops. In the dark a mobile phone rings unanswered. Then the lights come back on, quite low. The stage is empty.* DANIEL *is gone. The mobile stops ringing. No sound. One hand appears at the back in the hide, and palm-up it faces the audience for a moment and then slowly drops.* ROBERTO *steps onto the stage from stage right, looks around him as if lost, looks at the audience, shakes his head, and lifts a pair of binoculars.*]

ROBERTO: [*Whispers with a loud "s" sound.*] Please turn off your mobiles. [*He looks straight out to the back of the audience, and heads off in a circle around the stage.* ROBERTO *prepares to head off stage left but a hand comes up, flat palm upward, signalling that he cannot exit.*] Excuse me. . . Is this starting all over again? [*He faces the hand. He bows his head with resignation.*] Come on now. You're joking. [*He is very serious, nearly angry. The hand grows firmer.*] I want to get off, you hear me? [*Pleading softly.*] Why can I not continue on the way I was going? [*He stands listening. The hand slowly drops, and as it does so the lights go down slowly, in time to the hand, as if the hand was conducting the light. When the hand at last goes back in behind the curtain, the lights go out. Silence.*]

END

About the Editors

KEITH HOPPER teaches Literature and Film Studies at Oxford University's Department for Continuing Education, and is a Research Fellow in the Centre for Irish Studies at St Mary's University, Twickenham. He is the author of *Flann O'Brien: A Portrait of the Artist as a Young Post-modernist* (revised edition 2009), general editor of the twelve-volume *Ireland into Film* series (2001-7), and co-editor (with Neil Murphy and Ondřej Pilný) of a special "Neglected Irish Fiction" issue of *Litteraria Pragensia* (2013). He is a regular contributor to the *Times Literary Supplement* and is currently completing a book on Neil Jordan.

NEIL MURPHY teaches contemporary literature at NTU, Singapore. He is the author of *Irish Fiction and Postmodern Doubt* (2004) and editor of *Aidan Higgins: The Fragility of Form* (2010) and of the revised edition of Higgins' *Balcony of Europe* (2010). He co-edited (with Keith Hopper) a special Flann O'Brien centenary issue of the *Review of Contemporary Fiction* (2011) and *The Short Fiction of Flann O'Brien* (2013). He has published numerous articles and book chapters on contemporary fiction, Irish writing, and theories of reading, and is currently completing a book on John Banville.

The Collected Plays by Dermot Healy is part of a multi-volume sequence published by Dalkey Archive Press and edited by Neil Murphy & Keith Hopper. The series also includes Healy's *The Collected Short Stories* (2015); an edited reprint of his debut novel *Fighting with Shadows* (2015); and *Writing the Sky: Observations and Essays on Dermot Healy* (2016).

About the Author

Dermot Healy (1947-2014) was born in Finea, Co. Westmeath, and grew up in Cavan near the border with Northern Ireland. He edited the regional magazine *The Drumlin* (1978-80), and co-founded the Hacklers Theatre Group in Cavan in 1980. Following stints in London and Belfast, Healy settled in Ballyconnell, Co. Sligo, where he founded and edited the journal *Force 10: A Journal of the Northwest*. His debut collection, *Banished Misfortune and Other Stories*, first appeared in 1982, and this was followed by four novels – *Fighting with Shadows* (1984), *A Goat's Song* (1994), *Sudden Times* (1999), and *Long Time, No See* (2011) – and a memoir, *The Bend for Home* (1996). Healy wrote the screenplay for Cathal Black's *Our Boys* (1981), and played the lead role in Nichola Bruce's 1999 film, *I Could Read the Sky*. He also wrote five collections of poetry and thirteen stage plays. Elected to Aosdána in 1986, he was the recipient of two Hennessy Literary Awards, the Tom-Gallon Award, the Encore Award, and the AWB Vincent American Ireland Fund Literary Award. Dermot Healy died at his home in Sligo in June 2014.

Reviews of *The Collected Short Stories* and *Fighting with Shadows*

"Dalkey Archive Press has republished Dermot Healy's first novel, *Fighting with Shadows*, and issued his *Collected Short Stories*. These books provide an insight into the most extraordinary Irish literary consciousness of the last fifty years. [. . .] What lies before you in these books is both a gift to see the world with a clarity not often granted, and the immense will and virtuosity to render that vision as art." (Eoin McNamee, *Irish Times*, 2015)

"Before Murphy and Hopper's accomplished reissue of *Fighting with Shadows* the novel has been out of print since 1986. What was a reasonably chaotic text has become lucid and elegant under editorial guidance, and is now rigged with an introduction, a glossary of Irish terms and a list of published extracts from the novel that gives readers a view into Healy's methods of composition and revision. The clarity of the editorship supports an appreciation of Healy's style: his innovations with dialogue and reported speech have flowered, free of typographical weeds. Much the same can be said for the editors' work on *The Collected Short Stories*, which is a triumph of colourful and rational compilation." (Luke Maxted, *Times Literary Supplement*, 2016)

"If these stories haven't previously found favour with a popular audience, that's probably because the images contained within all of them are unsettling, violent and troublesome. But maybe that's the point: Healy doesn't want to make us feel warm or sentimental. Questioning everything – out past, our identity, our tribal allegiances, our quarrels, and our very existence – isn't supposed to be easy. But Healy's magisterial writing makes it a noble quest worth returning to." (John Paul O'Malley, *Sunday Independent* 2015)

"In a development that should help redress the neglect of a significant and highly distinctive Irish writer, Dalkey Archive Press has now published Healy's collected stories along with a reissue of his first novel, *Fighting with Shadows*. Encompassing more than four decades of work, *The Collected Short Stories* is a perfect introduction to Healy's voice, showcasing his intense engagement with language and his imagistic, often mesmeric writing style. Keith Hopper and Neil Murphy are conscientious, unpatronising editors. Their introduction locates their subject within the literary tradition from which he has been largely excluded. They point out that Healy is essentially a modernist, a descendant of Joyce, Beckett and other experimental writers such as Faulkner, Kafka and Borges. [. . .] But, as is so often the case with Healy, the brilliance lies beneath the surface of the work, which, like the majority of these stories, conjures up an entire world with all of its mind-sets, prejudices and shifting tensions." (Joanne Hayden, *Sunday Business Post*, 2015)

"The publication of this collection serves Healy scholars as well as readers fundamentally interested in the art of fiction. The pieces exemplify what's possible in fiction and likewise suggest how elusive those opportunities are but for the most capable creators." (John G. Matthews, *Library Journal*, 2015)